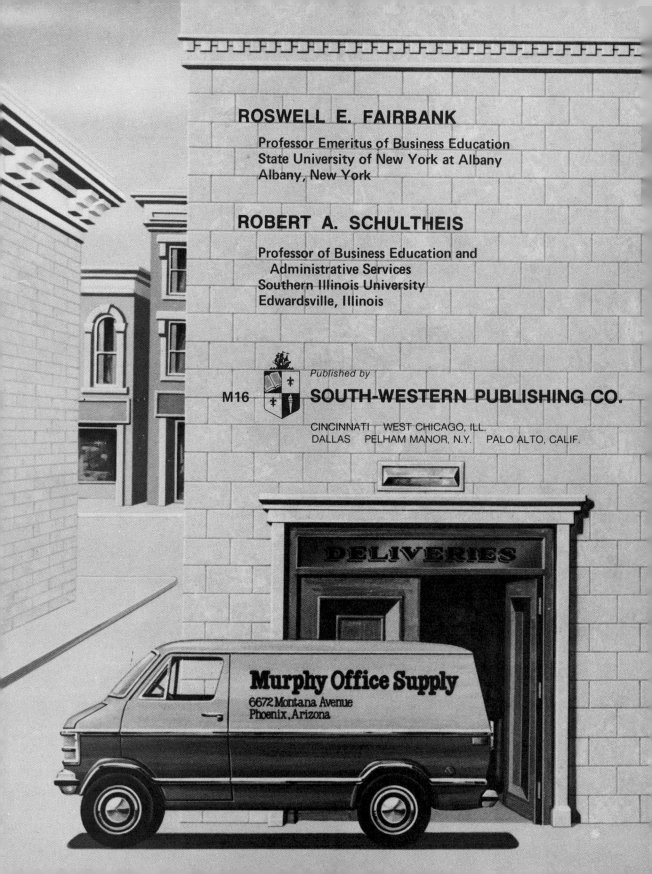

ROSWELL E. FAIRBANK

Professor Emeritus of Business Education
State University of New York at Albany
Albany, New York

ROBERT A. SCHULTHEIS

Professor of Business Education and
Administrative Services
Southern Illinois University
Edwardsville, Illinois

M16

Published by

SOUTH-WESTERN PUBLISHING CO.

CINCINNATI   WEST CHICAGO, ILL.
DALLAS   PELHAM MANOR, N.Y.   PALO ALTO, CALIF.

CONSUMER
MATH

Standard Book Number: 0-538-13160-8

Library of Congress Catalog Card Number: 80-51991

2 3 4 5 6 D 7 6 5 4

Printed in the United States of America

PREFACE

CONSUMER MATH is a totally new book, exclusively designed to develop the competencies needed to solve mathematical problems of consumers.

CONSUMER MATH is organized into five parts that appeal to high school students: Earning Money, Spending Money, Saving and Investing Money, Borrowing Money, and Understanding Business Operations. Those five parts are divided into 19 units and 84 sections.

Many new and vital topics are treated in CONSUMER MATH, such as fringe benefits, figuring equivalent pay, metrics, cost and energy saving, replacement cost insurance, figuring health and education costs, renting or leasing equipment, and using credit cards. Many problems require the student to figure comparative costs and to choose among alternatives. Optional topics and problems, marked by a star (★), challenge faster or more able students.

To strengthen the student's basic skills and knowledge, the fundamental processes of addition, subtraction, multiplication, and division of whole numbers, fractions, decimals, and percents are reviewed in early units. The review of fundamentals is interwoven with practical consumer problems that give purpose to mastery of basic skills.

In general, each topic in CONSUMER MATH is treated with these steps:

(1) A concise explanation to provide background for understanding the principle or process

(2) An example with a clear and simple model solution

(3) Graded practice problems, similar to the example, which immediately apply the new principle or process

(4) Periodic review of the principle or problem type at the ends of sections and parts to assure that essential skills and knowledges are fresh and functional

CONSUMER MATH is written for easy reading, with short, simple sentences and informal writing style. The general vocabulary is easy and familiar. Technical vocabulary is minimized. To promote mastery of technical terms, the most important new terms are shown in color and are defined where they first appear. Those new terms are then reviewed in a vocabulary "matching exercise" at the end of the section; they are also listed in the Terms section provided at the back of the book. Less important new terms are italicized where they first appear.

In CONSUMER MATH, objectives are stated in behavioral terms at the beginning of each unit so students can direct their own learning activities. Throughout the book, marginal reminders focus attention on key points. In early units, marginal reminders also direct attention to the need for accuracy and the importance of checking all work.

Color, cartoons, and illustrated business forms are used extensively in CONSUMER MATH to heighten interest and to strengthen comprehension of the subject matter.

v

The consumer problems provided in the "written practices" of CON-
SUMER MATH are realistic and practical. Within each written practice,
problems are graded according to difficulty. The answer to the first problem of a kind is given in color so the student can confirm the accuracy of
the method and the calculations as a guide to further correct practice.
Many more problems and drills are provided in a coordinated workbook.

In its entirety, CONSUMER MATH gives fair and equal treatment to
all individuals and groups.

The authors thank the many teachers, students, government agencies,
business persons, editorial staff, and others who have contributed in many
ways to CONSUMER MATH.

R. E. Fairbank
R. A. Schultheis

CONTENTS

part IV Borrowing Money

part V Understanding Business Operations

Part I

Earning Money

Like most other people, you will spend much of your life earning money to buy the things you need or want. You have probably already earned some money by working for pay. Maybe you have also earned some interest on a savings account or savings bond. The money you earned is called income.

During your lifetime you will earn hundreds of thousands of dollars of income — maybe even millions — so you will need to know the language of income, and how to solve many kinds of income problems. You will want to know how to figure or check gross and net pay, deductions, salaries, wages, commissions, and averages. You will want to compare jobs to figure which one really pays better.

That's what Part I is all about: Earning Money.

Unit One

SALARIES AND WAGES

During your working life you may get most of your income from salaries or wages. In Unit One you will learn when and how to use arithmetic to solve some common salary and wage problems. You will also review and build your skill in adding, subtracting, and multiplying whole numbers and decimals.

When you have done this unit, you should be able to:

- find gross income
- keep a cash receipts record
- add whole numbers and decimals, vertically (up and down) and horizontally (across), and check your work
- solve simple number sentences
- figure gross pay and net pay
- subtract whole numbers and decimals, vertically and horizontally, and check your work
- multiply whole numbers and decimals, and check your work
- round factors and estimate products in multiplication
- figure overtime pay
- figure deductions from pay
- figure piece-rate pay
- read, write, speak, and recognize the meanings of the terms shown in color

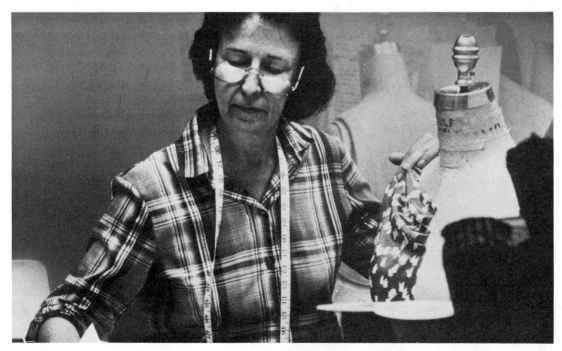

Greg Booth for Associates Corporation of North America

GROSS INCOME

Gross Income. People work at many different jobs to earn money, and their pay is called by many different names. Some people work by the hour, and their pay is called **wages**. Other people are paid a **salary**, which is a fixed amount of pay for a week, month, or year. Salespersons are often paid a **commission** based on the amount of their sales. Many workers in service businesses are given **tips** by customers. Self-employed persons make a profit or **net income** from their businesses.

In addition to the pay they get for their work, many persons also earn money on their investments in savings accounts, stocks, bonds, real estate, or other things of value.

Any of these amounts of money that are earned are called **income**. The sum of the income earned for a period of time is called **gross income** or **total income**. You can find your gross income for any period of time by adding (combining) all your income for that time.

Example

Last week, Rita Savona received $285.50 in wages from her job, $10 in tips, and $9.75 from interest on a savings account. What was her gross income for the week?

Solution		Explanation
Wages	$285.50	Gross income or total income is found by adding all the income amounts for a period. In adding, the decimal points in the amounts and in the total are put under each other. Dollar signs ($) are put only at the top of the column and by the total.
Tips	10.00	
Interest	9.75	
Gross income	$305.25	

Written Practice 1

Remember to line up the decimal points

Write $50 as $50.00 when you add; write $25 as $25.00

Do these problems on a sheet of paper. Arrange your work like the solution above. Check your answer by adding again.

1. For one month, Alex Bell had this income:

Wages	$900.00
Tips	382.50
Interest	6.05

What was his gross income for the week?* **$1,288.55**

2. Carla Mundo's income for the month of August was: salary, $862.50; commission, $479.20; bonus, $50; interest on savings, $13.56; interest on bonds, $25. What was Carla's gross income for the month?

---

*The answer is given for this problem and many others in the book. If you do not get the same answer, check the way you did the problem and your calculations.

3. Last week the Chong family had this income: Hak Chong's **wage**, $365.90; Soo Chong's salary, $372; profits from garage sale, $104.85; dividend on stock, $25; interest on savings bond, $50. What was the Chong family's gross income for the week?

4. A high school class had this income for one year: dues, $180; bake sale, $165.73; class dance, $238.65; car wash, $209; interest, $24.50. What was their gross income for the year?

5. Ramon Playa's income last year is shown below:

Income from own business	$24,468.00
Pay from part-time job	1,142.75
Interest on savings	953.00
Dividend on stock	277.00
Profit on sale of real estate	1,485.05

What was Playa's gross income for the year?

Cash Receipts Record. Many people keep a **cash receipts record**, which is a written record of all money actually received. In this record they list all the money they get, such as earned income, gifts, dividends, interest on savings, and refunds. The record helps them to make sure they have received everything they should. It is also useful in figuring income taxes and in planning spending.

Karl Wirth's cash receipts record is shown as an example:

Karl Wirth
Cash Receipts Record

Date		For	Amount	
April 19--	1	Interest on savings	60	34
	3	Salary for March	1,120	00
	3	Commission for March	547	65
	10	Sale of used car	695	00
	19	Birthday gift	25	00
	20	Dividend on insurance	104	72
	28	Income tax refund	268	08
		Total	2,820	79

Cash receipts record

In this record, Karl Wirth lists *all* money as he gets it. He shows the date, what the money was for, and the amount received. A vertical (up and down) line is used in the form, rather than decimal points, to separate dollars and cents.

At the end of each month, Karl adds (totals) the amounts to find his total cash receipts for that month. If you were keeping a cash receipts record for yourself, you might want to find the total every week, every month, every quarter, or every year.

Written Practice 2

1. Find the total of the O'Neal family's cash receipts record. To do this, put a separate sheet of paper under the column and write your answer on that paper as you add. *Do not write in your book.*

The O'Neal Family
Cash Receipts Record

The vertical line separates dollars and cents

Date			For	Amount	
19-- September	8		Jim's pay for a week	384	60
	8		Refund for purchase returned	69	95
	9		Sale of used carpet	35	00
	10		Dividend on stock	64	78
	12		Karen's salary for two weeks	438	50
	12		Karen's tips for a week	165	05
			Total		

2. Make a cash receipts record for yourself for the month of October. Use a separate sheet of paper and rule a form like the one shown above. Then, write in the information below and find your total receipts for the month.

Date		For	Amount
19-- October	1	Interest on savings	$ 17.85
	3	Gift	10.00
	8	Refund on purchase	9.95
	15	Pay for part-time job	148.00
	20	Sale of used tape player	15.00
	25	Pay for extra job	35.60
	29	Pay for part-time job	140.50

Terms to Remember

Can you read, write, speak, and recognize the meanings of these terms in color? To find out, write the letters *a* through *h* in a column on your paper. Then, match each term with the statement that means the same and write that term next to the correct letter on your paper. *Use each term only once.* As you write each term, pronounce it several times aloud or to yourself. When you've matched all the terms, make sure you are right by checking the meanings given where the terms first appear in the book.

cash receipts record	commission	gross or total income	income
net income	salary	tips	wages

a. Any amount of money earned
b. The total of all money earned
c. A self-employed person's profit
d. Pay based on amount of sales
e. Pay by the hour
f. Fixed pay for a week, month, or year
g. Given by customers
h. A record of all money taken in

Review 1

1. You earned these amounts of income last June: wages, $800; tips, $115.50; other, $23.40. What was your gross income last June?

2. The Kilgore family estimates that their income for next year will be: Steve's wages, $14,150; Etta's salary and commission, $14,200; interest on savings, $195; dividend on stock, $80. What is their estimated gross income for next year?

3. Find the total of Zuni's cash receipts record on a separate paper.

Alvira Zuni
Cash Receipts Record

Date		For	Amount	
19--				
September	2	Two weeks' pay	684	12
	5	Gift	15	00
	12	Part-time job pay	52	48
	16	Two weeks' pay	684	12
	26	Returned purchase	13	95
	30	Two weeks' pay	684	12
		Total		

4. Make a cash receipts record for yourself showing (a) these receipts for November of this year and (b) the total cash receipts: November 1, pay, $1,378.20; November 8, gift, $20; November 10, refund, $23.49; November 15, dividend, $56.21; November 29, pay, $1,378.20.

ADDITION

**section
2**

In Section 1 you used addition to find gross income and total cash receipts. Addition is the arithmetic process most often used by consumers, so you'll want to become skillful with it.

33 addend
12 addend
45 sum, or total

Terms in Addition. Addition is a process of putting numbers together to get one number. Each of the numbers to be added is called an **addend**. The result is called the **sum** or **total**.

Accuracy. All arithmetic, including addition, should be done accurately. Accuracy is vital because wrong answers are worthless and a waste of time. To be accurate in addition you must really *want* to be accurate and try to get the right answer the first time.

The best way to increase your accuracy in adding is to memorize the addition "facts" until you can recall them quickly without error. The addition "facts" are the one-hundred combinations of two one-digit numbers.* For example, some addition facts are: $0 + 2 = 2$; $3 + 4 = 7$; $8 + 9 = 17$; and $2 + 0 = 2$.

Checking Addition. To be sure of your answer, you must check your work. You can check by adding again in the same direction, but reverse addition is a better way to check. In **reverse addition**, you add again in the opposite direction. By adding in reverse you get new combinations of digits and may avoid making the same mistake twice.

**Written
Practice 1**

Copy and add these problems. Check the totals by reverse addition.

Remember to line up the decimal points!

1.	2.	3.	4.	5.	6.
$13.57	$65.78	$69.34	$ 84.33	5.42	1.21
2.43	12.72	41.56	64.55	3.28	24.58
1.85	49.17	58.78	137.02	0.34**	3.76
28.95	41.23	2.90	2.64	5.56	0.80
3.16	24.56	27.12	0.34**	4.54	0.46
6.54	6.54	33.51	19.12	1.45	9.05

*The digits are 0, 1, 2, 3, 4, 5, 6, 7, 8, and 9.
**In this book a zero is put in front of the decimal point to show the absence of a whole number. For example, 34 cents is written as $0.34 or 34¢, and 34 hundredths is written as 0.34.

Speed. You can increase your speed in simple addition problems by doing them mentally — "in your head." When you add mentally, you save the time of writing the numbers or of keying them into a calculator. With desire and practice, you'll build your skill and confidence in adding mentally, and you will have fun doing it.

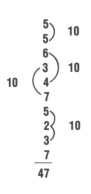

Another way to increase your speed is to combine mentally two or more numbers that equal 10, then add that 10 to other 10's or to other numbers. You can do this as shown in the example at the left.

To add from the top down, you would think 10, 20, 30, 40, 47. To check your work, you would add from the bottom up and think 10, 12, 17, 27, 37, 47.

You may find this way awkward and slow at first, but you'll really speed up as you practice it.

Oral Practice 2

Add from the top down. Use groups of two or three numbers when you can. Then, check your total by adding up.

a.	b.	c.	d.	e.	f.	g.	h.	i.	j.
6	7	8	4	3	1	8	2	3	0
4	3	2	6	9	6	4	1	7	1
5	5	2	1	6	0	5	8	6	5
8	5	5	4	4	2	5	2	8	5
2	6	5	3	6	5	7	4	2	3
3	9	1	7	3	2	7	6	5	3
3	5	9	5	7	7	3	3	5	4
4	1	8	5	5	6	6	0	4	6

Horizontal Addition. In adding, you usually put the numerals in a vertical (up and down) column and then add them. That is called **vertical addition**. Sometimes, though, you will find that the numerals to be added are already arranged horizontally (across). When they are horizontal, you can save time by adding across (**horizontal addition**) rather than rewriting the numerals. With practice you will find horizontal addition quite easy. Try it!

Oral Practice 3

Find these totals by horizontal addition.

a. $5 + 5 =$

b. $3 + 4 =$

c. $2 + 4 + 6 =$

d. $3 + 5 + 8 =$

e. $6 + 4 + 7 =$

f. $8 + 2 + 5 + 5 =$

g. $7 + 3 + 9 + 1 =$

h. $4 + 2 + 3 + 7 + 9 =$

i. $10 + 2 =$

j. $10 + 14 =$

k. $14 + 36 =$

l. $5 + 5 + 35 =$

m. $3 + 12 + 15 =$

n. $2 + 25 + 43 =$

o. $30 + 48 + 22 =$

p. $23 + 37 + 45 =$

Written Practice 4

Copy these problems and find the totals. Add across to find the line totals. Add up and down to find the column totals. Check by adding the column totals across and the line totals up and down. The two totals should be the same.

1.   **2.**   **3.**

$3 + 7 + 6 =$ _____ $10 + 12 + 14 =$ _____ $\$29 + \$33 + \$46 =$ _____
$4 + 5 + 8 =$ _____ $21 + 25 + 20 =$ _____ $51 + 72 + 84 =$ _____
$\underline{9} + \underline{2} + \underline{1} =$ _____ $\underline{35} + \underline{52} + \underline{48} =$ _____ $\underline{20} + \underline{34} + \underline{68} =$ _____
__ + __ + __ = _____   __ + __ + __ = _____   __ + __ + __ = _____

4.

Month	Wage	Tips	Interest	Gross Income
May	$720	$643	$24	
June	682	595	29	
July	765	824	31	
Totals				

Terms to Remember

Write the letters a through d on your paper. Then write the correct term next to the letter of the matching statement. Pronounce each term several times as you write it. Check your answers by looking back in the text.

addend   addition   horizontal addition
reverse addition   sum or total   vertical addition

a. Adding in the opposite direction
b. Each of the numbers to be added
c. The result or answer in addition
d. Adding up and down
e. Putting numbers together to get one number
f. Adding across

Review 2

Check your addition

1. You have these cash receipts for this week: salary, $182.40; tips, $136.75; gift, $20; purchase refund, $15.95; repaid loan, $25. What are your total cash receipts for this week?

2. Your income for three months is shown below. Find (a) the total of each kind of income, (b) the gross income for each month, and (c) the gross income for the three months.

Month	Wage	Commission	Other	Gross Income
March	$820	$430	$56	
April	790	425	71	
May	835	382	62	
Totals				

NUMBER SENTENCES

Numerals. When you use writing to solve arithmetic problems, you use marks or names to represent the numbers. These marks or names are called **numerals.** For example, the marks 9, 35, and 147 are numerals that stand for the numbers nine, thirty-five, and one hundred forty-seven.

Any number may be shown by many different marks or names. For example, the number nine is usually shown by the numeral 9. The number nine could be shown by the numerals $5 + 4$, $12 - 3$, 3×3, $18 \div 2$, $\frac{18}{2}$, IX, and others.

A
NUMBER
HAS MANY
MARKS OR NAMES

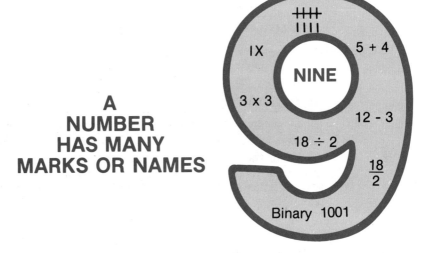

Number Sentences. To show that two different numerals are names for the same number, you may write an equal sign (=) between them. For example, you could write $5 + 4 = 3 \times 3$. The statement that you have written is called a **number sentence.** This number sentence says that the number named by $5 + 4$ is equal to the number named by 3×3. Such number sentences are also called equations.

A number sentence may be either true or false. For example, the sentence $18 \div 2 = 6 + 3$ is true, because $18 \div 2$ and $6 + 3$ are different names for the same number, nine. On the other hand, the sentence $3 \times 3 = 7 + 1$ is false, because 3×3 is a name for nine but $7 + 1$ is a name for eight.

Study each sentence. Is it true or false?

1. $3 + 5 = 5 + 3$	**7.** $4 \times 3 = 12$	**13.** $22 + 0 = 22$
2. $2 \times 3 = 3 \times 2$	**8.** $8 \div 4 = 6 \div 3$	**14.** $8 \div 2 = 8 - 2$
3. $4 \times 2 = 2 + 4$	**9.** $6 + 6 = 10 + 2$	**15.** $12 + 3 = 5 \times 3$
4. $6 - 3 = 5 - 2$	**10.** $15 - 5 = 10$	**16.** $6 = 12 \div 2$
5. $7 - 1 = 3 \times 2$	**11.** $18 \div 9 = 9 \div 3$	**17.** $3 + 2 + 1 = 2 + 2 + 2$
6. $3 \times 3 = 9$	**12.** $16 - 5 = 14 - 2$	**18.** $4 \times 2 \times 3 = 2 \times 2 \times 6$

Completing Number Sentences. A number sentence such as 6 + 3 = 5 + N is incomplete or "open" because a numeral is missing. The missing numeral is indicated by the N. An incomplete sentence is neither true nor false.

To solve many consumer math problems, you need to make such incomplete sentences into complete, true sentences. To make a complete, true sentence, you replace the N with a numeral that makes the sentence true. For example, in the sentence 6 + 3 = 5 + N, you replace the N with 4. You now have 6 + 3 = 5 + 4, which is a complete, true sentence because 6 + 3 is equal to 9, and 5 + 4 is equal to 9.

Sometimes a missing numeral in an incomplete sentence is shown by some letter other than N, or by a symbol such as a question mark (?).

Oral Practice 2

Replace the N or ? with a numeral that makes the statement true.

1. 6 + 2 = 5 + N
2. 3 + 3 = ? + 2
3. N + 7 = 6 + 3
4. 4 × 3 = ? × 6

5. N + 5 = 9
6. 4 × ? = 12
7. N = 5 + 0
8. ? = 9 − 3

9. N = 15 ÷ 5
10. N = 6 × 1
11. 5 × ? = 25
12. 6 × N = 18

Written Practice 3

As you rewrite these number sentences, replace the N or ? with a numeral that makes the statement true.

1. N + 3 = 8 + 2
2. 4 + 10 = ? + 6
3. 3 × N = 15

4. N = 12 ÷ 4
5. 9 − N = 8 + 0
6. N ÷ 6 = 4

7. N = 12 × 1
8. ? = 9 × 0
9. 5 × N = 20

Terms to Remember

Write the letters *a* and *b* on your paper. Then, write the correct term next to the letter of the matching statement. Pronounce each term several times. Check your answers by looking back in the book.

      number sentence   numeral

a. A mark or name for a number
b. A statement that says two numbers are equal

Review 3

1. As you rewrite these number sentences, replace the N or ? with a numeral that makes the statement true.

    a. 3 + 4 = 4 + N   **b.** ? + 5 = 5 + 4   **c.** 3 × N = 12

Check! Are your numbers right? Is your addition correct?

2. Your club had this income last year: dues, $210; profit from money-raising events, $1,643.90; interest on savings account, $102.58. What was the club's gross income last year?

3. Use the example on page 4 to rule a cash receipts record for yourself. Then, show these receipts for July of this year and find the total: July 1, interest, $40.65; July 14, two weeks' pay, $504; July 25, sale of used goods, $63.25; July 28, two weeks' pay, $520; July 31, dividend, $39.10.

GROSS PAY AND NET PAY

section 4

Figuring Net Pay. If you work for someone other than yourself, you are an employee. The person or business you work for is your employer. Your total pay is called your **gross pay**. Gross pay may also be called gross salary, gross wages, or gross commission.

From your gross pay, your employer has to hold back money for your deductions. **Deductions** include withholding (income) tax, social security tax, and other things that you want such as insurance and contributions.

The amount of money that you are actually paid, after these deductions have been made, is called your **net pay** or **take-home pay**. Net pay may also be called net salary, net wages, or net commission.

Gross Pay − Deductions = Net Pay

Look at this example to see how net pay is figured:

Example

Weng's gross pay for a week was $350. Weng's employer deducted $41.30 for withholding tax, $23.45 for social security tax, $5.75 for insurance, and $9.50 for other deductions Weng wanted. What was Weng's net pay for the week?

Solution			Explanation
Gross pay		$350.00	Deductions are added together. The total of the deductions is then subtracted from gross pay to find net pay. In subtracting, as in adding, the decimal points are put under each other.
Deductions:			
Withholding tax	$41.30		
Social security tax	23.45		
Insurance	5.75		
Other	9.50		
Total deductions		80.00	
Net pay		$270.00	

As shown in the example, the deductions are added to find the total deductions. The total deductions are then subtracted from gross pay to find net pay. Doing the problem that way, you have only two steps: one addition and one subtraction.

You could find net pay by subtracting the deductions, one after another, but that way you would have four steps: four subtractions. It is usually smart to do a problem in as few steps as you can. That way, you have fewer chances to make mistakes!

Written Practice 1

1. What is this worker's net pay?

Gross pay	$408.00
Deductions	122.40
Net pay	**$285.60**

2. Fran Volta's gross wages for a week are $295. Deductions from her pay total $59.60. What is her net pay?

Check your additions by reverse addition. Check your subtractions, too!

3. Kip Carner's weekly pay is $372.80. His employer withholds $53.50 each week for income tax and $24.98 for social security tax. What is Kip's net weekly pay?   **$294.32**

4. Your salary is $1,275 per month. From this salary your employer deducts $158.10 for withholding tax, $85.43 for social security tax, $9.67 for insurance, and $25 for savings bonds. What is your take-home pay each month?

Line up your decimal points!

5. A salesperson, Trudy Wilson, earned a gross commission of $1,494 during the month of April. What was Trudy's take-home pay for the month if her employer took out $300.50 for withholding tax, $100.10 for social security tax, and $25.40 for other deductions?

6. In a recent year, Joe Kemm's gross pay was $16,734. From this gross pay, Joe's employer had deducted $2,651 for withholding tax and $1,121.18 for social security tax. Also, Joe's employer had deducted a total of $117 for insurance, and $168 for contributions. What was Joe's net pay for the year?

★ **Self-employment Income.** Many persons are self-employed. That is, they run their own business or profession. They "work for themselves" rather than work for others. For example, many lawyers, doctors, farmers, barbers, and small shop owners are self-employed.

You figure a self-employed person's net income from the business in much the same way that you figure an employed person's net pay. The gross income that a self-employed person gets from the business is like an employee's gross pay. For example, a self-employed beauty shop owner's gross income is the total of all money paid in by customers. A doctor's gross income is the money received from patients.

Of course, a self-employed person's gross income is not all profit. Every business has to spend money for things such as buildings, heat, light, supplies, taxes, and employee's pay. These costs of running a business are called expenses. Expenses reduce gross income, so they are subtracted from gross income to find net income. A self-employed person's net income, also called net profit, is like an employee's net pay.

Net Income = Net Profit

Gross Income − Expenses = Net Income (Net Profit)

Look at the next page for an example of the way to figure net income.

Example

Tom Ravel is a self-employed repairer. His gross income this year from all customers is $50,000. His expenses for the year are: shop space, $7,000; part-time help, $10,000; supplies, $5,000; advertising, $500. What is Ravel's net income from his business for the year?

Solution			Explanation
Gross income		$50,000	The expenses are added to find
Expenses:			the total expenses. Total expenses
Shop	$ 7,000		are subtracted from gross income to
Help	10,000		find net income.
Supplies	5,000		
Advertising	500	22,500	
Net income		$27,500	

★Written Practice 2

1. Nicole is self-employed. Last year her gross income was $37,825 and her expenses were $9,276. What was her net income?

2. You are starting a new business. You estimate that your gross business income will be $45,000 a year and expenses will be $23,600 a year. What will be your estimated yearly net income from the business?

3. Ira Wukits has his own repair business. His expenses for the first year were shop rent, $4,800; heat, light, and telephone, $3,580; supplies, $6,734. Ira's gross income for the year was $43,374. What was his net income?

Terms to Remember

Match the terms and the statements as you have before. Pronounce the terms and check your answers.

deductions   ★expenses   gross pay   net pay or take-home pay

a. Total pay
b. Gross pay minus deductions
c. Amounts subtracted from gross pay
d. Costs of running a business

Review 4

1. Replace the N or ? with a numeral that makes a true sentence.

   a. $? + 8 = 9$ b. $5 \times N = 20$ c. $8 \times ? = 7 \times 8$

2. Your gross pay is $232.80 a week. Deductions are $33.40 for withholding tax and $15.60 for social security tax. What is your week's net pay?

Have you checked?

3. Lon O'Neal's record of cash receipts for August shows these amounts: $873.50, $1,246.25, $304.65, $29.86, and $6.95. What was the total of Lon's cash receipts for August?

★ 4. Your gross business income last year was $57,968. Business expenses totaled $19,325. What was your net business income last year?

SUBTRACTION

section

5

45 minuend
−12 subtrahend

33 difference

Check:
33 + 12 = 45

In Section 4 you used subtraction to find net pay or net income. Let's now review some of the processes of subtraction.

Terms in Subtraction. Subtraction is the reverse of addition. In subtraction you are given a known total of two addends, called the **minuend**, and a known addend, called the **subtrahend**. You are to find an unknown or missing addend, called the **difference**. You find the difference by subtracting (taking away) the known addend from the known total.

For example, in the problem $45 - 12$, 45 is the known total of two addends. The known addend is 12. You are to find the unknown addend to which 12 was added to make 45. In other words, $N + 12 = 45$. To find N, you reverse the addition by subtracting 12 from 45. The difference, 33, is the unknown addend.

Oral Practice 1

What is the value of N or $?$ in each of these sentences?

1. $7 - 5 = N$
2. $N = 12 - 9$
3. $N = 4 + 5$
4. $3 + 6 = N$
5. $N = 0 + 5$
6. $7 - 0 = N$

7. $N - 15 = 25$
8. $N - 8 = 14$
9. $N + 6 = 12$
10. $N + 3 = 16$
11. $25 = N - 4$
12. $19 = N - 6$

13. $10 = N + 8$
14. $15 = N + 6$
15. $N - 0 = 19$
16. $N + 0 = 8$
17. $25 = N - 0$
18. $23 = N + 0$

Accuracy. To be accurate in subtraction you must know your subtraction "facts." The one-hundred subtraction facts are the reverse of the one-hundred addition facts. For example, $5 - 2 = 3$ is the reverse of $3 + 2 = 5$ or $2 + 3 = 5$, and $15 - 8 = 7$ is the reverse of $7 + 8 = 15$ or $8 + 7 = 15$.

Checking Subtraction. Even the best mathematicians make mistakes. So, everyone needs to check subtractions to make sure they are right. The best check is to reverse the process and add the subtrahend and the difference. That sum should equal the minuend.

Example

What is $96 - 45$?

Solution	Check	Explanation
96 minuend	96 minuend	To check subtraction, reverse the process and add the difference and the subtrahend. *Do not rewrite the numerals; just add up instead of down.* The sum should equal the minuend.
−45 subtrahend	+45 subtrahend	
51 difference	51 difference	

Written Practice 2

Copy these problems and find the difference in each. Check each answer by adding the difference and the subtrahend. *Do not rewrite the numerals when you check the answer.*

Check by adding the difference and the subtrahend

Put the decimal points under each other

1. 645 −142	5. $469.75 −29.50	9. $65,700.00 −13,736.47	13. 75.6 −25.5
2. 7,531 −6,620	6. $8,642.00 −540.75	10. $52,002.05 −35,505.76	14. 46.25 −37.68
3. 45,862 −9,753	7. $39,596.45 −3,780.49	11. $30,330.30 −26,849.59	15. 37.06 −27.40
4. 63,007 −2,957	8. $45,217.37 −2,907.58	12. $87,462.75 −86,562.66	16. 4.8 −0.5

Subtracting Across. In subtraction, you usually arrange the numerals up and down (vertically). If the numerals are already arranged across (horizontally), you can save time by subtracting without rewriting the numerals. Try it!

Oral Practice 3

Find the difference by subtracting across.

1. 5 − 4 =
2. 7 − 2 =
3. 9 − 6 =
4. 8 − 5 =
5. 6 − 2 =

6. 10 − 5 =
7. 12 − 9 =
8. 15 − 6 =
9. 18 − 10 =
10. 22 − 12 =

11. 45 − 22 =
12. 76 − 34 =
13. $6 − $4 =
14. $3.50 − $2.00 =
15. $6.75 − $0.50 =

Written Practice 4

1. Your gross pay and deductions for four weeks of part-time work are shown below. Find your net pay for each week and for the four weeks. Find the totals of the gross pay, deductions, and net pay columns. Prove the total of your net pay by subtracting the total deductions from the total gross pay.

Subtract across

Week	Gross Pay	Deductions	Net Pay
First	$ 55	$15	$40
Second	78	24	
Third	84	26	
Fourth	105	32	
Totals			

2. The Cree family's earnings for a week are shown below. Find each person's net pay and all totals. Prove your work.

Check your additions and subtractions

Person	Gross Pay	Deductions	Net Pay
Jay	$280	$ 75	
Judy	295	105	
Jim	54	16	
Totals			

★ **3.** Alma Ponca has a part-time job. Her gross income and expenses for one summer are shown. Find her net income each month and all totals.

Month	Gross Pay	Expenses	Net Income
June	$ 58.50	$17.50	
July	165.25	33.00	
August	184.60	40.30	
Totals			

Terms to Remember

Match the terms and the statements. Pronounce the terms and check your answers.

difference   minuend   subtraction   subtrahend

a. The reverse of addition
b. The total of two addends in subtraction
c. A known addend in subtraction
d. An unknown addend in subtraction

Review 5

1. Replace the N or ? with a numeral that makes the sentence true.

a. $N = 20 + 0$ **c.** $6 + N = 9 + 5$ **e.** $13 - N = 12$
b. $? + 18 = 19$ **d.** $N - 5 = 10$ **f.** $3 \times N = 36$

2. Your wages, tips, and deductions for four weeks are shown below. Find your gross pay for each week by adding across. Find your net pay for each week by subtracting across. Find the totals of all columns.

Prove all figures to avoid errors

Week	Wages	Tips	Gross Pay	Deductions	Net Pay
One	$ 90	$30		$25	
Two	100	45		32	
Three	84	27		30	
Four	76	23		19	
Totals					

★ **3.** In her business last year, Jan Orr's gross income was $62,587.25. Her business expenses were $28,708.70. What was her net business income?

REGULAR-TIME PAY

Many workers are paid on an hourly rate basis. That is, they are paid a certain amount for each hour worked. They are usually paid each week. Their total pay for the week is called gross pay or gross wages.

Figuring Regular-Time Gross Pay. For an hourly rate worker, the number of hours of work expected in the usual workday or workweek is called **regular time** or straight time. To figure the gross pay for regular-time work, you *multiply* the regular-time pay rate by the number of regular-time hours worked.

Regular-Time Hours × Regular-Time Pay Rate = Gross Pay

For example, Linda Baker worked 40 regular-time hours in one week. Her regular-time pay rate was $8 per hour. Linda's gross pay for the week was 40 × $8 or $320.

Written Practice 1

1. Your regular-time pay rate is $6 per hour. What is your gross pay for an 8-hour day?   **$48**

2. Ada Trimm is paid $10 an hour. Last week she worked 35 hours. What was her gross pay last week?

3. Dom Vega's regular work time is 8 hours a day, 5 days a week. His regular-time pay rate is $7 per hour.
   a. What is Dom's gross pay per day?
   b. What is his gross pay per week?   **$280**

4. This week, Raul Sorrento worked these regular-time hours: Monday 8; Tuesday, 8; Wednesday, 7; Thursday, 8; Friday, 6. His regular-time pay rate is $5 per hour.
   a. How many hours did Raul work this week?
   b. What was Raul's gross pay for this week?

Figuring Regular-Time Hours and Overtime Hours. When you did Problem 4 above, you had to figure the number of regular-time hours worked before you could figure gross pay. To find total regular hours worked, you may have to separate time worked into regular-time hours and overtime hours. **Overtime** is time worked beyond regular time.

To separate regular-time and overtime hours, you need to know how many hours of work are expected by the employer in the usual day or week. In many businesses, the regular workday is 8 hours. In those businesses, 8 hours or less of work per day is counted as regular time. Any time worked beyond 8 hours in a day is overtime.

In other businesses, regular time is 40 hours or less per week. Over-time is paid only for hours beyond 40 per week, *even though the worker may work more than 8 hours in a day.*

Oral Practice 2

1. During a week, you worked these hours: Monday, 8; Tuesday, 7; Wednesday, 5; Thursday, 6; Friday, 9. How many hours did you work that week?

2. Your regular workday is 8 hours. Last week you worked 8 hours each day, Monday through Friday.
   a. How many hours did you work last week?
   b. How many regular-time hours did you work last week?

3. Jo Kem works on an 8-hour day basis. One week she worked these hours: Monday, 8; Tuesday, 4; Wednesday, 7; Thursday, 9; Friday, 10.
   a. How many total hours did Jo work that week?
   b. How many regular-time hours did she work?
   c. How many overtime hours did she work?

4. Greg Alda works on a 40-hour week basis. Last week he worked 8 hours a day for 5 days.
   a. How many hours did Greg work last week?
   b. How many regular-time hours did he work?
   c. How many overtime hours did he work?

5. You work on a 40-hour week basis. In two weeks you worked these hours:

	First Week	Second Week
Monday	8	8
Tuesday	8	9
Wednesday	7	10
Thursday	6	7
Friday	8	8

   a. How many hours did you work the first week? The second?
   b. How many regular-time hours did you work the first week? How many overtime hours the first week?
   c. How many regular-time hours did you work the second week? How many overtime hours the second week?

Figuring Regular Time and Gross Pay. If you have to figure both regular time worked and gross pay, you use two steps: (1) find the number of regular-time hours worked and (2) multiply the regular-time pay rate by the number of regular-time hours worked.

Example

	Solution			Explanation
Monday	7	$ 7.25	Total hours worked for the week
Tuesday	8	36	(36) were found by adding the hours
Wednesday	9	43 50	worked each day. All hours were regu-
Thursday	8	217 5	lar-time hours because the total was
Friday	4	$261.00	less than 40 hours. Gross pay was
Total			found by multiplying the hourly rate
hours		gross	and the hours worked. The decimal
worked	36	pay	point in the answer (product) was put

Mia Gonzales is paid $7.25 per hour. She is paid on the basis of a 40-hour week. Last week Mia worked these hours: Monday, 7; Tuesday, 8; Wednesday, 9; Thursday, 8; Friday, 4. What was Mia's gross pay for the week?

two places from the right because there were two places in the numbers that were multiplied.*

Written Practice 3

1. Your regular working hours are 8 hours a day, Monday through Friday. Your pay is $9.50 an hour. This week you worked these hours:

Monday	8
Tuesday	8
Wednesday	6
Thursday	4
Friday	8

   a. How many hours did you work this week?
   b. How many regular-time hours did you work this week?
   c. What is your gross pay for this week?   **$323**

2. Milt Domski is paid $8.50 an hour and is expected to work a 40-hour week at regular pay. In two weeks, he worked these hours:

	First Week	**Second Week**
Monday	8	10
Tuesday	7	8
Wednesday	8	4
Thursday	8	8
Friday	8	7

   a. What was Milt's gross pay the first week?
   b. What was his second week's regular-time pay?

---

*In multiplying, move the decimal point in the answer as many places from the right as there are decimal places in the two numbers multiplied.

Remember to
move the decimal
point as many
places from the
right as there are
decimal places in
the two numbers
multiplied

3. Helen King, a friend of yours, works on a 40-hour week basis and is paid $6.80 an hour. What should be Helen's gross pay for this week if she works these hours: Monday, 7; Tuesday, 9; Wednesday, 8; Thursday, 10; Friday, 6?

4. In one week you worked 8 hours a day, Monday through Thursday, but only 4 hours on Friday. You were paid $7.90 an hour and worked on an 8-hour day basis. What was your gross pay for that week?

5. Kaz Hermes works on an 8-hour day basis at $7.15 per hour. In a recent week he worked 10 hours a day for 5 days.
   a. How many total hours did he work?
   b. How many regular-time hours did he work that week?
   c. How many overtime hours did he work that week?
   d. What was his *regular-time pay* for that week? (Disregard overtime hours.)

Terms to Remember

Match the terms and the statements as you have before. Speak the terms several times and check your answers.

overtime   regular time

a. The expected amount of work time per day or week
b. Time worked beyond the expected time

Review 6

1. Replace the N or ? with a numeral that makes a true sentence.

   a. $N + 7 = 16$ c. $25 - N = 15$ e. $3 \times ? = 15$
   b. $10 + ? = 22$ d. $N - 8 = 20$ f. $5 \times N = 30$

2. Karen Rosen is paid $5.75 per hour. What is her pay for a week in which she works 38 hours, all regular time?

Check all your
calculations!

3. Herb Fels works on a 40-hour week basis at $5.60 per hour. During one week he worked these hours: Monday, 8; Tuesday, 6; Wednesday, 4; Thursday, 4; Friday, 8.
   a. How many regular-time hours did he work that week?
   b. What was his gross pay for that week?

4. Your gross salary is $1,720 per month. From that amount your employer deducts $360.40 for withholding tax, $115.24 for social security tax, and $22.36 for other deductions. What is your net pay per month?

5. You have been working a 40-hour week at $7 per hour. Your work is now being cut to 36 hours a week at the same pay rate.
   a. What has been your weekly pay?
   b. What will be your new weekly pay?
   c. How much less pay per week will you be getting?

MULTIPLICATION

In Section 6 you found regular-time gross pay by multiplying the number of hours worked by the rate of pay. Here you will review some important facts about multiplication.

Terms in Multiplication. **Multiplication** is a short way of adding two or more equal numbers. For example, multiplying 3×3 is the same as adding $3 + 3 + 3$. Multiplying is faster and easier than adding if you have learned your multiplication "facts" and can recall them correctly and quickly. The multiplication facts are the one-hundred combinations of the digits 0 through 9.

Factor   (F)
× Factor   (F)
Product   (P)

When you multiply you use two numbers: the multiplicand and the multiplier. The **multiplicand** is the number being multiplied. The **multiplier** is the number by which you are multiplying. The result or answer is called the **product**. Both the multiplicand and the multiplier are called **factors** of the product. In multiplication, the factors can be reversed and the product will be the same. You often reverse factors to get easier combinations to multiply, or to check multiplication.

Checking Multiplication. You can check multiplication by redoing it. A better check is to reverse the factors and multiply again. If the work is done right, the answers will be the same. Reversing and multiplying is a good check because it gives different combinations of numbers that help you avoid making the same errors.

Example
What is 25×34?

Solution				Check
Multiplicand (one factor)	(F)	34		25
Multiplier (other factor)	(F)	25		34
		170		100
		68		75
Product	(P)	850		850

Oral Practice 1

Find the value of N or $?$. As you do, remember that:
(1) Reversing factors does not change the product.
(2) Multiplying a number by 1 does not change the number.
(3) Multiplying with 0 gives 0 as a product.

1. $5 \times N = 3 \times 5$
2. $13 \times 6 = 6 \times N$
3. $7 \times 6 = ? \times 6$
4. $3 \times 9 = N \times 9$

5. $N = 1 \times 59$
6. $1 \times 1 = ?$
7. $N = 0 \times 38$
8. $N \times 73 = 73$

9. $N = 0 \times 7$
10. $33 \times N = 0$
11. $1 \times N = 1$
12. $69 \times ? = 0$

**Written
Practice 2**

Find the product in each problem. Check by reversing the factors and multiplying again.

	1.	2.	3.	4.	5.
a.	31 26	45 24	48 27	234 412	905 583
b.	69 27	48 35	38 79	642 105	759 642

Moving the Decimal Point in the Product. In Section 6 you were reminded to move the decimal point in the product as many places from the right as there are decimal places in the two factors. You did that in several problems involving dollars and cents. Here are some other examples of locating the decimal point.

Example

When multiplying, move the decimal point in the product as many places from the right as there are decimal places in the two factors.

$ 6.75	$ 8.92	3.245	4.02
35	1.5	0.22	1.25
33 75	4 460	6490	2010
202 5	8 92	6490	804
$236.25	$13.380	0.71390	4 02
			5.0250

**Oral
Practice 3**

Where does the decimal point go in these products?

Reminder: A zero before a decimal point shows that there's no whole number

	1.	2.	3.	4.
a.	$2.54 6 $1524	$6.07 0.25 $15175	0.17 5 085	0.06 5 030
b.	$ 6.29 5.5 $34595	$4.28 0.5 $2140	0.35 2 070	1.643 0.65 106795

Rounding Off. In many problems you need to round off an amount. When you **round off** an amount, you drop some numerals from it. You often round off to get a number that is easier to work with, but accurate enough for what you are doing.

When and how you should round off depends on the problem you are doing. The cent is the smallest coin in our money system, so you usually round a fraction of a cent to a whole cent *in an answer*. You may round up or down to the *nearest cent*, or you may round up to the *next whole cent*. What you should do depends on custom or special directions.

Rounding to the Nearest Cent. To round off to the nearest cent, you drop the numerals to the right of the cents place. Then, if the *first* numeral to the right of the cents place was 5 or more, you add 1 to the cents place. If the first numeral to the right of the cents place was less than 5, you do not add 1 to the cents place. (Disregard numerals to the right of the cents place, except for the first numeral.)

Example

Rounded to the Nearest Cent

$56.075 = $56.08	$56.044 = $56.04
$56.0785 = $56.08	$56.0449 = $56.04

Rounding to the Next Whole Cent. To round to the next whole cent, you drop all numerals to the right of the cents place. Then, if the *first* numeral to the right of cents place was 1 or more, you add 1 to the cents place. (Disregard numerals to the right of the cents place, except for the first.)

Example

Rounded to the Next Whole Cent

$35.761 = $35.77	$35.091 = $35.10
$35.765 = $35.77	$35.0906 = $35.09

REMEMBER THIS RULE In this book you are to
ROUND ANSWERS TO THE NEAREST CENT
unless told otherwise

Look only at the first numeral to the right of the place you want

You use the same ideas of rounding when you want to round off a number to the nearest hundred, thousand, and so on. For example, 25,379 rounded to the nearest hundred is 25,400; to the nearest thousand, it is 25,000.

To the nearest tenth, 5.9463 is 5.9; to the nearest hundredth, it is 5.95; to the nearest thousandth, it is 5.946.

In the same way, 4,793 rounded to the first numeral on the left is 5,000. The value of 7.45, rounded to the first numeral on the left, is 7.

**Oral
Practice 4**

1. Round each of these to the

   a. Nearest cent: $8.249; $3.684; $34.875; $42.6449; $65.503

   b. Next whole cent: $8.249; $3.684; $34.875; $34.641; $65.5009

Look at only the
first numeral to the
right of the place
you want

   c. Nearest tenth: 6.46; 7.33; 6.049

   d. Nearest hundredth: 3.617; 0.287; 0.434; 0.0409

   e. Nearest tenth of a cent: 9.77¢; 3.97¢; $1.4632; $9.4848

2. Round each numeral to the nearest million, then to the nearest hundred thousand, nearest ten thousand, and nearest thousand.

   a. 32,575,149   **c.** 5,622,374   **e.** 29,039,643
   b. 67,094,627   **d.** 6,394,550   **f.** 8,649,882

3. Round each numeral to the first nonzero digit at the left.

   a. 636   **e.** 2,892   **i.** 0.0685   **m.** $62.00
   b. 7,805   **f.** 499.9   **j.** 0.0075   **n.** $45.46
   c. 9,649   **g.** 8.075   **k.** 0.0447   **o.** $51.89
   d. 917   **h.** 54.92   **l.** 0.0729   **p.** $849.99

Estimating the Product. A good way to check the accuracy of multiplication is to estimate the product. When you **estimate** a product, you find a rough or approximate answer. By comparing your estimated product with your exact product, you can tell if your exact product is reasonable and probably right. For many problems, an estimated answer is close enough.

   To estimate a product, you round off one or both factors to numbers that you can easily multiply mentally. After you multiply, you compare your estimated product and the exact product to see if they are close.

Example

   What is the gross pay of a worker who works 38 hours at $7.88 an hour?

Exact Product	Solution	Estimated Product

$ 7.88
        38
    63 04
    236 4
  $299.44
	To find the estimated product, round off $7.88 to $8, and 38 hours to 40 hours. The estimated product, $320, is close to the exact product, $299.44, so the exact product is reasonable and probably right.	$ 8
		    40
		  $320

   In the example above, an exact product of $2.99, $29.94, or $2,994.40 would be unreasonable when compared with the estimate. If your estimated and exact products are not close, refigure your estimate to make sure it is right. If it is, refigure the exact product.

Oral Practice 5

How was the estimated product found?

	Estimated Product		Estimated Product
1. 5 × $7.89	$40	6. 9.9 × 9.75	100
2. 7.8 × $3	$24	7. 17.3 × 37.6	800
3. 6.2 × $4.98	$30	8. 20.1 × 69.4	1,400
4. 3.8 × $9.25	$36	9. 34.2 × 99.6	3,000
5. 2.5 × $19.95	$60	10. 195 × 205	40,000

Written Practice 6

For each problem, (a) find the exact product; (b) estimate the product; (c) check the exact product against the estimate; and (d) check the exact product by reverse multiplication.

1. 3.92 × 542   3. 29 × $19.75   5. 98 × $635
2. 6,297 × 4.95   4. 88 × $37.65   6. 490 × $975.50

Terms to Remember

Match the terms and statements as you have before.

estimate   factors   multiplicand   multiplication
multiplier   product   round off

a. A short way of adding
b. The number being multiplied
c. The number by which you are multiplying
d. The result of multiplication
e. The multiplicand and the multiplier
f. Drop some numerals from a number
g. Figure a rough or approximate answer

Review 7

1. Find the value of ? or N.
   a. $12 + N = 16$ c. $7 \times ? = 42$ e. $25 - N = 23$
   b. $28 - N = 6$ d. $24 - 6 = N$ f. $0 + ? = 39$

Be sure you're right! Check all your work

2. One week Erica Simms worked 8 hours on Monday, Wednesday, and Friday, and 6 hours on Tuesday and Thursday. At $7.42 an hour, what was her gross pay for the week?

3. Your salary, tips, and deductions from a part-time summer job are shown. Find your gross and net pay, and total all columns.

Month	Salary	Tips	Gross Pay	Deductions	Net Pay
June	$120	$ 49		$40	
July	240	125		87	
August	240	143		95	
Totals					

★ 4. You had business income last year of $36,575.42. Business expenses for the year were $12,094.68. What was your net business income?

OVERTIME PAY

Extra money that is paid for working more than the usual day or week is called **overtime pay**. Overtime pay is often figured at one and a half times the regular rate and is called **time and a half pay**. **Double time pay**, or two times the regular hourly rate, is sometimes given for work beyond time and a half work or for work on weekends and holidays.

Figuring Overtime Pay. To find time and a half pay, you first multiply the regular pay rate by 1.5 (1½) to get the time and a half rate. You then multiply the time and a half rate by the number of time and a half hours.

1.5 × Regular Pay Rate = Time and a Half Rate*
Time and a Half Hours × Time and a Half Rate = Time and a Half Pay

To find double time pay, you first multiply the regular pay rate by 2 to get the double time rate. You then multiply the double time rate by the number of double time hours.

2 × Regular Pay Rate = Double Time Rate
Double Time Hours × Double Time Rate = Double Time Pay

Example

During one week, Iris French worked 3 hours at time and a half pay and 4 hours at double time pay. Her regular pay rate was $8.40 per hour. What was her total overtime pay for the week?

Solution	Explanation
$1.5 \times \$ 8.40 = \$12.60$ time and a half rate $2 \ \times \$ 8.40 = \$16.80$ double time rate ――――――― $3 \ \times \$12.60 = \$ 37.80$ time and a half pay $4 \ \times \$16.80 = \underline{\ \ 67.20}$ double time pay $\$105.00$ total overtime pay	The time and a half rate and the double time rate were figured first. Then, the time and a half pay and the double time pay were figured and added to find the total overtime pay.

1. One week, Chip Barsam worked 5 hours at time and a half pay. His regular pay rate was $8 an hour. What was his overtime pay for the week? **$60**

---

*A fraction of a cent in an overtime rate is *not* rounded off. Instead, any fraction of a cent in the total overtime pay is rounded off. For example, if a regular pay rate is $8.75 an hour, the time and a half rate is $13.125 an hour (1.5 × $8.75 = $13.125). The pay for 5 hours of time and a half work at $13.125 an hour would be $65.63 (5 × $13.125 = $65.625, or $65.63).

CHECK! ! !

2. Rachael Henson's regular pay rate is $7.95 an hour. Her overtime last week was 4 hours on Saturday at the double time rate. What was her overtime pay for last week?   **$63.60**

3. During one week, Glenda Parsons worked 3 hours at 1.5 times the regular rate and 1 hour at the double time rate. Glenda's regular pay was $9.50 per hour. What was her overtime pay for that week?

4. Rupert Brown's regular pay rate is $6.75 an hour. This week Rupert's overtime is 4 hours at time and a half and 2 hours at double time.
   a. What is his time and a half pay for the week?
   b. What is his double time pay for the week?
   c. What is his total overtime pay for the week?

5. Last week you worked 48 hours. All work over 40 hours a week was at the time and a half rate. Your regular pay rate was $10.35 per hour.
   a. How many overtime hours did you work?
   b. What was your time and a half rate?
   c. What was your overtime pay for the week?

Combining Regular-Time Pay and Overtime Pay. You have now learned how to figure both regular-time pay and overtime pay. To figure the gross pay for a worker who has both regular pay and overtime pay, you just combine them. Here's an example:

Example

In one week, Dana Cord worked 40 hours at regular time, 6 hours at time and a half, and 4 hours at double time. Dana's regular pay rate was $8 an hour. What was his gross pay for the week?

Solution

$1.5 \times \$8$ = $12 time and a half rate
$2 \times \$8$ = $16 double time rate

$40 \times \$8$ = $320 regular pay
$6 \times \$12$ =   72 time and a half pay
$4 \times \$16$ =   64 double time pay
$456 gross pay for the week

Written Practice 2

Check all calculations!

1. Yesterday you worked 8 hours at regular time and 2 hours at time and a half pay. Your regular pay rate is $6 an hour. What was your gross pay for yesterday?   **$66**

2. Your regular pay rate is $6.40 an hour. During one week you worked 40 hours at regular time and 4 hours at time and a half pay. What was your gross pay for that week?

3. Jill Rostov is paid $7.20 an hour. This week she has worked 40 hours at regular time, 5 hours at time and a half, and 4 hours at double time pay. What is her gross pay this week?

4. Last February you worked 160 hours at regular time, 10 hours at time and a half, and 8 hours at double time pay. At a regular-time rate of $9 an hour, what was your gross pay for February?

Figuring Regular-Time Hours, Overtime Hours, and Gross Pay.

Sometimes you first have to figure how many hours were worked at regular time and at overtime, then figure gross pay. Look at this example:

Example

Kim Sanchez works on the basis of an 8-hour day at $6 an hour. Time and a half is paid for overtime on Monday through Friday. Double time is paid for weekend and holiday work. This week Kim worked these hours: Monday, 8; Tuesday, 9; Wednesday, 8; Thursday, 10; Friday, 8; Saturday, 4. What was Kim's gross pay for the week?

Solution

	Regular Time	Time and a Half	Double Time	
Monday	8	0	0	$1.5 \times \$6 = \$9$ time and a half rate
Tuesday	8	1	0	$2 \times \$6 = \$12$ double time rate
Wednesday	8	0	0	_____
Thursday	8	2	0	$40 \times \$6 = \$240$ regular-time pay
Friday	8	0	0	$3 \times \$9 = 27$ time and a half pay
Saturday	0	0	4	$4 \times \$12 = 48$ double time pay
Totals	40	3	4	$315 gross pay

As shown in the example, you can solve such problems with these steps: (1) find the number of hours worked at the regular and overtime rates; (2) figure the overtime pay rate or rates; and (3) figure and combine the regular pay and overtime pay.

Written Practice 3

1. You are paid $10 an hour. You are expected to work an 8-hour day and are paid time and a half for all overtime. Last week you worked these hours: Monday, 8; Tuesday, 8; Wednesday, 10; Thursday, 10; Friday, 8.
   a. What was your regular-time pay for the week? **$400**
   b. What was your overtime pay for the week? **$60**
   c. What was your gross pay for the week? **$460**

You can be right if you CHECK!

2. You are paid $9 an hour, with time and a half for overtime beyond 40 hours a week. This week you worked 8 hours a day on Monday, Tuesday, Wednesday, and Thursday. You worked 10 hours on Friday.
   a. How many regular hours did you work? How many overtime hours?
   b. What is your regular-time pay? Your overtime pay?
   c. What is your gross pay for the week?

3. Russ Welsh is paid on an 8-hour day basis, with time and a half for overtime. He worked these hours one week: Monday, 9; Tuesday, 7; Wednesday, 8; Thursday, 10; Friday, 8. Russ is paid $7.20 an hour.
   a. What was his regular-time pay for that week?
   b. What was his overtime pay for that week?
   c. What was his total pay?

4. Iola Keohu works in a factory at $12 per hour. Iola gets time and a half pay for all work beyond 40 hours a week. If she works 10 hours a day, Monday through Friday, what will be her pay that week?

Do not round the overtime rate

5. Craig Kermani works these hours: Monday, 9; Tuesday, 9; Wednesday, 10; Thursday, 8; Friday, 6. He is paid $7.25 an hour on the basis of an 8-hour day, with time and a half for all overtime. What was his gross pay for those five days?

6. You are paid $7 an hour for an 8-hour day, with time and a half for overtime Monday through Friday. Weekends and holidays are double time. In a recent week you worked these hours: Monday, 8; Tuesday, 9; Wednesday, 8; Thursday, 10; Friday, 10; Saturday, 2. What was your total pay for that week?

7. In one week you worked 9 hours a day, Monday through Friday. You also worked 8 hours ⅃ Saturday, which was a holiday. Your employer pays time and a half for work beyond 40 hours in a week, Monday through Friday, and double time for holidays. Your pay rate is $6.80 an hour. What was your gross pay that week?

Terms to Remember

Match the terms and the statements as you have before.

double time pay   **overtime pay**   **time and a half pay**

a. One and a half times the regular pay rate
b. Two times the regular pay rate
c. Any extra money paid for working more than the usual time

Review 8

1. What is the value of *?* or *N*?

   a. $N + 10 = 35$ c. $30 - N = 26$ e. $N = 15 - 0$
   b. $? = 0 + 8$ d. $8 \times ? = 64$ f. $3 \times N = 27$

Check all calculations!

2. You work on an 8-hour day basis at $6.50 an hour, with time and a half for overtime. Last week you worked these hours: Monday, 10; Tuesday, 9; Wednesday, 10; Thursday, 8; Friday, 6. What was your gross pay last week?

3. Your gross monthly salary is $1,142. Your monthly deductions are $193.70 for withholding tax, $76.51 for social security tax, and $28.55 for other deductions. What is your net monthly salary?

MULTIPLICATION SHORTCUTS

section 9

Some multiplication shortcuts are easy to learn and easy to use. You already know a good shortcut: reversing the factors. You can reverse the factors to get easier combinations or to check your work. Here are some other shortcuts that you can do mentally and save a lot of time.

Multiplying by 10, 100, or 1,000. The easy way to multiply by 10, 100, 1,000, and like numbers is to move the decimal point in the multiplicand. Just move the decimal point to the *right* as many places as there are zeros in the multiplier. If the product is a whole number, drop the decimal point. You may need to attach zeros.

**The easy way!
Move the decimal
point**

Example

To multiply by 10, 100, 1,000, and 10,000:

$$10 \times 3.64 = 36.4 \qquad\qquad 10 \times \$3.64 = \$36.40$$

$$100 \times 3.64 = 364 \qquad\qquad 100 \times \$3.64 = \$364.$$

$$1,000 \times 3.64 = 3,640 \qquad 10,000 \times \$3.64 = \$36,400.$$

**Oral
Practice 1**

Multiply each number by (a) 10, (b) 100, and (c) 1,000.

1. 0.317	**5.** 17	**9.** $3.68	**13.** $0.01	**17.** 25¢
2. 0.45	**6.** 34	**10.** $4.50	**14.** $0.06	**18.** 43¢
3. 6.4	**7.** 12	**11.** $0.376	**15.** $0.38	**19.** 2¢
4. 0.09	**8.** 50	**12.** $0.875	**16.** $0.79	**20.** 8¢

Multiplying by a Multiple of 10, 100, or 1,000. Multiples of 10 are numbers such as 20, 30, and 70. Multiples of 100 are numbers such as 200, 500, and 900. Multiples of 1,000 are numbers such as 3,000 and 12,000.

To multiply by a multiple of 10, 100, or 1,000, first multiply by the nonzero digits. Then move the decimal point to the right as many places as there are zeros in the multiplier. For example, to multiply $1.65 by 200:

(1) Multiply $1.65 by 2. The product is $3.30.

(2) Move the decimal point two places to the right. The product is $330.

**Written
Practice 2**

Multiply mentally, writing only the product on your paper.

	1.	2.	3.	4.
a.	0.21 × 20	2.2 × 300	20 × $0.41	80 × 22¢
b.	0.14 × 30	2.1 × 200	40 × $0.32	90 × 21¢
c.	0.35 × 50	4.1 × 500	70 × $0.12	20 × 73¢
d.	3.4 × 40	40 × 0.31	200 × $0.53	300 × $1.30
e.	4.5 × 80	60 × 0.43	400 × $0.33	21 × $6,000

**Move the decimal
point to the right**

Multiplying Other Numbers with End Zeros. Sometimes the multiplicand or the multiplier, or both, are whole numbers that have end zeros. An example is 2,000 × 150. An easy way of multiplying these is to multiply only the numerals to the left of the zeros. You then attach as many zeros to the product as there are zeros in the two factors.

In the examples below, notice that the numerals are arranged for multiplying as if there were no end zeros. The zeros are attached after multiplying the other numerals.

Examples		
2,000 × 150 = ?		520 × $34 = ?
Solution	**Explanation**	**Solution**
150 2000 ‾‾‾‾‾ 300,000	Arrange the numerals as though there were no end zeros. Multiply, then add zeros to the product.	$34 520 ‾‾‾‾ 68 17 0 ‾‾‾‾ $17,680

Written Practice 3

Multiply these numbers as shown in the above examples.

1. 340 × 58
2. 2,600 × 91
3. 15,000 × 246
4. 24 × 350
5. 13 × $4,600
6. 250 × $920
7. 370 × $6,500
8. 400 × $730
9. 1,200 × $3,450
10. 360 × $89.45
11. 1,600 × $57.05
12. 0.0215 × $5,600

Multiplying by 1¢ and 10¢. To multiply by 1¢, or $0.01, just move the decimal point in the multiplicand *two places to the left*. Attach a dollar sign (and a zero if the product is less than $1). Look at this example:

35 bolts × $0.01 = $0.35

If you are multiplying by 10¢, or $0.10, move the decimal point in the multiplicand *one place to the left*. Attach a dollar sign (and a zero if the product is less than $1). Look at this example:

8 hooks × $0.10 = $0.80

Oral Practice 4

Move the decimal point to the left

What is the product of each?

1. 24 × $0.01
2. 562 × $0.01
3. 88 × $0.10
4. 365 × $0.10
5. 74 × $0.01
6. 4 × $0.10
7. 329 × $0.01
8. 734 × $0.10
9. 489 × 1¢
10. 672 × 10¢
11. 1,200 × 10¢
12. 3,500 × $0.10

Multiplying by a Multiple of 1¢ or 10¢. If you are multiplying by a value such as $0.04 or $0.40, multiply mentally and write the product. Then move the decimal point *two places to the left* in the product, and attach a dollar sign. For example, to find 212 × $0.40,

(1) Multiply 212 by 40 mentally, and write the product: 8,480
(2) Move the decimal point two places to the left and
     attach a dollar sign. The product is: $84.80

Written Practice 5

Multiply mentally, then write the product on your paper.

	1.	**2.**	**3.**	**4.**
a.	32 × $0.03	65 × 6¢	63 × $0.20	45 × 30¢
b.	112 × $0.02	20 × 2¢	28 × $0.40	32 × 60¢
c.	91 × $0.05	72 × 8¢	26 × $0.70	145 × 90¢
d.	160 × $0.04	64 × 5¢	124 × $0.80	95 × 50¢
e.	205 × $0.07	48 × 9¢	140 × $0.50	72 × 20¢

Move the decimal point to the left

Review 9

1. Find the value of ? or N.

   a. $N = 0 \times 5$ **c.** $N = 8 \times 1$ **e.** $N - 7 = 6$
   b. $12 \times ? = 0$ **d.** $13 \times ? = 13$ **f.** $7 \times ? = 70$

2. **a.** Multiply $36.95 by 100   **c.** Multiply 87 by 10¢
   b. Multiply 42 by 600   **d.** Multiply $4.50 by 1,600
             e. Find the product of 2,400 × $320

3. Angie Modoc earns $7.95 per hour. Last week Angie worked 3 hours at time and a half and 4 hours at double time pay. What was Angie's overtime pay last week?

4. You worked these hours one week: Monday, 10; Tuesday, 8; Wednesday, 7; Thursday, 9; Friday, 9; Saturday, 4. You are paid $8.20 an hour, with time and a half for all time over 40 hours a week. What was your pay that week?

5. Irving and Mabel Zarr, and their young daughter Tanya, all have jobs. Their family income records for September are shown:

	Gross Pay	**Deductions**	**Net Pay**
Irving	$1,595	$435	
Mabel	1,604	527	
Tanya	372	69	
Totals			

You are to find (a) the family's total gross pay for September; (b) the family's total deductions; (c) each person's net pay; and (d) the family's total net pay.

WITHHOLDING AND SOCIAL SECURITY TAXES

section

10

You have already learned how to find net pay by subtracting total deductions from gross pay. Now you will learn how to figure the two most common deductions: withholding tax and social security tax.

Withholding Tax. An employer is required by law to deduct money from each employee's pay for federal income tax. That deduction is called the **withholding tax.** In some states, employers also have to deduct money for state income tax and city income tax.

The amount to be withheld for the federal tax is shown in tables such as this one:

INCOME TAX WITHHOLDING TABLE
WEEKLY PAYROLL PERIOD — EMPLOYEE NOT MARRIED

At least	But less than	0	1	2	3	4	5	6	7	8	9	10 or more
\$250	\$260	\$43.80	\$39.20	\$34.60	\$30.00	\$25.50	\$21.90	\$18.20	\$14.50	\$10.90	\$ 7.80	\$ 5.00
260	270	46.20	41.60	37.00	32.40	27.80	23.80	20.10	16.40	12.80	9.40	6.40
270	280	48.90	44.00	39.40	34.80	30.20	25.70	22.00	18.30	14.70	11.00	7.90
280	290	51.80	46.40	41.80	37.20	32.60	28.00	23.90	20.20	16.60	12.90	9.50
290	300	54.70	49.10	44.20	39.60	35.00	30.40	25.80	22.10	18.50	14.80	11.20
300	310	57.60	52.00	46.60	42.00	37.40	32.80	28.10	24.00	20.40	16.70	13.10
310	320	60.50	54.90	49.40	44.40	39.80	35.20	30.50	25.90	22.30	18.60	15.00
320	330	63.40	57.80	52.30	46.80	42.20	37.60	32.90	28.30	24.20	20.50	16.90
330	340	66.50	60.70	55.20	49.60	44.60	40.00	35.30	30.70	26.10	22.40	18.80
340	350	69.70	63.60	58.10	52.50	47.00	42.40	37.70	33.10	28.50	24.30	20.70

Column headers: "Wages are" (At least / But less than); "Number of withholding allowances claimed" (0–10 or more); "Amount of income tax to be withheld"

The amount of tax to be withheld depends on the worker's pay, whether married or single, and the number of withholding allowances claimed. A **withholding allowance,** sometimes called an exemption, reduces the amount of tax. Taxpayers may claim one withholding allowance for themselves, one for a husband or wife, and one for each child or other dependent.

Using a Withholding Table. To find the tax on a given amount of gross pay, first read down the "Wages are" column at the left until you reach that amount of gross pay in the column "At least . . . But less than." Then read across to the column headed by the number of withholding allowances claimed. The amount shown at that point is the amount of tax.

For example, an employee has gross pay of $255 and claims 4 withholding allowances. The tax is found on the first line of the table in the bracket "At least $250, But less than $260," under "4" withholding allowances. The tax is $25.50.

For another worker with $300.50 gross pay and one withholding allowance, the tax is $52.

Oral Practice 1

Use the table on page 34 to find the withholding tax on these amounts of pay:

	Total Pay	Withholding Allowances			Total Pay	Withholding Allowances
1.	$345	6		7.	$270.10	8
2.	$298	0		8.	$349.99	7
3.	$327	3		9.	$299.05	9
4.	$330	2		10.	$335.75	11
5.	$348	10		11.	$322.40	1
6.	$251	5		12.	$300	4

Social Security Tax. Employers are also required to deduct social security tax from each employee's pay. The social security tax is part of the *Federal Insurance Contributions Act*, so it is often called the FICA tax. The **social security** or **FICA tax** is a federal tax that provides benefits for retired or disabled workers and their dependents.

The FICA tax rate and the amount of an employee's pay on which the tax must be paid are changed from time to time. When this book was published, the rate was 6.7% (0.067) of the first $32,400 of an employee's annual pay.

To figure the FICA tax, you multiply the total pay for the period by 0.067, as shown below.

Remember: Round to the nearest cent unless told otherwise

$$0.067 \times \text{Total Pay} = \text{FICA Tax}$$

For example, Werner Kemper earns gross wages of $400 per week. The FICA tax on that amount would be $0.067 \times \$400$, or $26.80.

Written Practice 2

1. Your salary is $935 per month. The social security tax rate is 0.067. What amount must your employer deduct each month for social security tax?   **$62.65**

2. What is the FICA tax on a weekly wage of $364 if the tax rate is 0.067?

Remember the rounding rule!

3. Isis Nobata earned $276.50 during one week. Her employer deducted social security tax on that amount at the rate of 0.067. What amount did the employer deduct?

4. Your yearly salary is $32,900. Social security tax is charged on a maximum of $32,400 a year.
   a. How much of your salary is free from tax?   **$500**
   b. At a tax rate of 0.067, what is the maximum FICA tax you would pay per year?   **$2,170.80**

Using a FICA Tax Table. Employers often use a FICA tax table to find the amount of FICA tax. Part of a table is shown below.

SOCIAL SECURITY EMPLOYEE TAX TABLE 6.7%

Wages at least	But less than	Tax to be withheld	Wages at least	But less than	Tax to be withheld	Wages at least	But less than	Tax to be withheld	Wages at least	But less than	Tax to be withheld
$25.00	$25.15	$1.68	$30.08	$30.23	$2.02	$74.86	$75.00	$5.02	$99.03	$99.18	$6.64
25.15	25.30	1.69	30.23	30.38	2.03	75.00	75.15	5.03	99.18	99.33	6.65
25.30	25.45	1.70	30.38	30.53	2.04	75.15	75.30	5.04	99.33	99.48	6.66
25.45	25.60	1.71	30.53	30.68	2.05	75.30	75.45	5.05	99.48	99.63	6.67
25.60	25.75	1.72	30.68	30.83	2.06	75.45	75.60	5.06	99.63	99.78	6.68
25.75	25.90	1.73	30.83	30.98	2.07	75.60	75.75	5.07	99.78	99.93	6.69
25.90	26.05	1.74	30.98	31.12	2.08	75.75	75.90	5.08	99.93	100.00	6.70
26.05	26.20	1.75	31.12	31.27	2.09	75.90	76.05	5.09			
26.20	26.35	1.76	31.27	31.42	2.10	76.05	76.20	5.10	The FICA tax to be with-		
26.35	26.50	1.77	31.42	31.57	2.11	76.20	76.35	5.11	held on multiples of $100 is:		
26.50	26.65	1.78	31.57	31.72	2.12	76.35	76.50	5.12			
26.65	26.80	1.79	31.72	31.87	2.13	76.50	76.65	5.13	Wage	Tax to be withheld	
26.80	26.95	1.80	31.87	32.02	2.14	76.65	76.80	5.14	$100	$ 6.70	
26.95	27.09	1.81	32.02	32.17	2.15	76.80	76.95	5.15	200	13.40	
27.09	27.24	1.82	32.17	32.32	2.16	76.95	77.09	5.16	300	20.10	
27.24	27.39	1.83	32.32	32.47	2.17	77.09	77.24	5.17	400	26.80	
27.39	27.54	1.84	32.47	32.62	2.18	77.24	77.39	5.18	500	33.50	
27.54	27.69	1.85	32.62	32.77	2.19	77.39	77.54	5.19			

In the complete table, the FICA tax is shown for pay from $0.07 to $100, and for multiples of $100. To find the tax on pay of more than $100, you add the tax for $100, or multiple of $100, and the tax for the amount less than $100.

For example, suppose that Kim Clark's pay is $225.10. From the table, the tax for $200 is $13.40, and the tax for $25.10 is $1.68. So, the total FICA tax is $13.40 + $1.68 = $15.08.

For another example, the FICA tax on pay of $375 would be $25.13 ($20.10 + $5.03 = $25.13).

The tax that you find by using the table is the same amount that you would find by multiplying the pay by the tax rate, 0.067.

**Oral
Practice 3**

Use the social security tax table on page 36 to find the tax.

1. $26.30   3. $32   5. $100   7. $400
2. $27.24   4. $76.50   6. $130.10   8. $431.30

**Written
Practice 4**

1. Use the table on page 36 to find the social security tax on the pay of each of these workers. Check that amount by figuring the tax at 6.7% (0.067) on each worker's pay.

Worker	Pay	FICA Tax from Table	FICA Tax at 6.7%
Carlos Ray	$276.50	$18.53	$18.53
Nancy LeBarr	332.05		
Jean Fitzhugh	526.00		
Rufus Redding	199.50		
Nadia Kwan	427.68		

Have you checked all calculations?

2. Amon Karkim's gross pay last week was $326.75. Amon has 3 withholding allowances. He has no other deductions. Using the tables on pages 34 and 36:
   a. What was Amon's withholding tax for last week?
   b. What was his social security tax for the week?
   c. What were his total deductions for the week?
   d. What was his net pay for the week?

3. Your regular weekly gross pay is $275.30. You have one withholding allowance. In addition to withholding tax and social security tax, your employer deducts $15.60 for other items. Using the tables on pages 34 and 36:
   a. What are your total weekly deductions?
   b. What is your weekly net pay?

4. Copy and complete the table below. Use the tax tables on pages 34 and 36 to find the taxes. Add across to find the total deductions. Prove all your calculations.

Worker	Withholding Allowances	Gross Pay	Income Tax	FICA Tax	Other	Total	Net Pay
King	2	$332.70			$ –0–		
Lee	4	326.50			16.92		
Marco	0	299.20			30.00		
Quarr	5	277.35			6.62		
Totals	– – –						

★ **5.** A self-employed person has to pay social security tax at a higher rate than an employed person. At a FICA self-employment tax rate of 9.35% (0.0935), what is the tax on self-employment income of $18,750?

Terms to Remember

Match these terms and statements.

social security (FICA) tax   withholding allowance
                        withholding tax

a. A deduction for federal income tax
b. Reduces income tax
c. Provides benefits for retired and disabled workers

Review 10

1. What is the value of ? or N

   a. $6 + ? = 21$ **d.** $? \times 6 = 42$
   b. $35 - N = 20$ **e.** $29 \times ? = 29$
   c. $5 \times N = 65$ **f.** $63 \times N = 0$

2. **a.** Add across: $34 + 39 + 103 + 225$
   b. Subtract 75,368 from 79,023
   c. Find the product of $2,705 \times 21.03$
   d. What is $4,879 \times 1,000$?
   e. Multiply $\$7.56 \times 2,100$

3. What is the withholding tax on gross pay of $348 with 5 withholding allowances? (*Use the table on page 34.*)

4. What is the FICA tax on a salary of $384 at a rate of 0.067?

5. Using the table on page 36, what is the social security tax on weekly wages of $299.20?

6. Your weekly wage is $325.50. You have 2 withholding allowances. What is your net weekly wage if your employer deducts $15.24 in addition to withholding and social security taxes? (*Use the tables on pages 34 and 36.*)

7. Albert Copeland works on an 8-hour day basis, with time-and-a-half for overtime. His pay rate is $6.72 an hour and he had 4 withholding allowances. Last week he worked these hours: Monday, 10; Tuesday, 6; Wednesday, 12; Thursday, 8; Friday, 9.
   a. What was his gross pay for the week?
   b. Using the tables on pages 34 and 36, what was the total of his withholding tax and FICA tax?
   c. If he had no other deductions, what was his net pay for the week?

★ **8.** Trudy Harris is self-employed. Last year Trudy's gross income from her business was $41,195. Her business expenses for the year totaled $12,435. What was Trudy's net income for the year?

PIECE-RATE PAY

Many factory and service workers are paid on the basis of the number of items they produce or service. These items are called **pieces** and the workers work on a **piece-rate** basis. Piece-rate pay is supposed to increase workers' production by paying them in direct proportion to the work they do.

Figuring Gross Piece-Rate Pay. To figure gross pay for a piece-rate worker, you:

(1) Find the number of pieces produced, and
(2) Multiply the number of pieces produced and the piece rate.

Example

The Tron-X Company pays workers on a piece-rate basis. Dave Edner works in a department of Tron-X that pays $2 for each piece produced. In one week Dave completed these pieces: Monday, 32; Tuesday, 40; Wednesday, 34; Thursday, 38; Friday, 36. What was Dave's gross pay for the week?

Solution	Explanation
32 + 40 + 34 + 38 + 36 = 180 pieces produced 180 × $2 = $360 gross pay	The total number of pieces produced was found by adding the daily amounts. The number produced and the piece rate were multiplied to find gross pay.

Written Practice 1

1. You have a job in which you are paid $3.75 for each unit you assemble. Today you assembled 16 units. What is your gross pay for today? **$60**

2. Josh VanDyke works for a carpet installer. Josh is paid $1.35 for each square yard of carpet he installs. During one week he installed these square yards of carpet: Monday, 30; Tuesday, 45; Wednesday, 38; Thursday, 35; Friday, 42. What was his gross pay for that week?

3. The Airpress Company pays on a piece-rate basis. This week five workers produced the numbers of pieces at the rates shown below. Find each worker's total production and gross pay.

Worker	Pieces Produced						Piece Rate	Gross Pay
	M	T	W	Th	F	Total		
Bota	58	62	55	66	70		$0.98	
Ebert	23	34	28	31	26		2.20	
Huk	49	53	42	58	47		1.15	
Kisama	37	34	43	29	35		1.75	
Ruiz	38	44	46	39	40		1.42	

4. On weekends in September and October, the five members of the Du-kane family pick apples for fun and pay. They are paid 75¢ for each bushel they pick. One weekend they picked these bushels: Fred, 104; Eve, 88; Gene, 96; Greta, 112; Tina, 53. What was the family's total pay for the weekend?

5. Eva Perez works part-time in an auto service store where she installs shock absorbers and tires. She is paid at the rate of $3.25 for each pair of shocks and $1 for each tire she installs. On a Saturday she installed 12 pairs of shocks and 20 tires. What was her gross pay for the day?

6. Hans Okama is employed in a beauty and barber shop. He is paid at the rate of $4.25 for each haircut and $2.25 for each shampoo. If he averages 96 haircuts and 15 shampoos each week, what is his average weekly pay?

7. Wood Industries Corporation pays some of its workers on this piece-rate schedule:

40 pieces or less, $1.60 each
Next 10 pieces, $1.75 each
All over 50 pieces, $2 each

On a recent day, the six workers below produced the number of pieces shown. Find each worker's gross pay for that day.

a. Costeau 35
b. Gorski   39
c. LeBrun   40

d. Namook   46
e. Ogala   50
f. Rivera   55

Terms to Remember

Match the terms and the statements.

piece rate   piece

a. An item produced
b. Pay based on items produced

Review 11

1. Find the value of *N* or *?*
   a. $N + 25 = 40$ d. $18 + ? = 23$ g. $N \times 7 = 105$
   b. $N - 8 = 7$ e. $8 \times ? = 72$ h. $? + 10 = 24$
   c. $7 \times N = 56$ f. $? = 1,400 - 847$ i. $9 \times N = 108$

2. a. Subtract 8,196 from 9,205   d. Multiply $325 \times 10¢$
   b. From 12,462 subtract 8,572   e. What is $\$6.20 \times 1,500$?
   c. Multiply 304.07 by 1.06   f. What is 34.7682×100?

3. Your job pays $1.42 for each item you produce. If you produce 37 items in a day, what is your gross pay for that day?

4. Earl and Robin Magee are piece-rate workers in different departments of the Tonco Company. Last week, Earl produced 436 pieces at $0.85 per piece. Robin assembled 175 units at $2.15 per unit.
   a. What was Earl's gross pay last week?
   b. What was Robin's gross pay last week?
   c. Who earned more last week, and how much more?
   d. What was Earl and Robin's combined pay?

Are you checking carefully?

5. For the month of September you had these cash receipts: wages, $815.28; tips, $326.35; gift, $15; insurance dividend, $43.62; repaid loan, $50; sale of used sports equipment, $35. What was the total of your cash receipts for September?

6. What is the withholding tax on weekly pay of $347.20 for a worker who has 6 withholding allowances? (*Use the table on page 34*.)

7. What is the FICA tax on earnings of $432 at a rate of 0.067?

8. Your gross pay for a week is $276.80. Each week your employer deducts withholding tax, social security tax, and $12.75 for other deductions. You have one withholding allowance. What is your correct net pay each week? (*Use tables on pages 34 and 36*.)

9. You have been working 40 hours a week at $7.84 an hour. If your work week is cut back to 35 hours, how much pay will you lose per week?

★10. Golda Nueva, a self-employed person, has gross business income of $40,673 and expenses of $13,748 this year.
   a. What is Golda's net income for this year?
   b. At a FICA self-employment rate of 9.35% (0.0935), how much tax must Golda pay this year?

COMMISSIONS

Many salespeople and agents get their income from selling or buying goods and services for other people. Their pay is based on the amount they sell or buy, and it is called **commission**. Commission plans are designed to pay salespeople and agents in proportion to their efforts.

A commission may be a fixed amount for each item sold or bought, or it may be a percent of the money involved. The commission rate may increase as the amount of sales or purchases increases. The commission may be higher on things that are hard to sell than things that are easy to sell. Many times, salespeople and agents are paid a salary or a wage *and* a commission.

This unit deals with a variety of commission problems. When you have finished it, you should be able to:

- find straight commission
- figure salary and commission
- find graduated commission
- figure agent's commission
- find net proceeds and gross cost
- read, write, speak, and recognize the meanings of the terms shown in color

J. P. Stevens & Co., Inc.

SALES COMMISSIONS

If a salesperson is paid only a commission, the commission is called **straight commission**.

Figuring Straight Commission. To figure the amount of straight commission, you need to know the rate of commission and the amount of sales. If the rate of commission is given as a fixed amount for each item sold, you multiply the number of items sold by the rate per item.

Rate Per Item × Number of Items Sold = Commission

Example

A cheerleading team sells banners to raise money for uniforms. The team is paid a commission of $0.50 for each banner that is sold. Last year 342 banners were sold. What was the team's commission?

Solution

$0.50 × 342 = $171 commission

Written Practice 1

1. Trish Kent sells cookwear. Her commission is $25 per set. In August, she sold 32 sets. What was her commission for August?   **$800**

2. Birr Fosegan is a vacuum cleaner salesperson. He gets a commission of $34.50 for each cleaner he sells. What will be his total commission for selling 20 vacuum cleaners?

3. You want to earn some money. You can sell boxes of cards at a commission of $0.75 per box. What would be your total commission for selling 100 boxes of cards?

Check your work!

4. Enid Johnson delivers morning newspapers six days a week at a commission of 5¢ per paper. She has 50 customers on her route. What is her total commission for a week?

5. Afternoons after school, Kurt Kupic sells cookies door-to-door. Kurt is paid 35¢ for each box he sells. This week his sales were: Monday, 9 boxes; Tuesday, 14; Wednesday, 12; Thursday, 0; Friday, 26. What was his total pay for the week?

6. Emily Troka sells brushes door-to-door. Her commission on a hairbrush is $1.25. She has been selling 55 of these brushes per month. If she can increase her sales of these brushes to 75 per month, how much more commission will she make per month?

When the rate of commission is given as a percent of sales, you multiply the dollars of sales by the rate of commission.

Rate of Commission × Dollars of Sales = Commission

Example

Ruth Valona, a salesperson, is paid a straight commission of 5% on her sales. Her sales for June were $40,000. What was her commission for June?

Solution	Explanation
5% = 0.05 rate of commission 0.05 × $40,000 = $2,000 commission	The percent rate was changed to a decimal rate. The sales in dollars were then multiplied by the decimal rate.

You should note in the example above that the percent rate was changed to a decimal rate before multiplying. You change a percent rate to a decimal rate by dropping the percent sign and moving the decimal point *two places to the left*. Put a zero (0) in front of the decimal point if there is no whole number. For example:

1% = 0.01   4% = 0.04   25% = 0.25   150% = 1.5

Oral Practice 2

Change these percents to decimals.

1. 2%	**3.** 5%	**5.** 10%	**7.** 34%	**9.** 106%
2. 3%	**4.** 7%	**6.** 15%	**8.** 79%	**10.** 225%

Written Practice 3

In doing these problems, change the commission percent to a decimal.

1. You have a job that pays a straight commission of 2% on sales. If your sales are $57,500 in a month, what is your commission? **$1,150**

2. Noel York gets a commission of 4% on all sales. Last year his sales totaled $600,000. What was Noel's commission last year?

Change percents to decimals by moving the decimal point two places to the left
←

3. Nelly Chang is paid a 20% commission on her door-to-door sales of cosmetics. If she sells $950 worth of cosmetics during a week, what will be her commission?

4. As a salesperson, Neal Pruitt has a choice of working at a weekly salary of $310 or at a straight commission of 5% on all sales. He expects his sales to average $6,500 per week.
   a. What would be Neal's weekly commission?
   b. How much more would Neal earn per week on commission than on salary?

5. Ginny Kehou sells roofing on a 6% straight-commission basis. In June she sold $30,000 worth of roofing. In July she sold $28,000 worth of roofing.
   a. What was Ginny's June commission?
   ᴐ. What was Ginny's July commission?
   c. What was her total commission for the two months?
   d. By what amount was Ginny's July commission less than her June commission?

Have you CHECKED all your work?

6. Sid Romano sells cars on a commission basis. He is paid a 5% commission on small cars and a 9% commission on large cars. If he sells $25,000 worth of small cars and $17,000 worth of large cars, what will be his total commission?

Terms to Remember

Match the terms and the statements.

commission   straight commission

a. Commission is the only pay
b. Any pay based on the amount bought or sold

Review 12

1. Find the value of *?* or *N*.

   a. $33 + 64 = ?$ **c.** $57 - 22 = N$ **e.** $12 \times N = 72$
   b. $28 + ? = 73$ **d.** $49 - ? = 49$ **f.** $? \times 20 = 100$

2. **a.** What is $2.95 × 10?
   b. Find the product of 6,200 × $3.25
   c. Find the cost of 69 items at $0.10
   d. What is $2,004 − $1,896?
   e. Subtract $18.05 from $428.35
   f. Add $347.29 and $659.81

3. To raise money, your class is selling candy door-to-door at $2 a box. The class makes a commission of 45¢ on each box. If the class sells 500 boxes, what will be the total commission?

Change the percent rate to a decimal rate

4. Selig Cohen sells machine tools on a 4% straight-commission basis. His total sales last August were $65,362. What was his commission?

5. Carlotta Garcia sells and installs auto tires and batteries on a commission basis. She gets 8% commission on tires and 10% on batteries. Her total September sales were: tires, $15,460; batteries, $9,240.
   a. What was her total commission?
   b. How much more commission did she make on tires than on batteries?

6. Gus Rolandos works in a factory where he is paid $2.75 for each acceptable part he produces. This week he produced an average of 42 acceptable parts each day, Monday through Friday. What is his gross pay for this week?

SALES COMMISSIONS (concluded)

Salary (or Wage) and Commission. Some salespersons are paid both a salary (or wage) *and* a commission. The commission may be a percent of the total sales, or it may be a percent of the sales above a fixed amount. The fixed amount is known as a quota.

Example 1 shows how to figure salary plus commission on total sales.

Example

Ria Selsa, a salesperson, is paid a salary of $200 a week and a commission of 2% on all sales. Last week Ria's sales were $6,400. What was Ria's total pay for the week?

Solution

Salary	$200
Commission:	
0.02 × $6,400	128
Total pay for the week	$328

Example 2 shows how to figure salary plus a commission on sales above a quota.

Example

Thelma Quarels is paid a salary of $200 a week and a commission of 2% on sales above a quota of $5,000 a week. Last week Thelma's sales were $7,000. What was Thelma's total pay for the week?

Solution		**Explanation**
Salary	$300	The sales quota, $5,000, was subtracted from the total sales, $7,000, to find the amount of sales above the quota ($2,000). The commission was then figured (2% × $2,000) and added to the salary to find total pay for the week.
Commission:		
$7,000 sales		
−5,000 quota		
$2,000 sales above quota		
0.02 × $2,000	40	
Total pay for the week	$340	

Written Practice 1

1. A salesperson, Chad Lancer, is paid a salary of $900 a month and a commission of 5% on all sales. Chad's November sales were $17,500.
   a. What was Chad's commission for November? **$875**
   b. What was Chad's total pay for November? **$1,775**

2. Veda Osaki's sales for a week were $3,845. Veda was paid a salary of $220 per week and a commission of 6% on all sales. What was Veda's total pay for the week?

3. Roger DuPray is a salesperson for a business that pays a commission of 8% on all sales, plus a salary of $1,000 a month. During the month of April, Roger's sales totaled $25,000. What was his total pay for the month of April?

4. Doris Evans is paid $1,200 a month in salary, plus a commission of 3% on sales over a monthly quota of $20,000. Last month her sales totaled $70,000.
   a. By how much were her sales greater than her quota?   **$50,000**
   b. What was her commission for the month?   **$1,500**
   c. What was her total pay for the month?   **$2,700**

Read problems carefully!

5. Bret Hart's employer pays him a salary of $235 a week and a commission of 4% on all sales over a quota of $3,600 a week. What should be Hart's total pay for a week in which his sales totaled $5,075?

6. The Pedwear Company pays Cora Nelson a monthly salary of $980 and a commission of 7% on sales over a quota of $14,000 per month. Cora's sales for the four weeks of February this year were $7,650; $7,200; $6,845; and $7,605. What were Cora's total earnings for the month?

Graduated Commissions. Salespersons are sometimes paid a graduated commission to encourage and reward increased sales. Under the **graduated commission** plan, the *rate* of commission increases or "steps up" as sales increase. The rate of commission may be based on dollars of sales or on the number of units sold.

The way to figure total or gross commission under one such plan is shown in this example:

Example

Arno Hawk is paid a commission of 5% on monthly sales up to $30,000; 6% on the next $10,000 of monthly sales; and 7% on sales over $40,000 a month. During December, Hawk's sales were $45,000. What was Hawk's commission for December?

Solution

$45,000 − $30,000 = $15,000 sales above first quota
$15,000 − $10,000 = $5,000 sales above second quota

$0.05 \times $30,000 = $1,500 commission on first $30,000 of sales
$0.06 \times $10,000 = 600 commission on next $10,000 of sales
$0.07 \times $5,000 = \underline{350} commission on sales over $40,000
$2,450 total commission for December

Written Practice 2

1. Lisa Kelly is paid 8% on the first $3,800 of weekly sales and 10% on all weekly sales over $3,800. What was her commission on sales totaling $4,800 during one week?   **$404**

2. Rocco Volpo sold $52,500 worth of goods during March. Rocco's commission rate was 4% on the first $35,000 of monthly sales; 5% on the next $15,000; and 6% on all sales over $50,000. What was Rocco's total commission for the month?

3. As a salesperson, you are paid a commission of 3% on the first $50,000 of monthly sales and 4% on all monthly sales over $50,000. Your sales were $58,750 in May and $62,150 in June.
a. What was your May commission?
b. What was your June commission?

Watch this one!

4. Joan MacDuff is paid a commission of 9% on all sales. On sales over $350,000 per year she is paid an *extra* 1%. If her total sales last year were $400,000, what was her total commission for the year?

5. Floyd Mayo, a salesperson, is paid a weekly commission of 75¢ per unit on the first 300 units he sells; 90¢ on the next 100 units; and $1.05 each on units sold over 400. This week he has sold 420 units. What is his commission for the week? $336

Terms to Remember

Match the terms and the statements.

graduated commission   quota

a. A fixed amount above which commission is paid
b. Rate increases or steps up as sales increase

Review 13

1. Find the value of ? or N.
a. $35 + N = 42$ b. $54 - 6 = ?$ c. $6 \times N = 36$

2. a. Find the product of $4,700 \times 530$
b. What is 876.95×10?
c. Find the product of 368×0.012

3. Jeff Rivers, a salesperson, is paid a salary of $1,000 a month and a commission of 2% on all sales. His sales in August were $60,000. What was his total pay for August?

4. Kari Roma is paid a commission of 5% on the first $6,800 of her weekly sales and 6% on all weekly sales over $6,800. What is her commission for a week when her sales totaled $8,000?

5. Sam Yarter sells tools at a commission of 20% of sales. In March, Sam's sales were $8,500; in April, his sales were $11,472. What was his total commission for the two months?

Have you checked all your work?

6. Your employer deducts withholding tax and social security tax from your pay. You have one withholding allowance. What should be your net pay for a week when you worked 40 hours at $6.90 an hour? (Use tables on pages 34 and 36 for deductions.)

AGENT'S COMMISSION

Many people get most of their income by working as agents. An agent acts for someone else and can make contracts for that other person. The person or business for whom an agent works is called the principal.

For example, real estate agents or brokers act for their principals in selling property. Collection agents collect money owed to others. Auctioneers sell goods that belong to other people. Life insurance agents act for their companies. Advertising agencies and travel agencies represent their principals in selling services. Commission merchants, or factors, buy and sell goods for other people.

Agents are usually paid a commission for their work. They may also be paid for some expenses not covered by the commission.

Figuring Agent's Commission. An agent's commission is based on the amount of money involved in the transaction. The amount of the commission is the product of the commission rate and the amount of money involved.

Rate of Commission × Money Involved = Commission

For example, the Barker Real Estate Agency sells Lambert's house for $80,000 and is paid a commission of 6%. The agent's commission is 0.06 (6%) × $80,000, or $4,800.

As another example, a collection agent is paid a commission of 35% for collecting a $2,000 debt. The agent's commission is 0.35 × $2,000, or $700.

Written Practice 1

1. The Maxwell Real Estate Agency sold a house for Rubin Lenseth. The agency charged a commission of 7% on the sale price, which was $40,000. What was the agency's commission? **$2,800**

2. The Worldwide Travel Agency arranges a tour for you that costs $1,500. The agency collects a commission of 8% from the airlines and hotels that provide the tour services. What is the agency's commission?

3. Dr. Henry Kurum was unable to collect a bill of $2,580 for professional services. The doctor turned the bill over to a collection agent. The agent collected the $2,580 and charged a 30% commission. What was the agent's charge?

4. The Reliable Auction House sells household goods at auction and charges 20% for their services. If the total money involved in a sale is $4,375, what will be the auction house's charge?

Commission and Expenses. Most of an agent's expenses are paid by the agent from the commission. Some unusual expenses, though, may be charged to the principal. For example, an auctioneer might have unusual advertising expenses or high costs for moving the goods to the auction place. In such cases, the agent's charge to the principal is the total of the commission and the expenses.

Commission + Expenses = Agent's Charge

For example, a collection agent collected a bill of $5,000 for the principal. The agent's commission was 40%, and legal expenses of the collection were $173. The agent's charge to the principal was 0.40 (40%) × $5,000, or $2,000 + $173 = $2,173.

Written Practice 2

1. A purchasing agent bought goods for a customer for $1,200. The agent charged a commission of 10%, plus expenses of $37.50. What was the total of the agent's commission and expenses? **$157.50**

2. An advertising agent placed $15,000 worth of advertising in magazines. The agent charged the principal a 15% commission on that amount, plus $675 for unusual expenses. What was the agent's total charge to the principal for commission and expenses?

3. The Dunning Collection Agency collected a bill of $795 that was owed to the Coronado Department Store. The agency charged a 45% collection fee and $42.75 for legal costs. What was the agency's total charge to the store?

4. Harry Roberts, an auctioneer, sold some household goods for Maida Gibson. The total sale amounted to $2,000. Roberts charged a 20% commission and $120 for moving the goods to his auction place. What was Roberts' total charge to Maida Gibson?

★**Principal's Net Proceeds.** If you are the principal in a sale or collection by an agent, the amount that you get after the agent's charge is paid is called the **net proceeds**

Sale Price or Amount Collected − Agent's Charge = Net Proceeds

Look at this example:

Example

Swifty Callum, an auctioneer, sold some household goods for Anita Calvera at a price of $3,000. Callum charged a 20% commission and $140 for moving the goods to his auction place. What were the net proceeds of this sale for Anita Calvera?

Solution			Explanation
Sale price		$3,000	The agent's commission
Agent's charge:			was figured and added to the
Commission at 20%	$600		expenses to find the total
Expenses	140	−740	charge. The total charge was
Net proceeds		$2,260	then *subtracted* from the sale
			price to find the principal's
			net proceeds.

★**Written Practice 3**

1. Find the commission, expenses, total agent's charge, and net proceeds.

	Amount of Sale or Collection	Agent's Charge				Net Proceeds
		Commission				
		Rate	Amount	Expenses	Total	
a.	$ 6,000	15%	$900	None	$900	$5,100
b.	580	60%		$30.00	378	202
c.	57,325	7%		None		
d.	1,963	20%		54.40		
e.	831	35%		27.25		

2. Landmark Realtors sells Meewa's house for $67,500. Landmark charges a 6% commission.
   a. What is the amount of Landmark's commission?
   b. What are Meewa's net proceeds?

3. The Shurget Collection Agency collected a bill of $750 that was owed to Ertha Underwood. Shurget's collection fee was 30% and the expenses were $16. What were Underwood's net proceeds?

4. An agent sold some of your antique furniture for $875. The agent charged you a 25% commission and $15.50 for advertising costs. What were your net proceeds from the sale?

★**Principal's Gross Cost.** If you have an agent buy something for you, you should expect to pay for the cost of the item, the agent's commission, and the agent's unusual expenses. In such a case, the cost of the item is called the **prime cost** The sum of the prime cost and the agent's charge is called the **gross cost** or total cost.

Prime Cost + Agent's Charge = Gross Cost

Example

An agent buys some rare books for you that cost $3,500. The agent charges a 10% commission and $230 for expenses. What is the gross cost?

Solution			Explanation
Prime cost		$3,500	The commission at 10% of the prime cost, and the expenses, were added to find the agent's charge. The agent's charge was then *added* to the prime cost to find the gross cost.
Agent's charge:			
Commission at 10%	$350		
Expenses	230	580	
Gross cost		$4,080	

★**Written Practice 4**

Check all calculations!

1. Find the commission, expenses, total agent's charge, and gross cost.

	Prime Cost	Agent's Charge				Gross Cost
		Commission				
		Rate	Amount	Expenses	Total	
a.	$ 3,500	8%	$280	None	$ 280	$ 3,780
b.	478	10%		None		
c.	16,300	15%		$ 325.00	2,770	19,070
d.	1,842	12%		36.92		
e.	54,600	7%		1,098.00		

2. Hugh O'Malley had an agent buy some paintings for him. The paintings cost $4,600. The agent charged a commission of 8%.
   a. What was the amount of the agent's commission?
   b. What was the gross cost to O'Malley?

3. Tokay Importers, an agent, bought property valued at $7,375 for a principal, Ruby Soong. The agent charged 12% for a commission and $138.95 for expenses. What was the total cost to Ruby Soong?

4. Otto Grimaldi had an agent, the Grower's Cooperative, buy and store a supply of seed for the next year's planting. The prime cost of the seed was $5,628. The agent added storage charges of $224.60 and shipping costs of $343.20. The agent's commission was 10% of the prime cost. What was the gross cost to Grimaldi?

Match the terms and the statements.

agent   ★gross cost   ★net proceeds   ★prime cost   principal

a. A person who acts for and makes contracts for others
b. The person for whom an agent works
c. Sale price or amount collected minus agent's charge
d. Prime cost plus agent's charge
e. Cost of the item

Review 14

1. Find the value of *?* or *N*.

    a. $69 - ? = 43$ **b.** $9 \times N = 108$ **c.** $N \times 5 = 75$

2. a. What is $\$36.95 \times 0.055$?
    b. What is the cost of 300 items at 1¢?
    c. Find the product of $2,400 \times \$4.30$
    d. Multiply 606.1×2.08

3. A travel agent makes reservations for you at the Wayfarer Hotel for 3 nights at a total of $120. The hotel pays the agent a commission of 7% on the money involved. What is the amount of the agent's commission?

Are you checking all your work?

4. The Dunsmore Agency collected a bill of $1,672 for Gilda Perez. The agency charged a 45% commission and $35 for legal costs. What was the agent's total charge?

5. Rhonda Forrest sells cosmetics door-to-door. She gets a commission of $0.75 on each box of Beautymore powder that she sells. What will be her total commission on the sale of 150 boxes of the powder?

6. Rennie Lamont is a commission salesperson who sells furniture to retail stores. His principal, the Winthrop Products Corporation, pays Rennie a salary of $1,675 a month and a commission of 4% on sales over $56,000 a month. During November, Rennie's sales totaled $71,500. What was his gross pay for the month?

★ **7.** The Farmers' Auction House sold Bellott's animals and equipment at an auction, taking in $85,640 from the sale. The auction house charged a 15% commission, plus $483 for unusual expenses. What were Bellott's net proceeds from the sale?

★ **8.** Werfel bought some frozen turkeys through an agent. The prime cost was $810. The agent charged a 10% commission, plus $36.25 for storage. What was the gross cost to Werfel?

★ **9.** Carmen Verlott is self-employed. Her gross income from her business this year is $65,427, and her expenses for the year are $24,385.
    a. What is Carmen's net income from the business?
    b. At a FICA self-employment tax rate of 9.35%, what is her FICA tax for this year?

AVERAGE PAY

During your working life, the amount of your pay per hour, day, week, month, and year will change many, many times. You may have so many different amounts that comparing your present pay with your own past pay, or with other people's pay, will be difficult. To make comparing easier, you will need to figure your *average* pay.

This unit will show you how to figure average pay and use related skills. When you have done this unit, you should be able to:

- figure simple and weighted averages
- divide with whole numbers and decimals, and check your work
- estimate and check quotients
- read, write, speak, and recognize the meanings of the terms shown in color

SIMPLE AND WEIGHTED AVERAGES

section
15

Almost everyday you read or hear about averages such as average marks, batting averages, and average temperatures. An **average** is a single number that is used to represent or stand for a group of numbers. It is a number that is easier to use than a group of numbers.

For example someone might ask you, "How're you doing in math?" You would probably say something like, "My average is 86," rather than saying, "I got 85, 94, 80, 91, 79, and 87 on my tests."

"My Average is 86"

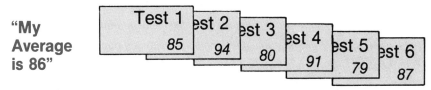

Test 1 — 85
Test 2 — 94
Test 3 — 80
Test 4 — 91
Test 5 — 79
Test 6 — 87

Put the decimal point in the quotient above the decimal point in the dividend:

X)XXX.XX

Simple Average. The simple average is the most often-used average. You find the simple average of a group of items by adding those items, then dividing that sum by the number of items.

Sum of the Items ÷ Number of Items = Simple Average

Example

During four weeks of October, Trina Kirk's weekly pay was $265, $300, $280, and $295. What was Trina's average weekly pay for the four weeks?

Solution	Explanation
$ 265 first week's pay 300 second week's pay 280 third week's pay 295 fourth week's pay ――――― $1,140 total pay for 4 weeks $1,140 ÷ 4 = $285 average pay per week	The pay for the four weeks was added to find the sum of the pay for the four weeks. That sum, $1,140, was then divided by the number of weeks, 4, to find the average pay per week, $285.

Written Practice 1

1. Two years ago your salary was $15,500. Last year it was $16,450. This year your salary is $17,670.
   a. What is the sum of your salaries for the three years? **$49,620**
   b. What is the average of your salaries for the three years? **$16,540**

2. Joel Homan works in a restaurant. His combined wage and tips for the five days of this week were: $36.50, $48.75, $51.20, $44.65, and $62.85. What was his average pay per day?

3. From January through June, Mavis Denver earned these commissions as a salesperson: January, $1,805; February, $2,362; March, $1,976; April, $2,174; May, $2,491; and June, $2,008. What was Mavis Denver's average monthly commission?

4. Rick's overtime pay for the four weeks of February was $69.24, $34.62, $51.92, and $80.78. What was Rick's average overtime pay per week?

5. The four best ticket sellers in your class sold these numbers of tickets to your class play: Seller *A*, 47; Seller *B*, 39; Seller *C*, 53; Seller *D*, 45. What was the average number of tickets sold by each of the four?

12 months = 1 year

6. Your pay for a year is $18,720. What is your average pay (a) per month and (b) per week?

52 weeks = 1 year

7. Kim's yearly pay is $12,504. Paul's pay is $1,050 per month.
   a. What is Kim's average monthly pay?
   b. Kim's monthly pay is how much less than Paul's monthly pay?

Weekly average × number of weeks = 1 year's commission

8. During January, Rory Krug's commissions averaged $345 per week. At that rate, what would be his commissions for the year?

9. Your commissions during the four quarters of last year were: January–March, $8,243; April–June, $9,382; July–September, $8,761; October–December, $8,438.
   a. What was your average quarterly commission last year?
   b. What was your average monthly commission last year?

4 quarters = 1 year

Weighted Averages. In figuring averages, you sometimes have more than one item at a given value. For example, in figuring your average monthly pay, you might find several months in which your pay was the same. The example below shows you how to solve such a problem.

Example
Your pay for the 12 months of last year was these amounts: 6 months at $1,800 per month; 3 months at $2,000 per month; 1 month at $1,848; and 2 months at $2,100. What was your average monthly pay last year?

Solution	**Explanation**
6 × $1,800 = $10,800	Each monthly amount was multiplied by the number of months in which that amount was earned. The sum of those products was then *divided* by the sum of the months to find the average monthly pay.
3 × $2,000 = 6,000	
1 × $1,848 = 1,848	
2 × $2,100 = 4,200	
12 $22,848 total pay	
$22,848 ÷ 12 = $1,904 average monthly pay last year	

The sum of the products ÷ the number of items = weighted average

As shown in the example, when you have more than one item at a given amount, you multiply that amount by the number of items. You then add those products and divide that sum by the total number of items. This average is called a **weighted average** because each amount has a "weight" proportional to the number of times it occurs.

Written Practice 2

1. At the end of a year, your records of overtime worked each month showed these figures: 5 months with 50 hours of overtime; 3 months with 26 hours of overtime; and 4 months with 20 hours of overtime. How many hours of overtime did you average per month?   34

2. Norbert Prinz worked 20 days one month at four different pay rates. He worked 8 days at $52 per day; 6 days at $50; 4 days at $48; and 2 days at $46. What was Norbert's average daily pay for that month?

3. Marybeth Wilber is a real estate salesperson. In two months she sold 10 houses at these prices: 4 at $45,000 each; 2 at $53,000; 3 at $55,000; and 1 at $60,000. What was the average price of the houses that Marybeth sold?

Have you checked your work?

4. Marybeth Wilber, in Problem 3 above, earned these commissions on the houses she sold: 4 at $1,575 commission on each; 2 at $1,855; 3 at $1,650; and 1 at $2,400. What was her average commission per house?

Unknown Item in a Series. Finding the unknown item in a series is another kind of problem that is related to averages. Look at this example:

Example

Your goal is to earn an average of $450 per week for 4 weeks. In 3 weeks you have earned $450, $440, and $500. How much must you earn in the fourth week to make your goal?

Solution	**Explanation**
(1) 4 × $450 = $1,800 to be earned in 4 weeks	(1) Multiply the average you want by number of periods to find total needed.
(2) $450 + $440 + $500 = $1,390 earned in 3 weeks	(2) Add amounts earned to find amount already earned.
(3) $1,800 − $1,390 = $410 must earn in fourth week	(3) Subtract amount earned from total needed to find unknown amount.

Written Practice 3

1. For the last three years, Jess Koff has earned $14,800, $15,680, and $16,900. How much must Jess earn this year to give him an average of $16,250 per year for the four years?   **$17,620**

2. Alma Fenton's commissions last year averaged $5,000 per quarter. Her commissions for the first three quarters were: first, $4,600; second, $5,350; third, $5,100. What were her commissions for the fourth quarter of the year?

3. Rosa Costain earned $22,800 during a recent year. For the first 11 months of that year, Rosa's average earnings were $1,890 per month. What were her December earnings?

4. Shawn Clancy, a car salesperson, has averaged 8 sales per month, January through September. Shawn wants to average 9 sales per month for the year. How many sales per month must he average for October, November, and December to reach his goal for the year?   12

5. Olaf Berger's total pay for a 5-day week was $324. His average daily pay for 4 days that week was $62. What was his pay for the fifth day?

Terms to Remember

Match the terms and statements. Use each term only once.

average   simple average   weighted average

a. Always figured as sum of the items ÷ number of items
b. Always figured as sum of the products ÷ number of items
c. Any number that represents a group of numbers

Review 15

1. Find the value of *?* or *N*.
   a. $N + 42 = 56$
   b. $85 - ? = 76$
   c. $7 \times N = 42$

2. a. What is $50 \times \$100$?
   b. Find the product of 362×0.05
   c. Multiply 2.145×0.63
   d. Subtract $649.26 from $890.05

3. For five weeks your pay was: $272; $268.50; $275.40; $281.20; and $277.30. What was your average pay per week?

4. Your yearly pay is $15,648. What is your average monthly pay?

5. Tara Monahan's average annual pay is $12,896. What is Tara's average weekly pay?

6. Clem Munger worked 8 hours at $6.50 per hour; 7 hours at $6 per hour; and 5 hours at $7.20 per hour. What was Clem's average pay per hour?

7. Your records show that your total pay for the last year was $19,420, and that your average monthly pay for the first 11 months was $1,620. You have lost the record of your pay for the twelfth month. What must have been your pay for that month?

8. An auctioneer sold some household goods for $834 and deducted a 25% commission plus $43.50 for expenses. What was the total of the auctioneer's charge for the sale?

★ 9. The Middler Agency bought several tons of fruit for the Hi-Cal Packing Company. The prime cost of the fruit was $12,000. The agency charged Hi-Cal $375 for trucking and 10% for commission. What was the gross cost of the purchase to Hi-Cal?

DIVISION

In Section 15 you used division to figure averages. Now let's look some more at division.

Division Indicators. As shown in the illustration below, the division process may be shown in several ways. They all mean the same.

$$15 \div 3 = 5 \qquad 3\overline{)15}^{\,5}$$

THEY ALL MEAN THE SAME

$$\frac{15}{3} = 5 \qquad 3\overline{)\,15\,}_{\,5}$$

What Division Is. Division is the opposite of multiplication. When you multiply, you combine two known factors to find an unknown product.

Known Factor × Known Factor = Unknown Product
(F)   (F)   (P)

When you divide, you break a known product (**dividend**) into two pieces or factors: a known factor (**divisor**) and an unknown factor (**quotient**). If the division is not exact, you have something left over (**remainder**).

Known Product ÷ Known Factor = Unknown Factor and Remainder
(P)   (F)   (F)   (R)

When you divide, you usually set up your problem this way:

$$\underset{\substack{\text{Known Factor} \\ \text{(divisor)}}}{}\Big)\overline{\underset{\substack{\text{Known Product} \\ \text{(dividend)}}}{\overset{\substack{\text{Unknown Factor} \\ \text{(quotient)} \quad \text{and Remainder}}}{}}}$$

Division may also be thought of as a short way of repeatedly subtracting a known amount (divisor) from a product (dividend) to find how many times the known amount is contained in the product.

Oral Practice 1

What is the quotient?

	1.	2.	3.	4.
a.	$8 \div 4 =$	$6\overline{)12} =$	$\dfrac{6}{2} =$	$2 \div 2 =$
b.	$8 \div 2 =$	$4\overline{)16} =$	$\dfrac{9}{9} =$	$0 \div N =$
c.	$2 \div 2 =$	$1\overline{)0} =$	$\dfrac{0}{5} =$	$N \div N =$
d.	$1 \div 1 =$	$5\overline{)5} =$	$\dfrac{N}{1} =$	$N \div 1 =$

Oral Practice 2

What is the quotient?

	1.	2.	3.	4.	5.
a.	$6 \div 2 =$	$8 \div 2 =$	$10 \div 2 =$	$12 \div 2 =$	$14 \div 2 =$
b.	$9 \div 1 =$	$32 \div 4 =$	$36 \div 4 =$	$40 \div 5 =$	$24 \div 6 =$
c.	$3 \div 1 =$	$0 \div 4 =$	$30 \div 5 =$	$24 \div 3 =$	$27 \div 3 =$
d.	$16 \div 2 =$	$18 \div 2 =$	$28 \div 4 =$	$36 \div 6 =$	$25 \div 5 =$
e.	$4 \div 4 =$	$6 \div 3 =$	$9 \div 1 =$	$24 \div 4 =$	$30 \div 6 =$
f.	$35 \div 5 =$	$8 \div 4 =$	$9 \div 3 =$	$1 \div 1 =$	$45 \div 5 =$
g.	$12 \div 6 =$	$21 \div 3 =$	$12 \div 4 =$	$12 \div 3 =$	$20 \div 5 =$

Identifying Factors and the Product. In multiplication and division sentences, you need to be sure which numbers are factors and which number is the product. To do so, you can imagine or write **F** or **P** over each numeral. For example:

$$\overset{\textbf{F}}{4} \times \overset{\textbf{F}}{3} = \overset{\textbf{P}}{12} \qquad \overset{\textbf{F}}{4} \times \overset{\textbf{F}}{N} = \overset{\textbf{P}}{12} \qquad \overset{\textbf{P}}{12} \div \overset{\textbf{F}}{3} = \overset{\textbf{F}}{4} \qquad \overset{\textbf{P}}{N} \div \overset{\textbf{F}}{3} = \overset{\textbf{F}}{4}$$

Oral Practice 3

Identify each numeral or N as **F** (factor) or **P** (product).

	1.	2.	3.
a.	$7 \times 5 = 35$	$N \div 6 = 5$	$8 \times N = 56$
b.	$5 \times 4 = 20$	$7 \times 4 = N$	$N \times 5 = 45$
c.	$32 \div 4 = 8$	$8 \times N = 32$	$N = 9 \times 9$
d.	$18 \div 9 = 2$	$14 \div 2 = N$	$N \div 8 = 5$
e.	$3 \times 7 = 21$	$N \times 9 = 45$	$28 = 4 \times N$

Written Practice 4

Copy each number sentence in Oral Practice 3 and identify each numeral or N by writing **F** or **P** above it.

Finding an Unknown Product or Unknown Factor. In the sentences $3 \times 4 = N$ and $N \div 3 = 4$, the two factors are known, but the product, N, is unknown. You find the unknown product, N, by *multiplying* the two known factors, 3×4. The unknown product is 12.

In the sentences $3 \times N = 12$ and $12 \div N = 3$, the product, 12, and one factor, 3, are known. The other factor, N, is unknown. To find the unknown factor, you *divide* the known product, 12, by the known factor, 3.

Oral Practice 5

Is N a factor or a product? What is the value of N?

	1.	**2.**	**3.**
a.	$12 \times 4 = N$	$N \div 6 = 9$	$40 = N \div 4$
b.	$8 \times N = 56$	$N = 8 \times 16$	$35 = 7 \times N$
c.	$N \times 6 = 42$	$80 = N \times 8$	$N \div 4 = 22$
d.	$63 \div 9 = N$	$N = 147 \div 7$	$3 \times N = 27$

Written Practice 6

Copy each sentence. Identify each numeral or N by writing F or P above it. Then find the value of N.

1. $15 \times N = 180$ 5. $27 \times N = 405$

2. $N \div 18 = 432$ 6. $N \div 15 = 34$

3. $133 \div N = 19$ 7. $24 = 288 \div N$

4. $N = 273 \div 21$ 8. $16 \times N = 368$

Showing a Remainder as a Fraction. When a division is not exact, there is a remainder. The remainder may be shown as a fractional part of the divisor by writing it over the divisor. Look at this example:

Example
$90 \div 12 = ?$

Solution:

$$\begin{array}{r} 7\frac{1}{2} \text{ Ans.} \\ \hline 12\overline{)90} \\ \underline{84} \\ 6 \end{array}$$

$$\frac{6}{6} = \frac{6}{12} = \frac{1}{2}^*$$

---

*A fraction is usually shown in lowest terms. A fraction is in lowest terms when both numbers are divisible only by 1.

Checking Division. You can check division by going over your work again. You can also check it by multiplying the divisor by the whole number in the quotient, then adding the remainder. That result should equal the dividend. The problem in the preceding example can be checked that way.

Example

$$90 \div 12 = ?$$

Solution	Check	Explanation
$7\frac{1}{2}$ Ans. $12\overline{)90}$ $\underline{84}$ $6 = \frac{6}{12}$ or $\frac{1}{2}$	$7 \times 12 = 84$ $\underline{+6}$ 90	The whole number in the quotient, 7, times the divisor, 12, is 84. 84 plus the remainder, 6, is 90. 90 is the same as the dividend, so the division is correct.

Written Practice 7

Divide, showing any remainder as a fraction in lowest terms. Check your answers.

1. $1{,}645 \div 7 =$
2. $2{,}592 \div 6 =$
3. $2{,}844 \div 9 =$
4. $1{,}400 \div 8 =$
5. $2{,}840 \div 5 =$

6. $2{,}731 \div 4 =$
7. $4{,}820 \div 9 =$
8. $3{,}229 \div 7 =$
9. $3{,}157 \div 8 =$
10. $1{,}368 \div 5 =$

11. $317 \div 12 =$
12. $420 \div 24 =$
13. $724 \div 16 =$
14. $1{,}328 \div 32 =$
15. $1{,}269 \div 36 =$

Putting the Decimal Point in the Quotient. You have already been reminded how to locate the decimal point when there is a decimal point in the dividend but *not* in the divisor. As shown in the example below, you put the decimal point in the quotient above the decimal point in the dividend.

Example

$$\$16.28 \div 4 = ?$$

Solution	Explanation
$\$\ 4.07$ Ans. $4\overline{)\$16.28}$	The dividend ($16.28) has a decimal point, but the divisor (4) is a whole number. So, the decimal point in the quotient ($4.07) is put above the decimal point in the dividend.

Written Practice 8

Divide, then check by multiplying.

1. $\$18.75 \div 5 =$
2. $\$48.42 \div 9 =$
3. $\$4.62 \div 7 =$
4. $\$238 \div 8 =$

5. $26.84 \div 4 =$
6. $3.768 \div 6 =$
7. $347.2 \div 8 =$
8. $305.06 \div 7 =$

9. $15.525 \div 25 =$
10. $700.35 \div 35 =$
11. $12.002 \div 34 =$
12. $1.4475 \div 15 =$

If a divisor has a decimal point, you remove the decimal point in the divisor by multiplying both the divisor and the dividend by 10, 100, 1,000, or other multiple of 10. You then divide as usual.

Example
350 ÷ 17.5 = ?

Solution

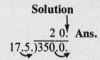

2 0. Ans.

17.5.)350.0.

Explanation

To remove the decimal point in the divisor, the decimal points in both the divisor and dividend were moved 1 place to the right. That multiplied both numbers by 10 and made the divisor a whole number. Multiplying both the divisor and dividend by the same number does not change the quotient. The decimal point in the quotient was put above the *new* position of the decimal point in the dividend.

Written Practice 9

Divide, then check your answers by multiplying.

1. $45.15 ÷ $2.15 =
2. $144 ÷ $3.20 =
3. $16.65 ÷ $0.45 =
4. $75 ÷ $0.375 =
5. $2,520 ÷ 6.3 =
6. 27.5 ÷ 0.055 =
7. 0.288 ÷ 0.0072 =
8. 8.10 ÷ 135 =
9. 0.5 ÷ 2.5 =

Terms to Remember

dividend   division   divisor   quotient   remainder

a. The known factor in division
b. The known product in division
c. The unknown factor, or answer, in division
d. The leftover in division
e. The opposite process of multiplication

Review 16

1. Copy each sentence and write **F** for Factor or **P** for Product over each numeral. Then find the value of the unknown number.

   a. $25 \times N = 600$ b. $N ÷ 15 = 30$ c. $336 ÷ N = 28$

2. a. Divide $6.25 by $0.25
   b. What is 36.55 ÷ 8.5?
   c. Divide 3.125 by 0.005

3. For four days, your pay was $50, $43.60, $57, and $55.20. What was your average daily pay?

4. Cyd's annual pay is $13,728. What is her average weekly pay?

5. Sol Ellsberg worked 20 hours at $5.80 per hour and 10 hours at $6.40 per hour. What was his average hourly pay?

DIVISION (concluded)

Dividing by 10, 100, or 1,000. You can easily divide by 10, 100, or 1,000 by moving the decimal point to the left as many places as there are zeros in the divisor.

Example

To divide by 10, 100, and 1,000:

$23.9 \div 10 = 2.39$	$\$8,900 \div 100 = \$89$
$520 \div 10 = 52$	$0.25 \div 100 = 0.0025$
$\$4,200 \div 10 = \$420$	$342.6 \div 1,000 = 0.3426$
$0.5 \div 10 = 0.05$	$875 \div 1,000 = 0.875$
$35.4 \div 100 = 0.354$	$\$10,431 \div 1,000 = \$10.431$
$432 \div 100 = 4.32$	$0.625 \div 1,000 = 0.000625$

Oral Practice 1

What is the quotient?

1.

a. $\$1,400 \div 10 =$

b. $\$73,000 \div 100 =$

c. $\$62,000 \div 1,000 =$

d. $9.3 \div 10 =$

e. $4,976.3 \div 1,000 =$

f. $4.8 \div 100 =$

2.

$70 \div 100 =$

$800 \div 1,000 =$

$9 \div 10 =$

$50 \div 1,000 =$

$0.5 \div 10 =$

$0.8 \div 100 =$

Written Practice 2

Move the decimal point to the LEFT
←

Find the quotient by moving the decimal point. Check by multiplying.

1. $\$350 \div 10 =$

2. $\$625 \div 100 =$

3. $\$9,860 \div 1,000 =$

4. $\$225 \div 100 =$

5. $\$25 \div 10 =$

6. $\$3,870 \div 1,000 =$

7. $6,540 \div 100 =$

8. $6.329 \div 10 =$

9. $0.4 \div 100 =$

10. $0.05 \div 1,000 =$

11. $7.05 \div 10 =$

12. $1.906 \div 10 =$

Dividing by Multiples of 10, 100, or 1,000. Multiples of 10, 100, or 1,000 are numbers that have zeros at the end, such as 40, 300, 480, 2,000, and 4,000. To divide by such a multiple, you cross out the zeros in the divisor and move the decimal point in the dividend to the left as many places as there were zeros in the divisor. Then you divide as usual.

An example of the way you would use this process in solving a practical problem is shown at the top of the next page.

Example

What is the average hourly pay of a worker who works 40 hours and is paid $314.40?

Solution

$314.40 ÷ 40 = ?

$$\frac{\$\ 7.86}{40\ \overline{)\ \$31\.4.40}}\quad\textbf{Ans.}$$

Explanation

When you cross out the zero in the divisor and move the decimal point one place to the left in the dividend, you are dividing both the divisor and the dividend by 10. This does not change the quotient. You then divide as usual and put the decimal point in the quotient above the *new* position of the decimal point in the dividend.

Oral Practice 3

What is the quotient?

	1.	**2.**	**3.**
a.	42 ÷ 20 =	660 ÷ 300 =	3,000 ÷ 2,000 =
b.	186 ÷ 60 =	840 ÷ 400 =	12,840 ÷ 4,000 =
c.	$320 ÷ 50 =	$2,170 ÷ 700 =	$18,060 ÷ 6,000 =
d.	$2,400 ÷ 30 =	$23,500 ÷ 500 =	$36,000 ÷ 3,000 =
e.	$3,420 ÷ 90 =	$12,800 ÷ $800 =	$60,000 ÷ $15,000 =

Written Practice 4

Find the quotient by moving the decimal.

1. 96 ÷ 30 =

2. 846 ÷ 200 =

3. 1,265 ÷ 500 =

4. 58.8 ÷ 70 =

5. 368.2 ÷ 2,000 =

6. 254.5 ÷ 5,000 =

7. 0.4 ÷ 80 =

8. 27,000 ÷ 900 =

9. $450 ÷ 20 =

10. $1,536 ÷ 40 =

11. $30 ÷ 600 =

12. $49,000 ÷ 7,000 =

Estimating the Quotient. Estimating a quotient and comparing it with your exact quotient is a good way to find large errors in division. Sometimes, also, an estimated quotient is accurate enough for your needs. For example, you might want to know how many items at $9.75 you could buy for $100. You could estimate that, because $9.75 is about $10, you could buy 10 items ($100 ÷ $10 = 10 items).

To estimate a quotient, you round the divisor to the first digit on the left. You then round the dividend to the nearest easy multiple of the rounded divisor, and divide. With practice, you can do this mentally.

Look at the example at the top of the next page.

Example

Find the estimated quotient and the exact quotient of 3,275 ÷ 306.

Estimated Quotient	Exact Quotient
Round the divisor, 306, to 300. Round the dividend, 3,275, to 3,300, the nearest easy multiple of 3. 3,300 ÷ 300 = 11, the estimated quotient.	10.7 **Ans.** 306) 3,275. (All figures for this division are not shown.)

In the example, the actual quotient, 10.7, is reasonable and probably correct because it is close to the estimated quotient, 11. If one quotient is ten or more times the other, at least one of the quotients is probably wrong. You should then refigure the quotients.

Here are some other examples of estimated quotients:

Examples

Find each estimated quotient.

	Approximate Divisor	Approximate Dividend	Estimated Quotient
9,544 ÷ 52	50	10,000	200
2,350 ÷ 28	30	2,400	80
432 ÷ 18.6	20	400	20
65 ÷ 0.084*	80	64,000	800

Oral Practice 5

How was the estimated quotient found?

1. 1,878 ÷ 577 is about 3

2. 757 ÷ 16 is about 40

3. 525.4 ÷ 47.5 is about 10

4. $4,850 ÷ 62 is about $80

5. $577 ÷ 84 is about $7

6. $9,324.50 ÷ 31 is about $300

Written Practice 6

Find the exact quotient and check it against the estimated quotient.

		Exact Quotient	Estimated Quotient
1.	$3,162 ÷ 31	$102	$100
2.	$4,134 ÷ 53		
3.	$625.05 ÷ 27		
4.	15.61 ÷ 2.23		
5.	$584.28 ÷ 3,246		
6.	0.39 ÷ 0.06		

*If the divisor is less than 1, change it to a whole number by moving the decimal point in the divisor and dividend to the right. In this way, 0.084 becomes 84, and 65 becomes 65,000.

Written Practice 7

Mentally estimate, then write your answers to these problems.

1. You are now making $51 per day in your job. About how many days must you work to earn $500? **10**

2. Flora Williams makes $4.75 on each item she sells. About how many items must Flora sell to earn $98 in commissions?

3. Enrico Vegas is paid a salary of $19,980 per year. At this rate, about how many years will it take Enrico to earn $200,000?

4. The 42 members of a school club are trying to earn $1,500 to take a trip. All students are expected to earn their equal share of the total. About how much should each student be expected to earn?

Rounding to a Stated Number of Decimal Places. If a division problem tells you to carry the answer to a stated number of decimal places, you should carry the division only *one* place farther. You then round back to the stated number of places. Look at this example.

Examples

Cindy Greentree works a 40-hour week and is paid a salary of $370.25 per week. What is Cindy's hourly pay (a) to the nearest cent and (b) to the nearest tenth of a cent.

Solutions		Explanation
(a)	**(b)**	The division was carried *one* place
6		beyond the stated number of decimal
$ 9.25̸6̸	$ 9.256̸3̸	places. The quotient was then rounded
40)$370.25	40)$370.25	back to the stated number of places.
Ans. $9.26	**Ans. $9.256**	

Remember this rule!

In this book, you are to round final answers in dollars and cents to the nearest cent, unless you are told otherwise.

Written Practice 8

In each problem, you are to:

a. estimate the quotient,
b. divide correct to the stated number of places, and
c. check the estimated and exact answers.

To *three* decimal places (nearest thousandth)	To *two* decimal places (nearest hundredth)	To the *nearest tenth of a cent*
1. 371.2 ÷ 3,524	4. 26.5 ÷ 2.62	7. $18.65 ÷ 605
2. 8.213 ÷ 9.07	5. 6.22 ÷ 0.721	8. $48.08 ÷ 415
3. 0.5642 ÷ 0.21	6. 48 ÷ 0.2412	9. $76.85 ÷ 246

Review 17   1. Copy each sentence and write **F** for Factor or **P** for Product over each numeral. Then find the value of the unknown number.

     a. $1.5 \times N = 60$ **c.** $0.25 \times N = 50$ **e.** $52.5 \div N = 1.25$

     b. $N \div 2.6 = 15$ **d.** $1.06 \times N = 84.8$ **f.** $N = 40 \div 64$

2. **a.** Divide 634.5 by 100
   b. What is $\$66.50 \div 70$?
   c. Divide 42.125 by 0.025
   d. Round 46.8245 to the nearest hundredth
   e. Multiply 23.6 by 0.075

3. Your goal is to average $80 in commissions per day. This week your daily commissions have been: Monday, $82.75; Tuesday, $71.45; Wednesday, $78.62; Thursday, $85.39. What commission must you make on Friday to reach your goal?

4. Larkin is paid a salary of $1,500 a month and a commission of 1% on all sales. During September, Larkin's sales totaled $62,850. What was Larkin's gross pay for September?

5. Tony Lorenzo upholsters chair seats in a furniture factory on a piece-rate basis. Tony is paid $1.20 for each seat he upholsters. One week his daily production was: Monday, 54 seats; Tuesday, 48; Wednesday, 51; Thursday, 53; Friday, 56. What was his gross pay for the week?

6. Kopec is now working a 38-hour week at $6.74 per hour. If Kopec's pay rate is increased to $7.06 per hour, what will be the increase in Kopec's weekly gross pay?

7. At a FICA tax rate of 6.7%, what is the FICA tax on Angela Delgado's wages of $452.20?

Get it right! Check everything

8. Joy's gross pay for a week is $429.60. If Joy's employer deducts $58.80 for withholding tax, $28.78 for FICA tax, and $5.82 for other deductions, what is Joy's weekly take-home pay?

★ 9. An agent bought some farm products for Tomcho at a prime cost of $9,482. The agent charged a commission of 12% and expenses of $178.25. What was the gross cost to Tomcho?

★10. The Admore Agency collected $12,876 for advertising they had sold for Station WKDL. The agency deducted their 15% commission, $1,040 for expenses, and sent the balance to the principal, Station WKDL. What amount did the agency send to the principal?

★11. Bruce Lufkin is a self-employed accountant who runs his business from his home. Last year Lufkin's gross income was $48,542 and his business expenses totaled $16,285.
   a. What was Lufkin's net income from his business?
   b. At a FICA self-employment tax rate of 9.35%, what was Lufkin's self-employment tax on his net income?

CHOOSING A JOB

You need to think about many things when you figure the total benefits of a job or compare the benefits of several jobs. For example, in deciding which one of several jobs to take, you need to consider the kind of work you would have to do, the working hours, and the working conditions. You need to think about your ability and desire to do the work, and your chances for success and promotion. These things are important, but they are hard to figure exactly because they involve judgments that often cannot be treated mathematically.

On the other hand, the pay, fringe benefits, and expenses of different jobs can be expressed and compared in dollars and cents. This unit is concerned with just that — figuring and comparing the financial benefits and expenses of jobs.

When you have finished this unit, you should be able to:

- figure pay for equivalent time periods
- figure fringe benefits and expenses of jobs
- compare the benefits and expenses of jobs
- read, write, speak, and recognize the meanings of the terms shown in color

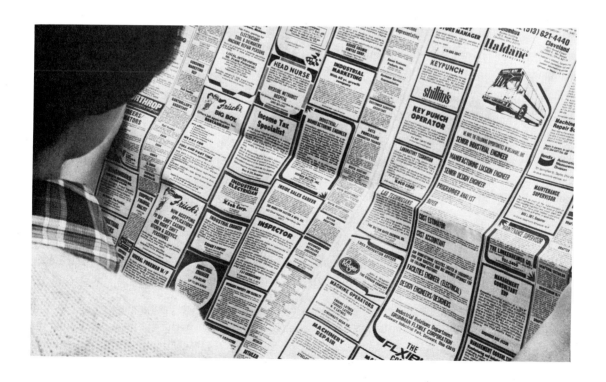

FIGURING EQUIVALENT PAY

The pay for different jobs may be given for different periods of time. For example, one job pays $250 per week; another job pays $1,125 per month. To compare the pay of such jobs, you must find the **equivalent pay** for the same time, such as a week, month, or year.

The table below shows you how to figure equivalent pay. The table is based on the fact that a work year generally has 12 months and 52 weeks, but that all work years, months, and weeks may not have the same number of hours or days.

FIGURING EQUIVALENT PAY

Given the pay per	To Find the pay per	Do This
Year	Month	Yearly pay ÷ 12
Year	Week	Yearly pay ÷ 52
Year, and number of hours per week	Hour	(Yearly pay ÷ 52) ÷ hours per week
Month	Year	Monthly pay × 12
Month	Week	(Monthly pay × 12) ÷ 52
Month, and number of hours per week	Hour	[(Monthly pay × 12) ÷ 52] ÷ hours per week
Week	Year	Weekly pay × 52
Week	Month	(Weekly pay × 52) ÷ 12
Week, and number of hours per week	Hour	Weekly pay ÷ hours per week
Hour, and number of hours per week	Year	Hourly pay × hours per week × 52
Hour, and number of hours per week	Month	(Hourly pay × hours per week × 52) ÷ 12
Hours, and number of hours per week	Week	Hourly pay × hours per week

To use the table, you locate in the first column the period for which you have a *given* pay. In the second column, you locate the period for which you are *to find* the pay. Then do as told in the "Do This" column.

For example, you are given a yearly pay of $18,000, and need to find the equivalent pay for a month. As shown in the table, you divide the yearly pay by 12 ($18,000 ÷ 12 = $1,500 per month).

Written Practice 1

1. Use the table on page 70 to find the equivalent pay for these amounts.

	Given		To Find	
	Pay	**For Time**	**Equivalent Pay**	**For Time**
a.	$1,600	Month	$19,200	Year
b.	$18,420	Year		Month
c.	$344	Week		Year
d.	$9.25	Hour for 40-hour week		Year
e.	$1,820	Month		Week
f.	$17,992	Year		Week
g.	$6.75	Hour for 40-hour week		Month
h.	$1,820	Month for 35-hour week		Hour

2. You can have a job that pays $15,600 per year at the Elmore Company. A similar job at Spartan Electronics would pay you $1,275 per month.
   a. What would be the yearly pay at Spartan?   **$15,300**
   b. Which job would pay more per year, and how much more?   **$300**
   c. What is the monthly pay of the job at Elmore?   **$1,300**
   d. What is the difference in monthly pay between the two jobs?   **$25**

3. Clara Quinn works at Allied Insurance Company and is paid $5.75 per hour for a 40-hour week. Ruth Wister works at the City Bank for $988 a month.
   a. What is Clara's weekly pay?
   b. What is Ruth's weekly pay?
   c. Who makes more weekly pay, and how much more?

Are you REALLY checking your work?

4. Faye Jordan's present job pays her $2,075 per month. She is considering a new job that will pay her $480 per week. Will the new job pay more or less per month than her present job, and how much more or less per month?

5. In one state, all state-employed clerks are to get an increase in their pay of 35¢ an hour. On the basis of a 40-hour week, what will be their pay increase:

   a. per week?   b. per year?   c. per month?

6. Burl Exberg is comparing the pay of two job offers. A job at Kirkwood will require him to work a 40-hour week at an annual salary of $13,312. A job at Coleville will pay him a weekly salary of $247 for a 38-hour week.
   a. What is the hourly pay for the Kirkwood job?
   b. What is the hourly pay for the Coleville job?
   c. What is the difference in weekly pay?
   d. What is the difference in annual pay?

Review 18

1. Find the value of N.

   a. $1.05 \times N = 3.15$ **b.** $16 \times N = 12$ **c.** $32 \times N = 20$

2. **a.** Multiply 8.53 by 0.07
   b. What is $20,400 \times 3,040$?
   c. Divide 0.207 by 45
   d. Divide 7 by 9, correct to 3 decimal places
   e. What is $\$27.86 \div 9.25$, to the nearest cent?

3. Weekly pay of $245 is equivalent to how much yearly pay?

4. You have a job that pays $9.40 an hour for a 40-hour week. You can get a new job that pays a salary of $400 a week.
   a. What does your present job pay per week?
   b. How much more per week would you make on the new job than on your present job?
   c. How much more per year would you make on the new job?

5. Desi Ortez is paid a yearly salary of $15,808 and is expected to work a 40-hour week. Jorges Shandu is paid a weekly wage of $294 for a 40-hour week. Which worker is paid the higher hourly rate, and how much higher? (Use the table on page 70, if you wish.)

6. Cora Matsu earns $332 a week and has 4 withholding allowances. Using the tables on pages 34 and 36, what is the total weekly deduction from Cora's pay for withholding tax and FICA tax?

7. Hoke Pampa is paid a commission of 4% on all monthly sales up to $50,000 and 6% commission on all monthly sales over $50,000. In October, Hoke's sales totaled $58,350. What was his total commission for October?

8. A real estate agency sold a house for $130,000 and charged a 6% commission on the sale.
   a. What was the amount of the agency's commission?
   b. What amount did the owner of the house get after the agency's commission was deducted?

9. The Mandan family's income for four weeks is shown below. Find the total of each kind of income, the gross income for each week, and the gross income for the four weeks.

Week	Salary	Wage	Commission	Other	Gross Income
First	$395.00	$284.00	$47.60	$20.00	
Second	395.00	284.00	38.10	0.00	
Third	395.00	284.00	52.36	37.64	
Fourth	395.00	284.00	49.84	0.00	
Total					

FRINGE BENEFITS AND EXPENSES

section
19

In addition to your pay, many jobs provide goods, services, and other things of value. These goods, services, and other things of value are called **fringe benefits**

Fringe benefits vary widely from job to job. They include such benefits as pensions, free or low-cost life insurance, health and accident insurance, sports and recreation facilities, free or low-cost meals, uniforms, paid sick leave and vacation time, use of a car, parking, purchase discounts, credit unions, and education and training.

Fringe benefits may be worth as much as 15% to 40% of gross pay

You should carefully consider fringe benefits when you look at jobs. The value of some of these benefits can be figured accurately; the value of others can only be estimated. In any case, the actual or estimated value of fringe benefits should be included when you figure total job benefits.

Gross Pay + Fringe Benefits = Total Job Benefits

Example

Nelda Webster works in the office of the United Electrical Company. Last year, Nelda figured these yearly benefits of her job:

Gross pay		$15,000
Fringe benefits:		
Paid pension contributions	$1,060	
Life and health insurance	950	
Vacation and sick leave	870	
Parking (estimated)	375	
Purchase discounts (estimated)	295	3,550
Total job benefits		$18,550

Written Practice 1

1. Vincent Felski has a job that pays him $14,750 a year in wages. His fringe benefits are worth these amounts per year:

Retirement plan	$1,180
Insurance	350
Paid time off	592
Low-cost lunches	250
Uniforms	200

   a. What is the total value of his fringe benefits per year? **$2,572**
   b. What are the total yearly benefits of his job? **$17,322**

2. You have an offer of a new job that would pay you $10.50 an hour for a 40-hour week. Your estimated weekly fringe benefits would be: insurance, $7.35; lunches, $8.25; parking, $12.50; purchase discounts, $1.25.
   a. What would be your weekly wage?
   b. What would your weekly fringe benefits be worth?
   c. What would be your total job benefits per week?

Gross pay plus fringe benefits equal total job benefits

3. You are looking at a new job that will pay you both a salary and a commission. The annual salary is $16,000. You estimate that the commission will amount to $5,000 per year. You figure that the yearly fringe benefits of the new job will be: paid pension plan, $1,050; insurance, $1,680; use of a car, $1,800; paid courses at a local college, $700.
   a. What is your estimated gross pay per year?
   b. What is the yearly value of your fringe benefits?
   c. What are the total yearly benefits of the job?

4. Adam Matthews estimates that all his fringe benefits are worth 30% of his annual pay. His annual pay is $16,200.
   a. What is the annual value of Adam's fringe benefits?   **$4,860**
   b. What are the total annual benefits of his job?

5. Nora Kilgore works at the Eagle Aircraft plant at a monthly salary of $2,000. She estimates that the monthly fringe benefits of her job are these: retirement plan, 8% of salary; insurances, 6% of salary; time off, $160; recreation facilities and events, $25; purchase discounts, $15.
   a. What is the estimated value of her retirement and insurance benefits per month?
   b. What is the total value of her fringe benefits per month?
   c. What are the total monthly benefits of her job?

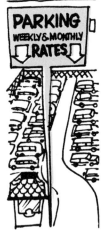

Job Expenses.
You are likely to have some expenses with any job you hold. For example, you may have expenses for traveling to and from work. You may have to spend money for such items as union or professional dues, special clothing, tools and equipment, parking, and insurance. These expenses vary from job to job. They may be great, so you need to consider them carefully.

Job expenses reduce your benefits from a job, so you subtract them from total job benefits to find net job benefits.

Total Job Benefits − Job Expenses = Net Job Benefits

Example

Nelda Webster, in the example on page 73, had total yearly job benefits of $18,550. From those benefits she subtracted her job expenses, as shown below, to find her net job benefits.

Total job benefits		$18,550
Expenses:		
Travel	$535	
Dues	25	
Birthday and holiday gifts	45	605
Net job benefits		$17,945

Written Practice 2

1. The total benefits of your job are $15,800. You estimate your job expenses to be $670. What are your net job benefits? **$15,130**

2. Aldo Hunter has a job for which he figures the total job benefits are worth $15,250 a year. He estimates his yearly job expenses to be: travel, $420; dues, $385; tools, $65; special clothing, $150.
   a. What are his total yearly job expenses?
   b. What are his net yearly job benefits?

Total job benefits minus expenses equal net job benefits

3. Frieda Sanger estimates that her total job expenses are 5% of her total job benefits. Her job benefits total $21,425 per year.
   a. What is the amount of her estimated job expenses? **$1,071.25**
   b. What is the net value of her job per year?

4. Kelly O'Connor is paid $17,650 a year on her job. She estimates the fringe benefits of the job to be worth $1,590 a year. She also estimates the job-related expenses to be $1,412 a year.
   a. What is the total of her job benefits per year?
   b. What are her net job benefits per year?

5. On his job at Spacetek, Incorporated, Phil Standish is paid an annual salary of $21,600. His fringe benefits are: pension and insurance, $1,945; vacation and sick time, $1,275; other, $220. He estimates his expenses to be: travel, $650; parking, $100; other, $375. What are the net annual benefits of his job?

Terms to Remember

Match the terms and the statements.

       equivalent pay   **fringe benefits**

   a. Pay for the same period of time
   b. Things of value above pay

Review 19

1. **a.** Divide $11.45 by 12, correct to the nearest cent
   b. Divide 14,000 by 400
   c. Multiply 16.3 by 4.08
   d. $15 \times N = 345$. What is the value of N?

2. Zelda Gray's job last year paid $10,200 in wages and $3,570 in tips. Fringe benefits were: free meals, $780; parking, $400; recreation facilities, $500. What were the total benefits of her job last year?

BE RIGHT! Check everything!

3. Your job pays you $23,400 per year. You estimate the value of your fringe benefits to be $5,150 per year. Your job-related expenses for a year are transportation and parking, $1,200; dues, $150; other, $370.
   a. What are your total job benefits per year?
   b. What are your net job benefits per year?

4. Davila normally works 40 hours per week on a job that pays $1,118 per month. What is Davila's hourly pay rate?

COMPARING JOBS

In choosing among jobs, you need to get the most complete and accurate data you can concerning the pay, fringe benefits, and expenses for each job. You can then compare the jobs to find which has the greatest money value. When you have done that, you can consider other factors and make an informed decision.

Written Practice 1

1. Debbie Havasu has a job with the Chenwan Company that pays her $1,550 per month. The yearly value of the fringe benefits of her present job are: pension and insurance, $1,674; free transportation to and from work, $565; low-cost credit union loans, $200. Her annual expenses on her present job are union dues, $375; special clothing, $250; tools, $50.

   If Debbie takes a new job with the Lomoto Corporation, her pay will be $20,500 a year. On the Lomoto job, the yearly value of fringe benefits would be: pension and insurance, $1,845; uniforms, $250; purchase discounts, $300. Her yearly expenses would be transportation and parking, $975.

   Complete the table below to find the net job benefits of each job.

	Yearly Values	Chenwan Company	Lomoto Corporation
a.	Gross pay	$18,600	$20,500
b.	Fringe benefits		
c.	Total job benefits		
d.	Expenses		
e.	Net job benefits		

2. You have a choice of two job offers. The Baker Corporation job would pay you an annual salary of $14,750, with fringe benefits worth $1,095. Your expenses on that job would be $740 per year. The Romco Corporation job would pay you a weekly wage of $285, with fringe benefits estimated at $985 a year. Your annual expenses on the Romco job would be $800.
   a. What would be the net job benefits per year of the Baker job?
   b. What would be the annual net job benefits of the Romco job?
   c. Which job would give you the greater net benefits per year, and how much greater?

Gross pay plus fringe benefits minus expenses equal net job benefits

3. Dillon's job with RKM Service pays him $7.50 per hour for a 40-hour week. He estimates the fringe benefits of that job to be worth $2,350 per year and his expenses to be $1,250 per year. If Dillon takes a new job with the ELCO Corporation, he will get $8 per hour for a 40-hour week. He estimates that the fringe benefits of the ELCO job will amount to 20% of his gross pay, and that his expenses will be 5% of his pay.
   a. What are the net job benefits per year with RKM?
   b. What will be the net job benefits per year with ELCO?

4. Holly Davis is choosing her first full-time job after graduation from high school. A job with AMCO Insurance would pay $6 per hour for a 40-hour week. A similar job with Rex Products would pay $5.50 per hour for a 40-hour week. Fringe benefits at AMCO average 15% a year, and at Rex Products they average 20% a year. Holly's expenses at AMCO would average $770 a year. Her expenses at Rex Products would average $260 a year. Which job would give her more net benefits per year? How much more?

Review 20

1. a. Divide $10.85 by 25, correct to the nearest cent
   b. Divide 52.74 by 1.8
   c. Multiply 2,900 by 4,000
   d. Multiply 0.056 by 2.5
   e. Subtract 3.2 from 64.095

2. Last year, Paula Yarrow earned $12,000 in salary and $9,620 in commissions as a salesperson. Fringe benefits of her job were: pension plan, $1,215; insurance, $1,324; use of car for personal driving, $800; paid vacation time, $1,080.
   a. What was the value of Paula's fringe benefits?
   b. What was the total of Paula's job benefits?

You can be sure of your answers if you check EVERYTHING!

3. Lars Benjak's job as a lab technician pays him an average of $18,096 per year. His average yearly expenses on the job are 7% of his average annual pay. What is the dollar amount of his average yearly expenses?

4. Jake Oporto is considering a new job that will pay $6.80 per hour for a 40-hour week. Fringe benefits on that job are estimated at $2,265 per year, and expenses at $570 per year. Oporto's present job pays $256 a week, with fringe benefits worth $1,600 per year and expenses of $665 per year. By how much would the net job benefits of the new job be greater than Oporto's present job benefits?

5. Olga Lamont is a piece-rate worker in an assembly plant. Her goal for this 5-day week is to assemble an average of 58 units per day. So far this week Olga has assembled 61 units on Monday, 54 on Tuesday, 58 on Wednesday, and 65 on Thursday. How many units must she assemble on Friday to make her goal?

6. Your annual salary is $20,280. What is your average pay:
   a. per week?
   b. per month?

7. Valerie Wheeler has a part-time job selling Kopper-Klad cookwear from house-to-house. Her commission on small sets is 20% of sales. On large sets her commission is 25% of sales. Last month Valerie sold $2,165 worth of small sets and $540 worth of large sets. What was Valerie's total commission last month?

1. **a.** $16 \times N = 96$. What is the value of N?
    b. Multiply $29.95 by 100
    c. Multiply 345 by 10¢
    d. Multiply $6.95 by 1,500
    e. Multiply 164.5 by 0.055
    f. Divide 36.25 by 1,000
    g. Divide 1.448 by 0.04
    h. Subtract 0.95 from 24.623

2. Rule a cash receipts record for yourself like the one on page 4. Show these entries in the record and find your total cash receipts for October: October 1, net pay, $520; October 1, interest for quarter, $30.25; October 12, gift, $20; October 15, net pay, $559; October 29, net pay, $568.75.

3. What is the FICA tax at 6.7% on pay of $240?

4. You are paid $7 an hour for a 40-hour week, with time and a half for overtime. You have one withholding allowance and no deductions other than withholding and FICA taxes. Last week you worked 45 hours.
    a. What was your gross pay last week?
    b. Using the tables on pages 34 and 36, what were your total deductions last week?
    c. What was your net pay last week?

5. The three members of the Curtis family pick fruit and are paid at the rate of $1.25 for each box they pick. Today Carl Curtis picked 25 boxes, Elsa picked 28 boxes, and Carl Junior picked 12 boxes. What total pay did they earn for the day?

6. Diane Crowfoot, a machine salesperson, is paid a salary of $1,600 a month, plus a commission of 3% on sales over $24,000. Her October sales totaled $44,000. What was her total October pay?

7. A collection agent collected a long-overdue bill of $1,876 that was owed to J. Z. Rolfe. The agent charged Rolfe a 50% collection fee and $40 for legal costs. What amount did Rolfe get?

8. For October, November, and December, Willie Ozark's monthly pay was $1,384.74, $1,523, and $1,490.26. What was Willie's average pay per month?

9. In reviewing his daily wages for 20 work days, Raul Veracruz found that he had these earnings: 10 days at $45.28 per day; 7 days at $53.50; and 3 days at $40. What were Raul's average daily earnings, to the *nearest cent*?

10. Pamela Yunan is paid $9 an hour for a 40-hour week. What would be Pamela's equivalent pay:
    a. for a year?
    b. for a month?

Part II

Spending Money

What is more fun than earning money? Spending Money! And that is what this part of the book is about.

In Unit Five you will learn how to use the metric system of weights and measures. You'll apply your knowledge of metric and other measures in Units Six, Seven, and Eight. Those units are concerned with buying food, clothing, and personal items; buying housing and household items; and spending for travel and transportation.

Unit Nine deals with spending for health, education, and personal development. In Unit Ten, you will learn how to figure income taxes and social security benefits.

Checks and checking accounts are treated in Unit Eleven.

THINK METRIC!

For many years metric weights and measures have been used in most of the world. In the United States, though, we have generally used Customary system weights such as the ounce, pound, and ton, and Customary measures such as the inch, foot, yard, mile, quart, and gallon.

The metric system is now being used more and more in the United States. Liquids such as milk, soda, and gasoline are often sold by the liter or milliliter rather than by the pint, quart, or gallon. Solids such as meat, fruit, vegetables, and hardware items are often sold by the kilogram, gram, or metric ton rather than by the pound, ounce, or Customary ton. Many times both the Customary and metric measures are shown. For example, the speedometer on your car may show both miles per hour and kilometers per hour.

The weight of a loaf of bread may be shown in both pounds and kilograms.

You probably already know how to use most of the Customary weights and measures. As a smart consumer, you also need to be able to use some of the most common metrics. When you have finished this unit, you should be able to:

- change from one metric unit to another by moving the decimal point
- add, subtract, multiply, and divide metric amounts
- solve common consumer problems using metrics
- make simple conversions between metric and Customary amounts
- read, write, speak, and recognize the meanings of the most often used terms and symbols for metric units of length, area, capacity, and weight

Johnson & Johnson

LENGTH

section

21

The metric system
is a decimal
system

Study the table of metric lengths that is shown below. Pay close attention to the names of the units, the symbols or abbreviations for the units, and the relative values of the units. Note that each unit is ten times the next smaller unit, or one-tenth the next larger unit. That is because the metric system is a decimal, or base-ten, system.

METRIC UNITS OF LENGTH

Unit	Symbol	Equivalent in Meters
millimeter	mm	0.001 m (one-thousandth meter)
centimeter	cm	0.01 m (one-hundredth meter)
decimeter	dm	0.1 m (one-tenth meter)
meter	m	1 m (one meter)
dekameter	dam	10 m (ten meters)
hectometer	hm	100 m (one hundred meters)
kilometer	km	1 000 m (one thousand meters)

Parts ⟶ { millimeter, centimeter, decimeter

Basic unit ⟶ meter

Multiples ⟶ { dekameter, hectometer, kilometer

Note: Large lengths or distances are usually measured in meters or kilometers. Small lengths or distances are measured in centimeters or millimeters. Decimeters, dekameters, and hectometers are seldom used.

As shown in the table, the meter is the basic unit of length in the metric system. A meter is equal to about 39 inches, or slightly more than a yard in the Customary system.

The parts of a meter are the *deci*meter, or one-tenth meter; the *centi*meter, or one-hundredth meter; and the *milli*meter, or one-thousandth meter.

Multiples of the meter are the *deka*meter, or ten meters; the *hecto*meter, or one hundred meters; and the *kilo*meter, or one thousand meters.

Remember deci, centi, milli, deka, hecto, and kilo

The prefixes deci- (tenth), centi- (hundredth), milli- (thousandth), deka- (ten), hecto- (hundred), and kilo- (thousand) are used with other metric measures. You will need to remember them.

Use small letter symbols and no "s" for plurals

In writing metric values, we generally use the symbols rather than the full names, and small letters rather than capital letters. The symbols indicate plurals as well as singulars, so we do *not* add an "s" for plurals. For example, 1 millimeter is written as 1 mm; 20 millimeters is written as 20 mm.

Use a space instead of a comma; write fractions as decimals

In metrics, a space rather than a comma is used to indicate thousands. For example, 4 000 cm; 5 000 000 m; or 0.000 1 m. Also, in metrics all fractions are written as decimals. For example, 0.5 m; 1.4 m.

**Oral
Practice 1**

1. What is the basic metric unit of length? What is its symbol?

2. What are the names of the parts of a meter? What symbols are used for the parts?

3. What are the names of the multiples of a meter? What are their symbols?

4. What part of a meter is a decimeter? A centimeter? A millimeter? How is each of these written?

5. How many meters are there in a dekameter? A hectometer? A kilometer?

6. Each metric unit is how many times greater than the next smaller unit?

7. Each metric unit is what part of the next larger unit?

8. How should you write one meter? Ten meters? One hundred meters? One thousand meters?

9. How should you write one millimeter? Ten millimeters? One hundred millimeters? One thousand millimeters? One-tenth millimeter?

10. What metric units are used most often for small lengths?

Adding, Subtracting, Multiplying, and Dividing Metric Lengths. Metric lengths are added, subtracted, multiplied, and divided in the same way as other amounts. Often, though, as a first step you have to change metric amounts to the same units. For example, before you can add 6 meters and 25 centimeters, you must show both amounts as meters or as centimeters.

25 cm = 0.25 m	6 m = 600 cm
6 m + 0.25 m = 6.25 m	*or* 600 cm + 25 cm = 625 cm

Because each metric unit of length is either ten times or one-tenth the next unit, you can change an amount easily by multiplying or dividing it by 10 as many times as needed to get the unit you want. To multiply or divide by 10, you just move the decimal point to the right or left.

For example, to change to a *smaller* unit, you move the decimal point to the *right*:

$$1 \text{ m} = 10 \text{ dm} = 100 \text{ cm} = 1\,000 \text{ mm, } or$$

$$1 \text{ km} = 10 \text{ hm} = 100 \text{ dam} = 1\,000 \text{ m} = 10\,000 \text{ dm} =$$

$$100\,000 \text{ cm} = 1\,000\,000 \text{ mm}$$

To change to a *larger* unit, you move the decimal point to the *left*:

$$1 \text{ mm} = 0.1 \text{ cm} = 0.01 \text{ dm} = 0.001 \text{ m, } or$$

$$1 \text{ m} = 0.1 \text{ dam} = 0.01 \text{ hm} = 0.001 \text{ km}$$

Oral Practice 2

What are the missing numbers?

	1.	**2.**	**3.**
a.	1 m = ? dm	1 km = ? dam	1 cm = ? m
b.	1 m = ? cm	1 km = ? m	2 mm = ? m
c.	1 m = ? mm	1 km = ? cm	5 m = ? mm
d.	1 cm = ? mm	1 m = ? km	250 mm = ? m
e.	1 km = ? hm	1 mm = ? cm	600 m = ? km

Written Practice 3

Just move the decimal point

	1.	**2.**	**3.**
a.	1 m = ? cm	1 km = ? m	750 mm = ? m
b.	1 cm = ? m	1 000 m = ? km	8 m = ? cm
c.	1 m = ? mm	100 cm = ? m	25 km = ? m
d.	1 mm = ? m	1 000 mm = ? m	12 cm = ? mm
e.	1 mm = ? cm	5 m = ? cm	300 m = ? km

Written Practice 4

1. Add:

    a. 3 m + 2 m + 4 m = ? m   **9 m**
    b. 3.5 km + 2.3 km + 5 km = ? km
    c. 2.5 m + 3.4 m + 7 m + 0.5 m = ? m
    d. 4 m + 50 cm + 30 cm = ? m   **4.8 m**
    e. 8 km + 12 km + 750 m = ? km
    f. 1 m + 35 cm + 20 cm = ? cm

2. Subtract:

a. 75 mm − 50 mm = ? mm **25 mm**		**d.** 125 m − 50 cm = ? m **124.5 m**
b. 8.75 m − 3.5 m = ? m		**e.** 75 cm − 250 mm = ? mm
c. 35 km − 16.3 km = ? km		**f.** 1 m − 65 cm = ? cm

3. Multiply:

Watch your decimal points!

a. 80 cm × 3 = ? cm **240 cm**	**d.** 7.5 cm × 4 = ? cm
b. 15 m × 2 = ? m	**e.** 14.6 mm × 5 = ? mm
c. 250 mm × 4 = ? m **1 m**	**f.** 500 m × 6 = ? km

4. Divide:

a. 15 km ÷ 3 = ? km **5 km**	**d.** 75.6 cm ÷ 3 = ? cm
b. 200 m ÷ 4 = ? m	**e.** 12.5 m ÷ 0.5 = ? m
c. 5 000 km ÷ 5 = ? km	**f.** 5.75 km ÷ 0.25 = ? km

Written Practice 5

1. Diane Shendo bought 1.75 m of wool cloth, 2 m of dacron cloth, and 2.25 m of cotton cloth. How many meters of cloth did she buy? **6 m**

2. Nick Cruz bought a board that was 4.9 m long to make shelves. When the shelves were done, Nick had 40 cm of board left. How many meters of board had he used?

3. How many meters of lamp cord would you need to make six pieces of cord, each 2.5 m long?

4. You have a bar of chocolate that is 12 cm long. You want to divide the bar into 3 equal pieces. How long should each piece be?

5. In 5 days you jogged these distances: 4.9 km, 5.6 km, 8 km, 6.5 km, and 9.5 km.
   a. How many kilometers did you jog in the 5 days?
   b. How many kilometers did you average per day?

6. If a mile is equivalent to 1.6 kilometers, 10 miles would be equivalent to how many kilometers?   **16 km**

7. A meter is equivalent to about 39 inches. So, a table that is 3 meters long would be about how many inches long?

Terms to Remember

Match the terms to the statements.

centimeter (cm)   kilometer (km)   meter (m)   millimeter (mm)

   a. The basic metric unit of length
   b. One-hundredth meter (0.01 m)
   c. One thousand meters (1 000 m)
   d. One-thousandth meter (0.001 m)

Review 21

1. a. Divide 26 by 16, correct to the nearest hundredth
   b. Divide 8.7 by 0.6
   c. $N = 460 \times 25$. What is the value of N?
   d. Add 15 m and 3.4 m
   e. Divide 235 km by 5

2. Each of the two sides of a lawn is 25 m long. The two ends are 18 m long. How many meters of fence will be needed to enclose the lawn?

3. Charles Karker bought a piece of cloth that was 4 m long. From it he cut 3 pieces, each 1.25 m long. How many meters of cloth did he have left? How many centimeters?

4. Flo Verdun has a job that pays her $425 per week. Fringe benefits amount to $3,095 per year and expenses are $1,440 per year. Kara Penn has a job that pays a yearly salary of $21,600, plus fringe benefits estimated at 20% per year. Expenses of Kara's job are estimated to be 8% of her salary.
   a. What are Flo's yearly net job benefits?
   b. What are Kara's yearly net job benefits?
   c. Who makes more per year, and how much more?

5. You are paid a commission of 5% on all sales up to $30,000 per month, and 6% on sales over $30,000 per month. Last month your sales totaled $32,850. What should be your commission for last month?

AREA

When you figure how much surface an object has, you are figuring its area. For example, if you measure the surface of a floor to find how much paint is needed to cover it, you are figuring the area of the floor.

An area measure is a square measure. You find area by multiplying the length of a surface by its width.

Area = Length × Width
(A) = (L) × (W)

For example, if a room is 12 feet long and 8 feet wide, its area is 12 feet × 8 feet, or 96 square feet.

12'

8' Area = 12' × 8' or 96 sq. ft.

In the Customary system, small areas are usually measured in square inches or square feet. Large areas are measured in square yards or square miles. In the metric system, the basic unit of area is the **square meter**. By comparison, a square meter is slightly larger than the Customary square yard (1 square meter = 1.2 square yards).

The parts and multiples of the metric units of area are these:

METRIC UNITS OF AREA

	Unit	Symbol	Equivalent in Square Meters
Parts →	square millimeter	mm^2	0.000 001 m^2 (one-millionth square meter)
	square centimeter	cm^2	0.000 1 m^2 (one ten-thousandth square meter)
	square decimeter	dm^2	0.01 m^2 (one-hundredth square meter)
Basic unit →	square meter	m^2	1 m^2 (one square meter)
Multiples →	square dekameter	dam^2	100 m^2 (one hundred square meters)
	square hectometer, or hectare	hm^2, or ha	10 000 m^2 (ten thousand square meters)
	square kilometer	km^2	1 000 000 m^2 (one million square meters)

You should remember these points about area measures:

Remember these facts!

(1) Metric units of area have the same prefixes as units of length: *milli*meter, *centi*meter, *deci*meter, meter, *deka*meter, *hecto*meter, and *kilo*meter. The special name, hectare, is used instead of square hectometer because it is easier.

(2) Area symbols are generally written using the exponent 2 (raised ^{2}) rather than with the abbreviation, sq. For example, square meter is written as m^2 rather than sq. m, and square centimeter is written as cm^2 rather than sq. cm.

(3) Each metric area unit is 100 times greater than the next smaller unit, or one-hundredth of the next larger unit.

(4) Small areas are measured in square millimeters or square centimeters. Large areas are measured in square meters, square hectometers (hectares), or square kilometers.

**Oral
Practice 1**

1. What is the rule for figuring area?

2. What is the basic metric unit of area? What is its symbol?

3. What Customary unit is about equal to a square meter?

4. What five metric units of area are most commonly used?

5. What two metric units of area are not often used?

6. Why is the term "hectare" used rather than square hectometer?

7. What symbols are generally used for metric area measures?

8. What area symbol is written without the exponent ^{2}?

9. **a.** How are metric units of area related to each other?
   b. How is this different from units of length?

10. What metric units are used for small areas?

11. What metric units are used for large areas?

Adding, Subtracting, Multiplying, and Dividing Metric Areas.

Metric areas are added, subtracted, multiplied, and divided just like other values. As with metric lengths, though, you may need to change values to the same units. For example, if you are adding m^2 and cm^2, you must first show the values in either m^2 or cm^2.

In changing square measures to the same units, you must remember that each square unit is 100 times the next smaller unit, or one-hundredth of the next larger unit. For example, a square centimeter is 100 times a square millimeter ($1\ cm^2 = 10 \times 10$ or $100\ mm^2$). A square meter is 10 000 times greater than a square centimeter ($1\ m^2 = 100 \times 100$ or $10\ 000\ cm^2$).

**Move the decimal
point two places
for each area unit**

So, to change from one metric area unit to another, you move the decimal point *two* places to the *right* for the next *smaller* unit, or two places to the *left* for the next *larger* unit. If you must skip a unit or units, you move the decimal point four, six, or more places. For example:

To a *smaller* unit	**To a *larger* unit**
1 cm² = 100 mm²	100 mm² = 1.00 cm²
1 m² = 10 000 cm²	10 000 cm² = 1.0 000 m²
1 ha = 10 000 m²	10 000 m² = 1.0 000 ha
1 km² = 1 000 000 m²	1 000 000 m² = 1.000 000 km²

Written Practice 2

1.
a. $1 \text{ cm}^2 = ? \text{ mm}^2$
b. $1 \text{ m}^2 = ? \text{ cm}^2$
c. $1 \text{ ha} = ? \text{ m}^2$
d. $1 \text{ km}^2 = ? \text{ m}^2$
e. $1 \text{ km}^2 = ? \text{ ha}$
f. $1 \text{ m}^2 = ? \text{ mm}^2$
g. $100 \text{ mm}^2 = ? \text{ cm}^2$
h. $10\ 000 \text{ cm}^2 = ? \text{ m}^2$

2.
a. $10\ 000 \text{ m}^2 = ? \text{ ha}$
b. $1\ 000\ 000 \text{ m}^2 = ? \text{ km}^2$
c. $0.2 \text{ m}^2 = ? \text{ cm}^2$
d. $5\ 000 \text{ m}^2 = ? \text{ ha}$
e. $0.4 \text{ m}^2 + 0.4 \text{ m}^2 = ? \text{ m}^2$
f. $50 \text{ mm}^2 + 50 \text{ mm}^2 = ? \text{ cm}^2$
g. $60 \text{ ha} - 20 \text{ ha} = ? \text{ ha}$
h. $35 \text{ m}^2 \times 2 = ? \text{ m}^2$

Written Practice 3

Remember to move the decimal point two places for each unit

1. Add:
a. $5 \text{ m}^2 + 3 \text{ m}^2 = ? \text{ m}^2$
b. $15 \text{ ha} + 8 \text{ ha} = ? \text{ ha}$
c. $9 \text{ cm}^2 + 100 \text{ mm}^2 = ? \text{ cm}^2$
d. $2 \text{ ha} + 10\ 000 \text{ m}^2 = ? \text{ ha}$
e. $6 \text{ m}^2 + 5\ 000 \text{ cm}^2 = ? \text{ m}^2$

3. Multiply:
a. $25 \text{ m} \times 3 \text{ m} = ? \text{ m}^2$
b. $5 \text{ ha} \times 6 = ? \text{ ha}$
c. $100 \text{ m}^2 \times 100 = ? \text{ ha}$
d. $40 \text{ mm}^2 \times 5 = ? \text{ cm}^2$
e. $1 \text{ km}^2 \times 0.5 = ? \text{ ha}$

2. Subtract:
a. $15 \text{ m}^2 - 9 \text{ m}^2 = ? \text{ m}^2$
b. $1 \text{ ha} - 5\ 000 \text{ m}^2 = ? \text{ ha}$
c. $1 \text{ cm}^2 - 50 \text{ mm}^2 = ? \text{ mm}^2$
d. $3 \text{ m}^2 - 1\ 000\ 000 \text{ mm}^2 = ? \text{ m}^2$
e. $4 \text{ km}^2 - 50 \text{ ha} = ? \text{ ha}$

4. Divide:
a. $40 \text{ m}^2 \div 4 = ? \text{ m}^2$
b. $0.25 \text{ ha} \div 5 = ? \text{ ha}$
c. $5\ 000 \text{ cm}^2 \div 2 = ? \text{ m}^2$
d. $6 \text{ km}^2 \div 3 = ? \text{ ha}$
e. $100 \text{ mm}^2 \div 4 = ? \text{ cm}^2$

Written Practice 4

1. The four rooms in Kate O'Dell's apartment have these floor areas: 8.8 m², 3 m², 20 m², and 15.6 m². What is the total floor area of Kate's apartment?   **47.4 m²**

2. You are papering the walls of a room. The total area of the walls, including doors and windows, is 40 m². The windows and doors, which will not be papered, have an area of 10 m².
   a. What is the area of the surface to be papered?   **30 m²**
   b. A large roll of paper will cover 6 m² of wall. How many large rolls will you need for the job?

3. Ted Stark is putting plastic covering on six chair seats. Each seat needs 2 600 cm² of covering.
   a. How many square centimeters of covering will he need?
   b. How many square meters of covering will he need?

4. Some notebook paper is 26.5 cm long by 20 cm wide. What is its area:
   a. in cm²?
   b. in mm²?

5. Kaz Ulna is putting in a new driveway, 30 m long by 3 m wide.
   a. What is the area of the driveway in m²?
   b. At $15 per m², what will the driveway cost?

6. Anya Jambo's house is on a building lot that is 25 m × 40 m in size.
   a. What is the size of the lot in square meters?
   b. What is the size of the lot in hectares?
   c. If land is worth $90,000 per hectare, what is Anya's lot worth?

Terms to Remember

hectare (ha)   **square centimeters (cm²)**   **square kilometer (km²)**
square meter (m²)   **square millimeter (mm²)**

   a. The basic metric unit of area
   b. One ten-thousandth square meter (0.000 1 m²)
   c. One-millionth square meter (0.000 001 m²)
   d. One square hectometer (10 000 m²)
   e. One million square meters (1 000 000 m²)

Review 22

1. a. Divide $673 by 15, correct to the nearest cent
   b. Multiply 73.68 by 2.4
   c. $7 \times N = 112$. What is the value of N?
   d. Subtract 36.5 m² from 85 m²
   e. Multiply 3.5 ha × 5

2. You are covering a surface that is 2.5 m long by 1.2 m wide. How many square meters of covering will you need?

3. Elna Ormond owns a plot of land that is 2 hectares in size. She is dividing the land into building lots that are 2 000 m² in size. How many lots will she have?

4. On a four-day auto trip, you drove these distances: 523 km, 602.5 km, 684 km, and 471 km. How many total kilometers did you drive?

5. A ski jumper jumped 90 meters. How many yards was that? (1 m = 1.09 yards)

6. Julian Laval's yearly salary is $19,760. His fringe benefits are: pension, $1,560; insurance, $975; other, $282.50. What are the total yearly job benefits of Julian's job?

7. Mid-State Auctioneers sells some of your property for $3,500 and charges you 22% for their commission. What is the amount of their commission?

★ 8. The Inter-City Collection Agency collected a bill of $2,874 for Lyle DeSousa and charged 45% for the collection. How much did DeSousa get?

CAPACITY AND WEIGHT

section

23

Capacity. The liter is the basic and most commonly used metric measure of capacity. A liter is slightly more than a Customary quart (1 liter = 1.06 quarts).·

METRIC UNITS OF CAPACITY

Unit	Symbol	Equivalent in Liters
milliliter	mL	0.001 L (one-thousandth liter)
centiliter	cL	0.01 L (one-hundredth liter)
deciliter	dL	0.1 L (one-tenth liter)
liter	L	1 L (one liter or one cubic decimeter)
dekaliter	daL	10 L (ten liters)
hectoliter	hL	100 L (one hundred liters)
kiloliter	kL	1 000 L (one thousand liters)

Parts ⟶ (milliliter, centiliter, deciliter)

Basic unit ⟶ liter

Multiples ⟶ (dekaliter, hectoliter, kiloliter)

You should remember these points about capacity measures:

The liter is the basic unit

(1) The parts and multiples of a liter have the same prefixes as other metrics: milli-, centi-, deci-, deka-, hecto- and kilo-.

(2) The symbol for liter is a capital L rather than a small L. This is to avoid confusing it with the number 1.

Each unit is ten times or one-tenth the next

(3) Each unit of capacity is ten times the next smaller unit, or one-tenth of the next larger unit.

(4) Small amounts are usually shown in milliliters (mL) or as decimal parts of a liter; for example, 250 mL or 0.25 L. Large amounts are shown in liters (L) or in kiloliters (kL); for example, 5 000 L, or 5 kL.

(5) You add, subtract, multiply, and divide capacity measures like all other values. You may first have to change them to the same units.

Oral Practice 1

1. What is the basic unit of capacity?

2. What is the closest Customary equivalent of a liter?

3. What are the parts of a liter, and what are their symbols?

4. What three units of capacity are most often used?

5. How is a unit of capacity related to the next smaller unit? To the next larger unit?

6. Are units of capacity related to their next units in the same way as units of length? In the same way as units of area?

7. How many milliliters are there in a liter?

8. What part of a kiloliter is a liter?

Oral Practice 2

	1.	2.	3.
a.	1 L = ? mL	1 L = ? kL	0.65 L = ? mL
b.	1 mL = ? L	500 mL = ? L	1.5 L = ? mL
c.	1 000 mL = ? L	0.5 L = ? mL	125 kL = ? L
d.	1 kL = ? L	250 L = ? kL	1 650 mL = ? L
e.	1 000 L = ? kL	750 mL = ? L	10 000 L = ? kL

Written Practice 3

1. Add:

a. 25 L + 130 L + 4 L = ? L   **159 L**
b. 34.5 L + 0.5 L = ? L
c. 250 mL + 1 L = ? mL   **1 250 mL**
d. 3.2 kL + 500 L = ? kL

3. Multiply:

a. 125 L × 6 = ? L   **750 L**
b. 1.5 kL × 8 = ? kL
c. 500 mL × 4 =? L   **2 L**
d. 0.6 L × 120 = ? L

Each capacity unit is ten times or one-tenth the next

2. Subtract:

a. 425 mL − 80 mL = ? mL   **345 mL**
b. 24.5 L − 5.25 L = ? L
c. 68 L − 250 mL = ? L   **67.75 L**
d. 2 kL − 1 500 L = ? L

4. Divide:

a. 480 mL ÷ 6 = ? mL   **80 mL**
b. 324.5 L ÷ 5 = ? L
c. 1 540 kL ÷ 5 = ? kL   **308 kL**
d. 1.5 L ÷ 3 = ? mL

Written Practice 4

1. You bought these amounts of gas on a car trip: 38 L, 45.4 L, 29 L, and 34.6 L. How many liters of gas did you buy?

2. Venus Reno has a one-liter bottle of cooking oil. If she uses 400 mL of the oil for baking, how many liters of oil has she left? How many milliliters?   **0.6 L, 600 mL**

3. The Costa family uses an average of 7.5 L of milk per week. The milk costs them 50¢ per liter.
a. How many liters of milk will they use in 52 weeks?
b. How much will they spend for milk per year?

4. Six people are sharing equally a 1.5 L bottle of beverage.
a. How many liters will each person get?
b. How many milliliters will each get?

Weight. The metric units of weight are shown in a table on the next page. You should remember these things about them:

(1) Units of weight are shown as parts and multiples of the gram, and have the usual prefixes: milli-, centi-, deci-, deka-, hecto-, and kilo-. The gram is very small (only 0.04 of a Customary ounce) and is *not* the most used measure. The kilogram is used as the basic unit. A **kilogram** is equal to 1 000 grams, or to 2.2 Customary pounds.

(2) Each unit is ten times, or one-tenth, the next unit.

(3) Small weights are usually measured in kilograms, grams, or milligrams. Large weights are measured in kilograms or metric tons. A metric ton is 1 000 kilograms, or 2,200 Customary pounds.

(4) You may need to change metric weights to the same units before you can add, subtract, multiply, or divide.

METRIC UNITS OF WEIGHT

Unit	Symbol	Equivalent in Grams
milligram	mg	0.001 g (one-thousandth gram)
centigram	cg	0.01 g (one-hundredth gram)
decigram	dg	0.1 g (one-tenth gram)
gram	g	1 g (one gram)
dekagram	dag	10 g (ten grams)
hectogram	hg	100 g (one hundred grams)
kilogram	kg	1 000 g (one thousand grams)
metric ton	t	1 000 000 g (one million grams), or 1 000 kg (one thousand kilograms)

Basic unit ⟶ kilogram

Oral Practice 5

1. To which metric unit of weight are the prefixes attached?

2. What is the basic metric unit of weight? What is its symbol?

3. What is the Customary equivalent of a kilogram?

4. What metric weights are most often used?

5. How many grams are there in a kilogram? A milligram?

6. How many kilograms are there in a metric ton?

7. What part of a kilogram is a gram?

8. What part of a metric ton is a kilogram?

Written Practice 6

Write the missing numerals.

Move the decimal point one place for each unit

	1.	2.	3.
a.	1 g = ? mg	500 g = ? kg	0.25 kg + 0.45 kg = ? kg
b.	1 mg = ? g	250 mg = ? g	3 kg + 500 g = ? kg
c.	1 kg = ? g	750 kg = ? t	25.5 t − 16.5 t = ? t
d.	1 g = ? kg	0.25 kg = ? g	1 kg − 750 g = ? g
e.	1 kg = ? t	0.6 t = ? kg	200 mg × 4 = ? mg
f.	1 t = ? kg	0.5 g = ? mg	600 g × 3 = ? kg
g.	1 t = ? g	125.5 kg = ? t	480 kg ÷ 20 = ? kg

Written Practice 7

1. You bought these items at the meat market: roast, 3.5 kg; hamburger, 500 g; chops, 1.5 kg; cold cuts, 1 kg. How many kilograms of meat did you buy at the market?   **6.5 kg**

2. Your weight was 61.5 kg before dieting. After dieting, your weight was 56 kg. How many kilograms of weight had you lost?

3. A loaf of bread weighs 500 grams. What is the weight of 10 loaves of the bread (a) in grams and (b) in kilograms?

4. A canned ham weighing 2.5 kg is to be served to 10 people. How many kilograms will each person get? How many grams?

5. You are shipping a package that weighs 6.5 kilograms. The shipping rate is 70¢ per kilogram, or fraction of a kilogram. What will be the cost of shipping the package?

6. Your recipe for jam requires 3 pounds of sugar per batch. You have on hand a bag of sugar that weighs 5 kg. You know that 1 kg = 2.2 pounds.
   a. How many whole batches of jam could you make with the bag of sugar you have on hand?
   b. How many pounds of sugar would you have left over?

Terms to Remember

Match the terms and the statements.

gram (g)   kilogram (kg)   kiloliter (kL)   liter (L)
metric ton (t)   milligram (mg)   milliliter (mL)

a. The basic metric unit of capacity
b. The basic metric unit of weight
c. One-thousandth liter (0.001 L)
d. One thousand liters (1 000 L)
e. One-thousandth kilogram (0.001 kg)
f. One-thousandth gram (0.001 g)
g. One thousand kilograms (1 000 kg)

Review 23

1. a. $12.4 L + 400 mL = ? L$ c. $750 g \times 10 = ? kg$
   b. $5 kL - 250 L = ? kL$ d. $3 t \div 6 = ? kg$

2. You are shipping a package that weighs 6 kg. The shipping charge is $2.15 per kg. What is the total shipping charge?

3. The Kroman family uses an average of 175 kilograms of potatoes in a year. There are 5 persons in the family. How many kilograms of potatoes per person do they use in a year?

4. Your doctor tells you to drink at least eight 250-milliliter glasses of fluid per day. How many liters of fluid is that?

5. The gas tank on Spander's car has a capacity of 50 L. What is the capacity of the tank in gallons (1 L = 0.26 gallons)?

6. How many square meters of wall-to-wall carpet are needed to cover a floor that is 7.5 m long by 4.6 m wide?

FOOD, CLOTHING, AND PERSONAL ITEMS

As a consumer, you will probably shop more often for food, clothing, and personal items than for other things. To get the most and the best for your money, you will need to be good at figuring with whole numbers, fractions, decimals, and percents.

In this unit, you will learn to solve some common problems in spending your money for food, clothing, and personal items. You will learn how to keep records of your cash payments, and how to plan your spending. You will also rebuild your skill with fractions, decimals, and percents.

When you have finished this unit, you should be able to:

- figure and check the extension, sales tax, and total sale amounts on sales slips
- add, subtract, multiply, and divide with fractions, decimals, and percents
- use fractions, decimals, and percents in solving common problems of buying food, clothing, and personal goods
- use aliquot parts of $1 and 100%
- solve simple problems using ratio and ★ proportion
- keep a cash payments record and cash record summary
- set up and use a budget
- read, write, speak, and recognize the meanings of many of the terms and symbols used in buying food, clothing, and personal items, in keeping records of expenses, in budgeting, and in using fractions, decimals, and percents

THE SALES SLIP

When you buy food, clothing, or personal items, you often get a cash register receipt or a sales slip. You should check this receipt or slip to make sure that you got all your goods and that all prices and calculations are correct. You can use the sales slip or receipt in keeping your expense records or as proof of purchase if you return part or all of the goods.

A sample sales slip is shown below.

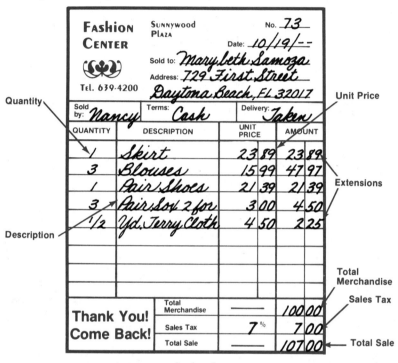

A sales slip

Sales slips may show:

(1) The quantity (number of units) and description of each item bought.

(2) The **unit price**, which is the price of one thing, or of a group of things that is treated as one thing. For example, in the sales slip above, "1 skirt" is a unit, and the unit price of $23.89 is for one skirt. But, a yard of terry cloth is one unit, so the unit price of $4.50 is for one yard of terry cloth.

(3) The **extension**, or extended price, which is the total price of an item on the sales slip.

(4) The total merchandise, or subtotal, which is the sum or total of the extensions.

(5) The sales tax.

(6) The total sale, or total, which is the sum of the total merchandise and the sales tax.

Figuring Extensions. You find the extension of an item on a sales slip by multiplying the quantity (number of units) and the unit price.

Quantity × Unit Price = Extension

For example, in the sales slip on page 94, the extended price of 3 blouses at $15.99 is $47.97 (3 × $15.99 = $47.97).

In figuring extensions, you need to know that "at," or @, refers to the price of a single unit. For example, "1 dozen cookies at $1.49" means "1 dozen at $1.49 *per dozen*," and "5 pounds of sugar @ 49¢" means "5 pounds at 49¢ *per pound*." On the other hand, "5 pounds hamburger, $8.95" means that 5 pounds sell for a total of $8.95.

Oral Practice 1

What is the extension of each of these prices?

1. 2 cans peas at 33¢
2. 3 boxes crackers at $0.90
3. 1 dozen lemons @ $1.39
4. 5 packages cookies @ 95¢
5. 4 bunches beets @ 45¢

6. 3 pounds meat @ $2.40
7. 2 gallons bleach, $1.59
8. 4 quarts milk @ 50¢
9. 6 liters soda at 75¢
10. 2 kilograms potatoes, 63¢

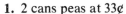

SPECIAL

JAM

3 FOR $2

If the unit price is for a group of things, you must first find the number of units. For example, suppose you are figuring the extension for 12 jars of jam at 3 jars for $2. You first find the number of three-jar units, then multiply that number of units and the unit price:

Example

Find the extension for 12 jars of jam at 3 jars for $2.

Solution

12 ÷ 3 = 4 three-jar units
4 × $2 = $8 extension

Oral Practice 2

Figure these extensions.

1. 6 bags raisins at 2 for 49¢
2. 4 boxes cereal @ 2 for $1.55
3. 2 bottles oil at 2 for $1.75
4. 8 bars soap, $2.95
5. 12 cans soup @ 3 for $1

6. 9 grapefruit at 3 for $1.25
7. 10 bottles catsup @ 2 for 89¢
8. 15 meters cord @ 3 m for $1
9. 10 m² plastic @ 5 m² for 25¢
10. 8 L vinegar at 4 L for $2

Written Practice 3

1. Figure these extensions

   a. 5 tubes toothpaste at 89¢   **$4.45**
   b. 8 oranges @ $0.15
   c. 3 skeins yarn, $3.95   **$3.95**
   d. 10 packages gum @ 5 for $1   **$2**
   e. 6 L soda @ 3 for $1.29

   f. ½ dozen cupcakes @ $2.20
   g. 0.5 m binding at $1
   h. 2.5 kg meat @ $2
   i. 500 mL hairset, $2.39
   j. 5 ties @ 2 for $6

2. On a separate paper, figure the extensions and the total merchandise of this sales slip.

Zembar's Market				
Old City Square **Tel. 368-4242**	Sold to: Roy Questor 6206 Hillcrest Avenue City			
	Cash ☐ Charge ☒		Date: 12/15/--	
Quantity	Item		Unit Price	Amount
3 pkg.	franks @		1.89	
5 lb.	beef roast @		2.75	
3 lb.	hamburger		5.75	
½ lb.	bacon @		2.60	
9	hard rolls @		0.12	
4 cans	tomatoes @	2 for	0.99	
Customer Copy No. 179 **Thank You**		Total Mdse.	—	
		Sales Tax	%	
		Total Sale	—	

3. List these items as they would look on a sales slip for Barnard Drugs. Figure the extensions and find the total merchandise.

6 rolls film @ 2 for $1.98   2 boxes cards @ $2.75
¼ doz. candy bars @ $2.40   1 package combs, 79¢
1 bottle shampoo, $1.59   1 bottle perfume, $5.95

4. List these items as they would look on a sales slip for Elins Sports World. Figure the extensions and find the total merchandise.

1 can tennis balls, $3.69   3 pair sport sox at $2.29
6 golf balls at 3 for $2.49   2 shirts, $14.95
2 canoe paddles at $9.95   12 batteries at 2 for $0.75

Figuring Sales Tax. You often have to pay a **sales tax** on things that you buy, except food. The seller collects the sales tax from you and pays it to the state, county, or city.

The sales tax is often 3 percent to 8 percent of your total purchase. The tax is figured this way:

Sales Tax Rate × Total Merchandise = Sales Tax

The total sale price that you pay is the sum of the merchandise total and the sales tax.

Total Merchandise + Sales Tax = Total Sale

In the sales slip on page 94, the sales tax rate is 7% (0.07) × $100, or $7. The total sale price is the total merchandise, $100, plus the sales tax of $7, or $107.

Oral Practice 4

1. What is the sales tax on:
   a. Total merchandise, $10; sales tax, 6%?
   b. Total merchandise, $200; sales tax, 3%?
   c. Total merchandise, $5; sales tax, 7%?
   d. A clock priced at $30; sales tax, 5%?
   e. A coat priced at $100; sales tax, 4%?
   f. A ticket priced at $6; sales tax, 8%?

2. What is the total sale price on these?

	Total Merchandise	Sales Tax	Total Sale
a.	$ 200.00	$14.00	
b.	33.00	1.65	
c.	76.50	3.06	
d.	5.60	0.28	
e.	1,300.00	52.00	

Written Practice 5

1. Find the sales tax and the total sale for each of these:

	Total Merchandise	Sales Tax Rate	Sales Tax	Total Sale
a.	$ 50.00	6%	$3.00	$53.00
b.	3.00	4%		
c.	170.00	7%		
d.	2,600.00	3%		
e.	75.95	8%		
f.	0.69	5%		

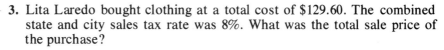

2. You bought a camera for $49.95. The sales tax rate was 5%.
   a. What was the sales tax amount?   **$2.50**
   b. What was the amount of the total sale?   **$52.45**

ONLY **$525** plus tax

3. Lita Laredo bought clothing at a total cost of $129.60. The combined state and city sales tax rate was 8%. What was the total sale price of the purchase?

4. The price of a moped is $525. The state sales tax rate is 4%, and the city sales tax rate is 2%.
   a. What is the combined state and city sales tax rate?
   b. What is the amount of the total sales tax?
   c. What is the total sale price of the moped?

5. You are going to buy a suit for $89.52. The sales tax rate at your local store is 7%. The sales tax rate in a nearby city is only 4%. How much less would the purchase cost you in the nearby city?

Checking Sales Slips. As a buyer, you should check your sales slips to be sure they are correct. You should check the extensions, the total merchandise, sales tax, and total sale figures. As you check each amount, put a check mark (√) next to it if it is correct. If the amount is wrong, write the correct amount next to it. Here is a sales slip with corrections:

BURSTEEN'S
at the Fairmont Center
Books   Office Supplies

Sold to: _Cash_

Sold by: *Sid*	Cash √	Charge	Deliver by: *Taken*	Order No.: —	Date: 1/15/--

Quantity	Description	Unit Price	Amount	
3	paperbacks @	2.25	6.75	√
6 pkg.	notebook paper @ 3 for	2.00	4.00	√
25	file folders @	0.12	3.00	√
½ doz.	pencils @	1.50	1.50	0.75
2 boxes	paper clips @	0.69	1.38	√

Total Merchandise	—	16.63	15.88
Sales Tax	6%	1.00	0.95
Total Sale		17.63	16.83

A sales slip with corrections

In the sales slip shown above, the correct extensions are indicated by a check mark. The extension for ½ dozen pencils @ $1.50 is incorrect, so the correct amount, $0.75, is shown next to it. The correct amounts for the total merchandise, sales tax, and total sale are also shown.

Written Practice 6

Copy each of these parts of sales slips on your own paper. Check the extensions, the total merchandise, sales tax, and total sale figures. If an amount is correct, put a check mark next to it. If an amount is wrong, put the correct amount next to it.

1. This is part of a sales slip from the Dad and Lad Shop:

Quantity	Description	Unit Price	Amount
1	sweater	21.95	21.95
2 pr.	slacks	18.00	36.00
6 pr.	socks	2 for $3	9.00
1 pr.	swim trunks	15.49	15.49
3	ties	3.75	10.25
Total Merchandise	—		92.69
Sales Tax	4%		3.71
Total Sale	—		96.40

2. These items were bought at Sew and Save:

Quantity	Item	Unit Price	Amount
$1\frac{1}{2}$ m	dacron	6.00	9.00
3 spools	thread	3 for 1.29	1.29
2 pkg.	buttons	2 for 0.65	0.65
2	zippers	0.79	1.58
Total Merchandise		——	12.52
Sales Tax		5%	0.75
Total Sale		——	13.27

3. You bought these items at a food store:

Quantity	Description	Unit Price	Amount
3 kg	carrots	0.27	0.91
2 kg	bananas	2 for 0.75	0.75
4 cans	beans	2 for 0.65	1.30
$\frac{1}{2}$ dozen	donuts	1.90	0.85
2 L	milk	0.56	1.12
Total Merchandise		——	4.93
Sales Tax		0%	——
Total Sale		——	4.93

Terms to Remember

extension   sales tax   unit price

a. The price of one thing, or a group of things as one
b. Number of units × unit price
c. A tax paid on things you buy

Review 24

1. a. 5.6 kg + 250 g = ? kg   **c.** 12 m × 4.5 m = ? m²
   b. 8 L − 500 kL = ? L   **d.** 0.5 km ÷ 2 = ? km

2. What are the extensions of these items?
   a. 6 boxes @ 59¢   **c.** 8 tubes @ 2 for 87¢
   b. 3 bottles, $2.29   **d.** 15 jars @ 3 for $1.35

3. What should be the sales tax at 4% on slacks bought at $19.95?

4. What is the total sale price of 8 packages of notebook paper @ 2 for $1.39, with a sales tax of 6%?

5. Edna Nogales has a job that pays $14,760 a year. Fringe benefits of the job are worth $1,995 per year. The estimated yearly expenses of the job are $310. What are Edna's net job benefits for a year?

6. Rod O'Casey earns $325 a week and has one withholding allowance. Use the tables on pages 34 and 36 to find Rod's:
   a. total withholding and FICA taxes.
   b. net pay per week, after withholding and FICA taxes.

FRACTIONS

Most of the problems in the previous sections have used whole numbers instead of fractions. In Section 24, though, you used easy fractions such as $\frac{1}{2}$ and $\frac{1}{4}$ in checking sales slips. In this section you will learn more about using fractions in other kinds of problems.

Call me the numerator

and call me the denominator

Fractional Numbers. Whole numbers, or integers, are numbers such as 1, 2, 3, 4, 10, 49, 163, and so on. Fractional numbers are the numbers that you get when you divide one number by another and the result is not a whole number. For example, dividing 3 by 4 ($3 \div 4$) gives $\frac{3}{4}$, which is a fractional number.

Fractions. A fraction is a symbol or name used to show a fractional number or a whole number. Fractions are also called common fractions or fractional numerals. A **fraction** has a numeral above and a numeral below a line. For example, $\frac{3}{4}$ is a fraction. In a fraction, the numeral below the line is called the **denominator**. The denominator tells you the size or number of equals parts into which a whole is broken. The numeral above the line is the **numerator**. The numerator tells how many of the parts you are dealing with.

The metric system uses decimals instead of fractions

Fractions such as $\frac{3}{4}$, $\frac{2}{3}$, $\frac{1}{2}$, $\frac{7}{3}$, $\frac{9}{7}$, and so on, are names for fractional numbers. Fractions such as $\frac{1}{1}$, $\frac{5}{1}$, $\frac{3}{3}$, $\frac{5}{5}$, $\frac{6}{3}$, and $\frac{12}{4}$ are names for whole numbers.

You can read a fraction in three ways. For example, you can read the fraction $\frac{3}{4}$ as "three fourths," as "three divided by four," or as "three over four."

Oral Practice 1

1. Which of these fractions name whole numbers?

a. $\frac{5}{3}$ **c.** $\frac{9}{5}$ **e.** $\frac{6}{6}$

b. $\frac{4}{2}$ **d.** $\frac{1}{1}$ **f.** $\frac{10}{4}$

2. Which fractions in Problem 1 name fractional numbers?

Written Practice 2

1. Write each of these as a fraction:

a. $7 \div 5$ $\frac{7}{5}$ **c.** $3 \div 3$ **e.** $15 \div 8$

b. $8 \div 4$ **d.** $9 \div 2$ **f.** $2 \div 3$

2. Write each of these with a division sign:

a. $\frac{4}{9}$ $9\overline{)4}$ **c.** $\frac{8}{8}$ **e.** $\frac{6}{5}$

b. $\frac{3}{1}$ **d.** $\frac{7}{2}$ **f.** $\frac{25}{8}$

Multiplying a Fraction by a Fraction. To multiply two or more fractions, you multiply the numerators to get the numerator of the product. You multiply the denominators to get the denominator of the product.

"Of" = "Times"

$$\frac{4}{5} \times \frac{2}{3} = \frac{4 \times 2}{5 \times 3} = \frac{8}{15}$$

A problem such as "$\frac{1}{3}$ of $\frac{2}{5}$" means the same as "$\frac{1}{3} \times \frac{2}{5}$." So, to find $\frac{1}{3}$ of $\frac{2}{5}$, you multiply the two fractions ($\frac{1}{3} \times \frac{2}{5} = \frac{2}{15}$).

Oral Practice 3

What is the product of each of these?

1. $\frac{1}{3} \times \frac{1}{4}$
2. $\frac{1}{2}$ of $\frac{1}{4}$
3. $\frac{1}{4} \times \frac{1}{6}$
4. $\frac{2}{3}$ of $\frac{1}{1}$
5. $\frac{1}{2}$ of $\frac{7}{8}$
6. $\frac{1}{4} \times \frac{2}{1}$
7. $\frac{2}{5} \times \frac{1}{4}$
8. $\frac{3}{4} \times \frac{1}{3}$

Finding Equivalent Fractions. In figuring with fractions, you may need to change them to equivalent fractions. An **equivalent fraction** is a fraction that names the same number as another fraction. For example, $\frac{1}{2}$, $\frac{2}{4}$, and $\frac{3}{6}$ are equivalent fractions.

You get an equivalent fraction by multiplying or dividing the numerator and denominator of a fraction by the same number. For example:

$$\frac{1}{2} \times \frac{2}{2} = \frac{2}{4} \qquad \frac{1}{2} \times \frac{3}{3} = \frac{3}{6} \qquad \frac{2}{4} \div \frac{2}{2} = \frac{1}{2} \qquad \frac{3}{6} \div \frac{3}{3} = \frac{1}{2}$$

Oral Practice 4

1. For each of these fractions, what equivalent fraction do you get by multiplying both the numerator and the denominator by 2, 3, 4, and 5?

   a. $\frac{1}{4}$
   b. $\frac{2}{3}$
   c. $\frac{3}{2}$
   d. $\frac{1}{1}$
   e. $\frac{3}{1}$
   f. $\frac{2}{10}$

2. What equivalent fraction do you get by dividing both the numerator and the denominator by the number shown?

   a. $\frac{2}{12}$, by 2
   b. $\frac{16}{20}$, by 4
   c. $\frac{21}{28}$, by 7
   d. $\frac{12}{8}$, by 4

Reducing Fractions to Lowest Terms. You should reduce fractions in answers to lowest terms. What is meant by "lowest terms"? The **terms** of a fraction are the numerator and the denominator. For example, in the fraction $\frac{4}{8}$ the 4 and the 8 are the terms. A fraction is in **lowest terms** when both terms are divisible only by 1. For example, the fraction $\frac{4}{8}$ is in lowest terms when it is reduced to the equivalent fraction, $\frac{1}{2}$.

You reduce a fraction to lowest terms by dividing both the numerator and denominator by the largest number that will exactly divide both of them. That number is called the *greatest common divisor*. For example, in reducing the fraction $\frac{4}{8}$, the largest number that will divide each term without a remainder is 4 ($\frac{4}{8} \div \frac{4}{4} = \frac{1}{2}$).

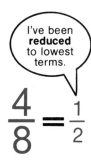

I've been **reduced** to lowest terms.

$$\frac{4}{8} = \frac{1}{2}$$

Oral Practice 5

Reduce each fraction to lowest terms.

1. $\frac{7}{14}$ 3. $\frac{6}{18}$ 5. $\frac{10}{15}$ 7. $\frac{9}{36}$ 9. $\frac{35}{50}$

2. $\frac{8}{20}$ 4. $\frac{18}{24}$ 6. $\frac{15}{18}$ 8. $\frac{7}{21}$ 10. $\frac{18}{30}$

Reducing the Product of Fractions to Lowest Terms. You can reduce the product of two or more fractions to lowest terms by *cancellation*. In cancellation, you divide the numerators and denominators by common factors before you multiply. Here are two examples:

$$\frac{1}{6} \times \frac{3}{4} = \frac{1}{\overset{}{\underset{2}{6}}} \times \frac{\overset{1}{3}}{4} = \frac{1}{8} \qquad\qquad \frac{5}{8} \times \frac{4}{10} = \frac{\overset{1}{5}}{\underset{2}{8}} \times \frac{\overset{1}{4}}{\underset{2}{10}} = \frac{1}{4}$$

Oral Practice 6

What is the product?

1. $\frac{1}{5} \times \frac{5}{12}$ 3. $\frac{3}{8}$ of $\frac{4}{9}$ 5. $\frac{1}{2} \times \frac{8}{9}$ 7. $\frac{1}{6}$ of $\frac{6}{1}$ 9. $\frac{2}{3}$ of $\frac{3}{5}$

2. $\frac{3}{4} \times \frac{1}{3}$ 4. $\frac{5}{8}$ of $\frac{4}{5}$ 6. $\frac{2}{5} \times \frac{5}{2}$ 8. $\frac{3}{7} \times \frac{5}{3}$ 10. $\frac{3}{4}$ of $\frac{4}{9}$

Written Practice 7

Show each product in lowest terms.

1. $\frac{5}{8} \times \frac{4}{7}$ $\frac{5}{14}$ 3. $\frac{5}{8}$ of $\frac{12}{15}$ 5. $\frac{2}{3}$ of $\frac{7}{12}$ 7. $\frac{3}{8} \times \frac{28}{12}$ 9. $\frac{3}{8} \times \frac{2}{1}$

2. $\frac{7}{9} \times \frac{18}{21}$ 4. $\frac{3}{4}$ of $\frac{5}{12}$ 6. $\frac{11}{12} \times \frac{30}{33}$ 8. $\frac{5}{6}$ of $\frac{3}{4}$ 10. $\frac{4}{5}$ of $\frac{8}{9}$

Changing Improper Fractions to Mixed Numbers. A **proper fraction** has a numerator smaller than the denominator. For example, $\frac{2}{3}$ and $\frac{7}{12}$ are proper fractions. An **improper fraction** has a numerator equal to or greater than the denominator. For example, $\frac{3}{3}$ and $\frac{7}{6}$ are improper fractions.

When you multiply fractions, the product may be an improper fraction. For example, $\frac{2}{3} \times \frac{4}{1} = \frac{8}{3}$. You usually change such improper fractions to mixed numbers. A **mixed number**, such as $2\frac{2}{3}$ or $4\frac{1}{4}$, has both a whole number and a fraction. You change an improper fraction to a mixed number by dividing the numerator by the denominator. For example, $\frac{8}{3} = 8 \div 3 = 2\frac{2}{3}$.

Oral Practice 8

Change each improper fraction to a mixed number or whole number.

1. $\frac{3}{2}$ 3. $\frac{9}{4}$ 5. $\frac{8}{8}$ 7. $\frac{9}{6}$ 9. $\frac{28}{8}$

2. $\frac{7}{3}$ 4. $\frac{11}{6}$ 6. $\frac{21}{7}$ 8. $\frac{10}{4}$ 10. $\frac{23}{10}$

Multiplying a Whole Number and a Fraction. Suppose you want to find the cost of $\frac{3}{4}$ pound of meat at $2.88 per pound. You would multiply the price, which is a whole number, by the quantity, which is a fraction:

$$\frac{3}{4} \times \frac{\$2.88}{1} = \frac{\$8.64}{4} = \$2.16$$

In this method, the unit price is shown as the numerator of a fraction, with a denominator of 1 ($\frac{\$2.88}{1}$). The numerators are multiplied, then the denominators are multiplied, giving a product of $\frac{\$8.64}{4}$. That fraction is reduced to \$2.16 by dividing the numerator.

You could also do this problem easily by cancellation:

$$\frac{3}{\underset{1}{4}} \times \frac{\overset{0.72}{\cancel{\$2.88}}}{1} = \$2.16$$

Oral Practice 9

What is the product? (Use cancellation if you can!)

1. $\frac{2}{3} \times 24$ 3. $\frac{3}{4} \times 28$ 5. $\frac{5}{6} \times \$30$ 7. $\frac{1}{6}$ of \$54   9. $\frac{1}{7}$ of \$3.50

2. $\frac{3}{5}$ of 35   4. $\frac{1}{3}$ of \$42   6. $\frac{1}{8} \times \$16$ 8. $\frac{3}{8} \times \$16$ 10. $\frac{7}{8} \times \$240$

11. A yard of cloth costs \$4.80. What is the cost of $\frac{5}{8}$ yard?

12. A cake that costs \$1.50 when fresh can be bought for $\frac{2}{3}$ of that price at a thrift store. What is the thrift store's price?

Terms to Remember

numerator   equivalent fraction   proper fraction   improper fraction
denominator   fraction   terms   mixed number   lowest terms

   a. Any symbol with a numeral above and a numeral below a line
   b. The numeral above the line
   c. The numeral below the line
   d. A fraction that names the same number as another fraction
   e. The numerator and denominator of a fraction
   f. A fraction with terms divisible only by 1
   g. A fraction with numerator smaller than denominator
   h. A fraction with numerator equal to or greater than denominator
   i. A number having both a whole number and a fraction

Review 25

1. **a.** $5 \times N = 95$. What is N?   **e.** 500 mL + 750 mL = ? L
   b. Multiply \$30 by $\frac{3}{8}$ **f.** 29 m² − 3.5 m² = ? m²
   c. What is $\frac{1}{2}$ of $\frac{1}{2}$?   **g.** 5.5 kg × 6 = ? kg
   d. Reduce $\frac{27}{36}$ to lowest terms   **h.** 3.6 m ÷ 4 = ? cm

2. If a dozen cupcakes cost \$2.40, what should 9 cupcakes cost?

3. Three 750-gram cans of coffee weigh a total of how many kilograms?

4. What is the cost of three shirts bought at \$12.95 each, plus a sales tax of 7%?

ALIQUOT PARTS OF $1

In the sales slip below, the unit prices are exact fractional parts of $1. That is, 25¢ is $\frac{1}{4}$ of $1, 50¢ is $\frac{1}{2}$ of $1, and $12\frac{1}{2}$¢ is $\frac{1}{8}$ of $1. These amounts, and other exact fractional parts of $1, are called **aliquot parts of $1**. Multiples of aliquot parts, such as 75¢ and $62\frac{1}{2}$¢, are also called aliquot parts.

$$\frac{25¢}{100¢} = \frac{1}{4}$$

5217 4413 006 172   **5382840**

1/1/--   12/31/-- *MC

SALES DRAFT	DEPT. NO. 5	CLERK'S NO. 27	CLERK'S INIT. a.c.	TAKE ✓
				SEND

ROSITA C. SHENG

QUAN.	CLASS	DESCRIPTION	UNIT COST	AMOUNT
12	pkg	tape	25¢	3 00
5	cards	buttons	50¢	2 50
32		clips	12½¢	4 00

DATE 11/25/--	AUTHORIZATION CODE 09373	SUB TOTAL	9 50
		TAX	57

NU-WAY DISCOUNT STORE

00123456

SALE CONFIRMED AND DRAFT ACCEPTED

CARDHOLDER'S SIGNATURE *Rosita C. Sheng* | **TOTAL** | 10 07

The issuer of the card identified on this item is authorized to pay the amount shown as TOTAL upon proper presentation. I promise to pay such TOTAL (together with any other charges due thereon) subject to and in accordance with the Agreement governing the use of such card.

CUSTOMER COPY

Sales slip with aliquot parts

If you wanted to figure or to check the extensions in the sales slip, you would multiply the quantity and the unit price. To save time you should multiply mentally, but multiplying numbers such as $32 \times 12\frac{1}{2}$¢ may be hard. You could multiply those figures easily and quickly, though, by using the equivalent fraction of the aliquot part.

Example

What is the extension of 32 clips @ $12\frac{1}{2}$¢?

Solution	Explanation
$12\frac{1}{2}¢ = \frac{1}{8}$ of $1	(1) Recall the equivalent fraction for the aliquot part of $1.
$\frac{1}{8} \times 32 = 4$	(2) Multiply the quantity by the equivalent fraction.
$4 \times \$1 = \$4$	(3) Multiply the product by $1.

Table of Aliquot Parts of $1. To use this method, you need to re-member the equivalent fractions for the most common aliquot parts of $1. They are shown in this table:

ALIQUOT PARTS OF $1

$25¢ = \frac{1}{4}$	$12\frac{1}{2}¢ = \frac{1}{8}$	$33\frac{1}{3}¢ = \frac{1}{3}$	$20¢ = \frac{1}{5}$
$50¢ = \frac{1}{2}$	$37\frac{1}{2}¢ = \frac{3}{8}$	$66\frac{2}{3}¢ = \frac{2}{3}$	$40¢ = \frac{2}{5}$
$75¢ = \frac{3}{4}$	$62\frac{1}{2}¢ = \frac{5}{8}$	$16\frac{2}{3}¢ = \frac{1}{6}$	$60¢ = \frac{3}{5}$
	$87\frac{1}{2}¢ = \frac{7}{8}$	$83\frac{1}{3}¢ = \frac{5}{6}$	$80¢ = \frac{4}{5}$

Oral Practice 1

$\frac{1}{4}$, $\frac{1}{2}$, and $\frac{3}{4}$. Explain the solution and give the product for each problem. For example, for the solution of 24 @ 25¢: 25¢ equals $\frac{1}{4}$ of $1; $\frac{1}{4} \times 24 = 6$; 6 × $1 = $6.

	1.	**2.**	**3.**	**4.**
a.	8 @ 25¢	24 @ 50¢	16 @ 75¢	32 @ 50¢
b.	16 @ 25¢	18 @ 50¢	36 @ $0.75	12 @ $0.25
c.	32 @ $0.25	34 @ $0.50	88 @ $0.75	48 @ $0.75
d.	42 @ $0.25	56 @ $0.50	28 @ 75¢	68 @ 25¢

Oral Practice 2

$\frac{1}{8}$, $\frac{3}{8}$, $\frac{5}{8}$, $\frac{7}{8}$. Explain the solution and give the product.

	1.	**2.**	**3.**	**4.**
a.	16 @ $12\frac{1}{2}¢$	32 @ $0.37\frac{1}{2}$	8 @ $0.87\frac{1}{2}$	72 @ $0.37\frac{1}{2}$
b.	24 @ $12\frac{1}{2}¢$	64 @ $62\frac{1}{2}¢$	48 @ $0.87\frac{1}{2}$	24 @ $0.62\frac{1}{2}$
c.	56 @ $0.12\frac{1}{2}$	88 @ $0.62\frac{1}{2}$	56 @ $37\frac{1}{2}¢$	32 @ $87\frac{1}{2}¢$
d.	8 @ $37\frac{1}{2}¢$	72 @ $0.62\frac{1}{2}$	88 @ $0.12\frac{1}{2}$	44 @ $12\frac{1}{2}¢$

Oral Practice 3

$\frac{1}{3}$, $\frac{2}{3}$, $\frac{1}{6}$, $\frac{5}{6}$. Explain the solution and give the product.

	1.	**2.**	**3.**	**4.**
a.	15 @ $33\frac{1}{3}¢$	48 @ $66\frac{2}{3}¢$	36 @ $0.83\frac{1}{3}$	27 @ $33\frac{1}{3}$
b.	9 @ $0.33\frac{1}{3}$	18 @ $16\frac{2}{3}¢$	72 @ $0.83\frac{1}{3}$	21 @ $0.66\frac{2}{3}$
c.	33 @ $0.33\frac{1}{3}$	42 @ $0.16\frac{2}{3}$	18 @ $66\frac{2}{3}¢$	84 @ $0.16\frac{2}{3}$
d.	12 @ $0.66\frac{2}{3}$	66 @ $0.16\frac{2}{3}$	96 @ $16\frac{2}{3}¢$	6 @ $0.83\frac{1}{3}$

Oral Practice 4

$\frac{1}{5}$, $\frac{2}{5}$, $\frac{3}{5}$, $\frac{4}{5}$. Explain the solution and give the product.

	1.	**2.**	**3.**	**4.**
a.	55 @ 20¢	25 @ $0.40	35 @ 80¢	125 @ $0.80
b.	95 @ $0.20	85 @ 60¢	45 @ 80¢	155 @ 80¢
c.	45 @ 20¢	65 @ $0.60	25 @ $0.60	225 @ $0.40
d.	15 @ $0.40	75 @ $0.60	85 @ $0.20	150 @ $0.60

**Written
Practice 5**

1. Use the equivalent fraction of the aliquot part of $1 to find the following extensions:

   a. 52 cans @ 25¢ $13
   b. 36 bottles @ 75¢
   c. 48 packages @ $37\frac{1}{2}$¢
   d. 15 boxes @ $33\frac{1}{3}$¢
   e. 72 units @ $16\frac{2}{3}$¢

   f. 64 lb. @ 0.62\frac{1}{2}$
   g. 85 kg @ $0.60
   h. 16 L @ 0.87\frac{1}{2}$
   i. 24 cm @ 0.66\frac{2}{3}$
   j. 25 m² @ $0.80

2. Copy the problems below and put a check mark next to the extension if it is correct. Write the correct amount next to the extension if it is wrong.

   a. 12 pkg. paper @ 0.83\frac{1}{3}$ = $10
   b. 4 bottles glue @ $0.75 = $2.50

   c. 24 rulers @ 0.33\frac{1}{3}$ = $8
   d. 36 erasers @ 0.12\frac{1}{2}$ = $6

3. What is the total cost of 14 bunches celery @ 50¢ and 16 cabbages @ $62\frac{1}{2}$¢, with no sales tax?

Review 26

1. **a.** $6.50 × N = $32.50. N = ?
   b. Multiply 18 by $33\frac{1}{3}$¢
   c. What is $\frac{3}{4} × \frac{1}{2}$?
   d. Reduce $\frac{35}{42}$ to lowest terms
   e. Divide 4.25 by 0.5

   f. 2.75 ha + 3.5 ha = ? ha
   g. 35 cm × 6 = ? m
   h. 24.5 L − 0.5 L = ? L
   i. 81 m² ÷ 12 = ? m²
   j. 35 kg × 0.5 = ? kg

2. What part of $1 is $83\frac{1}{3}$¢?

3. What is the cost of 16 pints ice cream @ $87\frac{1}{2}$¢?

4. What is the commission on sales of $12,500 at a rate of 4%?

Carpet
Buy by
the
square yard
or
square meter
Sale

5. A carpet warehouse is advertising 10 m² carpets on sale for $300.
   a. What is the price of the carpets per square meter?
   b. What is the size of the carpets in square yards? (1 m² = 1.2 square yards)
   c. What is the price of the carpets per square yard?

6. Your average allowance for food per day, Monday through Friday, is $11.25. Your meals for the first four days of this week have cost these amounts: Monday, $10.60; Tuesday, $13.50; Wednesday, $9.45; and Thursday, $11. How much can you spend on Friday and still stay within your allowance?

7. Berny Mosbey is paid an annual salary of $11,063 and has to work a 37-hour week. What is the equivalent hourly pay of Berny's job?

8. Connie Jambo's present job pays net job benefits of $17,645 per year. Connie is considering a new job that would pay a salary of $1,450 per month. Estimated fringe benefits would be worth $125 per month, and expenses would be $43 per month.
   a. What is the difference in the yearly net benefits of the jobs?
   b. Which job would pay the greater net benefits per year?

FRACTIONS AND MIXED NUMBERS

section

27

Like fractions have
the same
denominator

Adding and Subtracting Like Fractions. Fractions such as $\frac{1}{3}$ and $\frac{2}{3}$ are called **like fractions** because they have the same, or common denominator. To add or subtract like fractions, you add or subtract the numerators and write the result over the common denominator. Look at these examples:

$$\frac{1}{5} + \frac{3}{5} = \frac{4}{5} \qquad \frac{2}{7} + \frac{4}{7} = \frac{6}{7} \qquad \frac{4}{5} - \frac{3}{5} = \frac{1}{5} \qquad \frac{6}{7} - \frac{2}{7} = \frac{4}{7}$$

**Oral
Practice 1**

1. What is the sum?

   a. $\frac{1}{3} + \frac{1}{3}$ **d.** $\frac{1}{6} + \frac{5}{6}$ **g.** $\frac{7}{12} + \frac{11}{12}$

   b. $\frac{2}{5} + \frac{2}{5}$ **e.** $\frac{3}{8} + \frac{3}{8}$ **h.** $\frac{3}{5} + \frac{4}{5}$

   c. $\frac{3}{8} + \frac{2}{8}$ **f.** $\frac{4}{9} + \frac{7}{9}$ **i.** $\frac{3}{6} + \frac{5}{6}$

2. What is the difference?

   a. $\frac{5}{6} - \frac{4}{6}$ **d.** $\frac{7}{8} - \frac{1}{8}$ **g.** $\frac{9}{16} - \frac{5}{16}$

   b. $\frac{7}{10} - \frac{4}{10}$ **e.** $\frac{9}{10} - \frac{4}{10}$ **h.** $\frac{2}{2} - \frac{1}{2}$

   c. $\frac{3}{7} - \frac{2}{7}$ **f.** $\frac{11}{12} - \frac{6}{12}$ **i.** $\frac{5}{5} - \frac{3}{5}$

Raising a Fraction to Higher Terms. If you have two equivalent fractions, the fraction with the larger numbers in the numerator and denominator is in **higher terms**. To raise a fraction to higher terms, you multiply its numerator and denominator by the same number.

For example, suppose that you need to raise $\frac{2}{3}$ to twelfths. The denominator you want, 12, is 4 times greater than the denominator, 3. So, you would multiply both the numerator and the denominator by 4 ($\frac{4}{4} \times \frac{2}{3} = \frac{8}{12}$).

**Oral
Practice 2**

1. Replace the *?* with a numeral to make a true sentence.

   a. $\frac{1}{4} = \frac{?}{8}$ **c.** $\frac{3}{4} = \frac{?}{12}$ **e.** $\frac{2}{5} = \frac{?}{10}$ **g.** $\frac{7}{8} = \frac{?}{24}$

   b. $\frac{1}{2} = \frac{?}{6}$ **d.** $\frac{2}{3} = \frac{?}{9}$ **f.** $\frac{3}{8} = \frac{?}{16}$ **h.** $\frac{5}{6} = \frac{?}{30}$

2. Raise each fraction to the terms shown.

   a. $\frac{1}{2}, \frac{1}{3}, \frac{3}{4}, \frac{5}{6}$ to 12ths

   b. $\frac{1}{2}, \frac{1}{4}, \frac{3}{4}, \frac{5}{8}$ to 16ths

   c. $\frac{1}{2}, \frac{3}{4}, \frac{2}{5}, \frac{3}{10}$ to 20ths

   d. $\frac{1}{2}, \frac{1}{4}, \frac{3}{8}, \frac{9}{16}$ to 32nds

**Written
Practice 3**

Rewrite each fraction in the higher terms shown.

1. $\frac{1}{2}, \frac{1}{3}$ to 6ths

2. $\frac{1}{2}, \frac{1}{4}, \frac{3}{4}$ to 8ths

3. $\frac{1}{2}, \frac{2}{3}, \frac{5}{6}, \frac{4}{9}$ to 18ths

4. $\frac{1}{4}, \frac{3}{8}, \frac{5}{8}, \frac{7}{8}$ to 16ths

5. $\frac{2}{3}, \frac{3}{4}, \frac{3}{8}, \frac{11}{12}$ to 24ths

6. $\frac{5}{6}, \frac{3}{4}, \frac{2}{3}, \frac{1}{2}$ to 12ths

Adding and Subtracting Unlike Fractions.

Fractions that have different denominators, such as $\frac{1}{2}$ and $\frac{1}{5}$, are **unlike fractions**. To add or subtract unlike fractions, change them all to the same denominator. For example:

Unlike fractions
have different
denominators

I'm not
like
you!

No, we're
unlike
fractions.

$$\frac{1}{2} + \frac{1}{5} = \frac{5}{10} + \frac{2}{10} = \frac{7}{10} \qquad \frac{1}{3} - \frac{1}{6} = \frac{2}{6} - \frac{1}{6} = \frac{1}{6}$$

For the denominators of the new fractions, you can use any number that can be divided evenly by the original denominators. For example, to add $\frac{1}{3}$ and $\frac{1}{4}$, you can change the denominators to 12ths.

$$\frac{4}{4} \times \frac{1}{3} = \frac{4}{12} \qquad \frac{3}{3} \times \frac{1}{4} = \frac{3}{12} \qquad \frac{4}{12} + \frac{3}{12} = \frac{7}{12}$$

You usually use as a denominator the smallest number that can be divided by the original denominators. That number is called the **least common denominator**. For example, to add $\frac{1}{5}$ and $\frac{1}{6}$, you would use 30 as the denominator because it is the smallest number divisible evenly by 5 and 6.

$$\frac{6}{6} \times \frac{1}{5} = \frac{6}{30} \qquad \frac{5}{5} \times \frac{1}{6} = \frac{5}{30} \qquad \frac{6}{30} + \frac{5}{30} = \frac{11}{30}$$

The largest denominator of a group of fractions is often the least common denominator. For example, in the group $\frac{1}{2}$, $\frac{1}{3}$, and $\frac{1}{6}$, six is the least common denominator. Sometimes, though, you have to multiply the largest denominator by 2, 3, 4, or more to find the least common denominator.

Oral Practice 4

1. What is the least common denominator of each group?

   a. $\frac{5}{6}, \frac{1}{3}$ c. $\frac{1}{6}, \frac{7}{12}$ e. $\frac{3}{4}, \frac{2}{5}$ g. $\frac{3}{4}, \frac{1}{2}, \frac{5}{8}$ i. $\frac{7}{8}, \frac{5}{6}, \frac{1}{3}$
   b. $\frac{1}{2}, \frac{3}{8}$ d. $\frac{3}{5}, \frac{2}{3}$ f. $\frac{5}{8}, \frac{3}{4}$ h. $\frac{2}{5}, \frac{2}{3}, \frac{1}{2}$ j. $\frac{3}{10}, \frac{1}{2}, \frac{3}{4}$

2. Express each fraction of Problem 1 as a fraction with the least common denominator of its group.

3. What is the sum of each of these?

   a. $\frac{5}{9} + \frac{1}{3}$ c. $\frac{1}{2} + \frac{2}{3}$ e. $\frac{7}{8} + \frac{9}{16}$ g. $\frac{3}{8} + \frac{3}{4}$ i. $\frac{3}{4} + \frac{1}{2}$
   b. $\frac{1}{4} + \frac{5}{8}$ d. $\frac{3}{8} + \frac{1}{16}$ f. $\frac{1}{6} + \frac{2}{3}$ h. $\frac{1}{3} + \frac{5}{6}$ j. $\frac{3}{5} + \frac{2}{3}$

4. What is the difference in each of these?

   a. $\frac{3}{4} - \frac{1}{8}$ c. $\frac{3}{4} - \frac{1}{16}$ e. $\frac{3}{4} - \frac{5}{12}$ g. $\frac{2}{3} - \frac{1}{2}$ i. $\frac{5}{12} - \frac{1}{4}$
   b. $\frac{5}{8} - \frac{1}{16}$ d. $\frac{2}{3} - \frac{1}{6}$ f. $\frac{1}{2} - \frac{1}{4}$ h. $\frac{3}{4} - \frac{3}{8}$ j. $\frac{7}{8} - \frac{2}{3}$

Multiplying a Whole Number and a Mixed Number.

To multiply a whole number and a mixed number, you multiply by each part of the mixed number, then add the results. Here are two examples:

Examples

Multiply 17 by $6\frac{4}{5}$ Multiply $15\frac{2}{3}$ by 8

Solution	Explanation	Solution
17	The solution at the left shows how	$15\frac{2}{3}$
$6\frac{4}{5}$	to multiply a whole number by a	8
5) 68	mixed number. The whole number, 17,	3) 16
$13\frac{3}{5}$	is multiplied by $\frac{4}{5}$ by multiplying by 4,	$5\frac{1}{3}$
102	then dividing by 5. The result is $13\frac{3}{5}$.	120
$115\frac{3}{5}$	The whole numbers are then multi-	$125\frac{1}{3}$
	plied as usual.	

The solution at the right shows how to multiply a mixed number by a whole number. The whole number, 8, is multiplied by $\frac{2}{3}$ by multiplying by 2, then dividing by 3. The result is $5\frac{1}{3}$. The whole number is then multiplied as usual.

Written Practice 5

Find the product in these problems.

1. $24 \times 9\frac{1}{4}$ **222**   4. $48 \times 2\frac{7}{12}$ 7. $12\frac{5}{6} \times 54$ 10. $69 \times 10\frac{1}{3}$
2. $35 \times 6\frac{2}{5}$ **224**   5. $16\frac{5}{8} \times 32$ **532** 8. $35 \times 22\frac{3}{4}$ 11. $8\frac{4}{5} \times 75$
3. $42 \times 5\frac{5}{6}$ 6. $23\frac{3}{5} \times 35$ 9. $15\frac{2}{3} \times 38$ 12. $19 \times 5\frac{7}{8}$

Adding Mixed Numbers. To add mixed numbers, you may need to change the fractions to equivalent fractions. You can change them easily:

Example

Bud Darwin bought two chickens. One weighed $5\frac{3}{8}$ pounds; the other weighed $4\frac{13}{16}$ pounds. What was the total weight of the chickens?

Solution	Explanation
	16ths	The least common denominator of 8 and
5	6	16 is 16, so the fractions are shown as 16ths.
4	13	The numerators of the equivalent fractions
$9 + \frac{19}{16} = 10\frac{3}{16}$ lbs. **Ans.**	are written in a column at the right. The nu-

are written in a column at the right. The numerators are added and the sum, 19, is written as $\frac{19}{16}$. The whole numbers are added and the sum, 9, is combined with the sum of the fractions for a total weight of $10\frac{3}{16}$ pounds.

Written Practice 6

Find the sum of each problem.

1. $5\frac{1}{2}$	2. $8\frac{3}{4}$	3. $7\frac{5}{6}$	4. $12\frac{5}{8}$	5. $9\frac{5}{8}$	6. $3\frac{5}{6}$	7. $\frac{3}{4}$	8. $9\frac{2}{3}$
$4\frac{2}{3}$	$6\frac{1}{3}$	$3\frac{1}{2}$	$26\frac{1}{8}$	$4\frac{3}{4}$	$5\frac{7}{8}$	$8\frac{2}{3}$	$1\frac{3}{4}$
$10\frac{1}{6}$				$6\frac{1}{2}$	$7\frac{1}{4}$	$15\frac{1}{6}$	$4\frac{5}{6}$

Subtracting Mixed Numbers. To subtract mixed numbers, you may have to change the fractions to equivalent fractions.

Example

Subtract $15\frac{2}{3}$ from $24\frac{1}{2}$.

Solution	Explanation
6ths 23 | 9 2͢4 | 3 15 | 4 $8 + \frac{5}{6} = 8\frac{5}{6}$ **Ans.**	The least common denominator of the fractions is 6. The fractions are changed to sixths, and the numerators of the equivalent fractions are written in the column at the right. Because 4 sixths cannot be subtracted from 3 sixths, one unit (or 6 sixths) is borrowed from the 24. The 6 sixths are added to the 3 sixths in the column at the right for a total of 9 sixths. Then, the 4 sixths are subtracted from the 9 sixths, leaving 5 sixths, or $\frac{5}{6}$. The whole numbers are subtracted, and the difference, 8, is combined with the $\frac{5}{6}$ to give a total difference of $8\frac{5}{6}$.

**Written
Practice 7**

Do these subtractions and check all work.

1. $8\frac{1}{6}$ **2.** $9\frac{1}{4}$ **3.** $15\frac{7}{8}$ **4.** $6\frac{1}{6}$ **5.** $20\frac{1}{3}$ **6.** $7\frac{1}{5}$ **7.** $30\frac{3}{8}$ **8.** $6\frac{5}{12}$
    $\underline{3\frac{2}{3}}$ $\underline{6\frac{2}{5}}$ $\underline{9\frac{3}{4}}$ $\underline{2\frac{2}{3}}$ $\underline{12\frac{5}{8}}$ $\underline{1\frac{1}{2}}$ $\underline{20\frac{5}{6}}$ $\underline{5\frac{1}{3}}$
    $4\frac{1}{2}$

Changing Mixed Numbers to Improper Fractions. Suppose you want to change a mixed number to an improper fraction. You can use these steps:

Example

Change $4\frac{2}{3}$ to an improper fraction.

Solution	Explanation
$4 \times 3 = 12$	(1) Multiply the whole number by the denominator of the fraction.
$12 + 2 = 14$	(2) Add that product and the numerator of the fraction.
$\dfrac{14}{3}$	(3) Write the sum over the denominator of the fraction.

**Oral
Practice 8**

Change each of these mixed numbers to an improper fraction.

1. $3\frac{1}{4}$ **3.** $4\frac{2}{5}$ **5.** $15\frac{1}{2}$ **7.** $20\frac{5}{8}$ **9.** $5\frac{5}{12}$ **11.** $2\frac{3}{16}$
2. $5\frac{1}{8}$ **4.** $6\frac{2}{3}$ **6.** $7\frac{1}{6}$ **8.** $33\frac{1}{3}$ **10.** $25\frac{3}{4}$ **12.** $8\frac{7}{8}$

Multiplying Mixed Numbers by Mixed Numbers. To multiply a mixed number by a mixed number, you change both numbers to improper fractions and then multiply them. Study the following example.

$$2\frac{1}{4} \times 5\frac{1}{3} = \frac{\overset{3}{\cancel{9}}}{\cancel{4}} \times \frac{\overset{4}{\cancel{16}}}{\cancel{3}} = 12$$

Written Practice 9

Multiply these mixed numbers.

1. $4\frac{1}{2} \times 2\frac{1}{4}$ $10\frac{1}{8}$ 3. $3\frac{3}{4} \times 2\frac{1}{2}$ 5. $5\frac{1}{4} \times 2\frac{1}{3}$ 7. $15\frac{1}{3} \times 5\frac{1}{2}$
2. $3\frac{1}{5} \times 1\frac{1}{3}$ 4. $4\frac{2}{3} \times 3\frac{1}{4}$ 6. $1\frac{1}{8} \times 2\frac{1}{5}$ 8. $2\frac{1}{4} \times 24\frac{1}{2}$

Terms to Remember

aliquot parts of $1   higher terms   least common denominator
like fractions   unlike fractions

a. Exact fractional parts
b. Fractions having the same denominator
c. The fraction having a larger numerator and denominator
d. The smallest number divisible by the original denominators
e. Fractions having different denominators

Review 27

1. a. $9.80 \times N = 49$. What is N?
   b. Multiply 32 by $0.87\frac{1}{2}$
   c. What is $\frac{1}{4}$ of $\frac{5}{6}$?
   d. $\frac{2}{3} = \frac{?}{12}$
   e. $\frac{5}{6} - \frac{1}{2} = ?$
   f. $2\frac{1}{8} + 4\frac{5}{6} = ?$
   g. $3\frac{1}{2} \times 2\frac{3}{4} = ?$
   h. $3 \text{ L} \div 6 = ? \text{ L}$

2. A 0.5 kilogram package of sandwich spread costs 75¢. What would 6 packages of the spread cost?

3. You bought several items at a clothing store for a total price of $139.42. There is a state sales tax of 4% and a city sales tax of 3% on your purchase. What is the total amount of the sales tax?

4. Renaldo's gross pay for a week was $436.75. Renaldo's employer deducted $96.09 for withholding tax, $29.26 for social security tax, and $13.10 for insurance and other items. What was Renaldo's net pay?

5. Patsy Hanks works in an electronics plant. She is paid $4.35 for each part she assembles up to 15 per day, and $5 for each part over 15 per day. In three days, Patsy assembled this number of pieces: first day, 18; second day, 15; third day, 17. What was her gross pay for those three days of work?

6. Crane is paid a salary of $1,250 per month and a commission of 3% on all sales over $20,000 per month. During November, Crane's sales totaled $26,800. What was Crane's gross salary and commission for November?

★ 7. An agent bought raw materials that cost $35,670. The agent charged the principal 12% commission and $329 for other expenses. What was the total cost of the purchase to the principal?

UNIT PRICES

Oral
Practice 1

Treat a fraction of
a cent as a whole
cent

To get the most for your money, you need to compare the unit prices for competing brands or for different amounts of the same brand. But products are often packaged and priced in many different ways, and unit prices aren't shown on the package. So, unless the unit price is shown on the package or on the shelf, you have to figure the unit price for yourself.

Finding a Unit Price from a Group Price. The price of many products is given for a group of items rather than for one item. To figure the price of one unit, you divide the group price by the number of units in the group. You treat any fraction of a cent as a whole cent.

For example, canned pears are priced at 3 cans for $1.39. The price of 1 can is $1.39 ÷ 3, or $0.46\frac{1}{3}$ is rounded to $0.47. Two cans cost $2 \times \$0.47$, or $0.94.

What is the cost of one unit of each item?

1. 6 cans soda, $1.59
2. 3 lbs. onions, 69¢
3. 5 lemons, 73¢
4. 4 toothbrushes, $1.29

5. 2 boxes muffin mix, 88¢
6. 8 boxes cereal, $0.93
7. 3 tubes toothpaste, $2
8. 7 packs gum, $1.15

Finding the Unit Price When the Given Price Is for a Fraction of a Unit. Many items are packaged and priced at less than a full unit. For example, donuts may be boxed in fractions of a dozen, such as 6, 8, or 9. Cereal may be packaged in 12-ounce ($\frac{3}{4}$ pound) boxes. In such cases you need to find the price of a dozen, a pound, or some other unit.

To find the unit price, you divide the price by the quantity just as you did in finding a unit price from a group price. The only difference is that you divide by a fraction rather than by a whole number.

Example

A box of 8 donuts is priced at $0.90. What is the price per dozen?

Solution	Explanation
$8 = \frac{8}{12}$ or $\frac{2}{3}$ dozen $$\$0.90 \div \frac{2}{3} =$$ $$\$\overset{0.45}{\cancel{0.90}} \times \frac{3}{\cancel{2}} = \$1.35 \quad \textbf{Ans.}$$ Check: $\$1.35 \times \frac{2}{3} = \$0.90$	Show the eight as $\frac{2}{3}$ of 12, or $\frac{2}{3}$ of a dozen. So, the price of $\frac{2}{3}$ dozen donuts is $0.90. To find the price of a dozen, you divide the given price, $0.90, by the quantity, $\frac{2}{3}$ dozen. To divide $0.90 by $\frac{2}{3}$, you invert the fraction (turn it upside down) and multiply $0.90 by $\frac{3}{2}$. The product is $1.35. To check, multiply the unit you found, $1.35, by the fraction, $\frac{2}{3}$. That product is the same as the given price, $0.90.

To find the one-pound price of a 12-pounce package of cereal, you first express the 12 ounces as a fraction of a pound ($\frac{12}{16} = \frac{3}{4}$ pound). You then divide the price by the fraction, $\frac{3}{4}$. To divide, you invert the fraction, then multiply.

**Oral
Practice 2**

1. Express each of these as a fraction of the indicated unit.

   a. 10 ounces, as pounds   **e.** 1 pint, as quarts
   b. 2 feet, as yards   **f.** 3 quarts, as gallons
   c. 6 inches, as feet   **g.** 6 square feet, as square yards
   d. 9, as dozens   **h.** 500 pounds, as tons

2. Express each fraction in Problem 1 as an inverted fraction.

**Written
Practice 3**

1. What is the price per pound of instant coffee that costs $3.95 for a 6-ounce jar? **$10.53**

2. A package of 10 rolls costs 73¢. What is the price per dozen?

**Round the unit
price to the nearest
cent**

3. Cookies in 14-ounce packages costs $1.15. What is the price per pound?

4. A 2-foot piece of cloth is marked $2.75. What is the price per yard?

5. A 3-quart bottle of bleach is priced at 67¢. What is the gallon price?

**Use decimals with
metrics!**

Suppose the price of an item is for a metric measure. You then find the unit price by dividing the price by the metric measure shown as a decimal rather than as a fraction.

Example

A 400-gram box of cereal costs $1.20. What is the cost per kilogram?

Solution	Explanation
400 grams = 0.4 kilogram $1.20 ÷ 0.4 = $3 **Ans.** Check: $3 × 0.4 = $1.20	Four hundred grams would be equivalent to 0.4 kilogram, so you divide the price, $1.20, by the quantity, 0.4 kg. The quotient, $3, is the price per kilogram. Check the answer by multiplying the price per kilogram, $3, by 0.4 kilogram. The product is the same as the given price, $1.20.

**Written
Practice 4**

1. A 250-mL carton of milk costs 18¢. What is the price per liter? **72¢**

2. What is the price per kilogram of meat that costs $1.19 for 0.5 kg?

3. Remnants of dacron cloth are priced at $3.75 for 75 cm. What is the price per meter of the dacron?

To divide, invert
the fraction and
multiply

Dividing with Fractions. As you have seen in Written Practice 3, when you divide a number by a fraction, you first invert the fraction (turn it upside down). Then you multiply the number by the inverted fraction.

Actually, when you invert the fraction and multiply, you are multiplying by the reciprocal of the fraction. The **reciprocal** of any number is the number that gives a product of 1 when it is multiplied with the original number. For example, $\frac{3}{2}$ is the reciprocal of $\frac{2}{3}$, because $\frac{3}{2} \times \frac{2}{3} = 1$. In the same way, $\frac{1}{2}$ is the reciprocal of $\frac{2}{1}$, because $\frac{1}{2} \times \frac{2}{1} = 1$. As you can see, the easy way to find the reciprocal of any number is to "turn it upside down," or invert it.

Oral Practice 5

1. What is the reciprocal of each number?

a. $\frac{2}{3}$	**c.** $\frac{4}{5}$	**e.** $\frac{9}{5}$	**g.** 12	**i.** $\frac{1}{8}$	**k.** $\frac{6}{1}$
b. $\frac{1}{2}$	**d.** $\frac{8}{7}$	**f.** 2	**h.** 8	**j.** 6	**l.** $\frac{1}{6}$

2. What is the quotient of each of these?

a. $1 \div \frac{1}{3}$	**e.** $6 \div \frac{2}{3}$	**i.** $\frac{1}{2} \div \frac{1}{4}$	**m.** $\frac{2}{7} \div \frac{1}{2}$	**q.** $\frac{5}{6} \div 5$
b. $2 \div \frac{1}{4}$	**f.** $\frac{1}{4} \div \frac{1}{3}$	**j.** $\frac{1}{3} \div \frac{1}{6}$	**n.** $\frac{3}{4} \div \frac{2}{1}$	**r.** $\frac{5}{9} \div \frac{1}{3}$
c. $5 \div \frac{5}{6}$	**g.** $\frac{1}{5} \div \frac{1}{2}$	**k.** $\frac{3}{8} \div \frac{5}{8}$	**o.** $\frac{3}{5} \div 2$	**s.** $6 \div 18$
d. $3 \div \frac{3}{4}$	**h.** $\frac{1}{3} \div \frac{1}{3}$	**l.** $\frac{2}{5} \div \frac{1}{2}$	**p.** $\frac{5}{8} \div \frac{5}{8}$	**t.** $\frac{1}{15} \div 3$

Finding the Unit Price for a Quantity as a Mixed Number. Suppose the quoted price is for a mixed number quantity, such as $2\frac{1}{2}$ pounds. You find the unit price by dividing the quoted price by the mixed number.

Example

A $2\frac{1}{2}$-pound can of iced tea mix is $2.25. What is the price per pound?

Solution	Explanation
$2\frac{1}{2}$ pounds $= \frac{5}{2}$ pounds $\$2.25 \div 2\frac{1}{2} = \$2.25 \div \frac{5}{2} =$ $\overset{0.45}{\underset{1}{\$2.2\cancel{5}}} \times \frac{2}{\cancel{5}} = \$0.90$ **Ans.** Check: $\$0.90 \times 2\frac{1}{2} = \$2.25$	Two and one-half pounds would be equivalent to $\frac{5}{2}$ pounds, so the price of 1 pound is found by dividing $2.25 by $\frac{5}{2}$. To divide, invert the $\frac{5}{2}$, then multiply. Check by multiplying the pound price by $2\frac{1}{2}$.

Written Practice 6

1. What price would be paid for a dozen of oranges that sell at $2 for $1\frac{1}{2}$ dozen? **$1.33**

2. A $2\frac{1}{2}$-quart can of cooking oil costs $3.50. What is the price of the oil per quart?

To divide, invert
and multiply

3. A $3\frac{1}{4}$-pound box of soap powder is on sale at $1.17. What is the price per pound?

Use decimals in metrics

4. A 1.5-liter bottle of soda sells for 79¢. What is the price of the soda per liter?

5. A 9.2-kg bag of potatoes costs $2.30. What is the cost of the potatoes per kilogram?

Dividing with Mixed Numbers. When you divide, either or both the dividend and the divisor may be a mixed number. To divide with mixed numbers, you first change each mixed number to a fraction. Then you invert the divisor and multiply. For example:

$$62\frac{1}{2}¢ \div 2\frac{1}{2} = \frac{125}{2} \div \frac{5}{2} = \frac{\overset{25}{\cancel{125}}}{\underset{1}{\cancel{2}}} \times \frac{\overset{1}{\cancel{2}}}{\underset{1}{\cancel{5}}} = 25¢$$

Written Practice 7

What is the quotient?

1. $2\frac{5}{8} \div 3$ $\frac{7}{8}$
2. $3\frac{1}{5} \div 4$
3. $4\frac{2}{3} \div 6$

4. $3 \div 2\frac{1}{2}$ $1\frac{1}{5}$
5. $6 \div 4\frac{4}{5}$
6. $1\frac{1}{4} \div 1\frac{2}{3}$ $\frac{3}{4}$

7. $4\frac{2}{5} \div 2\frac{3}{4}$
8. $16\frac{1}{2} \div 3\frac{2}{3}$
9. $87\frac{1}{2} \div 3\frac{1}{2}$

Review 28

1. a. $N \times \$27.50 = \$13.75$. $N = ?$
   b. Multiply 68 by $0.62\frac{1}{2}$
   c. What is $\frac{5}{6}$ of $54?
   d. Reduce $\frac{54}{63}$ to lowest terms
   e. $\frac{3}{4} \times \frac{1}{8} = ?$
   f. $1\frac{2}{3} \div 4\frac{1}{6} = ?$
   g. $4\frac{1}{2} - 2\frac{5}{8} = ?$
   h. $1 \text{ m}^2 = ? \text{ cm}^2$
   i. $500 \text{ mL} \times 6.5 = ? \text{ L}$
   j. $8.5 \text{ kg} \div 2 = ? \text{ kg}$

2. What is the cost of 2 cans of beets when they are sale-priced at 3 cans for $1.15?

3. Pears are priced at 8 for $1. What would be the equivalent price per dozen?

4. A 1.5-kg bag of carrots costs 90¢. A 5-kg bag of carrots costs $2.60. What is the cost per kilogram of the carrots:
   a. in the 1.5-kg bag?
   b. in the 5-kg bag?

5. You are checking a sales slip for your purchase of 3 shirts at $15.97 each. The slip shows the extended price and the merchandise total as $47.91. The sales tax at 5% is shown as $2.40, and the total sale amount is $50.41.
   a. Are all the amounts on the sales slip correct?
   b. If an amount is wrong, what is the correct amount?

6. On a 3-day car trip, you traveled these distances: first day, 520 km; second day, 748 km; third day, 639 km. What was your average distance per day, to the nearest kilometer?

RATIO AND PROPORTION

Meaning of Ratio. Suppose that a recipe takes 2 cups of milk and 6 cups of flour. One way of comparing the amount of milk and the amount of flour is to say that the milk is to the flour as 2 is to 6. This way of comparing two amounts is a **ratio**. You may say that the ratio of milk to flour is 2 to 6. You may write the ratio of 2 to 6 as the fraction, $\frac{2}{6}$, as $2 \div 6$, or as 2:6.

You may also say that the ratio of flour to milk is 6 to 2. You may write that ratio as $\frac{6}{2}$, $6 \div 2$, or 6:2.

A ratio, like a fraction, can be reduced to lowest terms by dividing both terms by the greatest common divisor. For example, the ratio of milk to flour, $\frac{2}{6}$, can be reduced to $\frac{1}{3}$. The ratio of flour to milk, $\frac{6}{2}$, can be reduced to $\frac{3}{1}$.

To compare weights and measures in a ratio, you must show both terms in the same units. For example, to compare ounces and pounds, you must change both to either ounces or pounds.

Oral Practice 1

1. You have 10 jars of jam. Six jars are small jars, and 4 are large jars. What is the ratio of:
   a. small jars to large jars?
   b. large jars to small jars?
   c. small jars to the total?
   d. large jars to the total?

2. You earned $20 in a day. Of that amount you spent $15 and you saved $5. In lowest terms, what is the ratio of the:
   a. amount spent to the amount earned?
   b. amount saved to the amount earned?
   c. amount saved to the amount spent?
   d. amount spent to the amount saved?

3. What is the ratio of:
   a. 2 pounds to 9 pounds?
   b. 8 ounces to 2 pounds?
   c. 3 kilometers to 7 kilometers?
   d. 10 liters to 25 liters?
   e. 0.5 kilogram to 1 kilogram?
   f. 3 feet to 9 inches?

4. What is the ratio of:
   a. 23¢ to 43¢?
   b. 79¢ to 49¢?

Using Ratios. Suppose you decide that your earnings should be split between savings and spending in the ratio of 1 to 9. That ratio tells you that you should save $1 for every $9 you spend. It also tells you that you should save 1 part, or $\frac{1}{10}$, of your earnings and that you may spend 9 parts, or $\frac{9}{10}$, of your earnings.

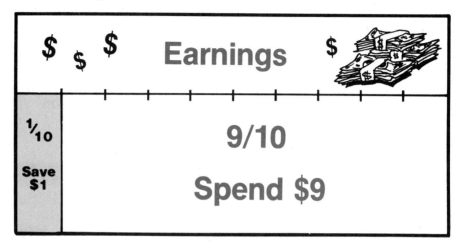

The ratio of 1 to 9 does not tell you how many dollars you will earn, save, or spend. But, if you know your earnings, you can use the ratio to find how much you should save or spend. For example, if you earn $2,000, you should save $\frac{1}{10}$ of $2,000, or $200. You can spend $\frac{9}{10}$ of $2,000, or $1,800.

Written Practice 2

Check by adding the amounts

1. You have $7,000 to spend for food and clothing. The ratio of your food expenses to clothing expenses is 5 to 2. How much of the $7,000 should you plan to spend for (a) food and (b) clothing?   **$5,000; $2,000**

2. A fruit drink has 1 cup of apple juice to each 4 cups of grape juice. How many cups of each juice are needed to make 40 cups of drink?

3. Ray and Jay are sharing food costs in the ratio of 3 to 2. What is Ray's share of a week's food bill of $42?

4. Boosters Club and Rooters Club are raising money for uniforms. They will share their profits in the ratio of 3 to 5, with the larger share to the Rooters. If they make $1,200 profit, how much money will each get?

5. Brenda Larkin earned $14,000 in a year and spent $2,800 of that amount for food. What was the ratio of her food expenses to her earnings?

6. Austin earned $1,500 last month. Of that amount, Austin spent $250 for food and $75 for clothing. What was the ratio of Austin's:
   a. food expenses to earnings?
   b. clothing expenses to earnings?
   c. food expenses to clothing expenses?
   d. clothing expenses to food expenses?

Cross products

$$\frac{9}{12} \diagdown \diagup \frac{6}{8}$$

9 × 8 = 72
6 × 12 = 72

are equal!

★**Meaning of Proportion.** The ratio $\frac{9}{12}$, when reduced to lowest terms, is $\frac{3}{4}$. The ratio $\frac{6}{8}$, when reduced, is also $\frac{3}{4}$. So, you can say that $\frac{9}{12}$ and $\frac{6}{8}$ are equal, and you can show that equality as $\frac{9}{12} = \frac{6}{8}$. A statement showing that ratios are equal is called **proportion**. You read this proportion this way: 9 is to 12 as 6 is to 8.

In a proportion, if the numerator of one fraction is multiplied by the denominator of the other fraction, the result is a **cross product**. *In all proportions, the cross products are equal.* For example, in the proportion $\frac{9}{12} = \frac{6}{8}$, the cross products are both 72. That is, 9 × 8 = 72, and 6 × 12 = 72.

★**Finding the Unknown Term in a Proportion.** You can use the fact that cross products in proportions are equal to find an unknown term in a proportion.

Example

Enough hamburger to make 12 patties costs $5. What would be the cost of hamburger to make 54 patties?

Solution	Explanation
$\frac{N}{\$5} = \frac{54}{12}$ 12 × N = $5 × 54 12N = $270 N = $270 ÷ 12 = $22.50 **Ans.**	Let N stand for the unknown cost, and show the ratio of the costs ($\frac{N}{\$5}$) equal to the ratio of the quantities ($\frac{54}{12}$). Write the cross products as a number sentence (12 × N, or 12N = $5 × 54, or $270). Then find the unknown factor, N, by dividing the known product, $270, by the known factor, 12.

★**Written Practice 3**

1. Six bananas weigh 2 pounds. How much would 15 bananas of the same size weigh?   **5 pounds**

2. A jam recipe takes 7 cups of sugar and makes 10 jars of jam. How many cups of sugar are needed to make 25 jars of the jam?

3. In 4 weeks you spent $305 for food. At that rate of spending, how much would you spend for food in 52 weeks?

4. Polyester cloth is on sale at 3 yards for $9.99. At that rate, what would 5 yards cost?

5. A jacket that was marked $40 is now marked down to $32. At that rate of markdown, what would be the price of slacks that were originally marked at $24?

6. This year, the 6 tomato plants in Selby's garden produced 24 kilograms of tomatoes. At the same rate, how many kilograms of tomatoes should Selby get next year from 25 tomato plants?

7. A school club sold 75 liters of soda and made a profit of $60. How many liters of soda would the club have to sell to make $100 profit at the same rate of profit?

8. In 3 weeks a family saved $26 on their food costs by shopping once a week rather than day-by-day. At that rate, how much would the family save in a year, to the nearest dollar?

Terms to Remember

★cross product   ★proportion   ratio   reciprocal

a. A way of comparing two amounts
b. A statement that two ratios are equal
c. A number that gives a product of 1 when multiplied with another
d. The result of multiplying a numerator and denominator in a proportion

Review 29

1. a. $42 \times N = 35$. What is N?
   b. Multiply 135 by $66\frac{2}{3}$¢
   c. $\$3.50 \times 2\frac{1}{2} = ?$
   d. $6\frac{3}{8} - 5\frac{2}{3} = ?$
   e. $56 \div \frac{7}{8} = ?$
   f. $2.5 \text{ m}^2 \times 6 = ? \text{ m}^2$
   g. $75 \text{ cm} + 60 \text{ cm} = ? \text{ m}$
   h. $12.4 \text{ kL} - 9.6 \text{ kL} = ? \text{ kL}$
   i. $5 \text{ t} \div 4 = ? \text{ t}$
   j. $3.5 \text{ ha} \times 20 = ? \text{ ha}$

2. What is the ratio of 12 ounces to 3 pounds?

3. Mike and Pete have a paper route. They share profits in the ratio of 3 to 1, in favor of Mike. What is each one's share of $38 profit?

4. A $1\frac{3}{4}$-pound can of peanuts costs $2.99. What is the price per pound, to the nearest cent?

5. Sandra Valdez is paid $9 an hour, with time-and-a-half for hours over 8 hours a day, and double time on weekends and holidays. Last week she worked these hours: Monday, 8; Tuesday, 9; Wednesday, 8; Thursday, 10; Friday, 6; Saturday, 4. What was her gross pay for the week?

6. What is the FICA (social security) tax at 6.7% on weekly pay totaling $336.80?

7. Ross Alund works a 5-day week for average daily pay of $73.76. What is Alund's average pay:
   a. per week?
   b. per year?
   c. per month, to the nearest cent?

★ 8. A three-pound box of detergent costs $1.17. At that rate, what would be the cost of 8 pounds of detergent?

FRACTIONS IN BUYING

You need to use fractions in solving many buying problems or other money problems. Here are four common kinds of problems using fractions:

(1) Finding a part of a number
(2) Finding a number that is a part greater or smaller than a number
(3) Finding what part one number is of another
(4) Finding what part one number is greater or smaller than another

A discount or markdown is an amount off the full price

Finding a Part of a Number. You often see signs or ads such as "$\frac{1}{3}$ off," or "Half-Price Sale." The amount "off" is a **discount** or **markdown.** To find the discount or markdown, you must find a fractional part of the full price. To find the part, you multiply the full price by the fraction.

Example

An ad for shirts says, "Factory seconds, $\frac{1}{3}$ off." The full price of the shirts was $15. What is the amount of the discount on these shirts?

Solution	Explanation
$\frac{1}{3} \times \$15 = \$5$ discount	"$\frac{1}{3}$ off" means that a discount of $\frac{1}{3}$ of the full price is being given. $\frac{1}{3}$ of $15 means the same as $\frac{1}{3}$ *times* $15.

You will also see phrases such as "$\frac{2}{3}$ as much as . . . ," "$\frac{2}{3}$ as great as . . . ," "$\frac{2}{3}$ as large as . . . ," or "$\frac{2}{3}$ as many as. . . ." All those phrases mean the same as "of" or "times," so you find the answer by multiplying the number by the fraction. The fraction is a known factor, the number is the other known factor, and the answer is the unknown product (F × F = P).

Sale Factory Seconds 1/3 off

Oral Practice 1

What is the unknown number?

1. $\frac{2}{3}$ of 45 is *?*
2. $\frac{3}{4}$ of 32 is *?*
3. *?* is $\frac{2}{5}$ of 35?
4. $\frac{1}{3} \times 15 = $ *?*
5. *?* is $30 \times \frac{5}{6}$
6. $72 \times \frac{3}{8}$ is *?*
7. *?* is $\frac{7}{8}$ as large as 40
8. *?* is $\frac{4}{5}$ as many as 75
9. *?* is $\frac{3}{10}$ as much as 50

Written Practice 2

1. A store is holding a "half-price sale." The full price of a sweater was $29.50. How much would you save by buying it at half price?   **$14.75**

2. A discount store ad says "$\frac{1}{3}$ off list price." If the list or full price of a watch is $69, how much is the discount?

3. An ad says, "Your food bill will be only $\frac{3}{4}$ as much if you use our purchase plan." Your food bill has been $482 per month. If the ad is right, how much would you save per month by the purchase plan?

4. Your income is $14,300 a year. You estimate that you will spend $\frac{1}{5}$ of that amount for food. What will be your annual food expense?

Finding a Number That Is a Part Greater or Smaller Than a Given Number. You may see ads such as "Buy from us and get up to $\frac{1}{3}$ more for your money," or "Our prices are $\frac{1}{4}$ less than at other stores." To judge the truth of these statements, you need to find the number that is $\frac{1}{3}$ more than a given number, or $\frac{1}{4}$ smaller than a given number.

"$\frac{1}{3}$ more than a given number" or "$\frac{1}{3}$ greater than a given number" means that $\frac{1}{3}$ of the number is added to the number. For example, the number that is $\frac{1}{3}$ more than \$12 is \$16:

$$\frac{1}{3} \times \$12 = \$4$$
$$\$12 + \$4 = \$16$$

"$\frac{1}{4}$ less than a given number" or "$\frac{1}{4}$ smaller than a given number" means that $\frac{1}{4}$ of the number is subtracted from the number. For example, the number that is $\frac{1}{4}$ less than \$24 is \$18:

$$\frac{1}{4} \times \$24 = \$6$$
$$\$24 - \$6 = \$18$$

Oral Practice 3

What is the unknown number?

1. *?* is $\frac{1}{3}$ more than 18
2. *?* is $\frac{2}{5}$ larger than 10
3. $\frac{1}{7}$ more than 14 is *?*
4. \$27 plus $\frac{1}{3}$ of itself is *?*
5. *?* is $\frac{1}{5}$ less than 35
6. $\frac{1}{8}$ less than 24 is *?*
7. \$15 minus $\frac{1}{3}$ of itself is *?*
8. *?* is \$16 less $\frac{3}{4}$ of \$16

Written Practice 4

1. A box of Vansweet cookies weighs 15 ounces and sells for \$1.09. At a special sale, a larger package is offered for \$1.09 and is advertised as having "$\frac{1}{3}$ more." If the advertising is correct, what is the weight of the larger package?   **20 ounces**

2. Store *A* advertises a well-known brand of slacks at \$22. Store *B* claims to sell the same brand of slacks for $\frac{1}{4}$ less than other stores. If Store *B*'s claim is correct, what is their selling price for the slacks?

3. A market has a weekly special on canned hams at $\frac{1}{3}$ off the regular price. If the regular price is \$7.29, what is the special price?

4. Your present job pays \$6.75 an hour. On a new job your pay would be increased by $\frac{1}{5}$. What would be your hourly pay on the new job?

5. Olga Helwig had been spending an average of \$73.60 per week for food. This week, by shopping only once and using a shopping list, she saved $\frac{1}{10}$ of her weekly food cost. What was her food cost this week?

6. During one year the Chomsky family's cost of living increased by $\frac{1}{8}$. If their cost of living had been \$18,000 a year, what was their yearly cost of living after the increase?

Imported
Cookies

Now
$2.50

Finding What Part a Number Is of Another Number. Suppose that a can of cookies is reduced from $3 to $2.50. Or, a set of books is marked, "Save $3 — usually sells for $10." In such cases you may want to figure what part either the reduced price or the discount is of the original price.

To find what part a number is of another number, you write the numbers as a fraction. As the numerator, you write the number that is the part. As the denominator, you write the number that is the whole with which the part is being compared. Then you reduce the fraction.

Example

A can of cookies is reduced from $3 to $2.50. What part of $3 is $2.50?

Solution	Explanation
$\dfrac{\$2.50}{\$3.00} = \dfrac{5}{6}$ **Ans.** Check: $\dfrac{5}{\cancel{6}} \times \dfrac{\overset{0.50}{\cancel{\$3.00}}}{1} = \$2.50$	The part, $2.50, is to be compared with the whole, $3. So, $2.50 is written as the numerator of a fraction, with $3 as the denominator. The fraction is then reduced to $\frac{5}{6}$. To check, the whole ($3) is multiplied by the fraction showing the part ($\frac{5}{6}$) to be sure that the product ($2.50) equals the part.

You should use this rough check on your answer when you are finding what part one number is of another:

Use this

———————→

rough check

(1) A number compared with itself equals 1. For example, 3 compared to $3 = \frac{3}{3} = 1$.

(2) When a number is compared with a larger number, the result is less than 1. For example, 3 compared to $4 = \frac{3}{4}$.

(3) When a number is compared with a smaller number, the result is greater than 1. For example, 3 compared to 2 is $\frac{3}{2}$, or $1\frac{1}{2}$.

Oral Practice 5

1. 6 is what part of 12? 8? 6? 4? 2?

2. 9 is what part of 54? 27? 18? 8? 3?

3. What part of 30 is 6? 10? 20? 25? 40?

4. What part of 15 is 10? 6? 8? 25? 12?

Written Practice 6

1. A hair dryer that usually sells for $15 has been reduced to $12 on special sale. What part of the usual price is the sale price? $\frac{4}{5}$

2. A discount of $10 is given on shoes that first sold for $35. The discount is what part of the first price?

3. Berries that were first priced at $1.25 a box are on sale now at 95¢ a box. The sale price is what part of the first price?

4. The same kind of meat that sold last year for $2 a pound is selling this year for $2.50 a pound.
   a. This year's price is what part of last year's price?
   b. Last year's price is what part of this year's price?

5. Last week the Silver Shear Shop raised the price of haircuts from $5 to $6.
   a. The new price is what part of the old price?
   b. The old price is what part of the new price?

Finding What Part a Number Is Greater or Smaller Than Another Number. Suppose that a necklace has been marked down from $9 to $6. You want to find what part the new price, $6, is smaller than the old price, $9.

To find what part a number is greater or smaller than another, you use the steps in this example:

Example
$6 is what part smaller than $9?

Solution	Explanation
$9 −6 $3 part	(1) Find the part by subtracting the smaller number from the larger number. The difference is the part.
$3 part $9 whole	(2) Write the part as the numerator of a fraction. As the denominator of the fraction, write the whole with which the part is being compared.
$\dfrac{\$3}{\$9} = \dfrac{1}{3}$ **Ans.**	(3) Reduce the fraction.

Remember this!

In doing problems like these, remember that the denominator of the fraction is the number with which the part is being compared. The *denominator may be either the larger or the smaller of the two numbers.*

Oral Practice 7

What is the unknown number?

1. 25 is what part greater than 20, 15, 10, 5?

2. 16 is what part smaller than 20, 24, 32, 48?

3. What part more than 8 is 10, 12, 14, 16, 24?

4. What part less than 20 is 18, 15, 10, 5?

5. 15 equals 10 increased by what part of itself?

6. 24 equals 30 decreased by what part of itself?

Written Practice 8

1. Last month you spent $260 for food. This month you spent $234 for food. What part smaller was your food expense this month than last month? $\frac{1}{10}$

2. Nona Columbo spent $1,200 for clothing and personal care last year. This year Nona plans to increase that amount to $1,400. What part greater will Nona's clothing and personal care expenses be this year than last?

3. Jerry Bauer bought a ski jacket on sale for $70. The jacket had been priced at $95. What part less did Jerry pay for the jacket?

4. A school club earned $250 last year by holding a food sale. The club plans another food sale this year and hopes to earn $350. What part greater would this year's earnings be than last year's?

5. At the Express Market, melons cost $1.44 each. At the Price Saver Market, melons of the same kind and size cost $1.68. What part less do the melons cost at the Express Market?

6. In one year the price of a pair of work shoes increased from $32 to $40. By what part did the price increase?

Review 30

1. a. $24 \times N = $204. What is N?
   b. Multiply 124 by $0.37\frac{1}{2}$
   c. $72 \div 4\frac{1}{2} = ?$
   d. $4\frac{2}{3} + 8\frac{7}{8} = ?$
   e. 62 cm − 125 mm = ? mm
   f. 6.5 m × 3.5 m = ? m²
   g. 350 mL + 2.5 L = ? L
   h. 0.5 kg ÷ 2 = ? g

2. You are selling some clothing at a garage sale for $\frac{1}{3}$ of its original cost. What should you charge for a coat that cost you $87?

3. A government report says that food prices have increased $\frac{1}{4}$ over the prices of two years ago. You spent $3,450 for food two years ago. How much should you expect to spend for food this year if you want to eat as well as before?

4. Last year your income was $13,800 and you spent $1,150 for clothing and personal items. What part of your income did you spend for clothing and personal items last year?

5. Fran Riata earned $1,760 in July and $1,672 in August. What part less were Fran's August earnings than the July earnings?

6. You are making a snack mix with 3 parts peanuts to 1 part cashews. How many ounces of each must you have to make 2 pounds of mix?

7. A 400-gram package of cheese costs $1.90. What is the cost of the cheese per kilogram?

8. What is the sales tax at 5% on a sales slip with a merchandise total of $136.29?

FRACTIONS IN BUYING (concluded)

In Section 30 you solved four kinds of problems with fractions. In this section you will solve two other kinds of problems with fractions. They are (1) finding the whole when a part is known, and (2) finding the whole when an amount that is a part greater or smaller than the whole is known. In both these kinds of problems you have to divide a known product by a known factor to find an unknown factor (P ÷ F = F).

★**Finding the Whole When a Part Is Known.** Here is an example of a problem in finding the whole when you know a part:

Example

The sale price of a suit is $80, which is only $\frac{2}{3}$ of the regular price. What was the regular price?

Solution	Explanation
F　　　　**F**　　　　**P** $\frac{2}{3}$ × regular price = $80 **P ÷ F = F** $80 ÷ $\frac{2}{3}$ = F (regular price) $80 × $\frac{3}{2}$ = $120　**Ans.** Check: $\frac{2}{3}$ × $120 = $80	The problem says that $\frac{2}{3}$ of (or times) the regular price is equal to $80. So, you have a problem in which one factor, $\frac{2}{3}$, and the product, $80, are known. You are to find the unknown factor which was multiplied by $\frac{2}{3}$. To find the unknown factor, you divide the product, $80, by the known factor, $\frac{2}{3}$. When you divide, you invert the fraction and multiply. The product is $120. To check, you multiply the regular price that you found by the known factor. That product should equal the given product.

★**Oral**
  Practice 1

What is the unknown number in each of these?

1. $\frac{1}{2}$ of *?* is 20
2. $\frac{1}{4}$ of *N* is 25
3. 20 is $\frac{2}{3}$ of *?*
4. 30 is $\frac{3}{4}$ as much as *?*

5. $\frac{1}{4}$ as much as *?* = 15
6. 8 is $\frac{1}{5}$ of *?*
7. *?* is $\frac{3}{2}$ of 28
8. $\frac{2}{3}$ of *?* is $\frac{3}{4}$ of 24

★**Written**
  Practice 2

1. Your food and clothing expenses last year totaled $3,900. That amount was $\frac{1}{4}$ of your earnings for the year. What were your earnings for that year?　**$15,600**

2. Don Jones spent $38 for meat last week, which was $\frac{2}{7}$ of his total food expense for the week. What was his total food expense for the week?

3. The treasurer of a high school club reported a balance of $1,530 on hand. That amount was $\frac{3}{4}$ of the amount needed for the club's trip. What amount was needed for the club's trip?

★Finding the Whole When an Amount That Is a Part Greater or Smaller Than the Whole Is Known. Look at these two examples:

Example

The price of a coat, as marked on the price tag, is $180. This is $\frac{1}{2}$ more than the coat cost the store. What did the coat cost the store?

Solution

$\frac{2}{2}$ = the store's cost (unknown factor F)

$+\frac{1}{2}$ = markup (increase)

$\frac{3}{2}$ = marked price (known factor F)

  F   F   P

$\frac{3}{2} \times$ store's cost = $180

$180 \div \frac{3}{2} = F$

$180 \times \frac{2}{3} = 120 **Ans.**

Explanation

The problem says that $\frac{1}{2}$ of the store's cost plus the store's cost (unknown factor) equals the marked price of $180. So, let the store's cost be $\frac{2}{2}$. Add $\frac{1}{2}$ for the markup or increase, and the marked price is then $\frac{3}{2}$ of the store's cost. The product (marked price) of $180 is then divided by the known factor, $\frac{3}{2}$, to find the unknown factor (store's cost) of $120. You check the answer by adding $\frac{1}{2}$ of the store's cost, $60, to the store's cost, $120. That sum, $180, is the same as the marked price.

Check: $120 + ($\frac{1}{2} \times $120)
    = $120 + $60 = $180

Remember:
$P \div F = F$

Example

A jacket is sale-priced at $50, which is $\frac{1}{3}$ less than the full price. What was the full price?

Solution

$\frac{3}{3}$ = the full price (unknown factor F)

$-\frac{1}{3}$ = discount

$\frac{2}{3}$ = sale price (known factor F)

  F   F   P

$\frac{2}{3} \times$ full price = $50

$50 \div \frac{2}{3} = F$

$50 \times \frac{3}{2} = 75 **Ans.**

Explanation

The problem says that the full price, less $\frac{1}{3}$ of the full price, equals the sale price of $50. So, let the full price be $\frac{3}{3}$, subtract $\frac{1}{3}$ for the discount, and the sale price equals $\frac{2}{3}$ of the full price. You divide the product (sale price) of $50 by the known factor, $\frac{2}{3}$, to find the unknown factor (full price) of $75. You check the answer by subtracting $\frac{1}{3}$ of the full price, $25, from the full price of $75. The difference, $50, is the same as the sale price.

Check: $75 - ($\frac{1}{3} \times $75)
    = $75 - $25 = $50

$P \div F = F$

★**Oral Practice 3**

What is the unknown number in these?

1. 15 is $\frac{1}{4}$ larger than ?
2. 24 is $\frac{1}{3}$ less than ?
3. ? increased by $\frac{1}{6}$ = 21
4. ? decreased by $\frac{1}{8}$ = 56

5. $\frac{1}{5}$ less than ? is 20
6. 50 is $\frac{2}{3}$ more than ?
7. 24 is ? reduced by $\frac{1}{4}$
8. 16 is $\frac{3}{5}$ more than ?

★**Written Practice 4**

1. Clark Hamlin's food expense last year totaled $3,960, which was $\frac{1}{8}$ more than the year before. What was Hamlin's food expense for the year before? **$3,520**

2. Because she took a new job, Cleo Odeon's clothing and personal expenses last year were $\frac{1}{6}$ greater than the year before. Her clothing and personal expenses last year were $1,470. What were her clothing and personal expenses for the year before?

3. During the peak season, tomatoes sold for 54¢ a pound, which was $\frac{2}{5}$ less than they sold for early in the season. What was the early season price? **90¢**

4. By planning their meals carefully and shopping wisely, the Beaumonts cut their average monthly food bill to $315. This was a decrease of $\frac{3}{10}$ from their old food bill. What was their old food bill per month?

★**Review 31**

1. **a.** $28 × N = $189. What is N?
   b. Multiply 90 by 0.83\frac{1}{3}$
   c. Multiply $2\frac{1}{6}$ by $3\frac{3}{4}$
   d. Divide 153.25 by 0.25
   e. 50 m² × 50 = ? ha
   f. 672 kL ÷ 4 = ? kL
   g. 500 kg × 10 = ? t
   h. 65 cm − 250 mm = ? cm

2. In June you spent $96.72, which was only $\frac{3}{4}$ of the amount you spent in May. What amount did you spend in May?

3. Lim Koza bought a new pair of work shoes for $29.75. In checking his records, he found that this amount was an increase of $\frac{1}{6}$ over the price he had paid for the same kind of shoes a year ago. What was the price he paid for the shoes a year ago?

4. In late August sweet corn was selling for $1 a dozen ears. This was a decrease of $\frac{1}{3}$ from the price in early July. What was the price per dozen ears in early July?

5. Louise Singer found that 2 quarts of berries would make 5 cups of juice for jelly. How many cups of juice would 15 quarts of berries make?

6. Ned Flores is self-employed. Ned's gross income from his business last year was $43,647, and his total expenses were $15,952.
   a. What was Ned's net income for last year?
   b. At a FICA self-employment tax rate of 9.35% on the net income, what was Ned's FICA tax for last year?

7. The Neverfail Collection Agency collected a bill of $3,645 for Malmud. The agency charged a collection fee of 35% and $73.65 for legal costs. What were Malmud's net proceeds?

EXPENSE RECORDS

As you learned in Section 1, many people keep a written cash receipts record of all money they actually receive. Many people also keep a cash payments record.

Cash Payments Record. A **cash payments record** is a written record of all money spent. Payments records are used to plan spending and to figure income taxes.

Karl Wirth's cash payments record is shown below. Karl lists all money he spends each day. He shows the date, what the money was spent for, and the amount. Karl totals his cash payments records at the end of each month.

Karl Wirth
Cash Payments Record

DATE		FOR	AMOUNT	
April	1	Insurance premium	32	65
	1	Rent for month	310	00
	4	Electric bill	37	57
	5	Food	36	42
	6	Gas and Oil	20	00
	22	Movies + stereo tapes	18	40
	23	Food	43	28
	26	Shirt and pants	31	49
	29	Gas and car repairs	44	93
			1,183	42

Cash payments record

Karl Wirth's record is easy to use except when he wants to find the total spent for one kind of expense, such as food. To find the total spent for any kind of expense, Karl has to pick out the items from his record and then add them.

Written Practice 1

Here is Toni Bond's cash payments record for the week of May 12 through May 18. You are to use that record to answer the questions below.

Toni Bond
Cash Payments Record

Date			For	Amount	
19-- May	12		Food	15	75
	14		Gas and oil	12	50
	14		Insurance	32	63
	15		Car payment	155	00
	16		Clothes	33	70
	17		Food	24	25
	18		Entertainment	6	17

1. What was the total of Toni's cash payments for the week?

2. How much did Toni spend for food during the week?

3. Toni's food expense for the week was what fractional part of her total payments for the week?

Cash Payments Record with Special Columns. Many people prefer to keep a cash payments record with special columns. In this kind of record, all payments for the same kind of expense are recorded in a special column. By keeping the record that way, the total payments for each kind of expense can be found easily. The Kruzan family's record is an example.

The Kruzan Family
Cash Payments Record

WEEK	FOR							TOTALS
	FOOD	CLOTHING/ PERSONAL	HOUSING	TRAVEL	HEALTH	EDUCATION/ RECREATION	SAVINGS	
19-- Jan 1-7	103 75		420 00	18 00	20 00	16 85	50 00	628 60
8-14	86 52	65 42		16 50	25 00	37 20		230 64
15-21	94 60	42 10		22 00	20 00	23 15	50 00	251 85
22-28	79 41	13 25	60 35	175 00	35 40	18 70		382 11
29-31	44 73		18 70	14 20	15 10	5 27	70 00	168 00
Totals	409 01	120 77	499 05	245 70	115 50	101 17	170 00	1,661 20

Cash payments record with special columns

As shown in the example, the Kruzan family records all of its payments for food, clothing, and so on in columns under descriptive headings. They record their payments for each week or part of a week, rather than day-by-day. At the end of each month, they add the columns to find how much they have spent for each kind of expense, and their total payments.

Written Practice 2

1. Burt Judd's cash payments record for June is shown below. Find the totals for each kind of payment by adding the columns vertically. Find the weekly totals by adding horizontally. The total of the weekly payments should equal the total of the different kinds of payments.

Burt Judd
Cash Payments Record

| Week | For | | | | | Totals |
	Food	Clothing	Housing	Car	Other	
June 1–7	56.20		150.00	182.00	91.80	**480.00**
8–14	49.74	24.50	42.60	16.50		
15–21	54.06		150.00	18.00	43.70	
22–28	52.25		17.40	76.00	26.10	
29–30	27.75	95.50		7.50	18.40	
Totals	**240.00**					

2. What fractional part of Burt Judd's payments for June (Problem 1) were paid for:
   a. food? $\frac{1}{5}$
   b. clothing?
   c. housing?
   d. car?
   e. other?

3. What fractional part of Burt Judd's total payments for June were paid in the first week?

Cash Record Summary. The Kruzan family keeps both a cash receipts record and a cash payments record. At the end of each month, the Kruzans transfer the totals from their cash receipts record and cash payments record to a **cash record summary**. Their summary is shown on the next page. At the end of the year, they total the summary. The Kruzans use their summary figures to review their income and expenses of the past year, to plan ahead, and to make their income tax reports.

The Kruzan Family
Cash Records Summary
For the year 19--

| MONTH | RECEIPTS | PAYMENTS | FOR | | | | | | |
			FOOD	CLOTHING/ PERSONAL	HOUSING	TRAVEL	HEALTH	EDUCATION/ RECREATION	SAVINGS
Jan.	1,725 00	1,661 20	409 01	120 77	499 05	245 70	115 50	101 17	170 00
Feb.	1,680 00	1,556 80	416 25	63 95	425 00	198 65	75 65	212 30	165 00
Mar.	1,635 00	1,630 24	420 80	84 08	425 00	305 16	70 15	265 05	60 00
Nov.	1,690 00	1,683 21	395 63	95 25	509 00	250 13	86 40	196 80	150 00
Dec.	1,675 00	1,674 50	432 84	105 59	475 20	278 10	92 50	245 27	45 00
Totals	20,000 00	20,000 00	5,000 00	1,000 00	5,600 00	3,000 00	1,000 00	2,400 00	2,000 00

Cash record summary

Written Practice 3

Use the information from the Kruzan family's monthly cash record summary to answer these questions.

1. What fractional part of the Kruzan's total payments last year were for
   a. food? $\frac{1}{4}$
   b. clothing and personal?
   c. housing?

2. a. How much money did the Kruzans save last year?
   b. What fractional part of the Kruzan's total payments was for savings?

3. The Kruzan's payments for clothing and personal were what fractional part of their payments for food?

4. What average amount per month did the Kruzans spend for
   a. travel? **$250**
   b. education and recreation?
   c. health?

5. To keep next year's spending the same as this year, how much should the Kruzans plan to spend next year for food?

6. a. If food costs should increase by $\frac{1}{10}$ next year, how much will the Kruzans need to spend for food next year?
   b. How much more would next year's food expenses be than this year's?

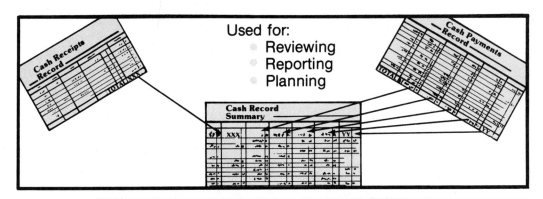

Used for:
  • Reviewing
  • Reporting
  • Planning

Terms to Remember

cash payments record   cash record summary   discount or markdown

a. An amount off a full price; a reduction in price
b. A review of cash receipts and payments
c. A written record of all money spent

Review 32

1. **a.** Multiply 120 by $37\frac{1}{2}$¢
   b. What is $\frac{2}{3}$ of $45?
   c. $32 ÷ $\frac{5}{6}$ = ?
   d. $1\frac{3}{4} \times 2\frac{1}{2}$ = ?
   e. 3.5 m + 2.6 m = ? m
   f. 5.25 km ÷ 0.5 km = ?
   g. 2.25 ha − 0.75 ha = ? ha
   h. 3 L ÷ 6 = ? mL

2. Nita Shirota's cash payments record for February is shown below. You are to find the weekly and monthly totals, then answer questions a, b, and c.

Week	Food	Clothing	Housing	Car	Savings	Other	Totals
Feb. 1–7	83.40	60.00	325.00	10.00		81.60	
8–14	78.00			160.00	35.00		
15–21	72.60	115.00		10.00	150.00	18.40	
22–28	74.00			27.00	100.00		
Totals							

   a. What fractional part of Nita's February payments were for clothing?
   b. What fractional part of Nita's total payments for February were her first week's payments?
   c. What was Nita's average weekly food cost?

3. You have $4,500 to spend for food and clothing. The ratio of your food expenses to your clothing expenses is 7 to 2, in favor of food. How much of the $4,500 should you plan to spend for (a) food and (b) clothing?

4. Hard rolls are priced at 6 for 79¢. You want to buy only one roll. What would be the cost of the one roll?

DECIMALS

You have already rebuilt your skill in adding, subtracting, multiplying and dividing with decimals. In this section you will learn more about decimals and how they are related to common fractions.

What Is a Decimal. In Section 32 you figured what part one number was of another and showed the answer as a fraction. You could have shown those fractions as decimals.

A decimal is a way of showing a fractional number

A **decimal**, or decimal fraction, is another way of naming a fractional number when the fraction has a denominator of 10, 100, 1,000, or another multiple of ten. For example, you can write $\frac{5}{10}$ as the decimal 0.5, $\frac{5}{100}$ as 0.05, or $\frac{5}{1,000}$ as 0.005.

Facts About Decimals. Here are some important facts about decimals:

(1) You can attach zeros to a decimal without changing the number it represents. For example, just as $\frac{5}{10}$, $\frac{50}{100}$, and $\frac{500}{1,000}$ are equivalent fractions, so 0.5, 0.50, and 0.500 are equivalent decimals.

(2) You can show any whole number as a decimal by attaching a decimal point and as many zeros as you want. For example, 39 = 39.0, or 39.00, or 39.000, and so on.

(3) You can make figuring easier by using decimals. For example, you can add $5.35 and $8.75 more easily than you can add 5\frac{7}{20}$ and 8\frac{3}{4}$.

(4) You can often compare decimals more easily than fractions. For example, you can see that 0.857 is larger than 0.778 more easily than you can see that $\frac{6}{7}$ is larger than $\frac{7}{9}$.

Changing a Fraction to a Decimal. You can change a fraction to a decimal by dividing the numerator by the denominator. If the division is not exact, you divide to one more place than the place you want, then round off.

Example

What is the decimal equivalent of $\frac{5}{7}$, correct to 2 decimal places?

Solution	**Explanation**
$\begin{array}{r} 0.714 \\ 7)\overline{5.000} = 0.71 \quad \textbf{Ans.} \\ \underline{4\ 9} \\ 10 \\ \underline{7} \\ 30 \\ \underline{28} \end{array}$	The numerator, 5, is divided by the denominator, 7. The division is carried to 3 decimal places, then rounded back to 2 places.

**Written
Practice 1**

Write each of these as a decimal.

1. **a.** $\frac{1}{10}$ 0.1   **e.** $\frac{35}{100}$ **i.** $\frac{635}{1,000}$ **m.** $\frac{9}{1,000}$

   b. $\frac{1}{100}$ **f.** $\frac{125}{1,000}$ **j.** $\frac{15}{1,000}$ **n.** $\frac{1}{10,000}$

   c. $\frac{1}{1,000}$ **g.** $\frac{7}{10}$ **k.** $\frac{7}{100}$ **o.** $\frac{56}{10,000}$

   d. $\frac{3}{10}$ **h.** $\frac{49}{100}$ **l.** $\frac{9}{10}$ **p.** $\frac{39}{100}$

2. Find the decimal equivalent of:

   a. $\frac{3}{7}$, to 3 places   0.429   **e.** $\frac{5}{7}$, to the nearest hundredth
   b. $\frac{5}{9}$, to 2 places   **f.** $\frac{4}{15}$, to the nearest tenth
   c. $\frac{8}{15}$, to 4 places   **g.** $\frac{8}{9}$, to the nearest thousandth
   d. $\frac{4}{11}$, to 1 place   **h.** $\frac{7}{12}$, to the nearest ten-thousandth

3. Opal Swift spent $\frac{1}{9}$ of her total payments last month for clothing. What part, expressed as a decimal correct to 2 places, did she spend for clothing?   **0.11**

4. Neil Zak's total expenses last year amounted to $16,500. Of that amount he spent $2,970 for food.
   a. What part did he spend for food, expressed as a fraction?
   b. What is the decimal equivalent of that fraction, correct to 2 places?

Changing a Decimal to a Fraction. To change a decimal to a fraction, you omit the decimal point and write the digits as the numerator of a fraction. To make the denominator of the fraction, you write 1 and as many zeros as there are decimal places in the decimal. Then reduce the fraction to lowest terms. For example:

$$0.5 = \frac{5}{10} = \frac{1}{2} \qquad 0.45 = \frac{45}{100} = \frac{9}{20} \qquad 3.5 = \frac{35}{10} = \frac{7}{2} = 3\frac{1}{2}$$

**Written
Practice 2**

1. Change these decimals to fractions in lowest terms.

   a. 0.48 $\frac{12}{25}$ **e.** 0.025   **i.** 0.4375

   b. 0.29   **f.** 0.125   **j.** 0.6

   c. 0.625   **g.** 0.75   **k.** 2.4

   d. 0.375   **h.** 0.05   **l.** 0.78

2. When you divided your food and clothing expenses by your total expenses, the quotient was the decimal, 0.32. What is the common fraction equivalent of that decimal, in lowest terms? $\frac{8}{25}$

3. Last year, Cindy Tripp spent $5,460 for food, clothing, and personal items. Cindy's total expenses for the year were $15,600.
   a. What decimal part of Cindy's total expenses were for food, clothing, and personal items?
   b. To what fraction is that decimal equivalent?

Move the decimal
point to the LEFT

←—————————

Multiplying by 0.1, 0.01, and 0.001. You multiply by 0.1, 0.01, or 0.001 by moving the decimal point in the multiplicand to the *left* as many places as there are decimal places in the multiplier. Prefix zeros, if needed. For example,

$$58.4 \times 0.1 = 5.84 \qquad 9.2 \times 0.01 = 0.092$$

$$167 \times 0.001 = 0.167 \qquad \$3,485 \times 0.01 = \$34.85$$

Written Practice 3

Multiply mentally, then write the product.

1. 46.7×0.01
2. 38.2×0.1
3. 6.9×0.1
4. 7.3×0.01
5. 354×0.001

6. 48×0.001
7. 675×0.001
8. 0.25×0.1
9. 0.3×0.01
10. 3.6×0.1

11. $\$256 \times 0.1$
12. $\$80 \times 0.001$
13. $\$9 \times 0.01$
14. $\$28.70 \times 0.1$
15. $\$340 \times 0.001$

Review 33

1. **a.** Multiply 0.382 by 3.4
   b. Subtract 6.45 from 8.3
   c. Divide 24.4 by 3.05
   d. Add 0.85 and 1.4
   e. 200 m ÷ 4 = ? m
   f. 400 cm² × 5 = ? m²
   g. 750 mL × 2 = ? L
   h. \$30 decreased by $\frac{1}{5}$ of itself gives what amount?
   i. \$20 is what fractional part greater than \$16?

2. What is the decimal equivalent of $\frac{2}{7}$, to 3 decimal places?

3. Change 0.3125 to a fraction in lowest terms.

4. Josh McLean spent \$15,000 last year. Of that amount, Josh spent \$2,250 for food.
   a. What fractional part of his total expense was his food expense?
   b. What is the decimal equivalent of that fraction?

5. A $2\frac{1}{2}$-pound box of Hurry muffin mix costs \$1.29. What is the price of the mix per pound?

6. What is the total sale price of slacks that cost \$21.95, plus a 7% sales tax?

7. Abby Juroz has a choice of two jobs. Job *A* pays \$230 a week. Fringe benefits of Job *A* are estimated to be worth \$1,495 a year, and expenses are estimated at \$688 a year. Job *B* would pay a salary of \$1,050 a month, with fringe benefits worth \$1,250 a year and expenses of \$820 a year. Which job pays the greater net benefits per year? How much greater?

8. Toby Marshall gets a commission of 5% on all sales, and an additional 2% commission on sales over \$30,000 a month. What was his commission for July on total sales of \$37,500?

BUDGETING AND PERCENTS

You can get more for your money if you plan your spending. To plan your spending, you first decide what *you* need and want over several months or a year. Then you decide when and how much you will spend to get the most for the money you will have. Your spending plan is called a budget .

Money records are a big help to you in budgeting. By looking back at your earning and spending records, you can get a good idea of what you can spend in the future.

Budget amounts are called "allowances"

Your budget should usually show what parts of your total income you want to spend for major kinds of expenses over a long period of time. For example, your budget might allow $\frac{1}{5}$ of your income for food in a month or year. You might show your budget allowances as fractions, but you probably would show them as percents.

A Sample Budget. The Kruzan family, whose cash record summary for a year is shown on page 131, budget their expenses each year. To budget, they first make a chart such as the one below. On the chart they show their income and expenses for the last year. They also show each kind of expense as a percent of their total cash income.

They find the percents by dividing the amount spent for each kind of expense by their total cash income. The decimal quotient is then changed to a percent by moving the decimal point two places to the right and adding a percent sign. For example, the expense for food, $5,000, when divided by the total cash income, $20,000, is 25%.

$5,000 ÷ $20,000 = 0.25, or 25%

TOTAL CASH INCOME: $20,000, or 100%

Food	Clothing and Personal	Housing	Travel	Health	Education and Recreation	Savings
$5,000	$1,000	$5,600	$3,000	$1,000	$2,400	$2,000
25%	5%	28%	15%	5%	12%	10%

In planning for next year, the Kruzans expect that their income will be increased by $2,000, to $22,000. They also expect that their expenses will be greater, but in the same ratio as last year. So, they plan next year's budget by multiplying their expected income by each percent shown in the chart.

For example, their food allowance for next year will be $5,500, figured this way:

25% × $22,000 = 0.25 × $22,000 = $5,500

The Kruzan's budget allowances for next year look like this:

EXPECTED CASH INCOME: $22,000, or 100%

Food	Clothing and Personal	Housing	Travel	Health	Education and Recreation	Savings
$5,500	$1,100	$6,160	$3,300	$1,100	$2,640	$2,200
25%	5%	28%	15%	5%	12%	10%

Written Practice 1

1. The year after next, the Kruzans expect to have a total income of $25,000. They will budget the same percents for expenses as shown on this year's budget. What amount will they allow for each kind of expense? **Food, $6,250**

2. Charo Mendez has a total income of $15,000 a year. Charo budgets her expenses this way: food, $3,000; clothing, $1,200; housing, $4,500; car, $2,700; savings, $2,100; other, $1,500. What percent of her income does Charo allow for each kind of expense?

Meaning of Percent. Percent means "per hundred," "parts per hundred," or "out of a hundred." A percent shows the comparison or ratio of a number to 100. For example, if you pay $7 sales tax on every $100 you spend, you can say that the tax is 7 percent.

A percent is a fraction with a denominator of 100

A ratio is another way of showing a fraction. For example, the ratio of 7 to 100 (7:100) is equivalent to $\frac{7}{100}$. So, the ratio of 7:100, the fraction $\frac{7}{100}$, the decimal 0.07, and the percent 7% are just different numerals that stand for the same number.

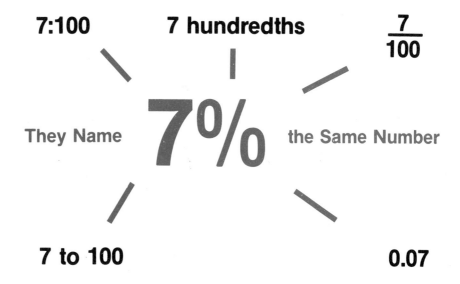

**Written
Practice 2**   Show each ratio as a fraction, a decimal, and a percent. Use this form:
7 to 100 = $\frac{7}{100}$ = 0.07 = 7%.

1. 55 to 100   55%
2. 79 to 100
3. 37$\frac{1}{2}$ to 100
4. 6$\frac{3}{4}$ to 100

5. 33$\frac{1}{3}$ to 100
6. 100 to 100
7. 105 to 100
8. 150 to 100

9. 200 to 100
10. $\frac{1}{2}$ to 100
11. 0.3 to 100
12. 0.9 to 100

Changing Fractions to Percents.

You can easily change any fraction with a denominator of 100 to a percent. You just write the numerator with a percent sign (%) after it. For example:

$$\frac{1}{100} = 1\% \qquad \frac{29}{100} = 29\% \qquad \frac{150}{100} = 150\%$$

Changing fractions with denominators of 1, 2, 4, 5, 10, 20, 25, or 50 to percents is easy, too. Just raise the fraction so the denominator is 100. Here are two examples:

$$\frac{1}{2} \times \frac{50}{50} = \frac{50}{100} = 50\% \qquad \frac{3}{1} \times \frac{100}{100} = \frac{300}{100} = 300\%$$

**Written
Practice 3**   Change each fraction to a percent.

1. $\frac{5}{100}$ 5%
2. $\frac{75}{100}$

3. $\frac{1}{5}$ 20%
4. $\frac{3}{4}$

5. $\frac{9}{10}$
6. $\frac{19}{50}$

7. $\frac{3}{25}$
8. $\frac{1}{1}$

9. $\frac{1}{4}$
10. $\frac{5}{1}$

Suppose that you cannot easily change the denominator of a fraction to 100. You must first change the fraction to a decimal, and then change the decimal to a percent.

Changing a Decimal or a Whole Number to a Percent.

The long way to change a decimal or a whole number to a percent is to change it first to a fraction with a denominator of 100. You then change that fraction to a percent. For example:

$$0.29 \times \frac{100}{100} = \frac{29}{100} = 29\%$$

Use the short way!   The short way is to move the decimal point two places to the right, then add a percent sign. For example:

$$0.29 = 29\%$$

Here are some other examples of the short way:

$$0.68 = 68\% \qquad 0.005 = 0.5\% \qquad 0.87\frac{1}{2} = 87\frac{1}{2}\%$$

$$0.09 = 9\% \qquad 0.6 = 60\% \qquad 7 = 700\%$$

Oral Practice 4

What percent is each decimal?

1. 0.26	**4.** 0.6	**7.** 0.083	**10.** $5.62\frac{1}{2}$
2. 0.04	**5.** 0.2	**8.** 0.0049	**11.** 3.5
3. 0.01	**6.** 0.362	**9.** $0.15\frac{1}{4}$	**12.** 10

Written Practice 5

Change these decimals to the nearest whole percent.

1. 0.42 42%	**3.** 0.08	**5.** 0.237 24%	**7.** 4.56
2. 0.5	**4.** 1.5	**6.** 0.079	**8.** 0.691

When changing a fraction to the nearest whole percent, the fraction must first be changed to a decimal, and the decimal is then changed to the nearest whole percent. Look at this example:

Example

Change $\frac{4}{7}$ to the nearest whole percent.

Solution	Explanation
$$\frac{4}{7} = 7\overline{)\begin{array}{l}0.571 \\ 4.000\end{array}} = 0.57 = 57\% \quad \textbf{Ans.}$$ $$\begin{array}{r}3\ 5 \\ \hline 50 \\ 49 \\ \hline 10\end{array}$$	The fraction was changed to a decimal by dividing the numerator by the denominator. The quotient was rounded to a two-place decimal. The decimal was then changed to a percent by moving the decimal point two places to the right and adding a percent sign.

Written Practice 6

Change these fractions to the nearest whole percent.

1. $\frac{6}{7}$ 86%	**3.** $\frac{5}{13}$ 38%	**5.** $\frac{3}{7}$	**7.** $\frac{5}{11}$	**9.** $\frac{8}{15}$
2. $\frac{7}{9}$	**4.** $\frac{2}{9}$	**6.** $\frac{6}{11}$	**8.** $\frac{8}{9}$	**10.** $\frac{11}{12}$

Changing a Percent to a Decimal. The long way to change a percent to a decimal has two steps. You change the decimal to a fraction with a denominator of 100. Then you change the fraction to a decimal:

$$39\% = \frac{39}{100} = 100\overline{)\begin{array}{l}0.39 \\ 39.00\end{array}} = 0.39$$

Use the short way. It's easy!

The short way to get the same result is to drop the percent sign and move the decimal point two places to the left. Look at these examples:

$$39\% = 0.39 \qquad \frac{3}{4}\% = 0.00\frac{3}{4} \qquad 140\% = 1.40 \text{ or } 1.4$$

Oral Practice 7

What is the equivalent decimal or whole number?

1. 73%	**4.** 6.5%	**7.** 0.5%	**10.** 300%	**13.** $62\frac{1}{2}\%$
2. 54.5%	**5.** 1%	**8.** 100%	**11.** 1,000%	**14.** $43\frac{1}{3}\%$
3. 13.2%	**6.** 8%	**9.** 150%	**12.** $133\frac{1}{3}\%$	**15.** $\frac{1}{3}\%$

Changing a Percent to a Fraction. To change a percent to a fraction, you first drop the percent sign, then you write the number as the numerator of a fraction, with a denominator of 100. Reduce the fraction to lowest terms. For example:

$$25\% = \frac{25}{100} = \frac{1}{4} \qquad 150\% = \frac{150}{100} = 1\frac{1}{2}$$

Written Practice 8

Change each of these percents to a common fraction in lowest terms, or to a mixed number.

1. 7% $\frac{7}{100}$
2. 5%
3. 24%

4. 6%
5. 15%
6. 48%

7. 40%
8. 25%
9. 50%

10. 175%
11. 225%
12. 140%

Terms to Remember		
budget	decimal	percent

a. A fraction with a denominator of 10, 100, or 1,000
b. A plan for spending
c. Means "per hundred"

Review 34

1. a. $27 decreased by $\frac{1}{3}$ of itself is what amount?
   b. What number is equal to $10 increased by $\frac{1}{2}$ of itself?
   c. 25 is what fractional part smaller than 35?
   d. Change $\frac{5}{9}$ to the nearest tenth percent
   e. Change 45% to a decimal
   f. Change 0.28 to a fraction in lowest terms
   g. Change $0.43\frac{1}{4}$ to a percent

2. Maria Corona's cash income is $18,000 per year. She budgets $4,680 of that amount for food. What percent of her income does Maria budget for her food?

3. You want to allow 12% of your budget for clothing and personal expenses. If your income is $21,500 a year, how much should you budget for your clothing and personal expenses?

4. During December, Dale Bogart's food cost $420. By comparison, Dale's food cost him $\frac{1}{6}$ less in June. What did Dale's June food cost?

5. The full price of a jacket was $75. The jacket has now been marked down and is on sale at $50. What fractional part of the full price is the:
   a. sale price?
   b. markdown?

★ 6. a. Express $3\frac{1}{2}$ as a decimal.
   b. 90 is $\frac{5}{6}$ of what amount?

PERCENTS IN BUDGETING AND BUYING

A percent is another way of showing a fraction, so you will often use percents instead of fractions.

Finding a Percent of a Number. You find a percent of a number by multiplying the number by the decimal equivalent of the percent.

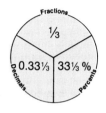

Example

Your income is $20,000. You want to allow 22% of your income for food. What amount should you allow for food?

Solution	Explanation
22% = 0.22 $ $ 0.22 × $20,000 = $4,400 **Ans.**	Change the 22% to its decimal equivalent, 0.22, by dropping the percent sign and moving the decimal point two places to the left. Then multiply the income, $20,000, by the decimal equivalent, 0.22.

Written Practice 1

1. Find the product. Multiply mentally if you can.

   a. 35% of $200 **$70**
   b. 5% of $50
   c. 6% of $400
   d. 100% of $9

   e. 500% of $29
   f. 8% of $750
   g. 1% of $235
   h. 130% of $500

   i. 40% of $129
   j. 65% of $300
   k. 9.5% of $1,000
   l. $13\frac{1}{2}$% of $2,000

2. The regular price of a suit is $150. How much would you save by buying the suit on sale at a 25% discount? **$37.50**

3. You plan to spend 30% of your weekly pay for food and clothing. If your weekly pay is $325, how much can you spend for food and clothing?

Finding 1%, 10%, 100%, and 1,000% of a Number. The easy way to find 1%, 10%, 100%, or 1,000% of a number is to move the decimal point as you would to multiply by 0.01, 0.1, 1, or 10. For example:

Just move the decimal point!

$$1\% \text{ of } \$372 = 0.01 × \$372 = \$3.72$$
$$10\% \text{ of } \$372 = 0.1 × \$372 = \$37.20$$
$$100\% \text{ of } \$372 = 1 × \$372 = \$372$$
$$1,000\% \text{ of } \$372 = 10 × \$372 = \$3,720$$

Written Practice 2

Multiply mentally and write the products. Round to the nearest cent.

   1. 1% of 25 **0.25**
   2. 1% of $382
   3. 10% of 94
   4. 10% of $8

   5. 100% of $35
   6. 100% of $4.25
   7. 1,000% of $68
   8. 1,000% of $94.20

   9. 10% of $0.75
   10. 1% of $23.50
   11. 100% of $15.99
   12. 10% of $3.85

$\frac{1}{2}$ and $\frac{1}{2}$% are NOT the same

Finding Part of 1% of a Number.
Suppose that you need to find $\frac{1}{2}$% of $600. The $\frac{1}{2}$% means $\frac{1}{2}$ of 1%, so you must find $\frac{1}{2}$ of 1% of $600. You may use either of these two ways, but Solution 1 is easier to do mentally.

Example

Find $\frac{1}{2}$% of $600.

Solution 1	Solution 2
1% of $600 = $6	$\frac{1}{2}$ of 1% = 0.005
$\frac{1}{2}$ of $6 = $3	$0.005 \times \$600 = \$3$

Explanation	**Explanation**
Find 1% of the number by moving the decimal point. Multiply that amount by the fraction.	Find the decimal equivalent of $\frac{1}{2}$%. Then multiply the number by the decimal equivalent.

Written Practice 3

Try to do these mentally, writing only the product. If you cannot do them mentally, write them out.

1. $\frac{1}{4}$% of $300   75¢
2. $\frac{1}{4}$ of $300 $75
3. $\frac{1}{2}$% of $800
4. $\frac{1}{2}$ of $800
5. $\frac{1}{3}$% of $600

6. $\frac{1}{3}$ of $600
7. $\frac{1}{5}$% of $500
8. $\frac{1}{6}$% of $120
9. $\frac{1}{8}$% of $400
10. $\frac{3}{4}$% of $2,000

11. $\frac{2}{3}$% of $60
12. $\frac{2}{5}$% of $250
13. $\frac{3}{8}$% of $48
14. $\frac{1}{4}$% of $8
15. $\frac{3}{4}$% of $200

Multiplying by Aliquot Parts of 100%.
To multiply by aliquot parts of $1, you can multiply by the equivalent fraction. You can use the same idea to multiply by percents that are aliquot parts of 100%. For example, suppose you want to find 50% of $800. Since 50% = $\frac{1}{2}$ of 100%, you can multiply the $800 by the fraction, $\frac{1}{2}$, instead of by the decimal, 0.5.

$$50\% \text{ of } \$800 = \frac{1}{2} \times \$800 = \$400$$

ALIQUOT PARTS OF 100%

These aliquot parts of 100% are easy to use

$50\% = \frac{1}{2}$	$20\% = \frac{1}{5}$	$12\frac{1}{2}\% = \frac{1}{8}$	$33\frac{1}{3}\% = \frac{1}{3}$
$25\% = \frac{1}{4}$	$40\% = \frac{2}{5}$	$37\frac{1}{2}\% = \frac{3}{8}$	$66\frac{2}{3}\% = \frac{2}{3}$
$75\% = \frac{3}{4}$	$60\% = \frac{3}{5}$	$62\frac{1}{2}\% = \frac{5}{8}$	$16\frac{2}{3}\% = \frac{1}{6}$
	$80\% = \frac{4}{5}$	$87\frac{1}{2}\% = \frac{7}{8}$	$83\frac{1}{3}\% = \frac{5}{6}$

Oral Practice 4

Use the fraction that is equivalent to the percent to do these.

1. 50% of $18
2. 25% of $16
3. 75% of $24
4. 20% of $30
5. 40% of $20

6. 60% of 150
7. 80% of $200
8. $12\frac{1}{2}$% of 32
9. $37\frac{1}{2}$% of $48
10. $62\frac{1}{2}$% of $72

11. $87\frac{1}{2}$% of $160
12. $33\frac{1}{3}$% of $75
13. $66\frac{2}{3}$% of $600
14. $16\frac{2}{3}$% of $300
15. $83\frac{1}{3}$% of $1,200

Finding a Number That Is a Percent Greater or Smaller Than a Given Number.

First you find the amount of the increase or decrease by multiplying the given number by the percent. Then you add the increase to the given number, or subtract the decrease from the given number.

Add the increase. Subtract the decrease

For example, suppose your clothing allowance last year was $1,000. You want to increase it by 15% this year. You would find your new clothing allowance this way:

Last Year's Allowance	+	**This Year's Increase**	=	**This Year's Allowance**
$1,000	+	0.15 × $1,000, or $150	=	$1,150

Or, suppose that your food expense last month was $400, and you want to reduce it by 10% this month. You would figure this month's food expense this way:

Last Month's Expense	−	**This Month's Decrease**	=	**This Month's Expense**
$400	−	0.1 × $400, or $40	=	$360

Written Practice 5

1. What amount is:

   a. 20% greater than $150 $180
   b. 15% more than $200
   c. 10% larger than $60
   d. 25% smaller than $300 $225
   e. 30% less than $60

   f. $25 increased by 20%
   g. $25 decreased by 20%
   h. $60 reduced by 15%
   i. $79 less 10%
   j. 100% greater than $35

2. At a clothing store, all items are on sale at 20% off. What is the sale price of shoes that were first sold for $40?

3. You paid $90 for an antique table 5 years ago. It has increased in value by 50%. What is its value now?

Finding What Percent One Number Is of Another.

As you know from working with budgets, you can find what percent one number is of another by dividing the one number by the other. Then you show the quotient as a percent. For example, suppose you want to find what percent this month's food expense, $425, is of your year's food allowance, $4,250. You do it this way:

$$\$425 \div \$4,250 = 0.10 = 10\%$$

As a rough check on your answer, remember that any number is 100% of itself. Or, when a number is compared with a smaller number, the result is more than 100%. Also, when a number is compared with a larger number, the result is less than 100%.

Written Practice 6

WATERMELONS

$\cancel{\$3}$
NOW $2

1. What is the unknown percent in each of these?

    a. 10 is ?% of 20   50%
    b. 15 is ?% of 60
    c. 20 is ?% of 10
    d. 39 is ?% of 39
    e. 15 is ?% of 75

    f. ?% of $240 is $30
    g. ?% of $120 is $9.60
    h. $9 is ?% of $45
    i. ?% is 99¢ of $3.30
    j. $11.25 is ?% of $15

2. Melons that sold for $3 have been reduced to $2. What percent is the new price of the old price? $66\frac{2}{3}\%$

3. A club buys candy for $2 a box and sells it for $3.50 a box. What percent of the cost is the selling price?

Finding the Percent That One Number Is Greater or Smaller Than a Given Number. Look at this example:

Example
Your October expenses were $1,200 and your November expenses were $1,500. By what percent were your November expenses greater?

Solution	Explanation
$1,500 − $1,200 = $300 difference $\dfrac{\$300}{\$1,200} = \dfrac{1}{4} = 25\%$	Find the part, which is the difference between the two numbers, by subtracting the smaller from the larger number. Then divide the part by the number with which the part is being compared. Show the quotient as a percent.

In doing problems like the example, be sure to compare the part with the correct figure. A decrease is compared with the larger figure; an increase is compared with the smaller figure.

Written Practice 7

Be sure to compare with the correct figure

1. What is the unknown percent?

    a. $6 is ?% greater than $4   50%
    b. $8 is ?% more than $5
    c. $10 is ?% less than $15

    d. $6 is ?% smaller than $8
    e. ?% more than $20 is $24
    f. ?% less than $12 is $10

2. Today you paid 39¢ per pound for bananas. Last week you paid 30¢ per pound. By what percent is this week's price higher than last week's price?   30%

3. Rose Tung paid $350 for food in June, and $315 for food in July. By what percent did her food cost less in July than in June?

4. Your school club increased its ticket price for a dance from $1.25 last year to $1.50 this year. What was the percent of increase in price?

5. By careful planning and buying, Asa Clum cut his average food cost from $120 a week to $100 a week. What was the percent of decrease in cost?

★**Finding the Whole Number When a Percent of the Whole Is Known.** Suppose you know the value of a certain percent of a number, and you want to find the whole number. For example, you know that your food allowance of $6,000 is 20% of your total year's budget. You want to find the amount of your total year's budget.

This is a problem of finding an unknown factor when the other factor and the product are known. So, you divide the product by the known factor to find the unknown factor:

$P \div F = F$

F	F	P	P	F	F
20% × Unknown Number = $6,000 $6,000 ÷ 0.20 = $30,000   Ans.
Check: 0.20 × $30,000 = $6,000

★**Written Practice 8**

1. What is the unknown number?

   a. 20% × ? = $75 $375
   b. $19.50 is 30% of ?
   c. 45% of $105 is ?
   d. $5 is 1% of ?

   e. $18 is 9% of ?
   f. $4 is $\frac{1}{2}$% of ?
   g. $16\frac{2}{3}$% of ? = $42
   h. $80 is 200% of ?

2. A hair dryer is on sale at $16.50, which is 75% of the full price. What was the full price? $22

3. Bea Hann spends 8% of her income for clothing. Last year she spent $1,800 for clothing. How much was Bea's total income last year?

4. By paying all bills on time, Chen Chou saved $672, or 12%, of his last year's bills. What was the total of Chen's bills last year?

★**Finding the Whole Number When an Amount That Is a Part Greater or Smaller Is Known.** Here are two examples:

Example 1

Your income in April was $1,540, which was an increase of 10% over your March income. What was your March income?

Solution	**Explanation**

100% = March income
     (unknown factor F)
+10% = increase in April
110% = April income
     (known product P)

  F   **F**   **P**
110% × March income = $1,540

$1,540 ÷ 110% = F
$1,540 ÷ 1.1 = $1,400   **Ans.**

Check: $1,400 + (10% × $1,400)
     = $1,400 + $140 = $1,540

The problem says that when 10% was added to your March income (unknown factor), the total was equal to your April income. So, let your March income be 100% and your April income be 110% of your March income. Your April income of $1,540 is a known product. You divide the known product, $1,540, by the known factor, 110%, to find the unknown factor, your March income. The answer, $1,400, is checked by adding 10% of itself ($140) to it.

Example 2

A jacket has been marked down 25% to a sale price of $33.75. What was the full price?

Solution	Explanation
100% = full price (unknown factor F) <u>−25% = markdown</u> 75% = sale price (known factor F) **F** **F** **P** 75% × full price = $33.75 $33.75 ÷ 75% = F $33.75 ÷ 0.75 = $45 **Ans.** Check: $45 − (25% × $45) = $45 − $11.25 = $33.75	The problem says that the full price, less 25% of the full price, equals the sale price, $33.75. So, let the full price be 100%. Subtract the markdown of 25%. The sale price is then 75% of the full price. Next, divide the product (sale price of $33.75) by the known factor, 75%, to find the unknown factor (full price). The answer, $45, is checked by subtracting 25% of the full price ($11.25) from the full price ($45). The difference, $33.75, is the sale price.

$P \div F = F$

★Written Practice 9

1. What is the unknown number?

   a. ? + 25% of itself = $300 **$240**
   b. $180 is $66\frac{2}{3}$% greater than ?
   c. $27 is 50% more than ?
   d. ? plus 40% of itself gives $84
   e. $230 = ? increased by 15%
   f. ? − 20% of itself = $2,460
   g. ? decreased by 60% is $336
   h. $54 is 25% less than ?
   i. ? less $12\frac{1}{2}$% of itself = $77
   j. $160 is $37\frac{1}{2}$% smaller than ?

2. The price of a shirt is now $20. That price is an increase of 25% over last year's price. What was last year's price? **$16**

3. Kent wants to sell his old bicycle for $30 after giving $33\frac{1}{3}$% off the marked price. What should be the marked price?

Review 35

1. **a.** What is 1% of $59?
   b. What is $\frac{1}{2}$% of $2,500?
   c. Show 75% as a common fraction
   d. $34 less 25% of itself is what amount?
   e. $15 is what percent of $22.50?
   f. $12 increased by $33\frac{1}{3}$% of itself is how much?

2. Juanita's income this year is 15% greater than last year's income of $14,600. What is her income this year?

3. In one year, toothpaste has increased from $1.25 to $1.50 a tube. What is the percent of increase in price?

4. Mort Shen wants to allow 35% of his $12,000 income for food and clothing. What amount should he allow?

★ 5. A snowsuit has been marked down by 40% to a sale price of $33. What was the full price?

HOUSING AND HOUSEHOLD EXPENSES

During your working and earning life, you may spend as much as 25% to 50% of your income for housing and household expenses. With so much money involved, you will want to spend in ways that will give you the greatest value and satisfaction. This unit will help you do that.

When you have finished this unit, you should be able to:

- figure total and average housing expenses, and budget those expenses, whether you own or rent
- find the cost of oil, gas, electricity, telephone, and water
- solve many problems in saving energy and cutting the cost of utilities
- figure costs of repair, redecoration, and maintenance in the home, including rental of tools and equipment
- figure the costs and "best buy" on furnishings and appliances
- solve problems in buying and collecting on homeowners insurance
- do real property tax problems
- figure the expenses of buying and owning a home, including mortgages
- read, write, speak, and recognize the meanings of many terms used in spending for housing and household (shelter) expenses

Courtesy of Evans Products Company — Portland, Oregon

FIGURING HOUSING AND HOUSEHOLD EXPENSES

Whether you rent or own your home, you need to be able to figure your total expenses and your average expenses of housing. You may also need to find what part or percent you have spent for housing, or how much to allow for housing expenses.

What Are Housing and Household Expenses. In budgeting and recording expenses, you treat any payment that is for shelter or home as a housing or household expense. One of those expenses may be rent.

If you use someone else's house or apartment and pay money for using it, you are a renter. The money you pay is called rent. Rent is often paid each month, but it may be paid for longer or shorter periods of time. Rent often pays only for the use of the property, but other items such as heat, water, trash disposal, repairs, and redecoration may be included in the rental price.

If you buy a home, you may have only enough of your own money to pay part of the purchase price and for other expenses of buying and moving. You will have to borrow money for the rest of the purchase price. You will borrow the money from a bank or other lender by means of a *mortgage loan*.

When you take a mortgage loan, you agree to pay back the amount of the loan, called the principal, and some more money, called interest. Interest is money that is paid for the use of money. You also sign a mortgage. The mortgage gives the lender the right to take the property if you do not repay the loan as agreed.

Many mortgages require you to pay back the principal and the interest on your loan in equal monthly payments for 20, 25, or 30 years. Part of each payment is for repaying the principal, and part is for interest.

Another kind of housing expense that you will probably have is for utilities. *Utilities* usually include fuel, electricity, telephone, and water. Utilities expense may also include such items as trash and garbage disposal. The cost of some utilities, such as heat and water, may be included in rent. Homeowners have to pay their own utility costs.

Repair, redecoration, and maintenance expenses include all costs of keeping the property in good condition, without increasing the original value. Some or all of these expenses may be included in rent, but homeowners must pay their own.

Taxes		Telephone		
Fuel	**+**	Repair	**=**	
Electricity		Redecoration		
Water		Insurance		**Housing Expenses**

If you rent a room, apartment, or house, the costs of furniture, carpets, drapes, stoves, refrigerators, and so on may be included in your rent. As a homeowner, you have to provide your own *furnishings and appliances*.

Whether you rent or own your home, you will probably pay for *insurance*. As a renter, you may want to insure your personal property for loss by fire or theft. You may also want personal liability coverage. As a homeowner, you may buy more complete coverage.

Property taxes are charged on real estate by cities, towns, villages, school districts, and some states. As a property owner and taxpayer, you must pay property taxes charged by one or more of those agencies. Renters do not pay property taxes directly.

"My home is my castle—and it sure cost a lot!"

Finding Total Housing Expenses. To find the total amount spent for housing and household items, you add all the expense amounts for the desired period of time.

Written Practice 1

1. The Lopez family's records showed these cash payments for housing and household expenses last year: rent, $4,500; electricity, $507; telephone, $156; furniture and supplies, $346; appliance repairs, $93; renter's insurance, $115. What was the Lopez family's total housing expense for the year?   **$5,717**

2. The Bardin's housing expenses for the month of April were these: rent, $425; fuel, $87.40; electricity, $38.95; telephone, $31.46; household supplies, $23.70; painting a room, $45.64. What was the Bardin's total housing expense for April?

3. Chester and Linn Nagel own their own home. Their cash payments record for a recent year showed these housing and household expenses: mortgage payments, $7,584; utilities, $1,695; repairs, redecoration, and maintenance, $1,472; furnishings and equipment, $863; insurance, $384; property taxes, $1,973. What was the total of their housing and household payments for the year?

4. Liza Rodriguez rents a college dormitory room. Last year her room rent was $1,225. She paid $55 to rent a small refrigerator, and $145.60 for telephone. She spent $78.42 for furnishings and other housing costs. What was Liza's total housing cost for the year?

Finding Average Expenses. You can find average housing and household expenses for a period of time by dividing the sum of the expenses by the number of time periods. For example, suppose that your housing expenses for a year totaled $7,200. To find your average monthly housing expenses for that year, you would divide the annual expense, $7,200, by the number of months in a year, 12.

$$\$7,200 \div 12 = \$600$$

Written Practice 2

1. The Omega's total housing expenses for the month of February were these: mortgage payment, $368.75; utilities, $162; insurance, $30.25; repairs and maintenance, $65. What was the Omega's average *weekly* housing cost for the four weeks of February? **$156.50**

2. Your cash payments record for last year showed a total of $7,824 spent for housing and household expenses. What was your average monthly expense for housing and household last year?

3. The Burkes own their own home. Their payments for housing and household expenses last year were: mortgage, $5,415; utilities, $1,592; repairs, redecoration, and maintenance, $500; furnishings and equipment, $200; insurance, $346; taxes, $1,475. What was their average monthly housing expense for the year?

Watch this one!

4. During October, the Yunan's housing and household expenses totaled $703.25. If this was an average monthly amount for that year, what would be their total housing and household expenses for the year?

5. The Marrs paid a total of $4,689.44 in mortgage payments last year. Of that amount, $375.12 was for repayment of the principal, and $5,314.32 was for interest.
   a. What average amount did they pay on the principal per month?
   b. What average amount of interest did they pay per month?

AVERAGES ARE ALL AROUND US

Finding What Part Is Spent for Housing. Suppose that your total expenses for a year were $20,000, and your housing and household expenses for that year were $7,000. You want to find what fractional part, and what percent, your housing and household expenses were of your total expenses.

This is a problem in finding what part or percent one number is of another. So, you divide the part by the whole, and show the answer as a fraction and as a percent.

$$\frac{\$\ 7,000}{\$20,000} = \frac{7}{20} = 0.35, \text{ or } 35\%$$

Written Practice 3

1. Amos Dodd spent $7,500 for housing and household expenses last year. Dodd's total expenses for the year were $25,000. What fractional part, and what percent, of the total expenses were for housing and household expenses? $\frac{3}{10}$; 30%

2. Ethel Rosa's income is $2,000 per month. Of that amount, Ethel spends $560 per month for housing and household expenses. What percent of her income does she spend each month for housing and household expenses?

3. During a recent year, the Culps spent $7,800 for housing and household expenses. Of that total amount, they spent $4,680 for mortgage payments, and $1,716 for utilities. What percent of their total housing and household expenses were for:
   a. mortgage payments?
   b. utilities?

4. Two years ago the Lings spent $5,120 of their $16,000 income on housing. Last year their income was the same, but they spent $5,600 on housing. What percent of their income did they spend on housing:
   a. two years ago?
   b. last year?

Figuring a Housing Allowance. Suppose that your income is $18,000 a year, and you want to allow 30% of your income for housing and household expenses. The problem is to find a percent of a number, so you multiply the number by the percent.

$$0.30 \times \$18,000 = \$5,400$$

Written Practice 4

1. Joy Nathan wants to allow 32% of her income for housing and household expenses. If her income is $15,000, how much should she allow? **$4,800**

2. Gil MacDill plans to spend $5,700 a year for housing and household expenses. He thinks he can spend no more than 70% of that amount for rent. How much can be spent for rent?

3. Glen and Hilda Valley have an income of $30,000, and are planning to move to a new home. Glen figures that they should allow 32% of their income for housing and household expenses. Hilda thinks they should allow 40%.
   a. How much does Glen figure they should allow?
   b. How much does Hilda think they should allow?

4. Your income is $21,000. You have been allowing 30% of your income for housing and household expenses. This year you want to increase your allowance by 10% of the *previous amount*.
   a. What was your old allowance?
   b. How much would the increase be?
   c. What would be your new allowance?

Terms to Remember

housing or household expense	mortgage	interest
principal	rent	

a. An amount borrowed
b. Money paid for the use of money
c. Money paid for the use of property
d. Payments to provide shelter or home
e. Gives the right to take property if not paid

Review 36

1. a. Multiply 8.5 L by 2.5   c. What is $\frac{3}{4}$% of $600?
   b. Add 43.2 and 0.5   d. What is $7\frac{2}{3} - 4\frac{3}{4}$?
   e. $2.50 is what fractional part of $22.50?
   f. Express $66\frac{2}{3}$% as a common fraction
   g. Change $0.15\frac{1}{2}$ to a percent
   h. $650 decreased by 20% of itself is how much?

2. The Moore's housing and household expenses for a year were: rent, $5,100; utilities, $480; insurance, $108; other, $96. What was their average monthly housing and household expense that year?

3. Oscar LeBrun's total income for a year was $12,000. Of that amount, Oscar spent $3,960 for housing and household expenses. What percent of his income did he spend for housing and household?

4. Your housing and household expenses last year totaled $4,480. If you increase that amount by 15% this year, how much will you spend for housing and household this year?

5. During a berry season, Denise Zuni bought 2 quarts at $1.55 each, 6 quarts at $1.35, and 10 quarts at 95¢. What average price per quart did she pay that season?

★ 6. a. Express 4.65 as a mixed number in simplest form.
     b. What amount decreased by 15% of itself is equal to $340?

FUEL

Many people use heating oil or natural gas for fuel in their homes. Oil is measured and priced by gallons or liters. Oil is often bought in large amounts and is stored in tanks that hold 275 gallons or more. Gas is piped into the home and is measured in cubic feet by a meter.

You are figuring an extension!

Finding the Cost of Oil Bought. To find the cost of oil you buy, you multiply the number of units bought by the unit price.

Written
Practice 1

1. During a heating season, Lee Plata bought 738 gallons of heating oil at $1.06 per gallon. What was the cost of the oil he bought? $782.28

2. Jean Corsair had these five deliveries of heating oil last season:

Date	Gallons	Cost
October 15	160.5	$170.13
November 30	207.1	227.81
January 10	210.6	211.70
February 8	194.0	223.10
March 22	188.3	210.90

   a. How many gallons of oil were delivered?
   b. What was the total cost of the oil for the season?

3. During the last heating season, you had four deliveries of oil: 786 liters; 695 liters; 757 liters; and 720 liters. The oil cost you $0.32 per liter.
   a. How many liters of oil were delivered to you?
   b. What was the total cost of the oil?

4. Olive Oporte received three deliveries of oil: 138 gallons at $0.99 per gallon; 154 gallons at $1.05 per gallon; and 196 gallons at $1.08 per gallon.
   a. How many gallons of oil were delivered?
   b. What was the total cost of the oil?

5. Pat Kovar bought 1,000 gallons of oil in one delivery. The regular price of the oil was $1.145 a gallon, but Pat got a discount of 2¢ per gallon because of the large quantity. What was the total cost of the oil?

Finding the Cost of Oil Used. Suppose you have some oil on hand at the start of a heating season, you buy more oil, and then have some oil left at the end of the season. How do you figure how much oil you have used? Look at the following example:

Example

Jody Lema had 120 gallons of oil in his tank at the start of a heating season. He bought 780 gallons of oil during the season, and had 75 gallons left at the end of the season. How many gallons had he used?

Solution	Explanation
120 gallons in tank at start +780 gallons bought 900 gallons available to use − 75 gallons left 825 gallons used	Add the amount in the tank at the start, and the amount bought, to find the amount available to use. Then, subtract the amount left to find the amount used.

Written Practice 2

1. Mae Sheng had 50 gallons of oil in her tank at the start of a heating season. She had 643 gallons delivered during the season. At the end of the season, there were 132 gallons left in the tank. How much oil had she used during the season? **561**

2. You bought 965 gallons of oil during a heating season. You had started the season with 104 gallons on hand, and you finished the season with 34 gallons on hand. How many gallons of oil had you used?

3. At the end of a heating season, Franz Kling had 474 liters of oil in his tank. Kling had started the season with 380 liters in the tank, and had bought 2 554 more liters during the season.
   a. How many liters of oil had Kling used?
   b. At 30¢ per liter, what was the cost of the oil used?

Finding Average Amount and Cost. In budgeting your heating expenses and in comparing costs or amounts of oil used, you often need to figure averages. You find the simple average or the weighted average as you have before.

Written Practice 3

1. The Marko's records show these amounts and costs of oil for three years:

Year	Gallons Used	Cost
First	1,050	$1,045.00
Second	843	885.00
Third	927	1,002.80

   a. What was the average number of gallons used per year? **940**
   b. What was the average yearly cost of the oil used?
   c. What was the average cost per gallon of the oil used? **$1.04**

2. Tish Yung budgets her annual heating costs in 12 equal monthly payments. She estimates that her heating costs for next season will be: oil, $980; repairs and cleaning of system, $76. What amount should she budget each month for heating costs?

This is a weighted average

3. In a heating season, Ben Mott had these oil deliveries: 210 gallons @ $1.09; 185 gallons @ $1.12; 205 gallons at $1.13. What was the average price per gallon, to the nearest cent?

Finding an Increased or Decreased Amount or Cost of Oil.

You often need to find an increased or decreased oil use or cost. If the increase or decrease is given as a percent of the old amount, you multiply the old amount by the percent. You can then find the new amount by adding the increase to the old amount, or subtracting the decrease from the old amount.

Written Practice 4

1. Last year Beth Egan spent $1,080 for oil. Beth will use the same amount of oil this year, but the price will increase by 6%.
   a. How much more will the oil cost this year?   **$64.80**
   b. What will be Beth's total oil cost this year?   **$1,144.80**

2. In recent years, the Carusos have used an average of 600 gallons of oil per year at an average cost of $1.15 a gallon. If the Carusos use an average amount of oil this year, but the price increases by 6¢ a gallon:
   a. What will be the increase in their oil cost?
   b. What will their oil cost this year?

3. Last year Ken Nema used 1,200 gallons of oil at a cost of $1,224. He plans to cut his use this year by 15% and to pay the same price per gallon.
   a. How much oil will he save?
   b. How much oil will he use?
   c. How much money will he save?
   d. What will the oil cost this year?

Finding a Percent of Increase or Decrease.

To find a percent of increase or decrease, you first find the amount of the increase or decrease. You then divide that amount by the amount with which it is being compared.

Written Practice 5

1. Two years ago the Bocks used 1,075 gallons of oil. Last winter they were away from home for a month, so they used only 946 gallons of oil.
   a. How much less oil did they use last winter?
   b. What percent less oil did they use last winter?

2. In November, the Freers used 75 gallons of oil. December was much colder, so they used 105 gallons of oil. By what percent did their oil use increase in December?

3. Two years ago the Sumios used 580 gallons of oil at a total cost of $667. Last year they used 551 gallons of oil that cost $733.70.
   a. Did they use more or less oil last year? What percent?
   b. Did their oil cost more or less than last year? What percent?

Checking Gas Bills. The amount of gas you use is recorded by a gas meter in units of 100 cubic feet. A meter reader reads the meter every month or two, and the company then sends you a bill. Jon Mota's bill is an example.

	KEEP THIS PART	
New City Gas Company Industrial Park New City, NC 27609-4890	**GAS BILL** JON MOTA 692 HILLVIEW LANE NEW CITY, NC 27614-2234	

Gas Service		Days	Readings		Usage in hundred cubic feet	Therm Factor	Usage in Therms (THMs)
From	To		Present	Previous			
11 22 —	12 22 —	30	0678	0598	80	1.0308	82

Next Reading	Account Number	Due Date	Gas Charge	Sales Tax	Total Amount
01 23 —	365-004-872	01 21 —	40.10	2.41	42.51 **PAY THIS AMOUNT**

PLEASE RETURN THIS PART WITH PAYMENT.

Route No.	Account Number	Due Date	Total Amount
43A	365-004-872	01 21 —	42.51 **MAKE CHECKS PAYABLE TO NEW CITY GAS COMPANY.**

A gas bill

Jon Mota's bill shows a present (December) reading of 678. The reading a month ago (November) was 598. The difference is 80 hundred, or 8,000, cubic feet of gas used during the period.

Hundreds of cubic feet × therm factor = therms (THMs)

Round off to the nearest therm

Because the amount of heat in gas varies from time to time, many gas companies charge for the amount of heat in the gas rather than for the number of cubic feet used. The amount of heat in gas in measured in therms, or THMs. To figure the cost of gas, the cubic foot measure has to be changed to therms.

To find the amount of heat in the gas they are delivering, the gas company constantly tests the gas. From these tests, the company gets a *therm factor* that shows the average heat content of the gas. The number of hundreds of cubic feet of gas used is then multiplied by the therm factor to find the number of therms used. For example, in Jon Mota's bill the 80 hundred cubic feet of gas used was multiplied by the therm factor, 1.0308. The product was 82 therms (80 × 1.0308 = 82.4, or 82 THMs). When the number of therms has been found, the cost of the gas is figured by using a rate schedule.

The New City Gas Company's rate schedule is this:

First 4 THMs, or less................. **$5.00**

Additional THMs, per THM....... **$0.45**

Jon Mota's bill was figured this way:

First 4 THMs............................	$ 5.00
Next 78 THMs = 78 × $0.45......	35.10
Gas charge	$40.10
Sales tax at 6%........................	2.41
Total bill	$42.51

Written Practice 6

Use the New City Gas Company's rate schedule at the bottom of page 156 for these problems.

1. Chom Shensky's present gas meter reading is 4275. Chom's reading last month was 4180. The therm factor on his bill is 1.02. A sales tax of 5% is charged on his bill.

Round therms to the nearest whole therm

   a. How many hundred cubic feet of gas has he used? **95**
   b. How many THMs has he used? (Round to a whole number.) **97**
   c. What is the correct gas charge? **$46.85**
   d. What is the correct total amount of his bill, including tax? **$49.19**

2. Ann Islin's March gas reading was 0596, and her April reading was 0648. The therm factor on her bill was 1.03.
   a. How many therms had she used?
   b. What was the correct gas charge?
   c. What was the correct total amount, with a 4% sales tax?

3. You used 38 hundred cubic feet of gas in a month. The therm factor of the gas was 1.025. A sales tax of 6% was charged on your bill. What was the correct total amount of your gas bill?

4. What is the total cost of 125 hundred cubic feet of gas if the therm factor is 1.02 and the sales tax is 7%?

Review 37

1. **a.** Divide 2.05 by 0.5
   b. Change $\frac{3}{20}$ to a percent
   c. Subtract 40 cm from 3.6 m
   d. What is $\frac{1}{4}$% of $600?
   e. Change $83\frac{1}{3}$% to a decimal
   f. Change $0.08\frac{1}{2}$ to a percent
   g. $50 decreased by what percent of itself gives $35?
  ★**h.** 25 is 40% of what amount?

2. Neva Mapur had 64 gallons of oil in her tank at the start of a heating season. During the season she had three deliveries of oil that totaled 586 gallons. She had 105 gallons left at the end of the season.
   a. How much oil had she used?
   b. At a cost of $1.20 a gallon, what was the cost of the oil used?

3. You used 70 hundred cubic feet of gas during a month. The therm factor was 1.04. A sales tax of 8% was charged. Using the New City rates at the bottom of page 156, what was your total gas bill?

ELECTRICITY

Electricity is commonly used for lighting and running household appliances. It may also be used for heating and cooling the home.

The electricity that you use is measured by an electric meter in units called *kilowatt-hours*, or KWHs.* A meter reader for the electric company records the reading of your meter, usually every month or two months.** The company then sends you a bill for the electricity you used.

Understanding and Checking an Electric Bill. Vera Soto's electric bill for April is shown as an example:

Valley Energy Corp. Caldor, CA 93765-7855	ELECTRIC BILL FOR: VERA SOTA 38 BORON ROAD CALDOR, CA 93770-1424 ACCOUNT NO: 825-342-006 ROUTE NO: 825				PLEASE SEND THIS STUB WITH PAYMENT ACCOUNT NO: 825-342-006 ROUTE NO: 825	

ELECTRIC SERVICE		NUMBER OF DAYS	METER READINGS		KWHS USED	TOTAL AMOUNT DUE
FROM	TO		PRESENT	PREVIOUS		
04/02/—	05/02/—	30	7684	7154	530	34.34

NEXT READING	ELECTRIC CHARGE	SALES TAX	TOTAL AMOUNT	DUE DATE	DUE DATE
06/01/—	31.80	2.54	34.34	06/02/—	06/02/—

An electric bill

As shown in the bill, Vera Soto's meter reading was 7154 on April 2, and 7684 on May 2. The difference of 530 was the number of kilowatt-hours used for 30 days.

The Valley Energy Corporation used this rate schedule to figure the bill:

Basic monthly charge $6.25

Plus total KWHs, per KWH....... $0.0482

---

*A watt is a basic unit of electric power. A *kilo*watt is 1,000 watts. A kilowatt-hour is the flow of 1,000 watts for one hour.

**You can check the reading on your own meter. Some meters have numbers like a gasoline pump. If the meter has dials and pointers, you read the number that the pointer is on. If the pointer is between numbers, read the lower number. The reading is in kilowatt-hours. The amount used is the difference between the present and previous readings.

Vera Soto's bill was figured this way:

Basic monthly charge......	$ 6.25
530 KWHs @ $0.0482	25.55
Electric charge	$31.80
Sales tax at 8%	2.54
Total bill	$34.34

Use the Valley Energy Corporation schedule on page 158.

Written Practice 1

1. Your electric meter reading in June was 965, and in July it was 1785. A 4% tax was charged on your bill.
   a. How many kilowatt hours (KWHs) of electricity did you use?   820
   b. What was the charge for electricity?   **$45.77**
   c. What was your total bill?   **$47.60**

Round all electric charges to the nearest cent

2. Cory Ebert's present electric meter reading is 6792. Last month his meter reading was 6068.
   a. What was the charge for electricity?
   b. What was the total amount due, including a sales tax of 5%?

3. The Zaboras used 1,146 KWHs of electricity in a month. What was the total amount of their bill, with a sales tax of 3.5%?

4. In August, Sue Leone used 642 KWHs of electricity. A sales tax of $5\frac{1}{2}\%$ was charged. Sue did not pay the bill until it was past due, so she had to pay a penalty of $1.60. What was the total amount she paid?

Using an Appliance Cost Table. Some power companies and consumer agencies publish tables that show the average cost of running appliances. You can use the tables to solve many cost problems.

AVERAGE COST OF RUNNING APPLIANCES

Appliance	KWHs per Month	Average Monthly Cost at 5¢ per KWH
Manual defrost refrigerator	99	$ 4.95
Automatic defrost refrigerator	187	9.35
Range with oven	98	4.90
TV (black and white)	10	0.50
TV (color)	37	1.85
Washing machine	8.5	0.42
Clothes dryer	83	4.15
Iron	12	0.60
Room air conditioner	860	43.00
Lighting	80	4.00

Written Practice 2

Use the appliance cost table on page 159 for these problems.

1. How much more does it cost to run an automatic defrost refrigerator than a manual defrost refrigerator:
   a. for a month?
   b. for a year?

2. How much more per year does it cost to run a color TV than a black-and-white TV?

3. What is the average yearly cost of electricity to run your own laundry with a washing machine, clothes dryer, and iron?

4. What is the average annual cost of lighting a home? How much less per year is this than the annual cost of running a manual defrost refrigerator?

5. Bob Carr runs two room air conditioners for six months a year. What is the cost of electricity for the air conditioners?

6. What percent more per month does it cost to run a range with oven than to light a home?

7. Eva Arroyo pays 4¢ per kilowatt-hour for electricity. At that rate, what would be the cost per month of lighting?

8. At 7¢ per KWH, what would be the average cost of the electricity to run an automatic defrost refrigerator for a year?

Review 38

1. a. Show 80% as a common fraction
   b. What amount is 70% of $49?
   c. Multiply 2.5 m² by 6
   d. Subtract 18.75 from 23.2
   e. $120 less 37½% of itself is how much?
   f. $36 is what fractional part greater than $32?
   ★g. $75 is 20% more than what amount?

2. Suellen Maddox used 850 KWHs of electricity in a month. The rate was $6.25, plus $0.0482 per KWH. The sales tax was 3%. What was the total amount of her bill?

3. In average use, a toaster uses 3 KWHs of electricity. At 5¢ per KWH, what is the average cost of the electricity to run the toaster:
   a. for a month?
   b. for a year?

4. Hugo Tregon started a heating season with 35 gallons of oil in his tank. He bought 728 gallons of oil during the season and had 75 gallons left.
   a. How much oil did Tregon use during the season?
   b. At $1.15 a gallon, what was the cost of the oil he used?

5. Una Kwon spent $6,048 for housing and household expenses in a year. Una's income that year was $16,800. What percent of her income did Una spend for housing and household?

ENERGY AND COST SAVING

section 39

Much of the energy for the heat, light, and power used in American homes comes from oil or gas, or from electricity made from them. Oil and gas are scarce and expensive, so we need to cut our energy use as much as we can.

You can cut your use of energy in many ways without giving up your comfort or spending money for improvements. Other ways of saving energy require you to spend some money but, with good planning, you may save more money than you spend.

Free or Low-Cost Energy Saving. You can save much energy in your home without buying energy-saving material or equipment. For example, you can save heat by lowering the temperature of your home, especially during the night or when no one is at home. You can close off unused spaces, pull shades or drapes at night, and close the fireplace damper to save heat waste. You can cut cooling costs by letting the house get a bit warmer, and by shutting out the sun with shades or drapes during the day.

SAVE HEAT  **TURN IT DOWN!**

You can save energy by lowering the temperature of your hot water. You can fix leaking hot water faucets and take shorter showers or baths with less hot water. You can wash and rinse clothes with cooler water.

You can save electricity by turning off unused lights and by using lower wattage bulbs. You can cut your use of heating devices such as electric ranges, ovens, quick-start TV's, irons, water heaters, space heaters, and electric blankets.

You may be able to figure accurately the amount of energy or cost you save by comparing old and new amounts or costs. For example, suppose that two years ago you used 640 gallons of oil. Last year was just as cold, but several heat-saving measures cut your oil use to only 500 gallons at $1.25 a gallon. By cutting your use, you saved 140 gallons of oil and $175 in cost.

If prices, weather, and other conditions change, you may not be able to make exact comparisons. In most such cases, though, you can at least estimate your savings in energy use and cost.

Written Practice 1

1. Last year you used 920 therms of gas at a cost of $474. By cutting your gas use this year, you used only 785 therms that cost $429.
   a. How many less therms of gas did you use this year? **135**
   b. How much less did your gas cost this year?

2. In July you ran your air conditioner often, and your electric bill was $70. August was as hot as July, but you reduced the use of your air conditioner and your electric bill was $43.75.
   a. How much less was your electric bill in August than in July?
   b. What percent less was your August electric bill than your July bill?

3. Dean Carter's average electric bill for a month had been $52. Carter then reduced the temperature of his electric hot water heater and also used less hot water. His average monthly electric bill dropped to $44.20.
   a. How much did Carter save per month?
   b. What percent of his previous electric bill did Carter save?

4. Before the last heating season, Erna Gibson had averaged 1,050 gallons of heating oil per year at an average cost of $1,200. Last winter Erna cut her oil use to only 840 gallons at a cost of $1,032.
   a. How many gallons less than her average did she use last winter?
   b. What percent less than her average did she use?
   c. How much less than average did Erna spend for oil last winter?
   d. By what percent did Erna reduce her oil cost last winter?

SAVE HEAT

INSULATE!

Figuring the Payback Period. Many ways of saving energy and cutting energy costs require that you spend money to make your home more energy efficient. For example, you might caulk and weatherstrip windows and doors. You could add insulation, or storm windows and doors. You could insulate your hot water heater, or buy a "setback thermostat" to automatically turn down your heat. To save electricity, you might change from an automatic defrost to a manual defrost refrigerator, or buy a microwave oven.

There are great differences in the cost of improvements and the amount of energy or dollars they might save for you. So, before you spend money for any energy-saving improvement, you should figure its payback period. The *payback period* is the number of years required for the estimated savings to equal or "pay back" the estimated cost.

Estimated Cost ÷ Savings per Year = Payback Period in Years

Example

Ava Lane estimates that adding insulation, storm doors, and storm windows would cost $2,600. Ava estimates that the energy saved would be worth $400 a year. What is the payback period for those improvements?

Solution	Explanation
$2,600 ÷ $400 = 6½ years, payback period	Divide the estimated cost of the improvements by the estimated annual savings. The quotient, or answer, is the payback period in years.

You should generally put your money first into the improvements with the shorter payback periods.

Written Practice 2

1. You estimate that adding to the insulation in your home would cost $920. You would save $160 a year in energy costs. What is the payback period of the insulation? $5\frac{3}{4}$ **years**

2. Pam Ursa plans to put some insulating glass doors and windows in her home. They will cost $1,500, but they will save an estimated $125 a year in heating and cooling costs. What is the payback period for these doors and windows?

3. Wayne Colt estimates that he would save $100 a year in energy costs by spending $200 to weatherstrip his home. He could also replace his automatic defrost refrigerator with a manual defrost refrigerator at a cost of $375, and would save an estimated $50 a year on electricity.
   a. What is the payback period for the weatherstripping?
   b. What is the payback period for the manual defrost refrigerator?
   c. Which improvement should he do first?

4. To save energy and money, Brian Foss put in a new heating system using a different fuel. The new system cost $1,800. Brian estimated that the fuel savings with the new system would average $240 a year. What was the payback period for the new system?

5. Ana Diaz figures that improvements to her home, costing $3,240, would cut her energy costs by 15% per year. Her energy costs have been averaging $1,800 a year.
   a. What amount would she save per year by these improvements?
   b. What is the payback period for these improvements?

Figuring Net Savings. Another way to measure the value of energy-saving improvements is to figure the net savings over a period of time. You find the net savings by subtracting the cost of the improvement from the gross savings for the given period of time.

Gross Savings − Cost of Improvement = Net Savings

Example

Leo Noyes insulated his home at a cost of $3,000. As a result, he is saving $400 a year in energy costs. What are his net savings over a period of ten years?

Solution	Explanation
10 × $400 = $4,000 $4,000 − $3,000 = $1,000 net savings	Multiply the yearly savings by ten years. Subtract the cost of the insulation to find the net savings over a period of ten years.

Written Practice 3

1. Meg Sonora plans to live in her home for ten years. She is spending $1,300 for storm windows and doors, which should save $145 a year in fuel costs. What would be her net savings in ten years? **$150**

2. If Noah Pells spends $850 now for energy-saving improvements, he will save an estimated $175 a year in fuel costs. What would be his net savings in five years? In ten years?

3. Mary Zeller expects to live in her home for at least 20 years more. She estimates that if she spends $6,000 now for energy-saving improvements she will save an average of $450 per year for the next 20 years. What would be her net savings for the 20 years?

4. Roxanne Johnson's average energy costs have been $1,600 a year. She thinks she can cut that amount by 10% a year if she now spends $1,200 for improvements. If she is right, what would be her net savings over a period of 15 years?

Review 39

1. **a.** Divide 4.2 by 0.25
   b. Multiply $19.99 by 100
   c. Change 140 m to kilometers
   d. Subtract 6.5 m² from 18 m²
   e. What is the decimal equivalent of $\frac{3}{7}$, correct to the nearest tenth?
   f. $40 is what percent greater than $30?
   g. Change $62\frac{1}{2}\%$ to a decimal
   ★ **h.** $\frac{2}{3}$ of what amount is equal to $9?

2. The Vogel family's electric costs had been averaging $696 a year. Last year they cut back on their use of electricity and cut their cost to $522 for the year.
   a. How much did they save in electric costs last year?
   b. What percent of their average electric costs did they save?

3. What is the payback period of energy-saving improvements that cost $825 and save $150 per year in energy cost?

4. If you spend $1,200 for some energy-saving improvements, you may save $250 a year in energy costs. What would be your net saving over 8 years?

5. Walter Osmond's housing and household expenses last month were $415. If Walter spends 12% less this month, how much will he spend?

6. The Modern Shop is having a "$\frac{1}{3}$ off" sale. How much is saved by buying a coat at the sale price if the coat originally sold for $79.95?

7. Concetta Doby is paid time and a half for all work beyond 40 hours a week. Last week she worked 43 hours. Her regular pay rate is $5.90 an hour. What was her gross pay last week?

★ 8. Last year your income was $18,630, which was an increase of 15% over your income for the year before. What was your income the year before?

TELEPHONE

If you understand telephone services and charges, you can save money and get good service too. For example, Jill Nakoma has an individual line, but she saves money with a limited service plan. Under that plan, Jill can make up to 60 local calls each month at less than the usual charge. She has to pay 9¢ for each local call beyond 60 calls. Jill prefers to save money that way rather than by using a two-party or four-party line.

A Telephone Bill. Telephone bills are usually sent out each month. Jill Nakoma's bill for November is an example.

Shawnee Telephone Company	BILL FOR: JILL NAKOMA 64 WEST FRONTIER STREET TOPEKA, KS 66609-3231	

DATE OF BILL: NOVEMBER 1, 19--   TELEPHONE NO: 913-439-2135

PREVIOUS BILL	29.18	
PAYMENTS THROUGH OCTOBER 30	29.18	
BALANCE DUE		0.00
BASIC MONTHLY SERVICE, NOVEMBER 1-30	10.90	
LOCAL CALLS ABOVE ALLOWANCE (SEE ENCLOSED STATEMENT)	2.70	
LONG DISTANCE CALLS (SEE ENCLOSED STATEMENT)	15.64	
TAXES: STATE, 4%, 1.18 - LOCAL, 3%, 0.88	2.06	
CURRENT CHARGES, WITH TAXES	31.30	31.30

PLEASE PAY BY NOVEMBER 25 ---------> TOTAL AMOUNT DUE-----------> 31.30
AND
RETURN THE ENCLOSED PUNCH CARD WITH YOUR PAYMENT

A telephone bill

Basic Monthly Service. Jill Nakoma's basic monthly service charge of $10.90 is payable in advance. The service charge includes the cost of lines from the central office to her home, lines inside the home, and phone sets furnished by the company. It also covers the cost of the 60 local calls she can make each month at no extra charge. If Jill had "flat rate service," the basic service charge would be higher but there would be no limit on "free" local calls.

Local Calls Above Allowance. The charge of $2.70 is for 30 local calls at 9¢ each. They were in excess of the 60 calls allowed by the basic service charge for October. The details of the calls and charges were shown on a statement enclosed with Jill's bill.

Long Distance Calls. Calls made to phones outside the local service area are long distance calls. The charges for long distance calls depend on the location of the number called, when the call is made, the length of the call, and whether operator assistance is required.

On Jill's bill, the long distance charge of $15.64 is for October calls. Details of the calls are shown on a statement enclosed with the bill.

Taxes. State and local taxes may be charged on telephone bills. On Jill Nakoma's bill, the total tax is $2.06. Each tax was figured on each part of the bill. The totals were found this way:

	Charge	State Tax @ 4%	Local Tax @ 3%
Basic monthly service............	$10.90	$0.44	$0.33
Local calls over allowance......	2.70	0.11	0.08
Long distance calls	15.64	0.63	0.47
Totals.............................		$1.18	$0.88

Written Practice 1

1. For each problem, find the total cost per month for flat rate service.

	Kind of Line	Basic Monthly Service Charge	State Tax	Local Tax	Total Cost
a.	Individual	$15.04	4%	3%	$16.09
b.	Two-party	11.80	4%	None	
c.	Four-party	10.24	None	2%	
d.	Individual	16.25	4%	4%	
e.	Four-party	9.42	3%	2%	

2. Based on the total cost in Problems 1a and 1b, how much less per month would a two-party line cost than an individual line?

3. A telephone company charges $9.75 for limited basic monthly service, plus 8.4¢ for each local call over 60 per month. The combined state and local tax is 8%. For each of these bills, find the monthly charge for service, the amount of taxes, and the total cost.

	Basic Monthly Service Charge	Total No. of Local Calls	Charge for Service	State and Local Taxes	Total Cost
a.	$9.75	25			$10.53
b.	9.75	60			
c.	9.75	70			$11.44
d.	9.75	92			

4. Your monthly charge for telephone service is $10.80, plus $9\frac{1}{2}$¢ for each call over 75 per month. The combined state and local tax is 6%. What should be your total bill for a month in which you made 83 calls?

Saving on Long Distance Calls. The table below shows charges for several kinds of long distance calls between two cities in different states.

LONG DISTANCE RATES TO ANOTHER STATE

Long Distance Calls	Weekday 8 a.m. to 5 p.m.	Evening 5 p.m. to 11 p.m.	Nights 11 p.m. to 8 a.m. (and weekends)
Dial-Direct First minute Each add'l minute	$0.50 0.34	$0.32 0.22	$0.20 0.13
Operator-Assisted, Station-to-Station 3 minutes Each add'l minute	$2.05 0.34	Weekday rates apply at all times	
Operator-Assisted, Person-to-Person 3 minutes Each add'l minute	$3.15 0.34	Weekday rates apply at all times	

You can see from this table how three simple rules help you to save money on long distance calls:

(1) *Keep calls short.* On a weekday, each additional minute you talk beyond the first minute costs you 34¢. So, an additional ten minutes of talk beyond the first minute would cost you $3.40.

(2) *Call when rates are lower.* The rate for the first minute of an evening call is only slightly more than half the one-minute rate for a weekday call (32¢ rather than 50¢). The night rate is less than half the day rate (20¢ rather than 50¢). Rates for additional minutes are comparably less.

(3) *Dial direct and avoid operator assistance.* When you dial a number yourself, you are making a dial-direct call. Dial-direct calls are much less expensive than operator-assisted calls.* For example, the table shows that a three-minute dial-direct call in the evening costs 76¢ (32¢ + [2 × 22¢]). But, if the operator calls that number for you (a station-to-station call), you pay $2.05. If the operator gets a particular person for you at that number (a person-to-person call), you pay $3.15.

---

*Operator-assisted calls include coin, collect, credit card, third-number, hotel guest, and time-and-charges calls.

**Written
Practice 2**

Use the table of rates on page 167 for these problems.

1. What is the cost of a 5-minute dial-direct call made at
   a. 10 a.m. on Wednesday? **$1.86**
   b. 8 p.m. on Friday? **$1.20**
   c. 11:30 p.m. on Tuesday? **$0.72**

2. How much would be saved on a dial-direct call made on a weekday by talking only 6 minutes instead of 10 minutes?

3. How much is saved by making an 8-minute dial-direct call at the evening rate rather than the weekday rate?

4. How much would you save on a 15-minute dial-direct call on Thursday by calling at 11:15 p.m. rather than 10:30 p.m.?

5. For a six-minute call on a weekday, how much would you save by calling:
   a. dial-direct rather than station-to-station? **$0.87**
   b. dial-direct rather than person-to-person?

**This is a
station-to-station
call** ——————➤

6. From a coin phone, you ask the operator to place a call for you to anyone at a number you give. You talk 15 minutes. What does the call cost?

7. What percent, to the nearest whole percent, is saved by making a 10-minute dial-direct call at the:
   a. evening rate instead of the weekday rate?
   b. night or weekend rate instead of the weekday rate?

Review 40

1. a. What is $3\frac{1}{4} + 5\frac{1}{5}$?
   b. Multiply 82 by $0.75
   c. 8.75 L × 3 = ? L
   d. Divide $87 by 1,000
   e. What is $62\frac{1}{2}\%$ of $360?
   f. Change 0.45 to a fraction in lowest terms
   ★g. What amount decreased by $33\frac{1}{3}\%$ of itself gives $28?

2. A telephone company's basic monthly charge for limited service is $11.40. Additional calls over 70 per month are charged at 10.5¢ per call. The state tax is 3% and the local tax is 2%. What is the total bill for a month in which 84 calls are made?

3. A dial-direct long distance call to a certain city at the weekday rate costs $0.75 for the first minute, plus $0.48 for each additional minute. What is the cost of a 7-minute call at that rate?

4. Chen Tiang used 85 hundred cubic feet of gas in January. The therm factor of the gas was 1.03. The sales tax on the gas was 6%. Use the New City gas rates on page 156 to find Chen's total gas bill.

5. What is the payback period in years of insulation that costs $1,235 to install but saves $260 a year in energy costs?

WATER

Water is measured by a water meter in gallons or cubic feet. Most water companies take readings every three, four, or six months, then send a bill for the amount used. You can check your own reading and bill.*

A Water Bill. Paul Junco's water bill for six months is shown below.

Meter read on	Present reading (gals.)	Previous reading (gals.)	Gallons used	Current bill	Unpaid balance	Gross bill	Due date
06/30/—	374580	326080	48500	43.65	00.00	43.65	07/30/—

Crystal Lake Water Department
602 Lake Street, Clearview, OH 43508-3222

"Our Water Is Crystal Clear"

Bill for water used by:

PAUL JUNCO
62 SPRUCE AVENUE
CLEARVIEW, OH 43509-2251

ACCOUNT NO. 22-835-06

PLEASE RETURN THE COPY OF THIS BILL WITH YOUR PAYMENT TO THE TAX OFFICE.

A water bill

As shown in the bill, Paul's meter reading on June 30 was 374,580 gallons. The previous reading was 326,080 gallons. So, in six months Paul had used 48,500 gallons (374,580 − 326,080 = 48,500).

The Crystal Lake Water Department used this rate schedule to figure the bill:

First 15,000 gallons, or less....... $13.50
Next 85,000 gallons .... $0.90 per 1,000
Next 900,000 gallons .... $0.80 per 1,000
Over 1,000,000 gallons .... $0.70 per 1,000

Paul's current bill of $43.65 was figured this way:

First 15,000 gallons	$13.50
Next 33,500 gallons @ $0.90 per thousand gallons	30.15
Total bill	$43.65

The first 15,000 gallons cost $13.50. The amount used over 15,000 gallons was found by subtracting 15,000 from the total, 48,500. The difference of 33,500 gallons was changed to 33.5 thousands of gallons by moving the decimal point 3 places to the left. The 33.5 thousands of gallons was then multiplied by the rate, $0.90.

*Water meters may have direct-reading dials like a gas pump, or several dials with pointers. If a pointer is between numbers, read the lower number.

In figuring water bills, the thousand gallon rate is not rounded. Also, no tax is usually charged.

Written Practice 1

Use the Crystal Lake Water Company's rates on page 169 for these.

1. For each of these readings, figure the amount of water used in gallons and in thousands of gallons.

Do not round the thousand gallon rates

	Meter Reading		Water Used	
	Present	**Previous**	**Gallons**	**Thousands of Gallons**
a.	68,560	26,350	42,210	42.21
b.	200,314	132,814		
c.	497,723	416,098		

2. Find the bill for each of these amounts of water used:
   a. 105,200 gallons $94.16
   b. 62,150 gallons $55.94
   c. 14,985 gallons $13.50

3. Figure the cost of the water for each of these readings.

	Present Reading	Previous Reading
a.	599,850	487,250
b.	255,841	243,169
c.	131,307	97,042
d.	803,562	582,666

4. Lona Solara's water bill shows these readings: present, 383,440; previous, 329,060.
   a. How many thousands of gallons had Lona used?
   b. What was Lona's water bill for the period? $48.94

5. Your water meter now reads 669,525 gallons. Six months ago it read 568,325 gallons. What should be your water bill for the six months?

STOP WASTE

TURN IT OFF!

Saving Water and Water Costs. Water may be scarce and expensive, so you will not want to waste it. Hundreds of gallons of water, and many dollars, can be saved in the home by stopping waste. For example, a faucet left running so that the water will get cold wastes 5 gallons a minute. Letting the water run while you brush your teeth may waste 5 to 10 gallons. A slow drip from a faucet wastes 15 to 20 gallons in 24 hours. A partly-filled automatic dishwasher uses 15 gallons of water — the same amount that it uses when it is full of dishes.

You can easily figure the amount of water wasted or saved, and the cost of the water. Here are some typical problems.

**Written
Practice 2**

1. You have a badly leaking faucet that wastes 100 gallons of water a day. Water costs $0.85 per thousand gallons.
   a. How many gallons of water are being wasted per year? **36,500**
   b. What is the cost per year of the water that is wasted? **$31.03**

2. Kay Vaca's automatic clothes washer uses 40 gallons of water per load. Water costs Kay $1.10 per thousand gallons. To save hot water, Kay cut her washing from 10 loads to 6 loads per week.
   a. How much less water per year did she use?
   b. How much money did Kay save per year?

3. Wes Lake took a 15-minute shower every day. The shower used 8 gallons of water per minute. The water cost $0.90 per thousand gallons.
   a. How many gallons of water per day did Wes use for the shower? How many gallons per year?
   b. What was the cost per year of the water used?

4. To save water and heat energy, Wes Lake (Problem 3) cut his showers to five minutes a day.
   a. How many gallons of water per year did Wes save?
   b. How much money per year did Wes save in water costs?

Review 41

1. a. What is $87\frac{1}{2}\%$ of $48?
   b. What is $\frac{2}{5}$ of $32.50?
   c. 3.5 L + 250 mL = ? L
   d. Multiply 34.22 by 0.5
   e. $20 increased by what percent of itself equals $25?
   f. Round 40.345 to the nearest tenth
   g. Show $0.16\frac{1}{4}$ as a percent
   ★h. $324 is 75% of what amount?

2. Briget Ryan's water meter read 421,396 gallons on June 30 and 530,046 gallons on December 31. Use the Crystal Lake rate schedule on page 169 to find Briget's water bill for that time.

3. By running their dishwasher with full loads rather than part loads, the Okshevski family cut their water use by 15 gallons a day. Their water cost $1.25 per thousand gallons.
   a. How much water did they save in a year?
   b. How much money did they save in a year?

4. Amy Geer is planning to spend $2,500 for energy-saving improvements. She estimates that she will save $350 a year in energy costs by these improvements. If she lives in the house for 15 years, what will be her net saving from the improvements?

5. In three years, Hale Noyes used 3,126 gallons of heating oil that cost $3,344.82.
   a. What average number of gallons did Hale use per year?
   b. What was Hale's average yearly cost of oil?

REPAIR, REDECORATION, AND MAINTENANCE

section

42

Figuring the Cost of Repair, Redecoration, and Maintenance. Keeping a home attractive and in good repair can be expensive. To figure the total cost, you include all money spent for materials and supplies, tools and equipment, and labor.

Materials and supplies are the goods used up in doing a job. For example, the material and supplies used in redecorating a room might be paint, paint thinner, wallpaper, paste, sandpaper, and patching plaster. Materials for repairing a floor might include tiles and cement. The materials used to maintain a lawn would include fertilizer, clean-up bags, gasoline and electricity for power tools, and so on.

Tools and equipment are the devices and machines needed to do a job. They are not used up in doing a job. For example, in redecorating you might use sanders, wallpaper removers, paint brushes and rollers, hammers, saws, and other hand tools. In maintaining grounds, you might use a lawnmower, snowthrower, cultivator, rake, hoe, shovel, and so on.

Labor is the human work used in doing a job. For example, you might hire someone to paint or to hang wallpaper, to do cleaning, to mow the lawn, or to remove snow.

Written Practice 1

1. Patty Shannon repainted two rooms, doing the work herself. The material, supplies, and equipment she used cost these amounts:

> 2 gallons ceiling paint @ $7.95
> 4 gallons wall paint @ $11.95
> 1 gallon trim paint @ $16.95
> 1 roller and tray set, $7.39
> 1 paint brush, $4.30
> Other supplies, $5.88

a. What was the total cost of the job? **$98.22**
b. What was the average cost per room? **$49.11**

2. Ira Gatos plans to redecorate his living room. He will do his own painting, but will hire a paperhanger. He estimates these costs: paint, $30; 16 rolls of wallpaper @ $9.75; paperhanger labor, $14 per roll; other supplies, $20. What is the total estimated cost of the job?

3. The Balog family take care of their own lawn and grounds. Their expenses for one year were these: fertilizer with weed and pest control, $48.95; loss in value of hand and power tools, $78; repairs to equipment, $53.75; gasoline, $9; hired labor during vacation, $25. What was their total cost to maintain the lawn and grounds for one year?

4. Chloe and Fred Ramsey have someone clean their apartment once a week. Their repair and maintenance expenses last year were these: supplies and equipment, $84.30; cleaning, $1,480; appliance repair, $167.55. What was their total annual cost of repair and maintenance?

5. Over a six-year period, Cesar Morales spent $483 for repairs on his appliances and $3,156 for repairs to his home. What was Cesar's average annual repair cost?

6. In one year, Nola Arkin's total expenses were $19,380. Of that amount, Nola spent $581.40 for repair, redecoration, and maintenance of her home. What percent were those expenses of her total expenses?

Renting Tools and Equipment. Some tools and equipment used in homes are expensive and seldom used, so you may want to rent them instead of buying them. You should compare the cost of renting and buying to find what is better for you.

Written Practice 2

1. You have rented a paint sprayer at a price of $15 for 4 hours, or $20 for a 24-hour day. You keep the sprayer for 27 hours. How much will it cost you for rental? $35

2. You are looking at this ad for a rental carpet cleaner:

4 hours	$4	*or*	5 p.m. to 8 a.m.	$6
24 hours	$9		Sat. 5 p.m. to Mon. 9 a.m.	$13.50
	Cleaning fluid:	2 qt. bottle	$6.98	
		1 gallon	$9.88	

You estimate that you can clean your carpets in 6 hours and can do the work at any time. You will need 3 quarts of cleaning fluid. What is the lowest cost for which you can do the job with this rental machine?

3. Quint Randles uses an extension ladder once or twice a year. He can rent a ladder for $6 a day, or he can buy a ladder for $165. For how many full days can he rent a ladder and spend less than the cost of buying a ladder?

4. To refinish some floors, Ellen Olsen rented a sander for 2 days at $11 a day, and an edger for 1 day at $4 a day. Ellen used 5 sheets of sandpaper at $1.75 a sheet, and 3 sheets of edger paper at 75¢ a sheet. What was the total cost of the equipment and supplies?

5. Sandy Samarka uses a snowblower an average of seven days a year. She can buy a snowblower for $639 that will last an estimated ten years. Service, repair, and storage on the machine will average $45 a year. She can rent a snowblower for $30 a day. Over ten years, how much would Sandy save by buying rather than renting a snowblower?

6. Todd LeLac needs a cement mixer for a week. He can rent a mixer for $21 a day. A deposit of $50 is required, but it would be refunded if the mixer is returned in good condition. Getting the mixer to his home and back to the rental agency would cost $18. He could buy a new mixer, delivered to his home, for $285. He would sell the new mixer for $100 when he had finished with it.
   a. If he returns the rented mixer in good condition, what would be the net cost of renting it for 7 days?
   b. What would be the net cost of owning the mixer?
   c. How much would Todd save by renting rather than buying a mixer?

7. A chain saw rents for $15 for 4 hours, or $18 for 8 hours. What percent greater is the 8-hour charge than the 4-hour charge?

Review 42

1. a. Multiply 34.8 by 100
   b. Divide $650 by 1,000
   c. Subtract 6.26 from 15.4
   d. 75 cm × 5 = ? m
   e. What amount is 35% of $840?
   f. 15.5 equals what percent?
   ★g. $540 is 8% more than what amount?

2. Milt Shedd spent these amounts to rebuild his lawn: 5 hours rototiller rental @ $12 for 2 hours, plus $6 for each additional hour; seed, $71.25; fertilizer, $31.50; topsoil, $45; labor, $56. What was the total cost of the job?

3. Eileen North's present water reading is 469,725 gallons and the previous reading was 393,165 gallons. The water rates are $11.25 for the first 10,000 gallons, and $1 a thousand gallons for the next 90,000 gallons. What is Eileen's water bill?

4. You are going to make a 10-minute long distance telephone call at weekday rates. The dial-direct rate is 44¢ for the first minute plus 30¢ for each additional minute. The person-to-person rate is $1.85 for three minutes plus 30¢ for each additional minute. How much would you save by the dial-direct call rather than the person-to-person call?

★ 5. Ramona Cardone's housing and household allowance of $4,900 is 35% of her total income. What is her total income?

FURNISHINGS AND APPLIANCES

Figuring the Value of Furnishings and Appliances. Sometimes you need to calculate or estimate the value of furnishings and appliances. *Household furnishings* include all the furniture in a home. Carpets, rugs, drapes, curtains, sheets, blankets, bedspreads, and towels are also furnishings. Dishes, silverware, and cooking utensils are furnishings, as are accessories such as lamps, pictures, and decorative devices. Stoves, refrigerators, freezers, portable air conditioners, humidifiers, dishwashers, washers and dryers, TV's, radios, and stereos are *household appliances*.

Written Practice 1

1. The Eglins keep a record of all their household furnishings and appliances, with the approximate cost. The costs of the different kinds of items they now have in their home are shown below. What is the total of these costs?

A list of things and their values is called an *inventory*

Furniture	$9,260
Floor coverings	2,745
Window coverings	1,450
Linens	1,100
China and silverware	1,230
Accessories	950
Kitchenware	400
Appliances	4,500

2. Gloria Kent lives in an apartment. For insurance purposes, she has listed all her furnishings and appliances, room by room. The values are shown below. What is the total value?

Living-dining room	$5,517
Bedroom	1,445
Bedroom	980
Kitchen	560
Bathroom	178
Storage area	430

3. Jim Lamont bought a dishwasher at a discount store for $459. The sales tax was 8%. He paid $19.50 to have the machine delivered to his home, and $38 for installation. What was the total cost of the appliance when installed in his home?

4. The Wuchans are planning to refurnish their living room. They estimate their costs as follows: furniture, $2,175; drapes, $650; carpet, $950; accessories, $375; TV and sound equipment, $1,350. The Wuchans think that the actual cost may be as much as 10% more or 10% less than their estimate.
   a. What is their estimated cost?
   b. If their estimate is 10% too high, what will be the cost?
   c. If their estimate is 10% too low, what will be the cost?

5. The actual cost of the furnishings bought by the Wuchans in Problem 4 was $5,885. Was the actual cost greater than, or less than, their estimated cost? By what percent?

6. Concetta Morena used an outdated mail order catalog to estimate the cost of some new furniture at $2,400. When she actually bought the furniture, the price had increased to $2,800. By what percent had the price of the furniture increased?

7. Jed Ames is buying some used furniture at a garage sale. The price of the furniture when new was $375. Jed thinks that he should pay not more than $\frac{1}{3}$ to $\frac{1}{2}$ of the original price. What is the least amount and what is the greatest amount that he should pay?

Be Smart!
Shop Our

August
White Sale

Getting the Best Buy. Furnishings and appliances are expensive, so you need to get the best buy that you can. You should plan to buy at regular sales such as the "white sales" on linens, and you should look for special sales. You need to learn about products in advance by reading about them and talking with informed people. You should "comparison shop" by reading ads and visiting several stores to learn about prices and features of the goods.

You may want to pay more to buy products that will last longer and give more satisfaction. For little or no extra cost, you may get added values such as delivery, credit, privilege of return, guarantees, and repair service. If you have the time and talent, you may want to make some of your own furnishings rather than buying them ready-made.

Written Practice 2

1. At the Price-Right Discount House, Renee Sesta can buy a new refrigerator for $589, including tax, on a "cash-and-carry" basis. She will have to pay $27 for delivery to her home, and $33 for installation. She can buy the same model machine at Gibson's Appliances for $629.75, including tax, delivery, and installation. Which store's machine would cost her less? How much less?

2. A sofa and chair set at Forsteen's Furniture sells for $725. The set would probably be usable for 10 years. A better set at Gresham's Furnishings sells for $900, but should be usable for 15 years.
   a. What would be the average yearly cost of the Forsteen set?
   b. What would be the average yearly cost of the Gresham set?
   c. How much less per year would the better set cost?

3. Tom Uvalde needs to replace some towels and sheets. The regular price of these "white goods" is $135. If Tom waits for the annual white sale, he can buy the goods for 30% off.
   a. How much would Tom save by waiting for the sale?
   b. What would these goods cost at the white sale?

4. A newspaper article reports that the cost of appliances will go up 15% next year. If the article is right, an appliance that costs $575 now would cost how much next year?

5. Bing Igoe needs new carpet for a room that is 3.5 m by 3.8 m in size. He would have to buy 14 square meters of carpet, regularly priced at $25 per square meter, to carpet the room. He has now found a remnant of the same carpet that is 3.65 m by 4 m in size. The remnant sells for $235.
   a. Is the remnant large enough for his room?
   b. If the remnant is large enough, how much would he save by buying it rather than the regular-priced carpet?

6. If Bess Gifford buys new custom-made drapes, they will cost $300. She can make the drapes herself by buying 18 yards of drapery fabric at $7 a yard, and some supplies totaling $39.
   a. How much would she save by making the drapes herself?
   b. What percent of the custom-made price would she save?

Review 43

1. a. Multiply 525 by 10¢
   b. Add 62.05 and 9.625
   c. Subtract 0.75 from 30.54
   d. 200 m ÷ 4 = ? m
   e. Divide $36.75 by 6, correct to the nearest cent
   f. $56 increased by $12\frac{1}{2}\%$ of itself is equal to what amount?
   g. Change $\frac{6}{25}$ to a percent
   ★h. Express 9.46 as a mixed number in simplest form

2. You estimate that a job of redecorating and refurnishing a room will cost $1,600. The actual amount may be 20% more or 20% less than your estimate. What is the least amount and what is the greatest amount that this job should cost?

3. You can buy an air conditioner from Store A for $250 or from Store B for $275. What percent greater is Store B's price than Store A's price?

4. Energy-saving improvements costing $450 saved $135 a year in energy costs for Saul Faber. What was the payback period for those improvements?

5. Arden Trent used 620 KWHs of electricity in a month. The basic monthly charge was $7.50, plus $0.051 per KWH. A 7% tax was charged on the bill. What was Arden's total bill for the month?

6. Upton Mako had 300 liters of heating oil in his tank at the start of a heating season. He had 4 500 liters of oil delivered during the season. At the end of the season, Upton had 250 liters of oil left in the tank. At an average cost of 30¢ a liter, what was his heating oil cost for that season?

★ 7. By buying lawn furniture at the end of the season, you saved $95. That amount was 25% of the original price. What was the original price?

★ 8. A coat that had been selling for $130 is now marked down to $104. At that rate of markdown, what would be the sale price of a coat that had been selling for $170?

Part II
Review A

1. **a.** Multiply 8.06 by 1,000
   b. Multiply $0.49 by 700
   c. Multiply 84.6 by 0.025
   d. Divide $1.25 by 0.5
   e. Multiply $\frac{1}{5} \times \frac{1}{3}$
   f. Multiply $18 by $6\frac{3}{4}$
   g. Multiply 2.540 by 25¢
   h. Divide $2.25 by $2\frac{1}{2}$
   i. 3.5 m − 75 cm = ? m
   j. 225 cm² × 10 = ? m²
   k. 12.5 L ÷ 5 = ? L
   l. 500 g × 20 = ? kg
   m. What is $\frac{3}{4}$ of $2.52?
   n. What is 44 × $0.62\frac{1}{2}$?
   o. What is $\frac{2}{3} + \frac{7}{8}$, in lowest terms?
   p. What is $\frac{1}{2}$ of $1\frac{1}{2}$?
   q. $380 increased by 25% of itself equals what amount?
   r. $60 is what percent of $30?
   s. Express 16% as a common fraction in lowest terms

2. Use the table on page 34 to find the withholding tax for a worker with weekly pay of $335.60 and 3 withholding allowances.

3. What is the FICA tax at 0.067 on weekly pay of $304.65?

4. Nuna Castro's gross pay per month is $2,042. Her employer deducts $581.97 for withholding tax, $136.81 for social security, and $42.06 for other deductions. What is Nuna's net monthly pay?

5. Erik Gruner is paid a salary of $1,200 a month and a commission of 3% on sales. What was his total pay for a month when his sales were $27,480?

6. For the four weeks of February, you want your food expenses to average $85 a week. In the first three weeks, you spent $79.84, $88.63, and $90.26. How much can you spend in the fourth week?

7. Helen Foss may take a new job that pays $23,600 a year. The fringe benefits of the job are worth an estimated 22%. Expenses of the job would amount to $1,425 per year. What are the net yearly benefits of the job?

8. What is the total sale price of 6 sets of curtains at $11.95 a set, plus a sales tax of 5%?

9. You are mixing peanuts and cashews in the ratio of 4 to 1. How many kilograms of each kind of nuts do you need to make 10 kilograms of the mix?

10. Waldo Varuna's commissions in October were $980 and in November they were $1,120. What fractional part greater than his October commissions were his November commissions?

11. Ezra Kamin can buy a staple gun for $15. He can rent the same model gun for $2.25 a day. For how many days could he rent the gun for less total rental than the cost of buying the gun?

★**12.** Dom Evolo's salary this year is $27,776. That is 12% more than last year. What was Dom's salary last year?

BUYING HOMEOWNERS INSURANCE

When you own or rent a home, you have many risks of losing money. For example, the buildings or the contents may be damaged or destroyed by fire, lightning, windstorm, hail, explosion, smoke, riot, vandalism, falling objects, ice, or snow. You may have costs of living elsewhere while your damaged home is repaired. Your personal property may be stolen. You may become liable for injury to other persons on your property.

You can reduce your chances of losing money from some risks through insurance. The basic idea of insurance is that you and others pay a small sum of money into an insurance company. Then, anyone who has paid in will be repaid a larger sum for any losses that may occur.

When you buy insurance, the insurance company is called the insurer. You are the insured. The written agreement between you and the company is the policy. The money you pay for the insurance is called a premium. Premiums are often paid annually.

Homeowners Insurance. Many homeowners and tenants (renters) buy a special kind of insurance that is called *homeowners insurance*. It is a "package" type of policy that covers many risks. The basic form of homeowners policy covers loss to buildings and contents from the greatest risks, such as fire, lightning, smoke, windstorm, glass breakage, and additional living expense. Liability for bodily injury or damage to property of other persons caused by negligence is also covered. You can buy other forms of homeowners insurance to cover other risks.

One form of homeowners insurance is called a *tenants* (or renters) *policy*. It covers all the risks of the basic homeowners policy, and some others, but does not cover damage to buildings.

Cost of Homeowners Insurance. The premium that you pay for homeowners insurance depends on the amount of insurance you buy, the form of coverage, the dwelling construction, and the amount of protection where the dwelling is located. (The dwelling is the building you live in.) The general rule is, "The greater the risk, the greater the cost." For example, property that is well protected from fire and theft costs less to insure than unprotected property.

Premiums for homeowners insurance are figured by using tables such as the one on the next page. As shown in the table, the annual premium for $25,000 of insurance on a protected brick dwelling is $118. The annual premium for $25,000 of insurance on a partly protected brick dwelling is $122. The difference in rates reflects the difference in risk of loss.

ANNUAL PREMIUMS FOR BASIC HOMEOWNERS INSURANCE

Amount of Coverage	Protected*		Partly Protected*	
	Brick	Frame	Brick	Frame
$25,000	$118	$125	$122	$134
30,000	131	137	136	148
35,000	144	151	149	163
40,000	166	174	172	187
45,000	184	194	191	210
50,000	208	220	216	236
55,000	228	239	236	258
60,000	251	265	260	286
65,000	278	292	288	314
70,000	301	317	312	342

*A protected dwelling has better fire protection than a partly protected dwelling.

Written Practice 1

Use the premium table above for these problems.

1. What is the annual premium for $35,000 of insurance on (a) a protected frame dwelling and (b) a partly protected frame dwelling?   **$151; $163**

2. What is the annual premium for $50,000 of insurance on (a) a partly protected brick dwelling and (b) a protected frame dwelling?

3. What is the difference in annual premium on $60,000 of insurance on a protected frame dwelling and a partly protected frame dwelling?

4. What is the difference in the annual premium for $55,000 and $60,000 of insurance on a protected brick dwelling?

5. Rena Lamarr owns and lives in a frame dwelling in a protected area. The dwelling is worth $70,000, but it is insured for only $65,000. What is the annual premium?

6. Lance Prawn owns a brick dwelling in a protected area. The dwelling is worth $60,000, but Lance insures it for only 75% of its value.
   a. How much insurance does Lance have on the dwelling?   **$45,000**
   b. What is the annual premium on the dwelling?

7. To the nearest whole percent, how much greater is the premium on $30,000 of insurance on a frame dwelling in a partly protected area than in a protected area?

You can reduce your premiums with safety devices such as burglar alarms, fire alarms, and sprinkler systems. You can also get lower premiums if you buy **deductible insurance**. With deductible insurance, you pay the first part of any loss, such as the first $100 or $250. The company pays losses above the deductible amount, up to the limits of the policy.

Written Practice 2

1. Sally Kerr's homeowners insurance premium has been $250 a year. When she installed burglar alarms in her home, the premium was reduced by 2% a year.
   a. How much did Sally save per year by installing the alarms? $5
   b. What was Sally's new premium per year?

2. Basil Drago saved 12% a year by buying deductible insurance rather than full-coverage insurance. His old premium had been $325 a year. What was his new premium?

3. The annual premium for $100-deductible insurance on Ella Foster's dwelling is $190. The premium on $250-deductible insurance is $171 per year. What percent per year would Ella save by buying the $250-deductible?

4. Guy Lapin insures his frame home in a protected area for $60,000 at the rates in the table on page 180. He gets a 20% discount from those rates by increasing the deductible amount and installing safety devices. What is his new annual premium?

Additional Coverages. The insurance you carry on your dwelling automatically provides insurance for other risks included in the form of coverage you buy. For example, you automatically get 50% of the dwelling amount for insurance on your personal property while it is at your home. That is, if you insure your dwelling for $40,000, you get $20,000 of insurance on your furnishings, clothes, and other personal property at your home.

Additional coverages are automatic!

You also get 10% of your dwelling amount for other buildings such as detached garages and sheds; 10% for living expenses elsewhere if your dwelling is unlivable; and 5% for personal property while it is away from home. With basic homeowners insurance, you automatically get $25,000 of personal liability insurance with any amount of dwelling insurance.

Written Practice 3

1. Mary Gage insured her dwelling for $40,000 on a homeowners basic policy. How much insurance did she have automatically on her personal property while it was:
   a. at home? $20,000
   b. away from home? $2,000

2. Harvey Imree has $35,000 of homeowners insurance on his dwelling. If the dwelling becomes unlivable because of a fire, what is the most the insurer will pay him for living expenses elsewhere?

3. Dan Yoko increases his personal property coverage to 70% of his dwelling coverage. This change increases his annual premium by 15%. The old premium was $280 a year. What is the new premium?

4. Yvonne Bolla has a basic homeowners insurance policy. How much personal liability insurance does Yvonne have that will cover an injury to someone in her home?

Tenants Policy. The premium on a tenants policy, and the additional coverages, are figured on the amount of insurance you buy on your personal property. A tenants policy automatically provides 20% of the contents coverage for additional living expenses elsewhere if your dwelling is unlivable, and 10% of the contents coverage for personal property while it is away from home.

A tenants policy is a form of homeowners insurance

Written Practice 4

1. Chun Soo insures the contents of his apartment for $18,000 under a tenants policy. How much insurance does he have on the building? On the contents?

2. Burr Crimm has a renters policy for $21,000. He is burned out of his apartment and has to live in a motel while the apartment is repaired. How much insurance does he have to cover this expense?

3. If Tracy Beach rents an apartment in a 6-family apartment house, the annual premium on her tenants policy will be $126. If she rents in a 2-family building, the annual premium will be $90. By what percent is the premium on the 6-family building greater?

Terms to Remember		
deductible insurance	insured	insurer
	policy	premium

a. The insurance contract
b. The person buying insurance
c. The insurance company
d. The amount paid for insurance
e. Insurance in which you pay part of a loss

Review 44

1. A frame house in a protected area is worth $50,000. It is insured for 90% of its value. Use the premium table on page 180 to find the annual homeowners insurance premium on the house.

2. The premium for $100 deductible insurance on a dwelling is $350. That premium can be reduced by 18% by increasing the deductible amount and installing safety devices. What would be the new premium?

3. You plan to spend $800 now for home improvements. You hope to save $250 a year in energy by the improvements. If you do, what would be the net saving in 5 years?

COLLECTING ON HOMEOWNERS INSURANCE

section

45

General Procedures and Rules. To collect on your insurance, you must first notify the insurance company of your loss. The company will have an adjuster estimate the value of the loss. You may then have to make a written claim. If your loss includes personal property, you may have to submit a list (inventory) of the property, showing when you got it and its value.

We can't begin to remember all the things we had in the house before it blew down!

After you and the company have agreed on the amount of the loss, the company will pay you according to the terms of your policy. Under some policies, you are paid the full amount of a loss up to the limits (face) of the policy. Under other policies, you are paid the full amount of the loss only if you have insured your property up to a certain amount, such as 80% of the replacement value or the actual cash value of the property. Under a deductible policy, you are paid the amount of a loss above the deductible amount.

Remember this! →

The insurer will never pay more than the amount of the insurance you have for that kind of risk. For example, suppose your dwelling is worth $60,000, but you have only $50,000 of insurance on it. The company will not pay more than $50,000, even if your dwelling is totally destroyed. If the contents are insured for the usual 50% of the dwelling insurance, you will be paid not more than $25,000 for loss of contents.

Written Practice 1

1. Dora Fiore has a basic homeowners policy for $50,000 on her dwelling. There is no deductible clause in her policy. A fire does $28,000 of damage to the dwelling and $13,250 damage to the contents. How much would Dora collect on her insurance for (a) the dwelling and (b) the contents? (a) $28,000; (b) $13,250

The insured cannot collect more than the limits of the policy

2. Frank Naylor's dwelling is worth $40,000, and the contents are worth $22,000. He has a homeowners policy on the dwelling for $35,000, with the usual 50% of the dwelling amount on the contents. The policy will pay the full amount of any loss up to the limits of the policy, with no deductible clause.

   a. If Frank's dwelling and contents are totally destroyed by fire, what is the most he can collect (1) for the dwelling and (2) for the contents?

   b. If Frank's dwelling has a $5,000 fire loss, with no damage to the contents, how much would he collect?

   c. If a thief steals contents worth $6,000, what is the greatest amount Frank could collect?

3. Gordon Kasenko has a tenants policy for $10,000 on the contents of his apartment. The policy has a $200-deductible clause. A windstorm damages the building and destroys Gordon's personal property worth $8,000. How much could Gordon collect?   **$7,800**

4. Lola Birch has $40,000 of insurance on her house. The policy has a $100-deductible clause. What is the most that Lola could collect on a claim for $20,000 damage to her house?

Dividing Loss Among Several Companies. Property is sometimes insured with more than one company, especially if the property is valuable. If a loss occurs, the amount of the loss is shared by the insurers. Each company will pay the part of the loss expressed by the ratio of that company's insurance to the total amount of insurance.

Example

A house is insured for $100,000 with Company A and for $50,000 with Company B. How much will each company pay on a loss of $60,000?

Solution

$100,000 + $50,000 = $150,000 total insurance

$\frac{\$100,000}{\$150,000} = \frac{2}{3}$, part of loss paid by Company A

$\frac{\$50,000}{\$150,000} = \frac{1}{3}$, part of loss paid by Company B

$\frac{3}{3}$, total loss paid by both companies

$\frac{2}{3} \times \$60,000 = \$40,000$ paid by Company A

$\frac{1}{3} \times \$60,000 = \underline{\quad 20,000}$ paid by Company B

$\$60,000$ total paid by both companies

**Written
Practice 2**

1. Find each company's share of the loss.

	Loss	Amount of Insurance With					
		Company F		Company K		Company M	
a.	$ 40,000	$100,000	$20,000	$75,000	$15,000	$25,000	$5,000
b.	20,000	120,000		40,000		None	
c.	12,000	40,000		60,000		20,000	
d.	125,000	90,000		None		90,000	

2. Tim Ogala buys homeowners insurance for $80,000 with the Acme Company and for $60,000 with the Peerless Company. What is each company's share of a loss of $35,000?

3. Your homeowners insurance is split into three policies: Faith Company, $90,000; Hart Company, $45,000; and Mainstay Company, $15,000. If you have a loss of $25,000, how much will each company pay?

4. Bertha Olander insures for $85,000 with the Empire Company and for $40,000 with the Formost Company. She has a loss of $8,500. What is each company's share of that loss?

★**Claims Based on Replacement Cost.** Many companies insure losses on the basis of *replacement cost*. That is, if your property is damaged or destroyed, the insurer will pay the amount needed to replace the property at present costs. Replacement cost is often higher than the actual cash value of property.

Under most replacement cost policies, to collect the full amount of a partial loss you must insure for 80% or more of the replacement value of the property. If you insure for less than 80%, the company may pay only part of your loss. The part that the company may pay is the ratio of the amount of insurance carried to 80% of the replacement cost.*

$$\frac{\text{Insurance Carried}}{80\% \times \text{Replacement Cost}} \times \frac{\text{Loss (at Replacement}}{\text{Cost)}} = \frac{\text{Amount Paid}}{\text{by Company}}$$

For example, suppose your house would cost $100,000 to replace if it were destroyed. Under "replacement cost" insurance, if you insure your house for $80,000 to $100,000, you will be paid the full amount of your loss up to the limits (face) of your policy. But if you insure your house for only $60,000, the company will pay only $\frac{3}{4}$ of any partial loss ($60,000 ÷ $80,000 = $\frac{3}{4}$). So, if you had a loss of $20,000, you would be paid only $\frac{3}{4}$ of $20,000, or $15,000.

---

*"Replacement cost" insurance is not the same as "coinsurance." Also, under some "replacement cost" policies, if less than 80% of the replacement cost is insured, the company may pay only the actual cash value of the loss.

★Written
  Practice 3

1. Colin Terry's dwelling would cost $70,000 to replace. His insurance policy requires him to carry 80% of the replacement value to collect the full amount of losses up to the face of the policy. There is no deductible clause in his policy.
   a. If Colin insures for $70,000, what is the most he can collect on a total loss? **$70,000**
   b. If Colin insures for $56,000, what is the most he can collect on a total loss? **$56,000**
   c. If Colin insures for $56,000, how much would he collect on a loss of $40,000? **$40,000**
   d. If Colin insures for $49,000, how much would he collect on a loss of $4,000? **$3,500**

2. Nina Sokarno has $40,000 of "replacement coverage" insurance on her house. The policy requires her to insure for not less than 80% of replacement cost for full coverage of partial losses. The policy has no deductible feature. When Nina's house is partly damaged by fire, the replacement cost of the building is $60,000. The cost to repair the damage is $12,000. How much would Nina collect?

3. Lily Niniva has homeowners insurance of $50,000 on her dwelling. That amount is only $\frac{2}{3}$ of the amount she needs to carry for full payment of partial losses. If Lily has a loss of $30,000 on her dwelling, how much would she collect?

Review 45

1. a. Multiply $0.85 by 500
   b. Divide 380.9 by 0.65
   c. 8 m² − 1.5 m² = ? m²
   d. 12.5 m × 8 m = ? m²
   e. What is the cost of 1,000 items at 1¢?
   f. Divide 125 by 8, correct to 2 decimal places
   g. What is $\frac{5}{8}$ of $140,000?

2. Ria Canova has $15,000 of tenants insurance on her apartment, with a $100-deductible clause. She has a loss of $2,750 on the contents. How much will the company pay her?

3. The Stellar Company has insured a building for $120,000, and the World Insurance Company has insured it for $24,000. If a fire does $18,000 of damage to the building, what is each company's share of the loss?

4. Betty Dodge used 126 hundred cubic feet of gas last month. The therm factor of the gas was 1.03. The gas company charges $6 for the first 5 therms, and $0.50 for each additional therm. What was Betty's total bill, including a 6% tax?

★ 5. The Pickett's home would cost $80,000 to replace. The "replacement cost" clause in their policy requires them to insure for at least 80% of the replacement value for full coverage of partial losses. They are insured for only $56,000. How much would they get on a loss of $12,000?

PROPERTY TAXES

section
46

A **property tax**, or real estate tax, is charged and collected by many tax districts such as states, cities, counties, towns, villages, and schools. Property taxes are usually charged only once a year by a tax district, but you may have to pay taxes to more than one district each year. Property taxes are a major expense of owning a home, so you need to know how they are figured.

Let's suppose that you pay property taxes on your home in Central City. Your tax is figured this way.

Step 1

Finding the Amount to Be Raised by Property Taxes. The city authorities plan their expenses for the next year. They also estimate the income they will get from sources other than the property tax, such as licenses, permits, fines, and state or federal aid. The difference between their planned expenses and their income from other sources is the amount they must raise by property tax.

For example, Central City plans to spend $1,500,000 next year. Their estimated income from sources other than property tax is $500,000. The city will have to raise the difference, $1,000,000, by property tax.

Total Budgeted Expenses	**$1,500,000**
Less Income from Other Sources	500,000
Amount to Be Raised by Tax	**$1,000,000**

Step 2

Assessed value is used for figuring taxes

Finding Assessed Value. The amount of tax to be raised has to be divided fairly among the taxpayers. To do this, the city puts a value on each piece of taxable property. This value is called the **assessed value**, or assessed valuation. The assessed value may be much less than the market value or the replacement value. The total assessed value of all taxable property in the city is the sum of the assessed values of the individual pieces of property.

For example, your home in Central City has been assessed at $6,500. The total assessed value of your home, plus all the other taxable property in the city, is $12,000,000.

Step 3

Finding the Tax Rate. The city then calculates a tax rate to use in figuring the tax on each piece of taxable property. The **tax rate** is a fraction in which the amount to be raised by tax is the numerator, and the total assessed value is the denominator.

$$\frac{\textbf{Amount to Be Raised by Tax}}{\textbf{Total Assessed Value}} = \textbf{Tax Rate}$$

Tax rates are often rounded to five places

For example, the amount to be raised by property tax in Central City is $1,000,000. The total assessed value of all taxable property is $12,000,000. So, Central City's decimal tax rate is 0.08333, stated as a decimal correct to five places ($1,000,000 ÷ $12,000,000 = 0.083333, or 0.08333).

Step 4

Finding the Tax on a Property. The tax on each piece of taxable property in a district is found by multiplying the assessed value of that property by the tax rate.

Tax Rate × Assessed Value of a Property = Tax on a Property

For example, the decimal tax rate in Central City is 0.08333. Your home is assessed at $6,500. So, your tax is 0.08333 × $6,500, or $541.65.

Written Practice 1

1. The city of Upton has to raise $3,400,000 in property taxes. The total assessed value of Upton is $28,000,000. What will be the decimal tax rate, correct to 5 places? **0.12143**

2. The Hartville school district's budget this year is $1,600,000. The total assessed value is $20,000,000. What is their decimal tax rate?

3. Trent Dyke owns property in Boonton that is assessed for $5,000. The tax rate in Boonton is 0.09265. What is Trent's tax bill? **$463.25**

4. Wendy Atkin's home is assessed for $7,600. The school tax rate in her district is 0.1125. How much is Wendy's school tax?

5. The town of Culdane plans to raise $950,000 from property tax this year. The assessed value of all property in Culdane is $10,000,000. Aram Saud owns property in Culdane assessed at $4,000.
   a. What is the tax rate in Culdane?
   b. How much is Aram's tax bill?

Showing a Tax Rate in Other Terms. Your Central City tax rate was shown as a decimal rate, correct to 5 places. Tax rates may be shown in other terms, such as dollars per $1,000, dollars per $100, cents per $1, or mills per $1. A mill is one tenth of a cent, one thousandth of a dollar, or $0.001.

You change a decimal rate to other rates this way:

Decimal Rate	Multiplier	Rate in Other Terms
0.08333	× $1,000	$83.33 per $1,000
0.08333	× $100	$8.333 per $100
0.08333	× 100 cents	8.333¢ per $1
0.08333	× 1,000 mills	83.33 mills per $1

Written Practice 2

1. Copy this table and fill in the blanks for the other rates. Do not round any rate.

	Decimal Rate	Rate in Other Terms			
		Dollars per $1,000	Dollars per $100	Cents per $1	Mills per $1
a.	0.07524	$75.24	$7.524	7.524¢	75.24
b.	0.06395				
c.	0.05216				
d.	0.10248				

2. The city of Kenton has a decimal tax rate of 0.04967. What is their tax rate in:
   a. dollars per $100? **$4.967**
   b. dollars per $1,000? **$49.67**

3. The town of Knox needs to raise $325,800 by property tax. The town's total assessed value is $6,000,000. What tax rate must they charge in:
   a. cents per $1? **5.43¢**
   b. mills per $1?

Divide the tax by
→
the assessed value

4. Peter Sanger pays a tax of $520 on property assessed at $8,000. What is his tax rate per $1,000? **$65**

5. The tax on property assessed for $15,000 is $1,200. What is the tax rate per $100 on the property?

Finding a Tax With Rates in Dollars per $100 or $1,000. Suppose a tax rate is given in dollars per $100, or dollars per $1,000. To find the tax, you first find the number of $100 or $1,000 units in the assessed value. Then you multiply the number of units by the tax rate.

For example, your property is assessed at $6,500. The tax rate is $8.333 per $100. You figure your tax this way:

$6,500 ÷ $100 = 65 units of $100
65 × $8.333 = $541.645, or $541.65, amount of tax

If the tax rate were $83.33 per $1,000, you would figure the tax this way:

$6,500 ÷ $1,000 = 6.5 units of $1,000
6.5 × $83.33 = $541.645, or $541.65, amount of tax

Written Practice 3

1. The tax rate in Ironton, is $6.825 per $100 of assessed value. What is the tax on property assessed at $9,000? **$614.25**

2. Stella Landry's home is assessed at $5,500. The tax rate is $7.382 per $100. What is the tax on Stella's home?

3. The school tax rate in Clearview is $83.67 per $1,000. What is the amount of tax on property assessed at $9,000 in that district?

4. Spring Valley's tax rate is $106.42 per thousand. What is the tax on property in Spring Valley assessed at $12,500?

Finding a Tax with Rates in Mills or Cents per $1. Suppose that your tax rate is in mills or in cents per $1. To find the tax, you change the mills or cents to dollars. Then you multiply that rate and the number of dollars of assessed value.

Example

Your property is assessed at $6,500. The tax rate is 83.33 mills, or 8.333 cents, per dollar of assessed value. What is your tax?

Solution	Solution
83.33 mills = $0.08333 6,500 × $0.08333 = $541.645, or $541.65 **Ans.**	8.333 cents = $0.08333 6,500 × $0.08333 = $541.645, or $541.65 **Ans.**
Explanation	**Explanation**
There are 1,000 mills in a dollar, so you find the dollar equivalent of 83.33 mills by dividing by 1,000. (Move the decimal point three places to the left.) That rate, $0.08333, is then multiplied by the number of dollars, 6,500, to find the tax. The tax is rounded to the nearest cent.	There are 100 cents in a dollar, so you find the dollar equivalent of 8.333 cents by dividing by 100. (Move the decimal point two places to the left.) That rate, $0.08333, is then multiplied by the number of dollars, 6,500, to find the tax. The tax is rounded to the nearest cent.

THIS IS A MILL—

$0.001

BUT SO IS THIS!

Written Practice 4

1. The tax rate in Sabin County is 43.5 mills per $1. What is the tax on property in Sabin that is assessed for $9,400?   **$408.90**

2. Theda Dobell owns property in Orange. The property is assessed at $7,500, and the tax rate is 96 mills per $1. What is Theda's tax?

3. A tax rate of 12.6 cents per dollar is charged on Drew Fong's property in Olive City. If Drew's property is assessed at $4,000, what is his tax? **$504**

4. Gerta Swenson owns a home worth $60,000 at market value. Her home is assessed at $12,000. The school tax rate on Gerta's home is 11.67 cents per dollar. What is the amount of Gerta's school tax?

Terms to Remember

assessed value   mill   property tax   tax rate

a. One tenth of a cent, or one thousandth of a dollar
b. Amount to be raised by tax divided by total assessed value
c. The amount that is multiplied by a tax rate to find tax
d. A tax on real estate

Review 46

1. a. Divide 18,000 by 500
   b. Multiply 0.0463 by 1,000
   c. $500 \text{ g} \times 8 = ? \text{ kg}$
   d. What is $\frac{1}{2}\%$ of $234?
   e. $24 is what percent of $240?
   f. $200 increased by $37\frac{1}{2}\%$ of itself is what amount?
   g. $15 is what fractional part of $105?

2. Next year the town of Smithvale will raise $900,000 from property tax. The total assessed value of property in Smithvale is $8,000,000.
   a. What will be Smithvale's decimal tax rate next year?
   b. What will be the tax on a property in Smithvale that is assessed at $6,500?

3. A decimal tax rate of 0.09063 is equivalent to what rate in:
   a. dollars per $100?
   b. dollars per $1,000?

4. The school tax rate in Sunburst is 79.88 mills per dollar. What is the tax on property in Sunburst assessed at $5,200?

5. Miguel Madera's annual premium on homeowners insurance has been $320. By installing safety devices and buying deductible insurance, Miguel's premium is now 15% lower than before. What is his premium now?

★ 6. Kirsten Blum's home would cost $80,000 to replace. She has a homeowners policy for $65,000 that requires her to carry 80% or more of the replacement value to get full payment for partial losses. How much would Kirsten collect on a fire loss of $12,000 to her property?

BUYING A HOME

section
47

Cost of Buying a Home. Instead of renting housing, you may want to buy a home. When you buy, you will have many expenses to pay. If you have not planned carefully for these expenses, you may be short of cash.

You will probably borrow much of the purchase price by a mortgage, but you will have to use your own money to pay part of the purchase price. That part is called a **down payment**. Down payments are often 10 percent to 30 percent or more of the purchase price.

The seller of the property will pay the agent's fee, but you will have to pay *settlement costs*, or closing costs. Settlement costs include charges for several kinds of legal fees, land surveys, insurance, and prepaid property taxes. Settlement costs may be 2 percent or more of the purchase price.

Written Practice 1

1. The Onestos bought a new house for $52,900. They made a down payment of 20% of the purchase price with their own money. They borrowed the rest.
   a. What was the amount of their down payment? **$10,580**
   b. What amount did they borrow? **$42,320**

2. You want to buy a house that sells for $65,000. A down payment of 30% is required. A bank will lend you the rest of the purchase price.
   a. How much down payment is required?
   b. How much can you borrow from the bank?

3. The Kirkers are buying a new house for $49,500. They plan for these expenses at the time they buy the house: down payment, 25% of the purchase price; settlement costs, 3% of the purchase price; moving costs, $850; furnishings and appliances, $1,225. How much cash do they need?

4. You would like to buy a home for $60,000. A down payment of 30% of the purchase price is required. You estimate that you will need $1,600 for settlement costs and $1,450 for other expenses. You have $21,500 cash.
   a. Do you have enough cash to buy the house?
   b. How much more or less cash do you have than you need to buy the house?

5. Aaron Cohen is buying a house for $80,000. He must make a down payment of $28,000, and must have $7,200 for other costs.
   a. What percent of the purchase price is the down payment?
   b. What percent of the purchase price are the other costs?

Borrowing on a Mortgage. When you borrow money to buy a home, you sign a note promising to repay the money. You also give the lender the right to take the property if you fail to repay the loan.

Most home mortgages run for 20 to 30 years and require you to repay a fixed amount each month until the loan is paid. Part of each payment is for repayment of the amount you borrowed, called the principal, and part is for interest.

On mortgage loans, the amount of your monthly payment is figured by using a table like the one shown below. This is called an *amortization table*.

MONTHLY PAYMENTS NEEDED TO PAY A LOAN

Amount of Loan	Interest Rate								
	12%			14%			16%		
	Time of Loan								
	20 yrs.	25 yrs.	30 yrs.	20 yrs.	25 yrs.	30 yrs.	20 yrs.	25 yrs.	30 yrs.
$30,000	$330.33	$315.97	$308.59	$373.06	$361.13	$355.47	$417.38	$407.67	$403.43
35,000	385.39	368.63	360.02	435.24	421.32	414.71	486.94	475.62	470.67
40,000	440.44	421.29	411.45	497.41	481.51	473.95	556.51	543.56	537.91
45,000	495.49	473.96	462.88	559.59	541.70	533.20	626.07	611.50	605.15
50,000	550.55	526.62	514.31	621.77	601.89	592.44	695.63	679.45	672.38
55,000	605.60	579.28	565.74	683.94	662.07	651.68	765.20	747.39	739.62
60,000	660.66	631.94	617.17	746.12	722.26	710.93	834.76	815.34	806.86
65,000	715.71	684.60	668.60	808.29	782.45	770.17	904.32	883.28	874.10
70,000	770.77	737.26	720.03	870.47	842.64	829.42	973.88	951.23	941.33
75,000	825.82	789.92	771.46	932.65	902.83	888.66	1,043.45	1,019.17	1,008.57

Using an Amortization Table. Suppose that you want to buy a home for $60,000. You have 25% of that amount, or $15,000, for a down payment. You will borrow the rest, $45,000, from a bank on a 20-year mortgage loan at 14% interest. The bank will use a table such as the one above to find your monthly payment.

On the ''$45,000'' line of the table, in the 20-year column under 14%, is the amount, $559.59. That is the amount you must pay each month for 20 years to pay off the loan.

Look at what the interest does to the total cost of the property!

In 20 years, there are 20 × 12, or 240 months. So, in 20 years you will pay 240 × $559.59, or $134,301.60. The amount of the loan, or principal, is $45,000, so you will pay $134,301.60 − $45,000, or $89,301.60 in interest over the 20 years. Your average interest cost per month will be $89,301.60 ÷ 240, or $372.09.

Written Practice 2

Use the table on page 193 to do these problems.

1. What is the monthly payment needed to pay each of these mortgages?
   a. A $30,000 loan at 16% for 30 years. **$403.43**
   b. A $60,000 loan at 12% for 25 years.
   c. A $75,000 loan at 14% for 20 years.

2. What is the difference in monthly payments on a $50,000 mortgage loan for 20 years at 12%, and the same loan at 14%?

3. How much more per month is the payment for a 14% loan of $50,000 for 25 years than for 30 years?

4. You take a $60,000 mortgage loan for 20 years at 16%. What is your:
   a. monthly payment on the loan?
   b. total of monthly payments?
   c. total interest cost?
   d. average monthly interest cost, to the nearest cent?

5. Con Cholak takes a $35,000, 30-year mortgage on his home. The interest rate is 12%. What is Con's total interest cost?

6. The Morgans buy a house for $70,000 and pay $20,000 down. They mortgage the rest for 30 years at 14%.
   a. What will be the total of the Morgan's payments?
   b. What will be the interest cost of the loan?

Using a Mortgage Payment Schedule. When you borrow money on a mortgage, the lender may give you a mortgage payment schedule. With it you can see how your payments are split between interest and principal. You can also figure how much interest and principal you have paid, and how much is left to be paid. Part of a mortgage payment schedule is shown below.

MORTGAGE PAYMENT SCHEDULE

ANNUAL PERCENT RATE	MONTHLY PAYMENT	LOAN PRINCIPAL
14%	$373.06	$30,000

TERM IN YEARS	TERM IN MONTHS	NUMBER OF PAYMENT PERIODS
20	240	240

PAYMENT NUMBER	INTEREST PAYMENT	PRINCIPAL PAYMENT	BALANCE OF LOAN
1	350.00	23.06	29,976.94
2	349.73	23.33	29,953.61
3	349.46	23.60	29,930.01
4	349.18	23.88	29,906.13
5	348.91	24.15	29,881.98
6	348.62	24.44	29,857.54
7	348.34	24.72	29,832.82
8	348.05	25.01	29,807.81
9	347.76	25.30	29,782.51
10	347.46	25.60	29,756.91
11	347.16	25.90	29,731.01
12	346.86	26.20	29,704.81

As shown in the schedule, the $30,000 loan is at 14% for 20 years. The loan is to be repaid in 240 equal monthly payments of $373.06 each. The first payment of $373.06 is split into $350 for interest and $23.06 for reducing the principal. When the $23.06 payment on the principal is subtracted from the original amount, $30,000, the balance of the loan is $29,976.94.

Only the first year's payments, and the balances, are shown in this part of the schedule. All 240 payments are shown in the full schedule.

Written Practice 3

1. What amount of the sixth payment is for:
   a. interest?   **$348.62**
   b. principal?   **$24.44**

2. What is the difference in the amount of interest between:
   a. payment 1 and payment 2?
   b. payment 11 and payment 12?

3. Is the amount of the monthly payments for interest increasing or decreasing?

4. What is the difference in the amount paid on the principal between:
   a. payment 1 and payment 2?
   b. payment 11 and payment 12?

5. Is the part of each monthly payment for principal increasing or decreasing?

6. How much interest is to be paid in the first six months of the loan?

7. How much is to be paid on the principal for the first year?

8. What amount is owed on the principal at the end of the first year?

9. By how much has the balance of the loan been reduced in one year?

10. What will be the balance of the loan after payment 240?

Review 47

1. a. $124 \times \$0.87\frac{1}{2} = ?$
   b. $2\frac{2}{5} \times 4\frac{1}{3} = ?$
   c. $500 \text{ mL} + 3.75 \text{ L} = ? \text{ L}$
   d. $26.5 \text{ m}^2 \div 2 = ? \text{ m}^2$
   e. $80 decreased by what percent of itself is equal to $45?
   f. Change $16\frac{1}{2}\%$ to a decimal

2. The Rameros are buying a house for $80,000. A down payment of 20% is required. Their settlement costs will be $2,600, and their other costs will total $1,575. How much cash will they need for these expenses?

3. What is the total interest cost of a 25-year mortgage for $40,000 at 14% interest? (Use the table on page 193.)

4. What is the tax on property assessed at $8,400 if the tax rate is $115.20 per $1,000?

OWNING A HOME

section
48

As a homeowner, you will have several housing expenses that a renter does not usually have. You will have to pay for property taxes, insurance on the home, repairs, and interest on your mortgage. You will also have depreciation and loss of interest on your cash investment.

Depreciation on a Home. Even though you keep your house in good repair, it will gradually wear out and go out of style. With these changes, the house may lose value and you may have to sell it for less than you paid for it. That loss of value caused by wear and aging is called **depreciation**. Depreciation is a "hidden expense," because you are losing value rather than paying out cash.

Depreciation is a loss of value

Depreciation takes place gradually and is hard to measure until you actually sell your house. So, depreciation is often estimated rather than figured accurately. Annual depreciation is often estimated to be in the range of 2% to 4% of the cost of the property.

For example, Peter Rabin paid $50,000 for his home. He estimates that his home will depreciate at the rate of 2% per year. His annual depreciation expense is $0.02 \times \$50,000$, or $1,000.

This method of depreciation is called the **straight-line method**. It spreads the depreciation evenly over the expected life of the property.

Written Practice 1

1. A house that cost $60,000 is depreciated at the rate of $2\frac{1}{2}\%$ a year. What is the annual depreciation on the house? **$1,500**

2. Bea King estimates that her house depreciates at the rate of 2% a year. The house cost $65,000. What is her annual depreciation expense?

3. Kim Shin owns a house in an area where depreciation is often figured at 4% a year. A that rate, how much annual depreciation would Kim take on his house that cost $30,000?

4. A house that cost $75,000 is depreciated at the rate of 3% per year. In 10 years, what will be the total depreciation expense?

5. A house that cost $80,000 is depreciated at the rate of $2\frac{1}{2}\%$ per year. In how many years will the house be fully depreciated?

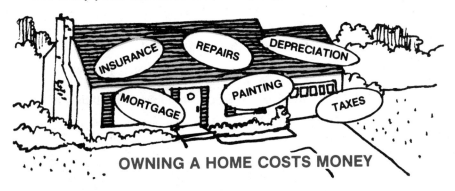

OWNING A HOME COSTS MONEY

Loss of Interest on Cash Investment. Suppose that you use some of your own cash to buy a home. By doing so, you lose the interest that your money would have earned if you had put it into a savings account or other investment. That loss of interest is an expense of owning the home.

Example

You pay $20,000 cash as a down payment on a house. The money would have earned 8% interest if you had invested it in savings certificates. How much interest are you losing per year?

Solution	Explanation
8% = 0.08 0.08 × $20,000 = $1,600 **Ans.**	A simple interest rate of 8% means 8% *per year*. To find the interest for one year, you change the 8% to its decimal equivalent, 0.08. You then multiply the amount of money, or principal, by the decimal interest rate to find the interest lost for a year.

An interest rate is for ONE YEAR!

Interest rates are always rates for *one year*, unless otherwise stated. You find the simple interest on any amount of money for one year by multiplying that amount, which is the *principal*, by the interest rate shown as a decimal.

Interest Rate × Principal = Interest for One Year
(F)   (F)   (P)

Written Practice 2

1. What is the simple interest on $12,000 at 6% for one year?   **$720**

2. How much will $15,000 earn in one year at 9%?

3. Edith Bono made a down payment of $18,000 to buy a home. She could have earned 7½% interest on her money by investing it in something else. How much interest did she lose per year by buying a home?   **$1,350**

4. The Bernays were earning 12% interest on money they had invested in bonds. They withdrew $25,000 of that money and put it into the purchase of a new home. How much interest did they lose per year?

5. Enos Montoya has put $28,000 into buying a new home. He could have earned 14% a year on that money by investing it elsewhere. What is his yearly expense from loss of interest?

6. The Ogamas are investing $30,000 of their savings in a new home. Their money has been earning 12% interest in another investment. Because of that lost interest, how much are they increasing their housing expense:
   a. per year?
   b. per month?   **$300**

Figuring Expenses of Home Ownership. Before you buy a home, you should review all the expenses of home ownership. You can figure some of those expenses accurately, but you will have to estimate other expenses. You may want to compare the costs of different kinds of homes.

Written Practice 3

1. Birk Harden has listed these expenses to own his home for a year:

Mortgage interest	$1,620
Property taxes	975
Insurance	210
Repairs	750
Depreciation	1,000
Loss of interest on investment	2,000

   a. How much per year is it costing Birk to own his home? **$6,555**
   b. What is Birk's average cost per month to own his home?

2. The Torka family bought their home many years ago for $30,000. Their average expenses per year to own the home are these: mortgage interest, $930; taxes, $620; insurance on home, $164; repairs, $450; loss of interest on cash investment, $800; depreciation, 2% of purchase price. What is their cost of home ownership:
   a. per year?
   b. per month?

3. Iva Ferris can buy a house for $75,000 with a down payment of $25,000. She estimates that the annual cost of mortgage interest, taxes, repairs, and insurance will be $7,150. If Iva buys the house, she will lose 8% interest per year on her cash down payment, and the annual depreciation will be 3% of the purchase price. What would be Iva's total cost per year to own the house?

4. Gerda Hansen is buying a house for $65,000. She estimates that her annual expenses for taxes, insurance, repairs, mortgage interest, and depreciation will be $7,630. For the down payment, Gerda will have to use $14,000 cash from an investment that is earning $8\frac{1}{2}\%$ per year. What will be her *monthly expense* of owning the house?

5. Ian Mason is comparing the ownership costs of two houses. House *A* costs $60,000, with a $15,000 down payment. House *B* costs $70,000, with a $17,500 down payment. The yearly expenses for taxes, insurance, repairs, interest, and depreciation on House *A* would be $3,500. On House *B*, those expenses would total $4,100 a year. To buy either house, Ian would lose 10% interest on his down payment money. How much more per year would the more expensive house cost him?

Renting or Owning a Home. Deciding whether to rent or to buy a home can be hard. You have to think about things such as comfort, convenience, your life style, and personal satisfaction. You also have to look closely at the costs of both renting and owning to see which would be less expensive for you.

Written Practice 4

1. The Motos are paying $450 a month to rent an apartment. They could buy a home with similar space for a $10,000 down payment. Their yearly expenses to own the house would be: mortgage interest, $2,703; insurance, $246; repairs, $400; and depreciation, $1,000. They could earn $900 a year on their down payment money by investing it in something else. How much would they save per year by buying rather than renting?   **$151**

2. Nora Nazamo can rent a house for $7,200 a year, or she can buy it by paying $15,000 down and mortgaging the rest. She estimates that taxes on the home would be $1,500; insurance, $225; interest, $3,240; and depreciation, $1,650 a year.
   a. If she can earn 8% on her money in another investment, what would be the yearly cost of owning the home?
   b. Would it be cheaper per year for her to rent or to buy the house?
   c. How much per year would she save by the less expensive method?

3. The Burdetts have owned their own home for several years. Last year their taxes, insurance, and repair expenses totaled $3,550. They paid 12% interest on their $30,000 mortgage last year. They allowed 2% depreciation on the purchase price of $60,000. They could have earned 12% interest on the $40,000 they have invested in their home.
   a. What was their total home ownership expense last year?
   b. If they had lived in an apartment at $900 rent per month, how much would they have saved in housing expenses for the year?

4. The Guzman family is renting housing for $550 a month. They can buy a house for $62,900. If they buy the house, their yearly expenses of ownership would be $4,650. They would also lose 9% interest per year on the $20,000 they would use for a down payment. If they buy the house, what amount will they save per month?

Terms to Remember

depreciation   down payment   straight-line method

a. Cash paid at time of purchasing a home
b. Loss of value caused by wear and aging
c. A way of spreading depreciation evenly

Review 48

1. a. Multiply $36 by $5\frac{1}{8}$
   b. Divide $6.75 by $2\frac{1}{4}$
   c. Divide 1 047 km by 3
   d. Divide 624 by 96
   e. What is the fractional equivalent of $87\frac{1}{2}\%$?
   f. 0.246 is equal to what percent?
   g. $62.50 is what percent of $100?
   h. Find the interest for 1 year on $5,000 at 12%

2. What is the yearly depreciation on a house that costs $78,000 if the depreciation is 3% a year?

3. The Carlsons invested $22,000 cash in their home. The money was earning 9% a year. How much interest did they lose per year by investing the money in the house?

4. The Wilmots bought a home for $60,000 and made a down payment of $15,000. They are losing 8% a year in interest on their down payment. They are depreciating the house at 2% per year on the purchase price. Their other ownership expenses total $6,000 a year. What is the cost of owning the house:
   a. per year?
   b. per month?

5. You borrow $35,000 on a 20-year mortgage to buy a home. Your monthly mortgage payment is $385.
   a. What total amount will you pay on the 20-year mortgage?
   b. How much of the total that you pay will be for principal?
   c. How much of the total will be for interest?

6. You want to insure a brick house in a partly protected area for 80% of its value. The value of the house is $75,000. Use the table on page 180 to find the annual premium.

★ 7. a. $966 is 15% more than what amount?
   b. Express 3.85 as a mixed number in simplest form.

Unit Eight

TRAVEL AND TRANSPORTATION

Travel by any method — car, plane, bus, train, ship — can be fun! Owning a car can be fun too — but expensive! In this unit you will learn about the costs of owning a car, traveling, and shipping goods.

When you have finished this unit, you should be able to:

- figure depreciation and rate of depreciation on a car
- find car insurance premiums
- figure costs of travel by different methods
- figure shipping costs by parcel post, express, and freight
- read, write, speak, and recognize the meanings of some special terms used in travel and transportation

Federal-Mogul Corporation

OWNING A CAR

Owning and using a car costs a lot of money! Car expenses include gas, oil, tires, repairs, license and inspection fees, insurance, garage rent, parking, tolls, taxes, and upkeep. You also lose interest on your investment in the car, and you have depreciation on it.

Depreciation on a Car. Cars wear out and change style much faster than houses. As with houses, though, the value that is lost through wear and aging is called *depreciation*.

The total depreciation of a car is the difference between its original cost and its trade-in value.

Original Cost − Trade-in Value = Depreciation

For example, suppose you buy a car for $8,000 and trade it in 3 years later for $3,200. The total depreciation is $8,000 − $3,200, or $4,800.

Finding Average Annual Depreciation on a Car. Depreciation on cars is often figured for a year. To find the average depreciation on your car for a year, you divide the total depreciation by the number of years you plan to keep the car.

Example

You buy a car for $8,000 and plan to keep it for 3 years. You estimate that its trade-in value will be $3,200. What is the average annual depreciation on the car?

Solution

Original cost	$8,000
Trade-in value	3,200
Total depreciation	$4,800

$4,800 total depreciation ÷ 3 years = $1,600 average annual depreciation

**Written
Practice 1**

1. Anya Embry buys a new car for $8,200. She thinks its trade-in value at the end of 5 years will be $2,500.
   a. What will be the total depreciation of the car for 5 years? **$5,700**
   b. What will be the average annual depreciation of the car? **$1,140**

2. Feng Li bought a new car 4 years ago for $9,000. Its trade-in value now on a new car is $2,900. What has been its average annual depreciation over the 4 years?

3. Your car is now worth $3,600 if you trade it in on a new car. You bought your car 3 years ago for $7,500. How much has the car depreciated per year?

4. Mona SanMarco bought a new car 9 years ago for $5,000. It will no longer run, so she can get only $50 junk value for it now. By what amount has the car depreciated each year?

5. You have bought a new car for $7,200. You estimate that its trade-in value will be $4,300 if you keep it for 2 years, or $2,200 if you keep it for 4 years. What will be your average annual depreciation if you keep it for (a) 2 years, and (b) 4 years?

Figuring Rate of Depreciation. When you allow an equal amount of depreciation on a car each year, you are using the *straight-line method.* In using straight-line depreciation, the annual depreciation is often shown as a percent of the original cost. To find the percent, or **rate of depreciation**, you make a fraction. The average annual depreciation is the numerator of the fraction, and the original cost is the denominator. Then you change the fraction to a percent.

$$\frac{\textbf{Average Annual Depreciation}}{\textbf{Original Cost}} = \textbf{Annual Depreciation Rate}$$

For example, suppose the average annual depreciation of a car is $1,600, and the original cost of the car is $8,000. The rate of depreciation is 20%.

$$\frac{\$1,600}{\$8,000} = 0.2, \text{ or } 20\%$$

Written Practice 2

1. Terry Vargas buys a car for $7,000. He estimates that he will get $1,400 trade-in allowance for it 5 years later. What is the estimated rate of depreciation? **16%**

2. You are buying a car for $6,500. You expect to trade it in after 3 years for $2,600. What is your estimated rate of depreciation?

3. Yvonne Tremont is trading in her 4-year old car for $2,560. It cost her $8,000 when she bought it. At what rate did the car depreciate?

4. Vida Green's car cost $8,800. When he traded the car for a new car 2 years later, he was given an allowance of $5,100 for the old car. What had been its average annual depreciation, to the nearest whole percent?

Figuring Annual Operating Costs. To find the total cost of running a car for a year, you add all the expenses. You include as expenses the depreciation and the interest lost on the purchase price of the car.

Example

Your car cost $8,000 when new. Last year your cash payments for gas, oil, repairs, insurance, and other items totaled $1,800. The car depreciated at 20% of the purchase price. Your investment in the car could have earned 12% interest. What was your annual operating cost?

Solution

Cash payments for gas, oil, etc.	$1,800
Depreciation @ 20% of $8,000	1,600
Loss of interest @ 12% of $8,000	960
Annual operating cost	$4,360

Written Practice 3

1. Alicia Bader's new car cost $6,600. Alicia's cash payments for car expenses the first year totaled $1,825. She allowed 25% for depreciation and 10% for loss of interest on her investment. What was Alicia's total car operating cost for that year? **$4,135**

2. Harry Noonan bought a new car for $7,300. His car expenses for a year were gas and oil, $835; service and repairs, $250; insurance, $425; license and inspection, $46; other cash payments, $83; depreciation at 25% of cost; loss of interest on investment, 12%. What was the total operating cost for that year?

3. Diane Poomau owns two cars. Her car expenses last year were gas and oil, $1,884; repairs, $483; insurance, $785; licenses and inspections, $66; depreciation, $2,610; loss of interest on investment, $1,450.
   a. What was the total of her car operating expenses last year?
   b. What was her average operating cost per car?

4. The estimated annual operating costs of two cars are shown below. The small car costs $6,500; the large car costs $10,000.

	Small Car	Large Car
Gas and oil	$510	$850
Repairs and maintenance	200	300
Licenses and inspections	23	40
Insurance	360	450
Other	100	150
Depreciation at 18%	?	?
Loss of interest at 10%	?	?

   a. What is the depreciation and loss of interest for each car?
   b. What is the annual operating cost for each car?
   c. What is the difference in annual operating costs between cars?

Written Practice 4

Your teacher will tell you to use the Customary or the metric measures, or both, with these problems. (The metric values in parentheses are only the approximate equivalents of the Customary measures.)

1. Duane Miller's car weighs 1,800 pounds (818 kg). What will be the cost of license plates for the car at a rate of $1.50 per 100 pounds ($3.30 per 100 kg)? **$27 ($26.99)**

2. On a trip of 800 miles (1 288 km), Nell Rourke's car used 32 gallons (121 L) of gas. How many miles per gallon (km per L) did the car average? (Show your answer to the nearest mile or kilometer.)

3. Sig Rombo used 85 gallons (322 L) of gas in one month. He traveled 2,720 miles (4 377 km) that month. How many miles (km) did Sig average per gallon (L)? (Show the answer to the nearest mile or kilometer.)

4. Sara Verdun's car averages 30 miles per gallon (8 kilometers per liter). Gas costs her an average of $1.60 per gallon (42¢ per liter). What is her average gas cost per mile (kilometer), to the nearest cent?

5. Simon Folger used 15 gallons (57 L) of gas on a trip of 360 miles (580 km). Gas for the trip cost him $22.50.
   a. How many miles (km) per gallon (L) did Simon average, to the nearest mile or kilometer?
   b. What was the cost of the gas used per mile (km), to the nearest cent?

6. Gretchen Huff drove her car 9,000 miles (14 500 km) last year. Her car expenses for the year were:

Gas, oil, lubes	$ 520
Repairs, service, tires	145
Insurance	410
Depreciation	1,350
Interest lost on investment	700
License and inspection	35
Garage, parking, tolls, washes	380

   a. What was Gretchen's total car cost for the year?
   b. What was her average cost per mile (km), to the nearest cent?

Written Practice 5

Your teacher will tell you to use the Customary or metric measures, or both, to do Problems 3, 4, 5, and 6. (The metric values in parentheses are only approximate equivalents.)

1. You left your home by car at 7:30 a.m. You arrived at your destination at 3:45 p.m. On the way you stopped a total of $1\frac{1}{2}$ hours for gas and lunch. What was your actual driving time? **$6\frac{3}{4}$ hours**

2. Hazel Kuwait drove her car from 8:15 a.m. to 4:15 p.m. During that time she stopped a total of 1 hour and 20 minutes. What was her actual driving time?

Distance = speed × time

3. How far will a car travel in 2 hours and 30 minutes if its average speed is 50 miles per hour (80 kilometers per hour)?   **125 mi (200 km)**

4. At an average speed of 46 miles per hour (74 km per hour), how far will you travel in 45 minutes?

Speed = distance ÷ time

5. Lila Hunt drove 245 miles (395 km) in 5 hours. What was her average speed in miles per hour? In kilometers per hour?   **49 mph (79 km/h)**

6. Ronald Yuma drove 300 miles (483 km) from St. Louis to Memphis. His actual driving time was 5.5 hours. What was his average speed to the nearest mile per hour? To the nearest kilometer per hour?

Review 49

1. **a.** What is $46.7349, rounded to the nearest tenth of a cent?
   b. Express 0.18 as a fraction in lowest terms
   c. $90 decreased by $16\frac{2}{3}\%$ of itself equals what amount?
   d. $48 increased by what percent of itself is equal to $64?
   e. What is the simple interest on $500 at 12% for one year?
   ★**f.** $180 is 120% of what amount?

2. Rodney Friar bought a new car five years ago for $7,000. He is trading it now for $1,400 on another car. What has been its:
   a. average annual depreciation?
   b. annual depreciation rate?

3. Grace LeClerc paid out $2,380 for car expenses last year. She also allowed $1,265 for depreciation and $790 for lost interest on her investment. What was her total car operating cost last year?

4. *Use Customary or metric measures, as directed by your teacher.*

   Jake Klinger used 10 gallons (38 L) of gas on a trip of 255 miles (410 km). The gas cost him $15.
   a. How many miles per gallon (kilometers per liter) did he average, to the nearest mile or kilometer?
   b. To the nearest tenth of a cent, what was his gas cost per mile? Per kilometer?

5. You drove 162 miles (261 km) in 3 hours and 30 minutes. To the nearest mile (kilometer), what was your average speed in miles per hour? In kilometers per hour?

6. Birch Elwin has homeowners insurance with the Faith Company for $150,000 and with the Hope Company for $100,000. What is each company's share of a fire loss of $60,000?

★ 7. Bianca Avila bought some produce through an agent. The prime cost was $6,500. The agent charged 10% commission, and $164.75 for expenses. What was the gross cost of the produce?

INSURING YOUR CAR

When you own and drive a car, you are liable if you injure other persons or damage their property. You may be injured, and your car may be damaged or stolen. To reduce your loss from such risks, you can buy insurance.

Kinds of Car Insurance. Most auto insurance policies are "packages" of protection for many kinds of risks. The most important part of the package is the liability insurance for bodily injury or for damage to the property of others.

Bodily injury (BI) insurance covers injuries to persons *other than* you or your family caused by a car accident that was your fault. Bodily injury insurance of at least $10,000 for injury to one person in an accident, and $20,000 for injury to two or more persons, is required by law in many states. Injury claims are often high, so you may want to carry at least $100,000 and $300,000 of bodily injury insurance.

Property damage (PD) insurance covers damage you cause to *other* people's property in driving a car. Many states require at least $5,000 of PD insurance. You may want to carry $25,000 or more.

Other kinds of coverage apply mainly to losses from injury to yourself and your family, or from damage to your car.

Medical payments insurance covers injuries to you and your passengers, no matter who is at fault. "No-fault" coverage for injuries is required in some states. It may cover loss of income, also, if the injuries keep you or your passengers from working.

Uninsured motorists insurance covers you and your passengers for injuries caused by an uninsured or hit-and-run driver.

Collision insurance covers damage to your car from collision or upset. Many people carry *deductible* collision coverage in which the company pays losses only above an amount such as $100 or $200. With deductible insurance, you collect only the actual value of a loss, less the deductible amount.

Comprehensive insurance covers theft of your car or loss from windstorm, glass breakage, and so on. It is usually deductible coverage.

Towing and labor cost insurance reimburses you for breakdowns.

Car Insurance Premiums. Premium costs for car insurance are based on the risks involved. Companies usually set their rates on factors such as where and how much the car will be driven. The age, sex, marital status, and accident or traffic offense record of the driver are also important in setting rates. Lower rates may be given for driver education. Rates may also vary with the kind and number of cars insured on one policy.

Written Practice 1

1. Nolan Jeng's car insurance coverages and premiums for a year are shown below. What is Nolan's total premium for a year?

Coverage	Premium
Bodily injury liability, $100,000/$300,000	$174
Property damage liability, $25,000	120
Medical payments	105
Collision, $200 deductible	136
Uninsured motorists	9
Comprehensive, $200 deductible	27
Towing and labor costs	4

2. Dody Smith uses her car for pleasure only. Her annual car insurance premium is $475. Helen Jory owns the same model car as Dody, but she uses her car for both pleasure and business. Helen's premium is $665. What is the difference in their premiums?

3. Kerry Soto owns two cars. The premium for Car *A* is $208, and for Car *B* it is $327.
   a. What is Kerry's total premium?
   b. What is Kerry's average premium per car?

4. Larry Parker is a young, unmarried driver who lives in a city. He owns a "high performance" car and has had several accidents and traffic violations. As a result, Larry's premiums are 325% of the standard $220 annual premium. What is Larry's annual premium?

5. Last year Susan Gorman paid an auto insurance premium of $540. The insurance company returned $129.60 of that premium to her at the end of the year because their claims had been lower than expected.
   a. What was Susan's net premium cost for the year?
   b. What percent of the original premium was returned?

Written Practice 2

1. Mark Tarrant uses his car to drive to work and for pleasure. His annual premium is $380.
   a. If Mark used the car for business, his premium would be increased by 18%. What would his premium then be, to the nearest dollar? **$448**
   b. If Mark used his car for pleasure only, the premium would be reduced by 12%. What would his premium then be, to the nearest dollar?

2. Celia Marone lives in a city and pays $720 premium for her auto insurance. Nina Sacco lives on a farm and pays $450 for her insurance. Both Celia and Nina have the same coverage. By what percent is Celia's insurance cost greater than Nina's?

3. Rex Zee changed his collision and comprehensive insurance from $100 deductible to $250 deductible. When he did, his premium was reduced from $220 to $165. What was the percent of decrease in premium?

4. Roberto Delgado has had driver training and a good traffic safety and accident record. Because of this, Roberto gets a reduction of 14% from the standard premium of $550 for the coverage he buys. What is Roberto's premium?

5. Adam and Curt have the same insurance coverage. Adam is a married male driver over age 25, with annual premiums of $240. Curt is an unmarried male driver, age 19, with annual premiums of $432. By what percent is Curt's premium greater than Adam's?

★ 6. Pauline Ewing pays a premium of $425 for her auto insurance. This is 15% less than her neighbor pays for the same coverage with another company. What is the neighbor's premium?

Terms to Remember

| bodily injury | collision | comprehensive | medical payments |
| property damage | | rate of depreciation | uninsured motorists |

a. Average annual depreciation divided by original cost
b. Covers damage you cause to other people's property
c. Covers damage from collision or upset
d. Covers theft and glass breakage of your car
e. Covers injuries to other persons only if you are at fault
f. Covers injuries to you and other persons no matter who is at fault
g. With medical payments coverage, also covers your injuries caused by another driver

Review 50

1. a. What is $300 \times 62\frac{1}{2}¢$?
   b. Divide $20.05 by 5
   c. Divide $6\frac{3}{8}$ by 3
   d. Multiply 15.6 m by 8 m
   e. What is the interest on $2,000 at 9% for one year?
   f. Show 0.165446 correct to the nearest thousandth

2. When she used her car for business, Rachel Blum paid auto insurance premiums of $520 a year. When she stopped using the car for business, the annual premium dropped to $364 a year. By what percent did the premium decrease?

3. Alan Hudson drove 9,000 miles last year. He paid out $1,876 for car expenses. Depreciation was 20% of the original cost of $6,800. He lost 8% interest on his investment. What was his operating cost per mile?

4. The decimal tax rate in Solview is 0.13524. What is the tax on a property in Solview that is assessed at $7,000?

5. This year, Kim Clark's housing expenses increased 12% over last year's expenses of $8,400. What were Kim's housing expenses this year?

★ 6. Gregor Orkin pays $678 a year for auto insurance. This is $\frac{1}{5}$ more than his brother pays. What does his brother pay?

TRAVEL EXPENSES

Like many other Americans, you will probably do a lot of traveling. You will travel by your own car, by rented car, by bus, taxi, train, plane, and ship. You will visit your friends and relatives, make business trips, take vacations, and tour the world.

To get the best buy for your travel dollar, you need to figure and compare the costs of different methods of travel. When you figure your costs, be sure to include items such as tips, snacks, and admissions. To compare costs, you may want to figure the average cost per day, week, or other unit.

Travel agencies can help you plan your travel and figure your costs. They will also issue tickets and make reservations. There is no direct charge to you for their service.

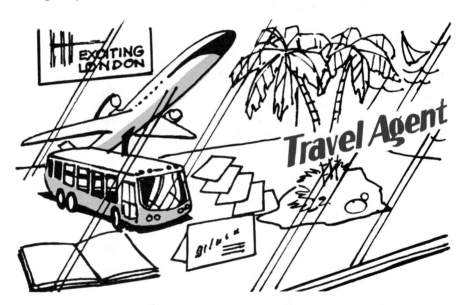

Written Practice 1

1. On a 7-day vacation trip by their own car, the Dorans had these expenses:

Gas, oil, tolls, parking	$189.00
Lodging and tips	475.00
Meals and tips	434.75
Admissions and other charges	82.50

    a. What was the Doran's total trip cost?
    b. What was their average cost per day?

2. Evelyn Jevons is making a one-day business trip to Detroit by plane. She estimates these costs: to and from airport by own car, $5; airport parking, $4; round-trip air fare, $241.50; taxi to and from destination in Detroit, $17. What is the total estimated cost of her trip?

A round trip is to a place and back again

3. John and Joyce Morales must travel to a nearby city. If they drive their own car, their round-trip cash expenses will be gas, $22.75; tolls, $9.50; parking, $15. If they take a bus, the expenses will be round-trip fare, *per person*, $33; transportation to and from bus terminals, $8. Which is less expensive, car or bus? How much less?

4. The one-way rail fare between two cities that are 150 miles apart is $21.50. The round-trip fare is $32.60.
   a. To the nearest tenth of a cent, what is the cost per mile of the one-way fare? Of the round-trip fare?
   b. How much is saved by buying a round-trip ticket rather than two one-way tickets?

5. Kip and Nan Osteen's travel agent estimates these per-person costs for a 7-day ship cruise: cruise fare, $945; air fare to and from the ship, $325; shore excursions, $85; tips, $75; incidentals, $75.
   a. What is the estimated cost for one person per week? Per day?
   b. What is the estimated cost for two people per week? Per day?

Written Practice 2

1. You are planning a round trip by car. You expect to arrive at a friend's home after supper on the third day (after two nights at a motel). You will stay with your friend for several days as a guest. The one-way distance is 1,500 miles. You plan to drive 500 miles per day. Your car averages 25 miles per gallon of gas. So far, your estimate of roundtrip expenses looks like this:

_____	gallons of gas at $1.75 per gallon	$_____
_____	nights' lodging at $40 per night	_____
6	days' meals at $18.50 per day	_____
	Tolls and other costs for round trip......	77

   a. What is the total estimated cost of your round trip?
   b. What is the average cost per day while you are on the road?

2. Felix Kramer is planning to rent a car for 5 days to drive a distance of 2,000 miles. The car rental will be $25 a day. Insurance on the car will cost $3.50 a day. Franz will furnish gas for the car at an average of $1.80 per gallon. Franz expects the car to average 25 miles per gallon.
   a. What will be the total car cost?
   b. What will be the average cost of the car per day?

3. Before taking a vacation trip, the Wongs estimated these expenses: round-trip air fare, $898; lodging, $770; food, $532; car rental and operation, $400; other, $200. When they had completed the trip, their total expenses had been $3,220.
   a. How much greater than their estimated expenses were their actual expenses?
   b. What percent greater than their estimated expenses were their actual expenses?

4. Calvin Beckwith is comparing the costs of driving his car or flying to a three-day meeting in a large city. His expenses while at the meeting will be the same whether he drives or flies. The one-way driving distance is 800 miles and will take two days of driving each way. He estimates his costs by car for the round trip to be 30¢ per mile for car expenses; lodging, 2 nights at $45 per night; meals while traveling, 4 days at $19.50; incidentals, $12. If he flies, his expenses will be round-trip air fare, $459; transportation to and from airports, $30; incidentals, $6.
   a. Which method of travel would be less expensive, and how much?
   b. What percent less would the cheaper method be?

Review 51

1. **a.** Multiply $368.75 by 10
   b. Divide $242.82 by 1,000
   c. 3 m + 25 cm = ? m
   d. Subtract 5 000 m² from 2 ha
   e. What is the interest at 8% on $10,000 for one year?
   f. $200 is what percent less than $250?
   g. Show $0.08\frac{1}{3}$ as a percent, correct to the nearest tenth

2. The Kimm's expenses on a 7-day vacation trip by car were these: car, $83.50; lodging, $376; food, $242.40; entertainment, $136; other, $16.80.
   a. What was the total cost of the vacation?
   b. What did the vacation cost per day?

3. Last year Leda Samona's auto insurance premium was $720. This year it has increased to $828. By what percent has her premium increased?

4. Using the amortization table on page 193, find the amount of interest paid on a mortgage loan of $40,000 for 20 years at 12%.

5. At a January "white sale," all goods are reduced by $\frac{1}{3}$. How much would you save by waiting for the sale price rather than buying towels fully priced at $75.99?

6. A 10-minute dial-direct telephone call on a weekday will cost you 50¢ for the first minute, and 34¢ for each additional minute. A 10-minute call made at the evening rate will cost you 32¢ for the first minute, and 22¢ for each additional minute. How much will you save by using the less expensive rate?

7. Your room air conditioner uses 860 KWHs of electricity per month during the cooling season. Electricity costs you 6¢ per KWH. What will be the cost of running the air conditioner for a month?

★ 8. At an end-of-season sale, gloves are marked down 30% to a sale price of $18.90. What was the original price?

★ 9. To get full coverage of partial losses, the Tourmas must insure to 80% of the replacement value of their dwelling. Their house is now valued at $60,000, but they have only $40,000 of insurance on it. How much would they collect on a $20,000 loss?

SHIPPING GOODS

If you ship goods, you will probably send them by mail, express, or freight. In choosing which method to use, you need to consider cost, speed, convenience, and the size, weight, and nature of the goods. Your choice may also depend on special services offered by the shipper, such as insurance, special handling, collect on delivery (C.O.D.), and door-to-door delivery.

Shipping by Mail. The United States Postal Service offers several kinds of service for shipping packages:

Express mail has a money-back guarantee of next-day delivery. Rates for this service are high.

Priority mail is the name used for first-class mailing of heavy pieces weighing over 12 ounces and up to 70 pounds. Rates are lower than for express mail but higher than for parcel post.

Parcel post, or fourth class mail, is the service most often used for shipping packages by mail. Parcel post packages cannot exceed certain weight and size limits, and some kinds of goods cannot be shipped by parcel post. For an extra fee, you can get added services such as insurance, registry, return receipt, C.O.D., special delivery, and special handling.

Parcel post charges are based on the weight of the package and the distance it is to be sent. Distance is measured by zones. Rates to all zones for parcels up to 10 pounds are shown in the table below. A fraction of a pound is counted as a full pound.

PARCEL POST ZONE RATES*

Weight 1 Pound and Not Over (Pounds)	Zones							
	Local	1 and 2 Up to 150 Miles	3 150 to 300 Miles	4 300 to 600 Miles	5 600 to 1,000 Miles	6 1,000 to 1,400 Miles	7 1,400 to 1,800 Miles	8 Over 1,800 Miles
2	$1.52	$1.55	$1.61	$1.70	$1.83	$1.99	$2.15	$2.48
3	1.58	1.63	1.73	1.86	2.06	2.30	2.55	3.05
4	1.65	1.71	1.84	2.02	2.29	2.61	2.94	3.60
5	1.71	1.79	1.96	2.18	2.52	2.92	3.32	4.07
6	1.78	1.87	2.07	2.33	2.74	3.14	3.64	4.54
7	1.84	1.95	2.18	2.49	2.89	3.38	3.95	5.02
8	1.91	2.03	2.30	2.64	3.06	3.63	4.27	5.55
9	1.97	2.11	2.41	2.75	3.25	3.93	4.63	6.08
10	2.04	2.19	2.52	2.87	3.46	4.22	5.00	6.62

*Rates effective when this book was published.

As shown in the table on page 213, local delivery of a package weighing 2 pounds or less costs $1.52. To ship a package weighing more than 2 pounds but not more than 3 pounds outside the local area but within 150 miles costs $1.63.

Oral Practice 1

What is the cost to ship these packages? (*Use the table on page 213.*)

1. A 5-pound package to your own city
2. A 10-pound package to a city in Zone 3
3. A $3\frac{1}{2}$-pound package to a city in Zone 8
4. A $9\frac{1}{4}$-pound package 300 miles
5. A 7-pound 3-ounce package 1,500 miles
6. An 8 lb. 15 oz. package locally

Written Practice 2

Use the table on page 213 to do Problems 1 through 4.

1. You mail a package by parcel post to a friend who lives in a city 1,200 miles away. The package weighs $2\frac{3}{4}$ pounds. Insurance on the contents, valued at $50, costs $0.85. What is the cost of shipping the package?   **$3.15**

2. Iris Cintron ships a package weighing $6\frac{1}{2}$ pounds by parcel post to a city that is in Zone 5. Insurance costs $0.45. What is the mailing cost?

3. Donald Frost sends a 10-pound package by parcel post to his mother, who lives in Zone 7. He pays a special handling fee of $0.75 for fast delivery. Insurance costs $1.25. What is the total cost?

4. You are sending a parcel post package to a person who lives 2,000 miles away. The package weighs 5 lb. 8 oz. You pay a special delivery fee of $3 to get fast delivery. You pay $0.60 for a return receipt as proof that the package was received, and $1.70 for insurance. What is the total cost of shipping the package?

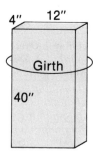

Girth is distance around widest part

5. To be shipped from the Middleburg Post Office, a parcel post package cannot weigh more than 70 pounds or exceed 100 inches in length and girth combined.

   Girth is the distance around a package at its thickest part. For example, a package is 40 inches long, 12 inches wide, and 4 inches thick. Its girth is 12 + 4 + 12 + 4, or 32 inches. The combined length and girth is 40 + 32, or 72 inches.

For each package, A through F, write "Yes" if it can be sent from Middleburg by parcel post. Write "No" if it cannot be sent by parcel post.

Package	Length	Width	Thickness	Weight	Yes or No
A	25 in.	18 in.	15 in.	60 lb.	
B	48 in.	16 in.	12 in.	20 lb.	
C	60 in.	6 in.	6 in.	15 lb.	
D	20 in.	12 in.	8 in.	72 lb.	
E	72 in.	8 in.	6 in.	8 lb.	

Shipping by Express. Express service provides fast shipment of goods that are small and light. You can send express shipments by plane, truck, bus, and train. Weight and size limits are often like parcel post limits.

Some express carriers, such as United Parcel Service and Federal Express, have door-to-door pick up and delivery, and C.O.D. service. Some express carriers will take goods, such as pets, that cannot be shipped by parcel post. Some will make guaranteed overnight delivery anywhere in the United States.

Express charges vary with speed, weight, distance, kind of goods, and special services used. Some insurance is often included in the shipping rate, and more can usually be purchased. Different express companies have many different rates and services, and they are changed often. You can get up-to-date information on charges and weight and size limits by talking with express agents.

Shipping by Freight. Freight service is usually slower than express and is used for shipping large amounts of heavy, bulky goods. Freight shipments can be sent by plane, truck, train, or ship. Charges are based on speed, weight, distance, size, kind of goods, and special services used. As with express, you should consult agents for up-to-date information.

Written Practice 3

1. Delma Kopal has a parcel service pick up a 15-pound package at her home for shipment. The charges are $3.25 for pickup; $7.33 for shipping; $0.75 for extra insurance; and $0.50 for a receipt showing delivery of the goods. What is the total charge?   **$11.83**

2. Lem Argus is sending two packages by a parcel service. The shipping charge on the first package is $3.47. On the second package, the shipping charge is $5.38. Added insurance on each package is 80¢. What is the total charge for shipment?

3. Del LeBec has ordered some goods shipped to him, C.O.D., by an express service. The price of the goods is $235.95. Delivery charges on the goods are $6.85, plus an insurance charge of 70¢. Del will also have to pay a C.O.D. charge of $2.10. What will be the total cost of the goods to Del?

4. If Martha Sinclair ships a package by truck express, the delivery time will be 5 days and the cost will be $16.50. If she ships the package by combined ground-air service, it will be delivered in 2 days at a cost of $46.20.
   a. What is the difference in cost?
   b. What percent greater is the cost of shipping by ground-air?

Find the number of
100-pound units,
then multiply by
the rate

5. Theresa Betar wants to ship 850 pounds of household goods by freight. The rate is $14.68 per 100 pounds. What is the freight charge?

6. A shipment of goods weighs 375 kilograms. The freight charge is $39.25 per hundred kilograms. What is the freight charge?

Terms to Remember

express   freight   parcel post

a. Fourth-class mail
b. Fast shipment for small and light goods
c. Used for shipping heavy, bulky goods

Review 52

1. a. Multiply $3\frac{3}{4}$ by 3
   b. Subtract 29.74 from 46.5
   c. 4.5 kg ÷ 12 = ? g
   d. 2.5 m × 6.5 m = ? m²
   e. Express $14\frac{3}{4}\%$ as a decimal
   f. What is the simple interest for one year on $250 at 6%?
   ★g. What amount decreased by 30% of itself equals $154?

2. What is the cost to send a 5 lb. 6 oz. package by parcel post to Zone 3, with 45¢ for insurance? (Use rate table on page 213.)

3. To ship a package by air express, Chet Moore paid a pick-up charge of $2.50, express charges of $7.92, and an additional insurance charge of $1.75. What was the total shipping cost?

4. On a vacation trip, Naomi Smith rented a car for 2 weeks at a weekly rate of $180. She paid $4.50 a day for additional insurance. She used 70 gallons of gas at an average of $1.75 per gallon.
   a. What was the total cost of operating the car for 2 weeks?
   b. What was the average cost per day, to the nearest dollar?

5. You are given a trade-in allowance of $1,300 on your old car. You paid $6,500 for it when it was new 5 years ago.
   a. What has been its annual depreciation?
   b. What has been its annual rate of depreciation?

6. Arturo Blanca added insulation to his home at a cost of $1,125. As a result, he saved an average of $250 a year in fuel costs. What was the payback period of the insulation?

7. Oki Ichiro has an apartment in a two-family dwelling. She now pays $80 a year for tenant's insurance. If Oki moves to a new apartment in an 8-family dwelling, her tenant's insurance will be $108. By what percent will her premium go up?

HEALTH AND EDUCATION

Deciding what kinds and amounts of life and health insurance you ought to have is not easy. When you are young and healthy, it is not easy to imagine the financial hardships that may be caused by your illness, injury, or death. Also, the many kinds of insurance, with many different benefits and costs, are confusing.

Shopping for education may be a lot more fun than buying insurance, but it can be confusing. To plan your education, you need to know your interests and your abilities, both now and in the future. You also need to know what educational programs are available, what they might do for you, what they cost, and how you might pay for them. That's a lot to know!

You have to start thinking about insurance and education sometime, so let's start right now! In this unit you will find much to learn about the benefits, the costs, and the ways of paying for life and health insurance, and for further education. When you have finished this unit, you should be able to:

- figure premium costs of life insurance
- find cash values of life insurance
- figure dividends and net premium costs of life insurance
- find the benefits of health insurance, including deductible and coinsurance features
- figure costs of further education
- solve problems of paying for further education
- read, write, speak, and recognize the meanings of some terms used in life and health insurance, and in education

University of Cincinnati

LIFE INSURANCE COSTS

Your death may cause financial hardship for other people. For example, if you are working and have a family, your family will lose your income. Someone will have to pay for your funeral. Someone will have to pay your debts, such as a mortgage on your home. You can provide money for these after-death expenses by buying life insurance.

Kinds of Life Insurance. Four basic kinds of life insurance are term life, whole life, limited-payment life, and endowment life.

Term life insurance covers you for a short time, such as a year or five years. You pay premiums for that time, then you have no more insurance. If you have *renewable term* insurance, you may renew the insurance but at a higher premium. Term insurance gives you the greatest amount of insurance coverage for your premium dollar, but it has no savings feature.

Whole life insurance is often called ordinary life or straight life insurance. It covers you for your whole life. You pay premiums for as long as you live, unless you take a lesser amount of paid-up insurance. Whole life has a savings feature.

Limited-payment life insurance covers you for all your life, but you pay premiums only for a limited time, such as 20 years. It has a savings feature.

Endowment life insurance covers you for a fixed period, such as 20 years. You pay premiums only for that time. At the end of that time, you are paid the face of the policy and the insurance is ended. It has a savings feature.

Figuring Premiums. Premiums differ greatly among companies, so you need to look closely at rates, coverages, and services. Premiums for life insurance depend, in part, on the kind of insurance you buy and your age when the policy is written.

The premiums that might be charged for each $1,000 of life insurance coverage are shown in the table on the next page. Using that table, the premium for a person buying $10,000 of 5-year term insurance at age 20 would be $26.50.

$10,000 ÷ $1,000 = 10 units of $1,000
10 × $2.65 = $26.50 annual premium

ANNUAL PREMIUMS FOR $1,000 OF LIFE INSURANCE

Age	5-Year Term	Whole Life	20-Payment Life	20-Year Endowment
20	$2.65	$10.15	$17.45	$38.70
25	2.85	11.45	19.00	38.85
30	3.20	13.85	22.00	39.10
35	3.85	17.15	25.75	39.65
40	5.35	21.15	29.80	40.85

Written Practice 1

Use the table above to do these problems.

1. What is the annual premium on each of these policies?

	Kind of Insurance	Issue Age	Amount of Insurance	Premium
a.	5-Year Term	25	$20,000	**$57**
b.	Whole Life	30	10,000	
c.	20-Payment Life	35	50,000	
d.	20-Year Endowment	40	30,000	

Take your time!

Be sure to use the right figures

2. How much more is the annual premium on a 5-year term policy for $10,000 issued at age 35 than on the same policy issued at age 30? **$6.50**

3. How much more is the premium on a whole life policy than on a 5-year term policy for $10,000 issued at age 25?

4. What is the difference in the annual premium at age 35 on a whole life policy and a 20-year endowment policy for $30,000?

5. At age 20, how much less is the premium on a $40,000 whole life policy than on a 20-payment life policy for the same amount?

6. How much more is the annual premium for a $50,000 whole life policy bought at age 40 than for the same coverage bought at age 20?

Written Practice 2

Use the premium table above for these problems.

1. When she was age 20, Lily Mutsu bought a 5-year term policy for $10,000. How much total premium would she have to pay in 5 years? **$132.50**

2. Nunzio Perma buys a 20-payment life policy for $25,000 when he is age 35. How much will he pay in premiums by the end of 20 years?

3. Hester Green is comparing the total premium cost for 20-payment life and 20-year endowment policies for $40,000. What is the difference in total premiums for those policies over 20 years if she bought at her present age of 30?

4. What percent greater, to the nearest whole percent, is the annual premium for $1,000 of whole life at age 40 than for 5-year term insurance at age 40?

5. Hubert Kapler is age 25. He can afford to spend $500 a year to buy life insurance. In even thousands of dollars, what is the largest policy he can get if he buys:
   a. 5-year term? **$175,000**
   b. whole life?
   c. 20-payment life?

Terms to Remember

| endowment life insurance | limited-payment life insurance |
| term life insurance | whole life insurance |

a. Also called ordinary life insurance
b. Pays you the face of the policy if you are alive
c. Covers you for a short time only; no savings feature
d. Covers your entire life, but you pay premiums for a fixed time only

---

Review 53

1. **a.** Multiply 1,600 by $37\frac{1}{2}$¢
   b. Multiply $1.45 by 3,000
   c. 1.5 L = ? mL
   d. 750 g = ? kg
   e. What is the simple interest at 9% for one year on $1,800?
   f. What fractional part of $16 is $12?

2. At age 30, Perry Jordan bought a 20-payment life policy for $50,000. The annual premium was $23.50 per $1,000. What total amount of premium would he pay in 20 years?

3. Bernice Gorgol has $600 a year to spend for life insurance. At an annual premium of $15 per thousand, how many thousands of dollars of insurance can Bernice buy?

4. You want to ship a parcel post package weighing $5\frac{1}{2}$ pounds to a friend in Zone 5. What will it cost, without insurance? (Use table on page 213.)

5. Rich Darwin paid $2,050 last year to operate his car. The car also depreciated at 18% of the original cost of $7,000, and Rich lost 10% interest on his $7,000 investment in the car. What was his total car operating cost for the year?

6. You have driven 295 miles in $6\frac{1}{4}$ hours. What was your average speed, to the nearest mile per hour?

LIFE INSURANCE BENEFITS

The main benefit of any kind of life insurance is the death benefit. The *death benefit* is the money that is paid to your beneficiary. The **beneficiary** is the person or organization named by you in the policy to get the face of the policy when you die.

Term insurance has no value other than the death benefit. Whole life, limited-payment life, and endowment policies have a savings feature as well as the death benefit. They build up cash values after the first few years. **Cash value** is an amount of money that will be paid to you if you cancel your policy. If you wish, you may use the cash value in other ways.

You can borrow part or all of the cash value as a *policy loan*. When you take a policy loan, the insurance continues. If you die while the loan is unpaid, the death benefit is reduced by the amount of the unpaid loan. Many people take policy loans because the interest cost is often low.

You can use the cash value to buy *extended term insurance*. This gives you the same amount of coverage as the original policy, but for a shorter period of time. You pay no more premiums.

If you wish, you can use the cash value to buy *paid-up insurance*. This is a smaller amount of insurance which covers you until you die. You do not pay any more premiums for it.

Table of Cash Values. Cash-value life insurance policies usually have a table showing the cash value after each year the policy has been in effect. Part of a cash-value table for a whole life policy is shown below.

TABLE OF CASH VALUES

End of Year	Cash and Loan Values per $1,000	Extended Term		Paid-Up Whole Life per $1,000
		Years	Days	
1	$ 0	0	0	$ 0
5	40.55	11	97	149
10	106.06	18	237	333
15	176.78	20	153	474
20	254.96	20	76	590

You read the table this way. Suppose you had paid premiums for 5 years on a $20,000 cash-value policy. If you then canceled the policy, you would be paid 20 × $40.55, or $811 in cash.

Rather than canceling the policy, you could borrow up to $811 on a policy loan. You could continue the insurance as term insurance of $20,000 for 11 years and 97 days. Or, you could take paid-up whole life insurance of $2,980 (20 × $149).

Written Practice 1

Use the table on page 221 for these problems.

1. How much cash would you get if you canceled a $50,000 policy after paying premiums for 15 years? **$8,839**

2. How much could you borrow on a policy loan after paying premiums for 5 years on a $30,000 policy?

3. You decide to cancel your $40,000 policy after you have paid premiums on it for 10 years. How many years and days of term insurance for $40,000 could you buy for the cash value?

4. Rolf Ludwig has paid premiums for 20 years on a $100,000 policy. He no longer needs that much coverage, so he takes paid-up insurance. What amount of paid-up insurance does he get?

5. Monica Beaumont has had a $50,000 policy for 20 years. She can no longer pay the premiums. She wants the most insurance coverage she can get for at least 10 years by using the cash values. If she cancels the coverage:
   a. How much extended term insurance would she get?
   b. How long would the extended term insurance continue?
   c. How much paid-up life would she get?
   d. Should she take the extended term or the paid-up insurance?

6. Chris Fong canceled his $25,000 policy after being insured for 10 years and paying $3,462.50 in premiums. He took cash when he canceled the policy.
   a. What was the cash value of the policy when it was canceled?
   b. What was the difference between the total premiums paid and the cash value of the policy?

Dividends. After you have been insured for several years, many insurance companies return part of your premium to you each year. The part that the company returns is called a **dividend**. The difference between the premium you pay and the amount you get back is called the *net premium*. Insurance on which dividends are paid is called *participating insurance*.

Dividend notices are usually sent with the next year's premium notice. When you get a dividend notice, you can usually do one of these things:

(1) Deduct the dividend from the premium due, and pay the difference.

(2) Leave the dividend with the company to buy more insurance.

(3) Take the dividend in cash.

Written Practice 2

1. You have a life insurance policy for $25,000. The annual premium is $280. You are now applying an annual dividend of $41.60 to your next premium. What amount should you send for your next premium? **$238.40**

2. Muriel Rurales has received notice of a $51.60 dividend paid on her life insurance policy. She will subtract that dividend from her next premium of $342.20. What will be her net premium payment?

3. Gert Lutka has finished paying premiums on a 20-payment life policy for $30,000. She paid annual premiums of $25.92 per $1,000. Over the 20 years, she received a total of $2,364 in dividends which she used to pay part of the premiums. What was the net cost of the premiums for the 20 years?

4. Sol Upata bought a whole life policy for $25,000 at an annual premium of $342.50. He held the policy for 10 years and was paid a total of $450 in dividends. At the end of ten years he canceled the policy and took the cash value of $2,205.
   a. What was the net cost of the insurance for the ten years?
   b. What was the average net cost per year?

Total premiums
– Dividends

Net premiums
– Cash value

Net cost

5. After paying premiums for 15 years, Vince Copollo canceled his $35,000 policy and took the cash value of $120 per thousand. Vince had paid an annual premium of $13.50 per thousand. Dividends had amounted to a total of $1,155. What was the net cost of the policy for the 15 years?

6. Della Starr is leaving her dividend of $203.50 with the insurance company to earn simple interest at the rate of 6% per year. How much interest will she earn on it the first year?

Terms to Remember

   beneficiary   cash value   dividend

   a. The amount that is returned if a policy is canceled
   b. Part of a premium returned by the company
   c. The person or organization to whom death benefits are paid

Review 54

1. a. Divide $432.50 by 1,000
   b. Subtract 0.805 from 6.5
   c. Multiply $14.75 by 0.2
   d. 5.6 L + 500 mL = ? L
   e. 250 g × 6 = ? kg
   f. 5 t ÷ 8 = ? t
   g. What is the simple interest on $560 for one year at 7%?
   h. Round 2.0749 to the nearest hundredth
   i. What percent greater than $2,500 is $3,100?
   ★**j.** $43.96 is $33\frac{1}{3}$% more than what amount?
   ★**k.** Express $5\frac{7}{8}$ as a decimal

2. At the end of 10 years, Abe Campo canceled his $30,000 life insurance policy and took the cash value of $108 per thousand. His premiums had been $16.50 per $1,000. His dividends had totaled $660.
   a. What total amount of premiums had he paid?
   b. What was the cash value of the policy?
   c. What was the net cost of the insurance for 10 years?

3. The Craigs paid $60,000 for their home. Their average yearly expenses of home ownership are mortgage interest, $2,760; taxes, $1,546; insurance, $294; repairs, $900; loss of interest on cash investment, $1,800; depreciation at $2\frac{1}{2}\%$ of the purchase price. What is their average cost:
   a. per year?
   b. per month?

4. Deborah Draper has $75,000 of homeowners insurance with the Frontier Insurance Company, and $50,000 with the Planet Company. What is each company's share of a $20,000 loss?

5. To insulate his home, Evan Davis rented a power stapler at $4.50 a day, or $1 an hour. He kept the stapler for 2 days and 4 hours. He also used 3 boxes of staples at $2.95 a box. What was the total cost of the stapler and the staples?

6. During a heating season, Serena Luan had 4 deliveries of heating oil: 597 L; 649 L; 579 L; and 673 L. The average price of the oil was $37\frac{1}{2}$¢ per liter. What was the total cost of the oil she bought?

7. A discount store advertises drapes at $\frac{1}{3}$ off the regular price. The full price is $19.95. What is the discount store's price?

8. A six-pack of canned soda costs $1.79. What is the price per can?

9. Melvin Okara is paid a 4% commission on all sales up to $375,000 a year, and 5% on sales over $375,000 a year. What is his commission for a year in which his total sales were $525,000?

10. Peggy Kafka's regular work time is $7\frac{1}{2}$ hours per day, 5 days a week. Her pay rate is $8 an hour. What is Peggy's pay rate:
    a. per day?
    b. per week?

11. What is the FICA tax on wages of $15,600 at a rate of 6.7%?

★12. Joseph Lobo is paying $624 a year for his car insurance premiums. This is 30% more than his sister is paying. How much is his sister paying?

★13. A lawn mower is on an end-of-season sale at $276.25. This is only 65% of the full price. What was the full price?

★14. Luisa Locarno is self-employed. Luisa's net income last year was $26,800. She paid self-employment tax on her income at 9.35%. What was her self-employment tax last year?

★15. Kenmore Realtors sold Ming Li's property for $59,990. The realtor's commission was 7%. What was the amount of Ming's net proceeds from the sale of his property?

HEALTH INSURANCE

The expenses of a serious illness or injury can quickly add up to many thousands of dollars. To reduce those risks of financial loss, you will want to have **health insurance**.

If you work for someone else, your employer may provide a *group health insurance* plan for you. You may carry *individual health insurance* for yourself and your family, in addition to or instead of group coverage.

Health insurance is sold by insurance companies and by organizations such as Blue Cross and Blue Shield. The federal government has the Medicare program for older and disabled persons. States have Medicaid programs for people with low incomes.

Kinds of Health Insurance. These are the general kinds of health insurance that you may have:

Hospital insurance pays in-hospital expenses such as room, meals, nursing care, operating room, lab tests, X-rays, and medicines.

Surgical insurance pays surgeons' fees.

Medical insurance pays doctors' fees and some other expenses.

All three of these kinds of insurance give limited protection. They are sometimes called "basic health coverage." For long and expensive illnesses or injury, you may have two other kinds of insurance:

Major medical insurance covers all or most of the hospital, surgical, medical, and other health care expenses of a major illness or injury. Major medical coverage may be in addition to basic health coverage, or it may replace basic health coverage.

Disability income insurance replaces part of the income you lose if you are out of work for a long time because of illness or accident.

Figuring Health Insurance Benefits. The benefits of health insurance are often stated as maximums that will be paid. For example, a policy may state the maximum number of days and the amount per day that will be paid for hospital care. The policy may have a schedule of surgeons' fees for different kinds of operations. It may limit the kind and amount of doctors' services and other expenses that will be paid. You must pay all amounts above those limits.

**Written
Practice 1**

1. Wanda Reese's insurance pays up to $90 a day for up to 60 days in the hospital, plus all surgeons' charges. Wanda had an operation and stayed 12 days in the hospital. The hospital charged $120 a day. The surgeon's fee was $900. What amount would the insurance pay? **$1,980**

2. Sigmund Firth's hospital bill for 8 days was $1,850. His surgical bill was $1,200. Sigmund's insurance covered $1,200 of the hospital bill, and $950 of the surgical bill.
   a. What total amount did the company pay?
   b. What total amount did Sigmund have to pay?

3. Faith Estey was injured in an accident. The expenses were 10 days of hospital care at $225 per day; tests, X-rays, and medicine, $985; surgeon's fee, $1,265. Faith's hospital insurance covered $1,250 of the hospital care and $500 of the tests, X-rays, and medicine. Her surgical insurance benefit was limited to $800.
   a. What was the total of all the expenses?
   b. How much did the company have to pay?
   c. How much did Faith have to pay?

4. Charley Benoit's disability income insurance pays him 50% of his regular wage for all days beyond the first 30 days that he is out of work because of illness or injury. Charley is injured and loses 45 days of work. His regular daily pay is $52. How much disability insurance will he collect? **$390**

Deductible and Coinsurance Features. The maximum benefits under major medical insurance are much greater than for basic coverage, so the cost is greater. To help keep down premium costs, many major medical policies have a deductible feature and a coinsurance feature. Both of these features result in your paying part of your expenses.

As with car and homeowners insurance, deductible health insurance requires you to pay the first part of the expenses before the company pays anything. The deductible amount you pay might be from $50 to $500, or more.

The **coinsurance** feature makes you cooperate in sharing the expenses above the deductible amount. For example, the company might pay 80% of the expenses above the deductible amount. You would have to pay the other 20% of the expenses above the deductible amount.

Here is an example of the way that deductible coinsurance works:

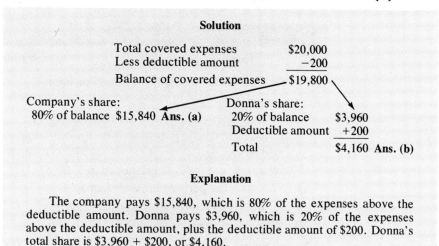

Example

Donna Britt is badly injured. Her hospital, surgical, and medical expenses that are covered by major medical insurance total $20,000. The policy has a $200 deductible feature and an 80% coinsurance feature. (a) What amount will the company pay? (b) What amount must Donna pay?

Solution

Total covered expenses	$20,000
Less deductible amount	−200
Balance of covered expenses	$19,800

Company's share:
  80% of balance $15,840 **Ans. (a)**

Donna's share:
  20% of balance $3,960
  Deductible amount +200
  Total $4,160 **Ans. (b)**

Explanation

The company pays $15,840, which is 80% of the expenses above the deductible amount. Donna pays $3,960, which is 20% of the expenses above the deductible amount, plus the deductible amount of $200. Donna's total share is $3,960 + $200, or $4,160.

Written Practice 2

1. Andre Delgado has health care expenses of $40,000 that are covered by major medical insurance. The policy has a $500 deductible feature and a 75% coinsurance feature. (a) How much of the expenses must Andre pay? **$10,375** (b) How much will the company pay? **$29,625**

2. You are injured in a car accident. Your major medical coverage has a $100 deductible feature and an 80% coinsurance feature. Your covered expenses total $43,500. (a) What will be the company's share? (b) What will be your share?

3. Elena Ramos was hospitalized with a serious illness for many days. The total hospital bill was $18,795. Surgeons' bills and other doctors' bills totaled $4,325. Home nurse visits, medications, and other treatments cost $2,648. Elena's major medical insurance paid 85% of the total medical expenses above the deductible amount of $250. (a) How much did the company pay? (b) What was Elena's share of the total expenses?

4. Gloria and Leon Barba's major medical insurance has a $100 deductible feature that applies to *each person's* claims in any year. The company pays 80% of each person's covered expenses above the deductible amount for the year. Last year, Gloria's covered expenses totaled $1,386, and Leon's covered expenses totaled $1,473.65. What amount did the company pay last year for (a) Gloria's expenses and (b) Leon's expenses?

5. Celeste Hogarth has major medical insurance with a $75 deductible feature and a 90% coinsurance feature. Last year Celeste made a claim to the company for a total of $1,682.50. The insurance company said that $134.50 of the expenses were not covered by the insurance, but paid 90% of the rest of the claim above the deductible amount.
  a. How much did the company pay?
  b. How much did Celeste have to pay?

Terms to Remember

coinsurance   health insurance

  a. Reduces risks of loss from illness or injury
  b. Makes you share in expenses above a deductible amount

Review 55

1. a. Express $102\frac{1}{2}\%$ as a decimal
   b. Add $6\frac{1}{2}$, $2\frac{3}{4}$, and $4\frac{7}{8}$
   c. 2.4 m = ? cm
   d. 1 m² = ? cm²
   e. What amount is $62\frac{1}{2}\%$ greater than $36?
   f. $2.80 is what percent greater than $2.40?
   g. What is the simple interest on $900 for a year at $5\frac{1}{2}\%$?
   h. Round $279.8981 to the nearest cent

2. Ivan Barzak had an operation that required 8 days in the hospital at $175 a day. The surgeon's bill was $1,275, and other doctors' charges totaled $250. Ivan's basic health coverage paid only $120 a day for the hospital, $1,000 for the surgeon, and $250 for other doctors.
  a. What total amount did the insurance pay?
  b. What amount did Ivan have to pay?

3. Callie Noonan has major medical insurance coverage, with a $250 deductible feature and a 90% coinsurance feature. Her total covered expenses last year were $870. Of that amount, what was (a) the company's share, (b) Callie's share?

4. After paying premiums on a $50,000 life insurance policy for 8 years, Royal Blake canceled the policy and took the cash value of $3,250. During those 8 years, he had paid $5,700 in premiums and had received a total of $722 in dividends.
  a. What was the net cost of the policy for the 8 years?
  b. What was the average net cost of the policy per year?

5. Claire Lenseth gets a discount of 20% on her auto insurance because she has had driver training and has a good driving record. Without the discount, the full annual premium would be $380. What is Claire's premium per year?

6. The Homeway Appliance Store will sell and install a dishwasher for a total of $489.50. Midtown Appliances sells the same model machine for $429.95, but charges $49.75 for delivery and installation. Which store charges less? How much less?

HIGHER EDUCATION

So far, you may not have thought very much about the benefits and costs of education. You've had to go to school, and somebody else has paid for it! For education beyond high school, though, you have to think about the benefits, the costs, and how you can get the money to pay for it.

Benefits of Higher Education. You cannot put an accurate dollar value on the benefits of education beyond high school. The amount of money you could hope to gain from further education depends on many things: how much and what kind of education you get; the job market for your skills and abilities over a working life of 35 to 50 years; your own basic skills, abilities, ambition, effort, and health.

Until recently, a college graduate could expect to earn as much as 50 percent or several hundred thousand dollars more in a working lifetime than could a noncollege graduate. Each additional year of education might add $1,000 or more per year to a worker's earnings. That advantage has decreased in recent years, partly because many college-educated people are competing for two few jobs requiring a college education. As a result, many college-educated people have had to take jobs that don't really require a college education.

These statements about higher education still seem to be true:

(1) A college education does not guarantee you a good job with good pay, but the more education you have the better your chances are of getting and holding good jobs, increasing your responsibility, and increasing your income.

(2) In technical and specialized fields, the kind of education you get is often more important than the amount. For example, to work as a skilled mechanic, technical training and experience are more important than a college degree.

(3) You must have certain amounts and kinds of college education to be a doctor, lawyer, engineer, nurse, teacher, or a professional in many other fields.

(4) Many of the benefits of higher education are not economic benefits: personal satisfaction, broader knowledge and understanding, greater ability to adapt to changing conditions, and increased ability to get along with other people.

Figuring Costs of Education. You can estimate the probable costs of higher education quite accurately. Costs among colleges differ greatly, so you need to get the best facts that you can, and then figure carefully.

A major expense that you have to plan for is *tuition*. Tuition is the basic instructional charge or fee that you pay to a school or college for being a student. Tuition for full-time study is often charged for a full academic year. Tuition may be charged for a semester ($\frac{1}{2}$ academic year), a trimester ($\frac{1}{3}$ academic year), or a quarter ($\frac{1}{4}$ academic year). For part-time study, tuition is often charged by the credit hour or semester hour. Those are basic units for measuring course credit.

Other than for tuition, you may have to pay fees such as a student activity fee, laboratory fee, and health-accident insurance fee. You will have to buy books and supplies. You may have expenses for room, meals, and transportation. You will also have to plan for clothing and personal care, recreation and entertainment.

Written Practice 1

1. Matt Barnes estimates that he will have these annual expenses to live on campus at a four-year college: tuition, $1,050; fees, including health insurance, $260; books, $285; room and board, $2,250; clothing and personal expenses, $400; transportation, $450; recreation and entertainment, $200. What is the total estimated cost for:
   a. one year? **$4,895**
   b. four years? **$19,580**

2. Dawn Janosek lives at home and attends the local two-year community college. She estimates these expenses for an academic year: tuition, $920; activity fee, $78; accident and health insurance, $31; books and supplies, $235; personal and entertainment expenses, $575; transportation by bus, $235. What will be her total estimated expenses for two years?

3. Kevin Sheng plans to take a one-year program at a private business school. He estimates these expenses for the year: tuition, two semesters at $1,375 per semester; books and supplies, $225; laboratory fees, $170; living expenses, $2,300; personal expenses, $1,000. What is the total estimated cost for one year?

4. Tricia Wicker is a second-year student at a two-year college. She lives with her parents and uses a family car to get to the college each day. She estimates that her expenses this year will be 10% greater than last year. Her expenses last year were tuition, $1,125; fees and insurance, $135; books and supplies, $275; personal, $675; transportation, $975.
   a. What were her total expenses last year?
   b. What will be her total estimated expenses for this year?

5. Vernon Katz has a full-time job, but he is taking courses in the evening at a local college. Each semester he takes two, 3-credit hour courses. The tuition is $60 per credit hour. Books average $25 per course, and transportation averages $95 a semester. What is Vernon's educational cost:
   a. per semester?
   b. per year?

6. Jenny Polito took a total of 32 credit hours of course work in two semesters. She paid tuition of $1,800 each semester. What was the tuition charge per credit hour?

Written Practice 2

1. Regaldo Montez spent a total of $5,900 to earn an associate degree at a two-year college. He then transferred to a four-year college and, in two years, earned a bachelor's degree. His total costs at the four-year college were $13,020.
   a. What were his total college expenses for four years? **$18,920**
   b. What were his average college expenses per year? **$4,730**

2. Norma Dorsey went to college for five years and earned a master's degree. Her expenses for the five years were $4,400, $4,710, $5,275, $5,590, and $6,725. What was her average college cost per year?

3. Chon Li can go to a local four-year college and live at home for an estimated cost of $3,200 a year. If he goes to another college and lives away from home, the cost will be $6,800 per year.
   a. How much more would four years cost at the more expensive college?
   b. What percent more would the cost be for the more expensive college?

4. Petra Omatta is planning her expenses for four years of college. She estimates that her first year's expenses will be $6,800, and that her fourth year's expenses will be 22% greater. What are her estimated expenses for the fourth year?

5. Harold Queen's college expenses for this year, and his estimated expenses for next year, are these:

	This Year	**Next Year**
Tuition	$4,000	$4,240
Fees	500	550
Books and supplies	450	450
Room and board	3,600	3,960
Other	1,500	1,750

To the nearest whole percent, what is the estimated percent of increase in:
   a. tuition?
   b. room and board?
   c. total expenses?

6. Sandra Talbot's employer pays the cost of tuition and books for courses she takes to increase her job effectiveness. Sandra pays all her other expenses. Last year, her employer paid $750, and Sandra paid $350. To the nearest whole percent, what percent of the total expenses were paid by:
   a. her employer?
   b. Sandra?

Paying for Higher Education. The costs of education are high, and they are rising. If you really want more education, though, you can find many ways to pay for it. You can be sure that your money is well spent for education, because it is an investment in your future.

To finance your education, you can use your own savings. Maybe your parents can help. You can earn a lot of money from summer and part-time jobs while you are in college. In some college programs you can work and get both academic credit and pay. Maybe you can get an academic, athletic, or music scholarship. You can borrow money at low interest rates from many government and private sources. Money for education may be available to you as the child of a deceased worker or veteran.

You may want to postpone further education, or to do only part-time study, until you can earn and save more money. If so, you might look for a job in a business that will pay part or all of your education expenses. The armed forces offer many kinds of education and training that you can use for a career in or out of the military service. They might finance part or all of your college degree.

Written Practice 3

1. Upton Webb estimates that two years at a community college would cost a total of $4,700. He has $2,250 in savings, $500 in scholarship aid, and $2,000 from his parents.
   a. Does he have enough money for the two years?   **Yes**
   b. How much more or less money than he needs does he have?
   $50 more

2. Carrie Elkins estimates that four years of college away from home will cost a total of $25,200. Carrie has these sources of money: savings, $3,000; estimated summer earnings, $4,000; part-time work in college, $9,000; scholarship aid, $1,000; help from parents, $2,000. To go to that college, how much will she need to borrow or get from other sources?

3. Fess Humbolt estimates that his college costs per year will be these: tuition, $1,900; fees, $300; books, $300; room and board, $2,500; clothing, personal, and transportation, $1,000; other, $500. He figures that he will have these amounts available per year: savings, $1,000; summer earnings, $1,200; student loan, $2,000. How much per year will he need from other sources?

4. Ingrid Jaffe is a high school senior. She plans to go to a junior college for two years at an estimated cost of $2,500 a year. She has only $500 in savings but she hopes to earn a total of $2,100 in two summers of work. She also hopes to work part-time during the school year at an average of $4 an hour. How many hours would she have to work during the two school years to earn the amount she will need?

5. Kenneth Storey plans to borrow $1,800 a year for four years to finance his education. The loan will be interest-free until graduation, but after that he will have to pay interest at 7% a year on the total loan.
a. What total amount does he plan to borrow?
b. What will be the yearly interest on the total loan?

6. After graduating from college, Terry Jarvis found that she had spent a total of $24,200 for her college education. Of that amount, $9,680 had come from her own savings and earnings. The rest was from other sources.
a. What fractional part of her expenses had she paid?
b. What fractional part had come from other sources?

7. As a full-time student, Kirt Wessel wants to work 15 hours a week during the 32 weeks of the college year. If he does that amount of work at $4.50 an hour, what will be his total earnings for a school year?

Review 56

1. a. Subtract $16\frac{5}{8}$ from $25\frac{1}{4}$
b. Multiply $5\frac{3}{4}$ by $2\frac{1}{3}$
c. Multiply 30.75 by 4.2
d. Divide $60.05 by 5
e. Round 0.06409 to the nearest thousandth
f. What is a year's simple interest on $695.50 at 10%?
★**g.** What amount decreased by $\frac{1}{7}$ of itself equals $258?

2. Roscoe Norwood's estimated expenses for his next year at college are tuition, $1,890; fees, $275; transportation, $870; books, $310; other, $900. To pay those expenses he has $875 in savings, $1,250 from his parents, and a scholarship for $500. How much more money must he get to pay his expenses?

3. Olivia Mora's health insurance has a $500 deductible feature and a 90% coinsurance feature. If she has $5,000 of covered health expenses in a year, how much would the company pay?

4. The Guzmans' expenses on a 7-day fly-drive vacation trip were these: air fare, $739; lodging, $418; food, $282; car rental costs, $225; other, $65.
a. What was the total cost of their trip?
b. What was the average cost per day?

5. Homer Audet's property in Oakdale is assessed for $9,000. The tax rate in Oakdale is 0.06472.
a. How much is Homer's tax?
b. What is the tax rate per $1,000?

6. Priscilla Denton pays an annual premium of $140 for her renters insurance on the contents of her apartment. If she moves to another apartment, the premium will be $126. By what percent would her premium decrease?

INCOME TAXES
AND SOCIAL SECURITY BENEFITS

You have already learned how to figure federal withholding taxes and social security taxes on your income. In this unit, you will learn more about federal, state, and local income taxes. You will also learn to figure some of the benefits that workers and their dependents get from social security.

When you have finished this unit, you should be able to:

- figure federal individual income taxes, using tax tables

- find refund or balance due on federal income taxes
- ★● figure federal individual income taxes, using tax rate schedules
- find state and city income taxes
- find workers' social security retirement and disability benefits, using a table
- figure dependents' social security benefits, using a table
- read, write, speak, and recognize the meanings of some basic terms used in figuring income taxes

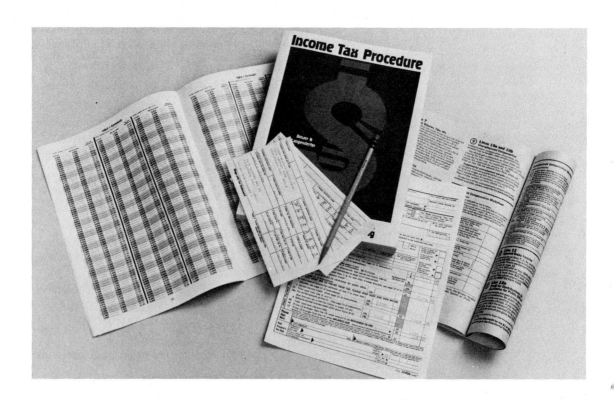

FEDERAL INCOME TAX

The income of citizens and others who live in the United States is taxed by the federal government. The tax is called the **U.S. individual income tax**. If you are a taxpayer, you must file a tax return by April 15 of each year, reporting your tax for the year before. The **tax return** shows how your tax was figured.

I NEED

YOUR TAX!

Figuring Adjusted Gross Income. In the first part of your income tax return, you report your gross income. Gross income includes money received from sources such as wages, salaries, commissions, bonuses, tips, interest, dividends, prizes, pensions, rents, gain on sale of property, and profits from a business or profession.

From your gross income, you may subtract some kinds of expenses called *adjustments to income*. Adjustments to income include payments for moving expenses, employees' business expenses, payments to retirement plans, alimony, and interest penalty for early withdrawal of savings. The amount left after the adjustments are made is your **adjusted gross income**.

$$\begin{array}{ccc} \textbf{Gross} & \textbf{Adjustments} & \textbf{Adjusted Gross} \\ \textbf{Income} & - \quad \textbf{to Income} & = \quad \textbf{Income} \end{array}$$

Written Practice 1

1. Last year, Jeanne Osata earned a salary of $20,000, commission of $8,000, and interest of $275. During the year Jeanne had moving expenses of $800 and $150 of business expenses not paid by her employer.
   a. What was Jeanne's gross income for the year? **$28,275**
   b. What was the total of her adjustments to income? **$950**
   c. What was Jeanne's adjusted gross income? **$27,325**

2. Peter Sutro's gross income for a year was $26,438. Adjustments to his income totaled $1,693. What was his adjusted gross income?

3. Your income for a year was salary, $18,750; commission, $4,283; profit from a part-time business, $3,681; other, $449. Your adjustments to income totaled $605. What was your adjusted gross income?

4. Al and Golda Kagle's wages totaled $36,742 for a year. They got $1,855 from tips and $1,261 from interest. They paid $1,800 into a retirement fund and had a penalty of $94 for withdrawing savings early. What was their adjusted gross income?

5. Last year, Lenore Keola earned $8,725 in wages and $10,436 in tips. Lenore's employer paid her a bonus of $375 at the end of the year. She made a profit of $675 on the sale of some property, and she earned $247 from dividends on stock. Lenore had no adjustments to income. What was her adjusted gross income for the year?

Figuring Taxable Income. After figuring adjusted gross income, you figure your taxable income. *Taxable income* is the amount on which you actually pay tax; it is your adjusted gross income less deductions and exemptions.

Deductions are expenses that you may claim to reduce the amount of tax you pay. You may deduct interest paid; property, sales, and state or local income taxes; losses on sale of property; many business and professional expenses; and contributions to many kinds of organizations. A "zero bracket amount" or "standard deduction" is included in the tax tables. If you want to claim a greater amount than the zero bracket amount, you may itemize your deductions and subtract the excess deductions from your adjusted gross income.

An **exemption** is an amount of income, such as $1,000, that is free from tax. You can claim one exemption for yourself, one for a spouse, and one for each dependent. For example, a single (unmarried) person with one dependent parent can claim two exemptions. A married couple with three dependent children has five exemptions.

You figure your taxable income by subtracting your excess deductions, if any, from adjusted gross income. From that amount, you then subtract your exemptions, as shown in the following example.

Example

Both Roy Brown and Hudson Maxon have adjusted gross incomes of $30,000. Brown has deductions of $1,500 more than the zero bracket amount. Maxon has no excess deductions. Both Brown and Maxon claim 2 exemptions at $1,000 each. What is Brown's taxable income, and what is Maxon's taxable income?

Solution

	Brown	Maxon
Adjusted gross income	$30,000	$30,000
Excess deductions	1,500	–0–
Total	$28,500	$30,000
Exemptions (2 × $1,000)	2,000	2,000
Taxable income	$26,500	$28,000

Written Practice 2

1. Last year, Nanette Quayle's adjusted gross income was $23,500. She itemized her deductions and had an excess of $2,480 more than the zero bracket amount. Nanette claimed 3 exemptions of $1,000 each. What was her taxable income last year? **$18,020**

2. Starr Jenks had adjusted gross income last year of $19,750. He did not itemize deductions, but he claimed 4 exemptions at $1,000 each. What was his taxable income for the year? **$15,750**

3. In filling out her tax return, Sonja Olafsen found that her allowable deductions were $3,245 more than the zero bracket amount. Her adjusted gross income for the year was $23,940, and she claimed 5 exemptions at $1,000 each. What was her taxable income?

Using Tax Tables. If your taxable income is $50,000 or less, you may use a tax table like the one shown below to figure your tax. An average or zero bracket amount of deductions is provided in the table.

19-- TAX TABLE

Taxable Income		Filing Status			
At least	But less than	Single	Married filing jointly	Married filing separately	Head of household
$15,500	$15,550	$2,728	$2,138	$3,272	$2,580
15,550	15,600	2,743	2,149	3,290	2,593
15,600	15,650	2,758	2,159	3,308	2,606
15,650	15,700	2,772	2,169	3,327	2,618
15,700	15,750	2,787	2,180	3,345	2,631
15,750	15,800	2,802	2,190	3,363	2,644
15,800	15,850	2,817	2,200	3,381	2,657
15,850	15,900	2,832	2,211	3,400	2,670
15,900	15,950	2,846	2,221	3,418	2,683
15,950	16,000	2,861	2,232	3,436	2,695
20,000	20,050	4,133	3,191	5,060	3,825
20,050	20,100	4,150	3,202	5,081	3,841
20,100	20,150	4,167	3,214	5,102	3,856
20,150	20,200	4,184	3,226	5,123	3,871
20,200	20,250	4,200	3,239	5,145	3,887
20,250	20,300	4,217	3,253	5,166	3,902
20,300	20,350	4,234	3,267	5,187	3,917
20,350	20,400	4,251	3,280	5,208	3,932
20,400	20,450	4,267	3,294	5,230	3,948
20,450	20,500	4,284	3,308	5,251	3,963

To use the tax table, you first find the amount of your taxable income in the "At least . . . But less than" column. You then read across that line to the column that indicates your filing status as "single," "married filing jointly," "married filing separately," or "head of household." The amount shown where your income line and your filing status column meet is the amount of your tax.

For example, if your taxable income is $15,530 and you are single, your tax is $2,728. If you are married and filing a joint return with your spouse, your tax on income of $15,530 is $2,138.

---

*In general, a "head of household" is an unmarried or legally separated person who pays more than half the cost of keeping a home for a dependent father or mother, or for an unmarried child, grandchild, or stepchild.

Oral Practice 3

What is the income tax on these amounts of taxable income? (*Use the table on page 237.*)

$15,800 is at least $15,800, but less than $15,850

	Taxable Income	Filing Status
1.	$15,775	Single
2.	$15,775	Head of household
3.	$15,800	Married filing jointly
4.	$15,800	Married filing separately
5.	$15,999	Single
6.	$20,100	Married filing jointly
7.	$20,495	Head of household
8.	$20,005	Single
9.	$20,200	Married filing separately
10.	$20,349	Single

Written Practice 4

1. Mr. and Mrs. Himstreet's taxable income last year was $20,350. They filed a joint tax return. What was their tax?   **$3,280**

2. Igor Savitch is single. His taxable income for a year is $15,620. What is his income tax?

3. What is the amount of income tax to be paid by a head of household whose taxable income is $15,749?

4. Jorge and Jessica Santana are married but are filing separate tax returns. Their taxable income last year was $20,480. What was the amount of their tax?

5. Keiko Okano is unmarried and has taxable income of $20,400 per year. How much less tax will she pay if she qualifies as a head of household rather than as single?

6. Patrick and Sheila McKeon are married and have an annual taxable income of $20,375. How much more tax must they pay if they file separately rather than jointly?

Figuring Refund or Balance Due. If you have been employed during a tax year, your employer will have withheld money for your income tax. If you have been self-employed, you will have paid self-employment tax. In either case, the amount of tax paid in advance is probably too much or too little.

When you have figured your tax on the tax return, you can then figure whether you owe more money or are entitled to a refund. If too much withholding or self-employment tax has been paid, the government will refund the difference. If less than the amount of your tax has been paid, you must pay the difference to the government.

Written Practice 5

1. Your employer withheld $3,712 from your wages last year for income tax. Your tax return for last year shows a total tax of $3,489. How much should the government refund to you?

2. Beryl Imree is self-employed. During last year she paid the government $7,836 in self-employment tax. Her tax return shows her total tax last year as $7,920. How much additional tax does Beryl owe the government?

Use the tax table on page 237 for Problems 3 and 4.

3. Jordan Ogamma is single and is not the head of a household. Last year, his taxable income was $15,640 and his employers withheld $2,995.20 from his wages for income tax.
   a. What was Jordan's actual tax for last year?
   b. What was the amount of Jordan's refund?

4. Mr. and Mrs. Tansey showed a taxable income of $20,280 on their joint tax return for a year. Their employers had withheld $2,716 for their income tax.
   a. What was the Tansey's actual tax for the year?
   b. What balance of tax did the Tanseys owe?

Terms to Remember

adjusted gross income $\qquad$ deductions $\qquad$ exemption
tax return $\qquad$ U.S. individual income tax

   a. A federal tax on incomes
   b. A form showing how income tax was figured
   c. Gross income less adjustments to income
   d. Expenses claimed to reduce amount of tax
   e. An amount of income that is free from tax

Review 57

1. a. Show $137\frac{1}{2}\%$ as a decimal
   b. Add 3.4 m + 6.05 m + 14.75 m
   c. What is the simple interest on $1,500 at $8\frac{1}{2}\%$ for a year?

2. Carmello Canso's taxable income last year was $15,600. She is single. Her employer withheld $2,704 from her wages for income tax. Using the tax table on page 237, how much additional tax does she owe for the year?

3. Last year, Doug Humbolt's college expenses totaled $4,250. He expects his expenses to be 8% greater this year. To the nearest hundred dollars, what will be his expected college expenses this year?

4. Using the table of cash values on page 221, how much could be borrowed on a policy loan after paying premiums for 10 years on a $25,000 insurance policy?

5. Bert Marden traveled 630 km on 45 L of gas. How many kilometers per liter of gas did he average?

FEDERAL INCOME TAX (concluded)

Using a Tax Rate Schedule. In most cases, if your taxable income is $50,000 or more, you have to figure your tax with Tax Rate Schedule X, Y, or Z instead of the tax tables. A part of each of those tax rate schedules is shown below.

Schedule X is for single persons who do not qualify for Schedule Y or Schedule Z.

Schedule Y is for married couples who file joint returns, and for qualifying widows and widowers.

Schedule Z is for unmarried or legally separated persons who are heads of households. A *head of household* is an unmarried person who has a home shared by a dependent, or by an unmarried child, grandchild, or stepchild who is not a dependent. The rates in Schedule Z are lower than the rates in Schedule X.

Schedule X — SINGLE TAXPAYERS not qualifying for rates in Schedule Y and Z

If the taxable income is:		The tax is:	
Over —	But not over —		of the amount over —
$41,500 —	$ 55,300	$12,068 + 50%	— $ 41,500
$55,300 —	$ 81,800	$18,968 + 50%	— $ 55,300
$81,800 —	$108,300	$32,218 + 50%	— $ 81,800
$108,300 —	. . . . .	$45,468 + 50%	— $108,300

Schedule Y — MARRIED TAXPAYERS FILING JOINT RETURNS and QUALIFYING WIDOWS AND WIDOWERS

If the taxable income is:		The tax is:	
Over —	But not over —		of the amount over —
$ 45,800 —	$ 60,000	$11,457 + 44%	— $ 45,800
$ 60,000 —	$ 85,600	$17,705 + 49%	— $ 60,000
$ 85,600 —	$109,400	$30,249 + 50%	— $ 85,600
$109,400 —	$162,400	$42,149 + 50%	— $109,400

Schedule Z — UNMARRIED (or legally separated) TAXPAYERS WHO QUALIFY AS HEADS OF HOUSEHOLD

If the taxable income is:		The tax is:	
Over —	But not over —		of the amount over —
$ 44,700 —	$ 60,600	$12,498 + 49%	— $ 44,700
$ 60,600 —	$ 81,800	$20,289 + 50%	— $ 60,600
$ 81,800 —	$108,300	$30,889 + 50%	— $ 81,800
$108,300 —	$161,300	$44,139 + 50%	— $108,300
$161,300 —	. . . . .	$70,639 + 50%	— $161,300

Tax rate schedules

This example shows you how to use a tax rate schedule:

Example

Alexis Barr has taxable income of $53,000. She is single and is not the head of a household. What is her tax income?

Solution		Explanation
Tax on first $41,500	$12,068	Alexis uses Schedule X. The
50% of $11,500	5,750	schedule shows that the tax on
Total income tax	$17,818	$55,000 is $12,068 plus 50% of the amount over $41,500. The amount over $41,500 is $11,500. ($53,000 − $41,500 = $11,500) So, the tax is $12,068 + 50% of $11,500, or $17,818.

★Written Practice 1

Use the tax rate schedules on page 240 for these problems.

1. Use Schedule X to find the tax on these taxable incomes:

   a. $63,500 $23,068   **b.** $50,000   **c.** $88,200

2. Use Schedule Y to find the tax on these taxable incomes:

   a. $52,000 $14,185   **b.** $60,000   **c.** $92,250

3. Use Schedule Z to find the tax on these taxable incomes:

   a. $64,000 $21,989   **b.** $54,102   **c.** $83,600

★Written Practice 2

Use the tax rate schedules on page 240 for these problems.

1. Agatha Zeller had taxable income of $56,500. She was single and did not qualify to use Schedule Z. What was her tax for that year? **$19,568**

2. Mr. and Mrs. Bernarski had taxable income of $61,900 for a year. They filed a joint federal tax return. What was the correct amount of their tax for the year?

Be sure to use the correct tax rate schedule!

3. For a tax year, Hans Norge qualified as the head of a household. His taxable income that year was $55,100. What amount of federal income tax did Hans have to pay on that income?

4. Omar Yemen's employer withheld $23,240 in federal withholding tax from Omar's wages during a year. When Omar completed his tax return, he found that his taxable income for the year was $68,720. Using Schedule X, what was Omar's balance of tax due? **$2,438**

5. Mr. and Mrs. Riva's joint federal income tax return showed taxable income of $53,980 for the year. They had paid a total of $15,285.20 in withholding tax during the year. By how much was their tax overpaid?

6. During a recent year, Glenda Luang qualified as the head of a household. Her adjusted gross income for the year was $108,460. Her excess deductions totaled $5,460, and she claimed 3 exemptions at $1,000 each. What was Glenda's tax for the year? **$39,989**

7. Perry and Ada Lomax are married and they file a joint federal income tax return. On this tax return, their adjusted gross income is $72,735. They claim $4,285 in excess deductions. They also claim 6 exemptions at $1,000 each. They report that $18,467 has been withheld from their salary and wages during the year. What is the balance of tax due on their tax return?

★Review 58

1. **a.** $480 is 8% of what amount?
   b. What amount increased by 25% of itself is equal to $800?
   c. Express 15.625 as a mixed number in simplest form.
   d. What amount decreased by $\frac{1}{6}$ of itself equals $2,000?
   e. Show $23\frac{5}{8}$ as a decimal correct to two decimal places

2. Roberta Torres is single and is not the head of a household. Her taxable income is $50,500. Using Tax Rate Schedule X on page 240, what is her tax?

3. Karen Forbes pays an annual premium of $1,008 for auto insurance with Company A. This is 12% greater than Carol Denny pays for insurance with Company B. What is Carol Denny's annual premium?

4. The Gellers have $50,000 of homeowners insurance on their home. The policy requires that they insure for at least 80% of the replacement cost to collect the full amount of partial losses. Suppose that the Gellers have a fire that causes $15,000 of damage. At the time of the fire, the replacement cost of the building is $75,000. How much of the loss will the insurance company pay?

5. A sofabed has been marked down 30% to a sale price of $696.50. What was the full price?

6. Helene Holcomb's salary increased this year by $2,500. This was an increase of $\frac{1}{8}$ over her last year's salary.
   a. What was Helene's salary last year?
   b. What is her salary this year?

7. Julio Romero had an auction agency sell some household goods for him. The agency sold the goods for $1,680. The agency charged 20% commission and $65.70 for transporting the goods to the auction house. What were Julio's net proceeds from the sale?

STATE AND CITY INCOME TAX

Nearly all states tax the incomes of their residents. Many cities also have an income tax. State and city income tax rates are often shown as percents of taxable income. State tax rates may range from 1% to 16% or more of taxable income. City tax rates may range from $\frac{1}{2}$% to 2% of taxable income. *Taxable income* is gross income less adjustments, deductions, and exemptions.

Here is a table of tax rates that might be used by a state:

STATE TAX RATES

2% on the first $1,000 of taxable income
3% on the next $2,000 of taxable income
4% on the next $2,000 of taxable income
5% on the next $5,000 of taxable income
6% on the next $5,000 of taxable income
8% on the next $10,000 of taxable income
10% on the next $10,000 of taxable income
12% on all over $35,000 of taxable income

The state income tax is figured this way:

Example

Coretta Frish has taxable income of $13,500. What is her state income tax, using the rates shown in the table above?

Solution	Explanation
$0.02 \times \$1,000 = \$\ 20$ $0.03 \times \$2,000 = \ \ \ 60$ $0.04 \times \$2,000 = \ \ \ 80$ $0.05 \times \$5,000 = \ 250$ $0.06 \times \$3,500 = \ \underline{210}$ Total tax $\ \ \ \ \ \$620$	You multiply each part of the taxable income by the tax rate shown for that part in the table. You then add the amounts to find the total tax.

Use the state tax rate schedule above for these problems.

1. Willard Kipp's taxable income last year was $3,500. What was his state tax last year? **$100**

2. Your state income tax return for a year shows a taxable income of $10,000. What is your tax on that amount of income?

3. Ursula Young's total taxable income on which she must pay state income tax is $39,500.
   a. How much of that income is over $35,000?   **$4,500**
   b. What is the state tax on the amount of Ursula's income that is over $35,000?   **$540**

4. Gilbert Dumont's total taxable income is $44,650.
   a. How much of that income is taxed at 12%?
   b. What is the tax on the income that is taxed at 12%?

5. Hope Agan files a state income tax return that shows taxable income of $42,675. What is her tax on that amount?

6. Nolan Okara's gross income last year was $17,480. After subtracting his adjustments, deductions, and exemptions, Nolan's taxable income was $13,265. What was his state tax for that year?

Written Practice 2

1. In the city where they live, Mr. and Mrs. Laval have to pay a city income tax of 1.5% on their taxable income. If the Lavals' taxable income last year was $28,950, what was their tax?   **$434.25**

2. Noreen Boyle lives in the city of Spring Harbor. Spring Harbor charges an income tax of $\frac{1}{2}$% on the taxable income of its residents. Last year, Noreen's taxable income was $16,930. What was her city income tax for the year?

Use the table of state tax rates on page 243 for Problems 3 and 4.

3. Mario Lugo lives in the city of Tolliver. Mario's taxable income last year was $20,500. In addition to a state income tax, Mario had to pay a city income tax of 1% on his taxable income.
   a. What was Mario's state income tax last year?
   b. What was his city income tax last year?
   c. What was the total of his state and city income taxes?

4. The city of Beachview charges a 2% tax on the taxable income of its residents. The tax is in addition to the income tax charged by the state. Ester Alonzo lives in Beachview and has taxable income of $14,600. What is Ester's total city and state income tax?

Review 59   1. **a.** $84 is what percent less than $112?
    b. What amount is $66\frac{2}{3}\%$ greater than $21?
    c. What is $12\frac{1}{2}\%$ of $32.96?
    d. $9.32 is what percent greater than $6.99?
    e. What is the simple interest on $5,000 at $14\frac{1}{4}\%$ for a year?

2. Using the state tax rate schedule on page 243, what is the tax on taxable income of $12,800?

3. Last year, Mr. and Mrs. Okola had taxable income of $20,295. They filed a joint federal income tax return and used the tax table shown on page 237 to figure their tax.
    a. What was their tax for last year?
    b. They had paid $3,568 in withholding tax. How much refund should they get from the government?

4. Patti Ulster's major medical coverage has a $100 deductible feature and an 80% coinsurance feature. Patti's covered medical expenses last year were $1,600. Of that amount, how much would be paid by (a) Patti, and (b) the insurance company?

5. Vic Waite is buying a 10-year term life insurance policy for $25,000 at age 30. Each monthly payment is to be $7.84. What will be his total premium payments if he lives 10 years?

6. Inez Santo is shipping three packages by parcel service. The charge on each package is $4.38 for shipping, plus 90¢ for insurance. What is the total cost to ship the three packages?

7. Yul Londos drove 310 miles (499 km) in 6 hours and 30 minutes. To the nearest mile (kilometer), what was Yul's speed in miles per hour? In kilometers per hour?

8. The Generos invested $30,000 of their savings in a down payment on a new home. The money had been earning $10\frac{1}{2}\%$ per year in another investment. How much interest per year did they lose on their down-payment money?

9. To buy a home, Hulda Norse takes a loan of $60,000 for 30 years at 12%. Using the amortization table on page 193:
    a. What is the monthly payment on the loan?
    b. What will be the total of the monthly payments over 30 years?
    c. What will be the total interest cost of the loan for 30 years?

★ 10. Oley Kado had adjusted gross income last year of $56,750. On his federal income tax return, Oley claimed $1,250 of excess deductions, and one exemption at $1,000.
    a. What was Oley's taxable income last year?
    b. Using Schedule X on page 240, what was Oley's tax for last year?

SOCIAL SECURITY BENEFITS

Social security benefits for workers include retirement benefits, disability benefits, and Medicare. Spouses and children of retired or disabled workers, and survivors of deceased workers, are also eligible for social security benefits.

Figuring a Worker's Retirement or Disability Benefit. If you are a worker covered by social security (FICA), you can retire and draw partial benefits at age 62. You will not get full retirement benefits unless you wait until age 65 or older to retire.

Benefits are paid each month and are called the *monthly benefit*. The amount of your monthly benefit depends on how many years you have worked, how much your pay has been, your age, the benefit plan in effect when you start to draw benefits, and other factors. Social security benefits have been changed often, so figuring exact benefits is not easy. You may be able to roughly estimate your benefits, however, by using a benefits table. Part of a benefits table for the "new plan" that became effective in 1981 is shown below.

SOCIAL SECURITY BENEFITS FOR 1981 — NEW PLAN

Average Indexed Monthly Wage	For Workers		For Dependents		
	Primary Insurance Amount (PIA)	Old-Age Benefit Age 62	Wife or Husband Age 65	Age 62	Maximum Family Benefits
$135 or less	$135.70	$108.60	$ 67.90	$ 51.00	$ 203.50
250	225.10	180.10	112.60	84.50	337.70
500	314.10	251.30	157.10	117.90	488.00
750	402.00	322.40	201.50	151.20	730.00
1,000	492.00	393.60	246.00	184.50	891.50
1,250	581.00	464.80	290.50	217.90	1,017.30
1,500	627.20	501.80	313.60	235.20	1,098.30
1,750	668.90	535.20	334.50	250.90	1,171.20
2,000	710.60	568.50	355.30	266.50	1,244.20
2,250	752.30	601.90	376.20	282.20	1,317.10

Before you can use the table, you must find your "average indexed monthly wage." To find that amount, you must know the number of years you have worked and how much of your earnings were subject to FICA tax. You then relate or "index" your earnings to average earnings for those years and express your earnings as a monthly wage.

When you have found your "average indexed monthly wage," you locate that amount in the benefits table, then read across that line to the appropriate benefit column.

For example, suppose your average indexed monthly wage is $135 or less. If you retire at age 65, or are disabled before retiring, your monthly benefit will be the primary insurance amount (PIA) of $135.70, as shown in the table. If you retire at age 62, your monthly benefit will be the "old-age benefit" of $108.60. If you retire between the ages of 62 and 65, the benefit will be an amount between $108.60 and $135.70.

Written Practice 1

Use the social security benefit table on page 246 for these problems.

1. Christie Farrell's average indexed monthly wage is $500. What will be her monthly benefit if she retires:
   a. at age 65? $314.10
   b. at age 62? $251.30

2. Gary Boone has been disabled and can no longer work. Before being disabled, his average indexed monthly wage was $1,250 and his primary insurance amount was $581. How much will Gary get as a monthly disability benefit?

3. Katrine Osenko is age 62 and has an average indexed monthly wage of $750.
   a. If she retires at age 62, what will be her monthly benefit?
   b. If she waits to retire at age 65, what will be her monthly benefit?

4. Pedro Valdiva's average indexed monthly wage is $2,000. How much more per month will his benefit be if he retires at age 65 rather than at age 62?

5. Winifred Perdue plans to retire at age 65 with an average indexed monthly wage of $1,500.
   a. What will be her yearly benefit after she retires?
   b. If she had decided to take early retirement at age 62, what would have been her yearly benefit?

Figuring Dependents' Benefits. When a worker gets retirement or disability benefits, the worker's dependents can usually get benefits also. The amounts of some of those benefits are shown in the table on page 246.

If the worker has no dependent children, a wife or husband (spouse) who starts benefits at age 65 may get the full dependents' benefit shown in the table. Starting benefits at age 62, the spouse would get the lesser benefit that is shown. For example, suppose that a retired worker's average indexed monthly wage is $135 or less, and that the worker's monthly benefit is $135.70. The worker's dependent spouse, starting benefits at age 65, would get a monthly benefit of $67.90. If starting benefits at age 62, the dependent spouse would get a monthly benefit of $51.

If the worker has no spouse but has a dependent child, the child may get the same benefit as a spouse at age 65.

The total benefits for two or more dependents may be the same as, or more than, the benefit for a spouse at age 65 or for a child. The combined worker's and dependents' benefits, however, can not exceed the "maximum family benefits" shown in the table. For example, if a worker has a primary insurance amount of $225.10, the maximum family benefit, including the worker's own benefit, is $337.70.

Written Practice 2

1. Maida Jenkins retires at age 65 with an average indexed monthly wage of $1,750. She has no children but has a dependent husband who starts benefits at age 65.
   a. What is Maida's monthly benefit?   **$668.90**
   b. What is Maida's husband's monthly benefit?   **$334.50**
   c. What is their combined monthly benefit?   **$1,003.40**

2. Kermit Zell is retired and drawing his primary insurance amount of $710.60. Mrs. Zell is drawing the full amount of a wife's benefit at age 62.
   a. How much is Mrs. Zell's benefit?
   b. What is the Zells' total monthly benefit?

3. Gladys Osage has one dependent child. Her husband is deceased. She retired at age 62 and is drawing her old-age benefit on an average indexed monthly wage of $2,250.
   a. What is the child's monthly benefit?   **$376.20**
   b. What is their total benefit per month?

4. Benji Endo will retire at 65 with an average indexed monthly wage of $1,500. His wife will draw dependent's benefits at age 65. Benji also has two dependent children. What is the maximum monthly family benefit they can get?   **$1,098.30**

5. For a worker whose average indexed monthly wage is $1,000, what percent of the worker's PIA is the benefit of a spouse at age 65?

Review 60

1. **a.** $7 is what percent greater than $4?
   b. $4.90 is what percent less than $5.60?
   c. What is the simple interest on $5,000 for 1 year at 15%?
   d. Express in grams: 6 kg ÷ 8

2. Dwight Fritts is retiring at age 62 with average indexed monthly wages of $2,000. Mrs. Fritts will begin to draw her dependent's benefits at age 62. What will be their combined monthly benefit?

3. Using the social security tax table on page 36, what is the social security tax on wages of $299.50?

CHECKING ACCOUNTS

You will probably make most of your large payments by check. Checking accounts are easy and safe to use, and the canceled checks are a good record of your payments.

Starting a checking account is easy. Generally, you only have to go to a bank to fill out and sign a signature card, put some money into your account, and get a supply of blank checks.

In using your checking account, you will probably not put money into your account very often, but you will write checks quite often. Every time that you put money into your account, write a check, or have some other kind of charge or credit to your account, you will record it in your checkbook record. You will also prove the accuracy of your checkbook record every month or so by comparing it with the statement you get from your bank. You will use your arithmetic skills mostly in keeping the checkbook record and in checking its accuracy.

When you have finished this unit, you should be able to:

- prepare deposit slips and checks
- keep a check register
- check the accuracy of checkbook and bank statement records
- read, write, speak, and recognize the meanings of the terms that are most commonly used in handling checking accounts

USING A CHECKING ACCOUNT

Making Deposits. Money that you put into a checking account is called a deposit. To make a deposit, you must present the money to the bank with a special form that you have prepared, called a **deposit slip** or *deposit ticket*.

TRANSIT NUMBERS

For the Account of	DATE *March 20*, 19--	70-1699	
		713	
SONIA OMATA	CURRENCY	125	00	**D**
439 Sixth Avenue	COIN	5	35	**E**
Lake City, IL 60600-5005	CHECKS 70-342	240	00	**P** **S**
	80-16	10	00	**O** **L**
CHECKS AND OTHER ITEMS ARE RECEIVED FOR DEPOSIT ACCORDING TO THIS BANK'S COLLECTION AGREEMENT.				**S** **I**
				I **P**
Lake City Bank	TOTAL DEPOSIT	380	35	**T**
Lake City, IL 61699-7178	(LIST OTHER CHECKS ON BACK)			

⑆0713 ⑈16998⑆ 224 00 350 8⑈

TRANSIT NUMBER

A deposit slip

The deposit slip shown above is for a deposit that Sonia Omata made to her checking account in the Lake City Bank. The total amount of bills or paper money is shown as "Currency." The total of the coins is shown as "Coin." Each check is listed separately and is identified by the transit number of the bank on which the check was drawn. The transit number identifies the bank and is the top part of a group of numbers. Transit numbers are shown on the deposit slip above, and on the check on page 251. The total of the currency, coin, and checks is shown on the last line as "Total Deposit."

**Written
Practice 1**

For each of these problems, list the total currency, total coin, and each check in a column as they would look on a deposit slip. Then add the items to find the total deposit.

1. Cher Golden deposited these items in her checking account:

Bills:	3 twenty-dollar bills; 5 ten-dollar bills; 12 one-dollar bills
Coin:	6 quarters; 7 dimes; 4 nickels
Checks:	$25; $39.75; $15.50

2. Irvin Kemper is treasurer of a club. Irvin deposited these items in the club's checking account:

Bills:	6—$20's; 4—$10's; 9—$5's; 18—$1's
Coin:	3 halves; 15 quarters; 20 dimes; 25 pennies
Checks:	$119.50; $62; $84.25; $5.40

Writing Checks. When you want to pay out money from your checking account, you write a check. Your check tells your bank to pay a certain amount of your money to the person or business you specify, called the *payee.**

| SONIA OMATA
439 Sixth Avenue
Lake City, IL 60600-5005 | Lake City Bank
Lake City, IL 61699-7178 | No. 378
March 17 19 — 70-1699⁄713 | TRANSIT NUMBER |

Pay to the order of *The Decorator Shop* $24.76

Twenty-four and 76⁄100 _____ Dollars

Memo *Sewing materials*   *Sonia Omata*

⑈0713 16998⑈ 224 00350 8⑈

A check

Sonia Omata's check that is shown above directs the Lake City Bank to pay $24.76 from her account. The money is to be paid to The Decorator Shop. The memorandum (memo) shows that the check is to pay for sewing materials.

Keeping a Checkbook Record. You need to know how much money you have in your checking account at any time. To be sure of the amount, you must keep an accurate record of all deposits, checks, and other charges or credits to your account. You may keep your record in a **check register**, or on *check stubs*.

A page of Sonia Omata's check register is shown below.

CHECK NO.	DATE	CHECKS ISSUED OR DEPOSITS MADE	AMOUNT OF CHECK (—)	√	OTHER CHARGES	AMOUNT OF DEPOSIT OR CREDIT (+)	BALANCE
							293 26
378	3/17	*The Decorator Shop* *Sewing materials*	24 76				24 76 268 50
Dep.	3/20	*Deposit* *Wages, tips, gifts*				380 35	380 35 648 85
379	3/30	*City Power Company* *Gas and electricity*	85 43				85 43 563 42
380	3/31	*Landmark Realty Agency* *Rent due 4/1*	300 00				300 00 263 42
SC	3/31	*Service charge on* *checking account for Mar.*			2.00		2 00 261 42
IN	3/31	*Interest on checking* *account for March*				1 95	1 95 263 37

A check register page

_____

*A payee may endorse a check and make it payable to someone else.

The amount of money that Sonia has in her account at any time is called the **balance**. Sonia's balance of $293.26 at the top of the check register page was carried over from the page before.

Checks and other charges decrease (−) the balance

Sonia *subtracts* each check or charge from the old balance to get a new balance. For example, on March 17 she wrote check number 378 for $24.76 to the Decorator Shop. She subtracted that amount from the old balance of $293.26 to get the new balance of $268.50.

Deposits and other credits increase (+) the balance

Sonia *adds* each deposit or other credit to the old balance to get a new balance. For example, she added her deposit of $380.35 on March 20 to the old balance of $268.50. Her new balance was then $648.85.

To cover their costs of handling checking accounts, most banks have a **service charge**. The Lake City Bank makes a service charge of $2 for any month in which Sonia's account balance falls below $500. The bank also pays her interest on the average balance of her account during the month. When her bank reported a service charge of $2 and an interest credit of $1.95 for March, Sonia recorded them in her check register as of March 31.

Written Practice 2

1. James Sovachik's check register is shown below. Find the new balance after each item is recorded in the Balance column.

Item No.	Date	Checks Issued or Deposits Made	Amount of Check (−)		Amount of Deposit or Credit (+)		Balance	
							1,274	30
106	9/15	Roamer Car Sales	225	50				
		Car payment					Bal.	
107	9/15	Arkay Insurance Co.	124	00				
		Car insurance prem.					Bal.	
DEP	9/27	Deposit			525	00		
		Paycheck, 9/13–9/27					Bal.	
108	9/30	Ben's Bootery	58	85				
		Purchases					Bal.	
IN	9/30	Interest credited to			6	19		
		account for Sept.					Bal.	

2. Sharon Wexler's check register for a part of May shows the balance of her account on May 1, the interest earned on her account for April, her deposits, and her checks. Find her correct balance after each item.

Do not write in your book!

May 1 Balance $864.58   May 8 Deposit $324.65
       1 Interest for April   3.40   Balance
         Balance   10 Check   200.00
       3 Check   39.95   Balance
         Balance   14 Deposit   60.72
       4 Check   25.00   Balance
         Balance

3. Put these items in a vertical column as they would appear in a check register. Then find the new balance after each.

   July 1, balance, $43.29; July 1, check, $14.67
   July 3, deposit, $135.50; July 7, check, $20.75
   July 10, check, $10.99; July 11, deposit, $98.06

4. On a Monday, Jose Romero's checking account balance was $371.05. Jose wrote a check that day for $75.25. On Wednesday, he deposited $250 and wrote another check for $139.76. What was Jose's balance after those transactions?

Terms to Remember

balance	check register	deposit
deposit slip	service charge	transit number

   a. Money put into a checking account
   b. The amount in a checking account at any time
   c. Identifies a bank
   d. Another name for a deposit ticket
   e. Pays the cost of handling a checking account
   f. A record of deposits, checks, and other charges or credits

Review 61

1. a. Round $19.55349 to the nearest tenth of a cent
   b. 1 ha equals how many m²?
   c. $25 increased by 30% of itself is how much?
   d. Find the simple interest for 1 year on $10,000 at $12\frac{1}{4}\%$
   ★e. What amount decreased by 40% is equal to $227.40?

2. Sal Zorba's checking account balance on July 1 was $639.50. On July 5, Sal wrote a check for $243.25. He deposited $410.80 on July 15. He wrote a check for $57.69 on July 20, and another check for $142.95 on July 25. On July 31, Sal recorded a bank service charge of $2 for the month, and a credit of $2.53 for interest earned. What was Sal's balance on July 31 after these transactions?

3. Winnie Roberts is retiring at age 65 with an average indexed monthly wage of $750. Using the table of social security benefits on page 246, what will be Winnie's monthly benefit?

4. Patricia Germaine figures these average costs per year to go to a certain four-year college away from home: tuition, $5,200; fees and health insurance, $600; books, $460; room and board, $4,100; clothing and personal, $650; transportation and other, $900. What would be the total cost for four years?

5. If they travel by car, Lynn and Lillian Marsh will have these trip expenses: gas, $35.20; tolls, $8.90; parking, $13.50. If they travel by train, the round trip will cost $36.25 per person. How much would they save by traveling the less expensive way?

RECONCILING THE BANK BALANCE

If you have a checking account, your bank will send you a report of your account, probably each month. The report shows items such as your beginning balance, deposits, interest earned, checks paid by the bank, service charges, and your ending balance. Other charges and credits may be shown also. You should use the report to bring your checkbook record up to date and to prove the accuracy of your records and the bank's records.

The Bank Statement. The report that a bank sends to a checking account customer is called a **bank statement**. Sonia Omata's bank statement for the month of March is shown below.

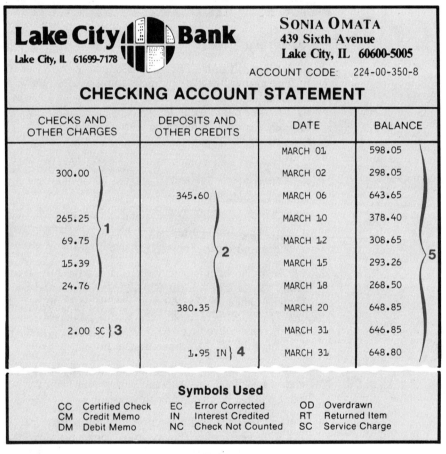

Lake City Bank
Lake City, IL 61699-7178

SONIA OMATA
439 Sixth Avenue
Lake City, IL 60600-5005
ACCOUNT CODE: 224-00-350-8

CHECKING ACCOUNT STATEMENT

CHECKS AND OTHER CHARGES	DEPOSITS AND OTHER CREDITS	DATE	BALANCE
		MARCH 01	598.05
300.00		MARCH 02	298.05
	345.60	MARCH 06	643.65
265.25		MARCH 10	378.40
69.75		MARCH 12	308.65
15.39		MARCH 15	293.26
24.76		MARCH 18	268.50
	380.35	MARCH 20	648.85
2.00 SC } 3		MARCH 31	646.85
	1.95 IN } 4	MARCH 31	648.80

1 (checks)   2 (deposits)   5 (balance)

Symbols Used

CC	Certified Check	EC	Error Corrected	OD	Overdrawn
CM	Credit Memo	IN	Interest Credited	RT	Returned Item
DM	Debit Memo	NC	Check Not Counted	SC	Service Charge

A bank statement

Sonia Omata's bank statement shows five checks paid by the bank (No. 1), and two deposits received by the bank (No. 2). The statement also shows a $2 service charge by the bank (No. 3), and a $1.95 credit for interest earned (No. 4). The beginning balance, balances after each transaction, and the balance at the end of the month are also shown (No. 5).

Outstanding Checks. The bank also sent Sonia Omata her canceled checks with the bank statement. A **canceled check** is a check that has been received and paid by the bank, then marked in some way (canceled) so it cannot be used again.

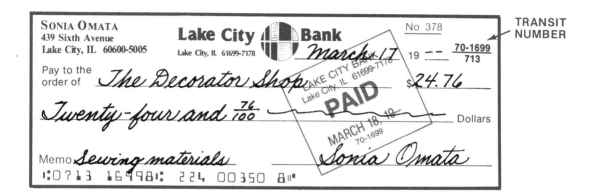

A canceled check

Sonia compared the canceled checks with her check register and found that two checks had not been returned by the bank. She had written check number 379 on March 30, and check number 380 on March 31, so there had not been time for them to get back to her bank. Checks that have been written but have not yet been paid by the bank are called **outstanding checks**.

The Reconciliation Statement. Sonia Omata found several other differences between her check register and the bank statement. But before she made any changes in her register, she prepared the reconciliation statement shown below. A **reconciliation statement** is a form used to bring a checkbook balance and a bank statement into agreement with each other.

Sonia Omata
Reconciliation Statement
March 31, 19--

Checkbook balance	$263.42	Bank statement balance		$648.80
Deduct		Deduct		
Service charge	2.00	Outstanding checks:		
	$261.42	No. 379	$ 85.43	
Add		No. 380	300.00	385.43
Interest for March	1.95			
Correct checkbook balance	$263.37	Available bank balance		$263.37

A reconciliation statement

The "checkbook balance" is the balance shown in the check register

Sonia set up her reconciliation statement with the checkbook figures on the left side and the bank statement figures on the right side. She listed her checkbook balance for March 31 of $263.42, and the bank statement balance of $648.80. To bring those balances into agreement, Sonia then added or subtracted the differences that she had found between her check register and the bank statement.

Sonia subtracted (deducted) the bank service charge of $2 from her checkbook balance because that charge decreased the amount of money in her account. She added the March interest credit of $1.95 because the interest increased the amount of money in her account. With these two changes, her *correct checkbook balance* on the statement was $263.37.

Sonia then deducted the total of the two outstanding checks, $385.43, on the bank statement side. She deducted that amount because the two checks had already been issued and would be deducted from her balance by the bank when they were received. With this deduction, Sonia's *available bank balance* was $263.37. This amount agreed with her correct checkbook balance.

The process of bringing the checkbook balance and the bank balance into agreement is called *reconciling the bank balance*. After Sonia had reconciled her bank balance, she recorded both the service charge and the interest earned in her check register.

Written Practice 1

Use the form shown on page 255 for your statements

You want to make the checkbook balance and the bank statement balance agree

Make a reconciliation statement for each of these.

1. On July 31, your checkbook balance was $589.65. Your bank statement balance was $598.36. The bank statement showed a service charge of $3 and an interest credit of $1.86. Check No. 49 for $9.85 was outstanding. **$588.51**

2. Ramos Creek's checkbook balance on September 30 was $135.40. The bank statement balance on that date was $180.15. Ramos found that one check, No. 133, for $45.95 was outstanding. The bank service charge was $1.20 for the month. There was no interest on the account.

3. Irene Samson's bank statement for the month of January showed a balance of $525.90 on January 31, a service charge of $2, and interest earned of $1.75 for the month. These checks were outstanding: No. 464 for $350, and No. 466 for $75.90. Her checkbook balance on January 31 was $100.25.

4. Teri Volens is reconciling her bank balance for June. Two checks that she has written, No. 809 for $215.75, and No. 815 for $87.46, are not shown on her bank statement. The bank statement shows interest of $8.20 credited for the month, and a balance of $1,965.76 in her account on June 30. Teri's check record shows a balance of $1,654.35 on June 30.

5. Verne Bazan reconciled his bank balance on April 30 and found four outstanding checks: No. 55, $6.75; No. 58, $106.50; No. 61, $33.89; and No. 62, $67.84. His bank statement showed a balance of $672.80 on April 30, and a service charge of $2.25 for April. Verne's checkbook balance on April 30 was $460.07.

★**Special Reconciliation Problems.** You may have many kinds of problems in reconciling bank balances. You must study each one to see whether the checkbook side or the bank statement side is affected, and whether there is an increase or a decrease in the balance.

For example, Mack Pember's bank statement for May showed a balance of $1,376.38 on May 31. His checkbook balance on that date was $734.70. When Mack compared his bank statement and canceled checks with his checkbook record, he found these items:

A service charge of $1.80 was reported by the bank for the month of May but had not yet been recorded in the checkbook record.

He had failed to record and subtract check number 593 that was written on May 16 for $37.65.

Check number 597 written on May 23 for $29.95 was recorded in the checkbook record as $19.95. This was $10 less than it should be.

He had not recorded a deposit of $586 made on May 22.

On May 31, the bank had credited his account with $5.25 interest for May. The interest had not been recorded in the checkbook record.

Check number 601 for $175.42 was outstanding.

A deposit of $75 he had made on May 31 was not shown on the bank statement.

The bank had made an error on his check number 588. The bank had paid $12.93 rather than $12.39 for which the check was written. This was a difference of 54¢.

Mack Pember's reconciliation statement for May looked like this:

Mack Pember
Reconciliation Statement
May 31, 19--

Checkbook balance		$ 734.70	Bank statement balance		$1,376.38
Deduct			Deduct		
Service charge $	1.80		Outstanding check No.		
Check No. 593			601		175.42
not recorded	37.65				$1,200.96
Amount of					
check No.			Add		
597 too			Deposit not		
small	10.00	49.45	recorded	$75.00	
		$ 685.25	Error on check		
Add			No. 588	0.54	75.54
Deposit not					
recorded	$586.00				
Interest for					
May	5.25	591.25			
Correct checkbook					
balance		$1,276.50	Available bank balance		$1,276.50

A reconciliation statement

The unrecorded service charge of $1.80, the unrecorded check number 593, and the error in recording check number 597 made the checkbook balance too large by $49.45. So, Mack deducted that amount on the checkbook side. The unrecorded deposit of $586 and the interest for May of $5.25 made the checkbook balance too small by $591.25, so he added that amount to the checkbook balance. The correct checkbook balance was $1,276.50.

The outstanding check number 601 made the bank balance too large by $175.42, so Mack deducted that amount from the bank balance. The unrecorded deposit of May 31, and the bank's error on check number 588, made the bank balance too small by $75.54. So, Mack added $75.54 to the bank balance. The available bank balance on May 31 was $1,276.50, which was the same as the correct checkbook balance.

★**Written Practice 2**

Make a reconciliation statement for each of these problems. Use the statement on page 257 as a guide. Use your own name in the heading, and April 30 as the date of the statement and of the balances.

	Checkbook Balance	Bank Statement Balance	Outstanding Checks	Other Adjustments
1.	$ 487.63	$ 414.08	#87, $ 23.50 #90, $ 52.20	Service charge, $1.40. Interest credit, $2.15. Late deposit of $150 omitted on bank statement. **$488.38**
2.	$ 393.27	$ 475.80	#56, $ 89.42 #59, $ 7.65 #60, $104.21	Service charge, $2.50. $100 late deposit omitted on bank statement. Check #52 for $16.25 not in register.
3.	$ 852.04	$1,055.24	#34, $ 65.95	Interest credit, $3. $140 deposit omitted from register. Check #38 for $5.75 omitted from register.
4.	$1,436.22	$1,567.02	#93, $195.00 #94, $264.00	Service charge, $2.25. $325 deposit recorded twice in register. Check #89 for $59.95 shown as $59 in register.
5.	$ 604.29	$ 879.69	#68, $ 34.50 #69, $ 89.74 #70, $132.06	Service charge, $0.90. Check #62 for $37 shown as $57 in check register.
6.	$ 230.79	$ 255.26	#81, $ 44.67	Service charge, $2. Deposit of $68 in register as $86. Bank paid $14.99 on check #77 instead of $14.79.
7.	$ 791.06	$1,010.21	#16, $ 6.35 #21, $ 14.95 #22, $124.05	Service charge, $1.20. Deposit of $225 shown as $200 in register. $50 deposit credited twice on bank statement.

★Written Practice 3

Make a reconciliation statement for each of these problems.

1. On October 31, Myron North's checkbook balance was $485.20 and his bank statement balance was $325.55. Myron's outstanding checks were No. 29 for $16.75 and No. 31 for $43.90. The bank statement showed a service charge of $2.50 and interest credited of $2.20 for the month. A deposit of $220 made on October 31 was too late to show on the statement.

2. Natalie Vance's bank statement for June 20 showed a balance of $917.92. Her checkbook balance for that date was $876.42. In reconciling the bank balance, Natalie found that check No. 423 for $139.95 was outstanding. She also found that she had not recorded a check No. 418 for $23.45 in her checkbook, and she had recorded a deposit of $75 twice in her record.

3. Oliver Pardee reconciled his bank balance on August 31. The bank statement balance was $675.63 and his check register balance was $629.83. Oliver found that no checks were outstanding, but he had not recorded a deposit of $47.60 in his register. He had also written a check for $36.48 but had recorded it in the register as $34.68.

Terms to Remember

bank statement   canceled check   outstanding checks
reconciliation statement

a. A check that has been written but not yet paid by the bank
b. A bank report sent to a checking account customer
c. A check that has been paid and marked by a bank
d. A form used to bring the checkbook and bank statement balances into agreement

Review 62

1. **a.** $2.45 is what percent greater than $1.96?
   b. Find the simple interest on $12,000 for a year at 9%
   c. 3.5 L ÷ 5 = ? L

2. Hale Morrow's checkbook balance on February 28 is $570.45. Hale's bank statement for February shows a balance of $604.95 on February 28. The statement also shows a service charge of $1.50 and an interest credit of $1.15 for February. Hale's check No. 95 for $34.85 is outstanding. Prepare a reconciliation statement for Hale.

3. Akim Jabul has a life insurance policy for $30,000. Last year, Akim paid a premium of $347.50 on the policy but he got a dividend of $52.75 at the end of the year. What was his net premium for the year?

★ 4. Roseann Zapata's bank statement for December shows a balance of $553.77 on December 31. Roseann's checkbook balance was $699.82 on that date. Her check No. 483 for $275 is outstanding. A deposit of $328.45 she made on December 31 was too late to show on the statement. She had not recorded her check No. 63 for $92.60 in her register. What was her correct checkbook balance and her available bank balance on December 31?

**Part II
Review B**

1. a. Multiply 26.3406 by 1,000
    b. Divide $343.25 by 100
    c. Multiply $4,200 by 0.055
    d. Divide $15.75 by $3\frac{1}{2}$
    e. 8.6 m + 40 cm = ? m
    f. 4.2 m × 3.5 m = ? m²
    g. 750 mL × 6 = ? L
    h. What is $\frac{1}{4}$% of $800?
    i. What is one year's simple interest on $2,000 at $15\frac{1}{2}$%?
    j. $79 decreased by 30% of itself is what amount?

2. Julia Rem works on a 40-hour week basis at $9 an hour, with time and a half for overtime. Last week Julia worked 43 hours.
    a. What was her gross pay for the week?
    b. Julia's employer deducted $84.40 for withholding tax, $26.83 for social security tax, and $9.50 for other. What was her net pay?

3. Rob Seng works in a factory and is paid $3.50 for each item he assembles. Last week he assembled these numbers of items: Monday, 20; Tuesday, 17; Wednesday, 24; Thursday, 26; Friday, 18. What was his gross pay?

4. Lena Koke bought 4 boxes of cereal at 95¢ each, 3 boxes at $1.05 each, and 2 boxes at $1.16 each. What was the average cost per box?

5. On a 5-day car trip, you drove these distances: 728 km, 603.5 km, 648 km, 402 km, 474.5 km. You used a total of 408 L of gas.
    a. How many kilometers did you drive on the trip?
    b. How many kilometers per day did you average, to the nearest kilometer?
    c. How many kilometers did you average per liter of gas?

6. What is the total sale price of 3 pairs of slacks at $21.99, and 3 shirts at $12.57, plus a sales tax of 5% on the total purchase?

7. Madge Lapin is spending $3,000 for energy-saving home improvements. She estimates that in 15 years the improvements will save $6,750 in fuel costs. What is her estimated net saving over 15 years?

8. The price of a dishwasher at Breen's Appliances is $529, delivered and installed. Save-Mart's price for the same model is $449, plus $22.50 for delivery and $39.75 for installation. Which store's machine would cost less? How much less?

9. The Faithful Insurance Company has insured a building for $50,000, and the Stellar Insurance company has insured it for $70,000. What is each company's share of a $36,000 fire loss?

10. Plainview's tax rate is $83.75 per $1,000 of assessed value. What is the tax on Plainview property that is assessed at $15,000?

11. A new car bought now for $9,000 will have a trade-in value of $2,520 at the end of 4 years. What is its annual rate of depreciation?

★12. At an end-of-season sale, you got a $33\frac{1}{3}$% discount on some furniture. The sale price was $386. What was the original price?

Part III

Saving and Investing Money

At some time in your life, or maybe many times, you will want to buy a car, a boat, or a home. You will want to buy new furniture, take a long and expensive vacation, travel, or go to college. Perhaps you will lose your job, or be out of work because of illness or accident. After working most of your life, you will want to retire and "take it easy."

To provide money for those costly needs and wants, you will have to set aside part of your current income. You will want to put your savings where the money will be safe and where it will grow by earning more money. That is what Part III is about: Saving and Investing Money.

In Unit Twelve, you will learn more about interest and savings accounts. You will meet bonds and stocks in Units Thirteen and Fourteen, and real estate in Unit Fifteen.

Unit Twelve

SAVINGS ACCOUNTS

This unit is concerned with figuring simple and compound interest, and with investing money in regular or special savings accounts.

When you have finished this unit, you should be able to:

- figure simple interest by the exact and banker's interest methods
- find rates of simple interest

- figure compound interest and balances on passbook savings accounts
- figure interest earned on savings certificates
- find penalties on withdrawals from savings certificates
- read, write, speak, and recognize the meanings of some terms that are commonly used in working with interest and with savings accounts

SIMPLE INTEREST

$I = P \times R \times T$

In figuring interest, you work with three factors: principal, rate, and time. Those three factors are related as shown by the basic interest rule or formula:

Interest = Principal × Rate × Time (in years)
(I)   (P)   (R)   (T)

The **principal** is the amount of money on which interest is paid. For example, if you borrow $500 and pay interest on it, the $500 is the principal. Also, the amount of money that you put into a savings account to earn interest for you is called the principal.

An interest rate is a rate for *one year*!

The **rate of interest**, or just *rate*, is the part or percent of the principal that is paid for using the money *for one year*. For example, a bank may pay an interest rate of 8%, or $8 for each $100 of principal on deposit with the bank *for one year*.

Time is shown in years or parts of years

In the interest formula, **time** is the number of years or the fraction of a year for which the principal is used and the interest is paid.

In figuring **simple interest**, which is also called *ordinary interest* or *interest*, the principal stays the same for the whole time the money is used. Interest is *not* added to the principal to form a new principal as is done in compound interest.

Interest for One Year. You have already done many problems in this book in which you were given a principal and a rate and were to find the interest for one year. In those problems, you found the interest by multiplying the principal by the rate:

Principal × Rate = Interest for 1 Year

For example, the interest on $2,000 at 6% for 1 year is $2,000 × 0.06, or $120. You do not have to multiply by the time factor of 1 year because multiplying any amount by 1 does not change that amount.

**Oral
Practice 1**

What is the interest on these amounts?

1. $500 @ 6% for 1 year
2. $1,000 @ 8% for 1 year
3. $2,000 @ 10% for 1 year

4. $600 at 5% for 1 year
5. $3,000 @ 7% for 1 year
6. $400 at 12% for 1 year

Paying Interest Is Like Paying Rent To Use Someone Else's Money.

Interest for Time in Multiples or Fractions of a Year. To figure interest for more than one year, you multiply the interest for one year by the number of years. For example, the interest on $1,000 at 8% for 3 years is $240.

$$\$1,000 \times 0.08 \times 3 = \$240$$

To figure the interest for part of one year, you multiply the interest for one year by the part. For example, the interest on $1,000 at 8% for $\frac{1}{4}$ of a year is $20.

$$\$1,000 \times 0.08 \times \frac{1}{4} = \$20$$

Oral Practice 2

What is the interest on:

1. $500 @ 6% for 2 years?
2. $1,000 @ 8% for 4 years?
3. $2,000 @ 10% for 3 years?
4. $5,000 @ 12% for 5 years?
5. $100 @ $5\frac{1}{2}$% for 2 years?

6. $400 @ 6% for $\frac{1}{2}$ year?
7. $2,000 @ 8% for $\frac{1}{4}$ year?
8. $800 @ 10% for $\frac{3}{4}$ year?
9. $1,000 @ 12% for $2\frac{1}{2}$ years?
10. $5,000 @ 10% for $1\frac{1}{2}$ years?

Written Practice 3

What is the interest on:

1. $100 @ 7% for 3 years? $21
2. $400 @ 8% for $\frac{1}{2}$ year? $16
3. $300 @ 9% for 2 years?
4. $600 @ 10% for $2\frac{1}{2}$ years?
5. $2,000 @ $8\frac{1}{2}$% for 4 years?

6. $1,200 @ 6% for $1\frac{1}{4}$ years?
7. $1,000 @ $5\frac{1}{2}$% for 2 years?
8. $500 @ 12% for $\frac{1}{3}$ year?
9. $400 @ 15% for $\frac{5}{6}$ year?
10. $6,000 @ $8\frac{1}{2}$% for $1\frac{1}{2}$ years?

Interest for Time in Months. Suppose that you need to figure interest for a number of months. You show the number of months as the numerator of a fraction, with a denominator of 12. Then you reduce the fraction. For example, the interest on $1,000 @ 8% for 6 months is $40.

$$6 \text{ months} = \frac{6}{12} \text{ or } \frac{1}{2} \text{ year}$$

$$\$1,000 \times 0.08 \times \frac{1}{2} = \$40 \text{ interest for 6 months}$$

Written Practice 4

Find the interest on:

1. $800 @ 5% for 3 months $10
2. $600 @ 8% for 9 months
3. $1,200 @ 10% for 8 months
4. $2,000 @ 12% for 6 months
5. $3,000 @ 8% for 7 months

6. $1,500 @ 7% for 2 months
7. $7,200 @ 10% for 1 month
8. $3,600 @ 5% for 5 months
9. $400 @ 12% for 11 months
10. $10,000 @ 15% for 4 months

Exact Interest for Time in Days. Suppose that you are to figure the interest on $2,000 at 10% for 25 days. You would show the number of days (25) as the numerator of a fraction, with the *number of days in a year* as the denominator. But, the number of days in a year may be either 365 days or 360 days, depending on the method you use.

Exact interest uses a 365-day year

The U.S. Government, many banks, and some other businesses use the exact interest or *accurate interest* method. That method uses a 365-day year. So, if you are figuring by the exact interest method, you show the time as $\frac{25}{365}$. The interest by that method is $13.70, figured this way:

$$\$2,000 \times 0.10 \times \frac{25}{365} = \$200 \times \frac{\overset{5}{\cancel{25}}}{\underset{73}{\cancel{365}}} = \frac{\$1,000}{73} = \$13.70$$

Written Practice 5

Find the exact interest to the nearest cent.

1. $500 @ 8% for 120 days   **$13.15**
2. $1,200 @ 5% for 50 days
3. $800 @ 6% for 200 days
4. $5,000 @ 4% for 180 days
5. $4,000 @ 7% for 100 days
6. $14,600 @ 10% for 75 days

7. What is the exact interest on $800 at 7% for 40 days?

8. Cindy Irwin owns a $10,000 government bond. The bond pays 12% exact interest per year. How much interest will Cindy earn on the bond in 30 days?   **$98.63**

9. You have $1,000 in a long-term deposit at a bank. The bank pays you 8% per year and uses the exact interest method. How much interest will you earn on the deposit for 90 days?

Banker's Interest for Time in Days. As you have seen, figuring exact interest with a 365-day year is not easy. The denominator, 365, is an awkward number to use. For that and other reasons, many banks and businesses figure interest by the banker's interest method. The banker's method uses a 360-day banker's year or *commercial year*, with 12 months of 30 days each. The banker's method is easier to use in many problems, and gives more interest than the exact interest method.

Banker's interest uses a 360-day year

Using the banker's method, a time of 25 days would be shown as $\frac{25}{360}$. The interest on $2,000 at 10% for 25 days is $13.89, figured this way:

Use a 360-day year for further interest problems in this book

$$\$2,000 \times 0.10 \times \frac{25}{360} = \$200 \times \frac{\overset{5}{\cancel{25}}}{\underset{72}{\cancel{360}}} = \frac{\$1,000}{72} = \$13.89$$

You are to use a 360-day year for all interest problems in this book unless you are told otherwise.

Written Practice 6

Find the banker's interest to the nearest cent.

1. $600 @ 8% for 60 days $8
2. $800 @ 9% for 30 days
3. $400 @ 10% for 45 days
4. $1,000 @ 12% for 90 days

5. $3,000 @ 7% for 180 days
6. $5,000 @ 6% for 240 days
7. $8,000 @ 15% for 300 days
8. $10,000 @ 5½% for 36 days

9. What is the banker's interest on $6,000 at 11% for 60 days?

10. An investment of $4,000 pays interest at 12% per year, figured by the banker's interest method. What is the interest for 90 days?

11. Judy Romer earns 12% per year on an investment of $6,000. What is the interest for 30 days, using the banker's method?

Finding a Rate of Interest. You can find a rate of interest easily if you know the principal and the amount of interest for one year. To find the rate, you divide the interest for one year by the principal.

$$\text{Rate of Interest} = \frac{\text{Interest for 1 Year}}{\text{Principal}}$$

Use the 360-day banker's year

If the given interest is not for one year, you first find the interest for one year. For example, Sam Amora earned $120 interest for 180 days on an investment of $2,000. The time of 180 days is ½ of the banker's year of 360 days. So, the interest of $120 for 180 days is equal to interest of $240 for 360 days (2 × $120 = $240). The rate of interest is 12%, figured this way:

$$\frac{\$\ 240}{\$2,000} = 0.12 = 12\%$$

Written Practice 7

Find the interest rate for each of these problems.

An interest rate is an annual rate unless otherwise specified

	Principal	Interest	Time	
1.	$400	$3	30 days	9%
2.	$800	$24	90 days	
3.	$200	$8	180 days	
4.	$1,500	$50	120 days	
5.	$2,000	$20	60 days	
6.	$1,200	$45	3 months	15%
7.	$5,000	$225	6 months	
8.	$10,000	$1,050	18 months	7%
9.	$8,000	$1,000	30 months	

Written Practice 8

1. Josef Hammer is paid $60 interest every 3 months on his investment of $3,000. What annual rate of interest is he paid?   8%

2. In the first 9 months of last year, Imogene Costa received $450 interest on an investment. The principal of the investment was $5,000. What yearly rate of interest did she receive?

3. An ad says that interest of $350 will be paid on an investment of $5,000 for 6 months. What annual rate of interest will be paid?

4. In 2 years, you were paid a total of $120 interest on an investment of $1,500. What was the annual rate of interest?

Terms to Remember

banker's interest   banker's year   exact interest   principal
rate of interest   simple interest   time

a. Uses a 365-day year
b. Uses a 360-day year
c. Also called a commercial year
d. The number of years for which interest is paid
e. The principal stays the same all the time the money is used
f. The amount of money on which interest is paid
g. A part or percent of the principal paid for using money for a year

Review 63

1. a. $16 is what percent less than $24?
   b. Show $107\frac{7}{8}\%$ as a decimal
   c. What is 40.5 m − 20.8 m?
   d. What is the simple interest on $600 at 8% for 2 years?
   e. Find the exact interest to the nearest cent on $800 @ 10% for 20 days
   f. Find the banker's interest to the nearest cent on $400 @ 9% for 120 days

2. What is the difference in the amount of the exact interest and the banker's interest at 8% for 60 days on $6,000?

3. Dominick Scarza's checkbook balance on October 31 was $706.30. His bank statement balance on October 31 was $725.21. The bank statement showed a service charge of $2 and an interest credit of $3.06 not shown in the check register. His check No. 91 for $17.85 was outstanding. Make a reconciliation statement for Scarza, showing the correct checkbook balance and the available bank balance.

4. The balance in Hattie Evert's check register on June 1 was $460.25. She deposited $325.80 on June 4. On June 12, Hattie wrote one check for $136.40 and another check for $23.50. On June 20, she deposited $75 and wrote a check for $9.95. What was her correct check register balance after those transactions?

PASSBOOK SAVINGS

You may want to put some of your money into a regular savings account at a savings bank, commercial bank, savings and loan association, or credit union. The money will be safe and it will earn some interest. You can easily withdraw all or part of your money if you want.

Regular savings accounts are also called passbook accounts

The Savings Passbook. When you start a savings account, you fill out a signature card, make a deposit, and get a **passbook**. The passbook shows your withdrawals, deposits, interest earned, and balances after each transaction.

You usually make a deposit to a savings account by presenting a deposit slip, your passbook, and your money. Interest is credited to your account, generally every quarter year, and is entered in your passbook when you next present it. Deposits and interest are *added* to your previous balance.

With a regular savings account, you take money out, or "withdraw" it, by presenting a withdrawal slip with your passbook. Withdrawals are recorded in your book immediately and are *subtracted* from the previous balance.

Pablo Cardona's passbook for his savings account at the Sandhill Bank is shown below.

		In account with:		Account No.	
SANDHILL BANK		PABLO CARDONA 37 DUNES COURT YUMA, AZ 85365-1425		10-376-24	
Date	Withdrawal	Deposit	Interest	Balance	
JULY 15, 19--		100.00		100.00	
AUG 5, 19--		50.00		150.00	
AUG 20, 19--	25.00			125.00	
SEPT 8, 19--		130.00		255.00	
OCT 1, 19--			1.88	256.88	

A savings passbook

Written Practice 1

For each of these problems, make a form like the passbook shown above. Show only the columns and column headings. Then record the deposits, interest, and withdrawals. Figure and show the balance after each transaction.

1. April 3, deposit, $500.00; April 20, deposit, $250.00; May 15, withdrawal, $100.00; June 10, withdrawal, $225.00; July 1, interest, $6.38. **$431.38**

2. February 20, deposit, $75.00; March 20, withdrawal, $15.00; April 1, interest, $0.36; May 16, withdrawal, $10.00; June 2, deposit, $165.00; July 1, interest, $0.69.

3. December 1, balance, $1,349.28 (enter in Balance column only); December 18, withdrawal, $200.00; December 28, deposit, $80.00; January 2, interest, $18.43; January 5, withdrawal, $49.75; January 24, withdrawal, $367.00.

A quarter year is three months

Interest on Savings Accounts. Interest is usually added to savings accounts at the end of each quarter year on April 1, July 1, October 1, and January 2. (January 1 is always a holiday, so interest is credited on January 2.)

To figure the interest for a quarter year, you multiply the principal by the interest rate, then by $\frac{1}{4}$. For example, the interest on $1,000 at 6% for one quarter of a year is $15.

$$\$1,000 \times 0.06 \times \frac{1}{4} = \$15$$

Interest is often paid on whole dollars only

Interest on savings accounts is often paid on *whole dollars only*. For example, if you have $425.68 on deposit, the interest is paid on $425. If you have $936.22 on deposit, interest is paid on $936.

Written Practice 2

$I = P \times R \times T$

Find the quarterly interest to the nearest cent on each of these balances. Figure the interest on *whole dollars only*.

1. $758.50 at 6% a year **$11.37**
2. $1,624.96 at 5% a year
3. $346 at $5\frac{1}{2}$% a year **$4.76**
4. $93.12 at $5\frac{1}{2}$% a year

5. $3,262.74 at 6% a year
6. $6,000 at $5\frac{1}{4}$% a year
7. $583.06 at $5\frac{3}{4}$% a year
8. $709.33 at 7% a year

Last balance plus interest equals new balance and new principal

Figuring Interest and New Balances. At the end of each interest period, the interest due is figured and added to the last balance in the passbook. The new balance then becomes the principal on which interest is figured for the next period, if no deposits or withdrawals are made. This process of figuring interest and adding it to the old principal to form a new principal is called **compounding interest**

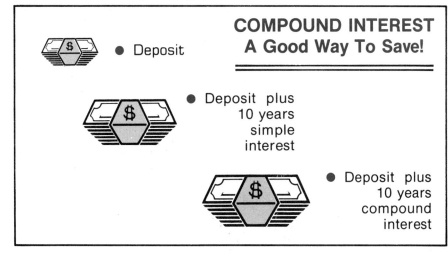

Here is an example of compounding interest:

Example

On July 1, Mae Crimmins opened a savings account with a deposit of $500. The account paid 6% interest, and the interest was added quarterly on January 2, April 1, July 1, and October 1. If Mae made no other deposits or withdrawals, what was her balance on the next January 2?

Solution

In account with: Mae Crimmins			Account No. 320-68-075	
Date	Withdrawals	Deposits	Interest	Balance
19-- July 1		500.00		500.00
Oct. 1			7.50	507.50
Jan. 2			7.61	515.11

Explanation

Mae's passbook is shown above. Her opening deposit of $500.00 on July 1 made a new balance of $500.00 on that date. On October 1, interest for the quarter was figured ($500 × 0.06 × $\frac{1}{4}$ = $7.50) and added to the old balance. The new balance and new principal was $507.50. On January 2, interest for the quarter was figured on *whole dollars only* of the new principal ($507 × 0.06 × $\frac{1}{4}$ = $7.61). The interest of $7.61 was added to the old balance to make a new balance and new principal of $515.11.

Compound interest is greater than simple interest

The amount of money earned by compounding interest is called **compound interest**. In the example, the compound interest on the deposit of $500 at 6% for 6 months was $15.11 ($515.11 − $500.00 = $15.11 compound interest).

Compound interest is *always greater* than simple interest for the same rate and time, because interest is paid on interest. As shown in the example, the compound interest on $500 at 6% for 6 months was $15.11. The simple interest is only $15 ($500 × 0.06 × $\frac{1}{2}$ = $15).

Written Practice 3

Do each of these in the form of a passbook like the one above.

1. On April 2, Duke Gladwin deposited $2,000 in a savings account that paid 6% interest per year. Interest was credited to the account each quarter on July 1, October 1, January 2, and April 1. Duke made no other deposits or withdrawals.
   a. Figuring interest on whole dollars only, what was Duke's account balance on April 2 of the next year?   **$2,122.72**
   b. How much compound interest did Duke earn in one year?   **$122.72**

Figure interest on whole dollars only

2. Your savings bank pays $5\frac{1}{2}\%$ interest per year. The bank adds interest quarterly on January 2, April 1, July 1, and October 1. You deposited $800 on April 1 and made no other deposits or withdrawals.
   a. What should be your balance on October 2 of the same year?
   b. How much interest should you have earned by October 2 of that year?

3. Hilda Mendez opened a savings account on July 1 with a deposit of $250. Interest was credited on the account each quarter at the annual rate of 6%. Hilda made no other deposits or withdrawals for a year.
   a. What was the balance of her account on July 2 of the next year?
   b. How much interest had been paid on the account for the year?

4. The Westview Bank pays $5\frac{1}{4}\%$ interest per year on savings accounts. It credits the interest each quarter. How much compound interest will the bank pay in six months on a deposit of $5,000 made on October 1?

★Written Practice 4

Figure interest on whole dollars only

1. Howard Kinsul opened a savings account in the Palmetto Savings Bank with a deposit of $800 on July 1. He deposited $300 more on October 1. The bank pays interest at 6% per year and credits the interest to accounts on January 2, April 1, July 1, and October 1. If Howard made no further deposits or withdrawals after October 1, what was his balance on the next January 2?   **$1,128.68**

   Figure and add the interest for October 1 before showing the deposit of October 1. For January 2, figure the quarter's interest on the balance after the deposit of October 1.

2. The Homestead Bank compounds interest on passbook savings accounts each quarter at an annual rate of 6%. On October 1 last year, after the interest had been credited, Lita Prevost's account balance was $3,600. On that date, she deposited $400 more in her account. On April 1 of this year, Lita deposited an additional $800. If she makes no other deposits or withdrawals, what will be Lita's balance after the interest is credited on October 1 of this year?

3. The Desert Savings Bank pays $5\frac{1}{2}\%$ interest per year, compounded quarterly. Rosalie Yuan's balance in that bank on January 2 was $1,200. She deposited $500 more on April 1, and withdrew $250 on July 1. If she made no other deposits or withdrawals, what was her balance on October 1?

   Figure and add the interest on April 1 before showing the deposit of April 1. Figure and show the interest on July 1 before the withdrawal of July 1. Figure the interest for October 1 on the balance after the withdrawal of July 1.

4. What is the difference in the compound interest for one year at 5% on $500, compounded quarterly on whole dollars only, and the simple interest at 5% on $500 for one year?

5. One kind of investment will pay you simple interest of 7% a year. Another kind of investment will pay you 7% interest per year, compounded quarterly on whole dollars only. How much more interest would you earn the first year on $5,000 in the better-paying investment?

★**Interest on Minimum Balances.** Interest on savings accounts may be paid in many different ways. Interest on some accounts is paid from the day of deposit to the day of withdrawal. In those accounts, all money on deposit earns interest for the actual amount of time it is on deposit.

Interest may be paid on the *average* amount on deposit during a quarter. Sometimes a full quarter's interest is paid on deposits made as late as the tenth day of a quarter. Interest may be compounded daily but credited to the account at the end of each quarter.

Interest may be paid on whole dollars only

Interest may be paid on the minimum (smallest) balance on deposit during a quarter. For example, the Exeter Bank pays 6% a year, adding the interest each quarter on January 2, April 1, July 1, and October 1. The bank figures the interest on the smallest balance of the quarter. As shown below, the smallest balance from July 1 through September 30 was $795.80. So, the interest for the quarter was $11.93 ($795 × 0.06 × $\frac{1}{4}$ = $11.93).

The smallest balance from October 1 through December 31 was $1,057.73. So, the interest for the quarter, credited on January 2, was $15.86 ($1,057 × 0.06 × $\frac{1}{4}$ = $15.86).

≡ Exeter Bank ≡

In account with ___LENA OSAKA___   Account No. 606–320–55

(We pay interest on whole dollars of minimum quarterly balances)

Date	Withdrawals	Deposits	Interest	Balance
19--				
JULY 1				945.80
AUG 3	150.00			795.80
SEPT 10		250.00		1,045.80
OCT 1			11.93	1,057.73
DEC 26		400.00		1,457.73
19--				
JAN 2			15.86	1,473.59

A savings passbook for Lena Osaka

★**Written Practice 5**

Do these problems in the form of a passbook like the one above. Use your own name on the account. Figure the interest on whole dollars only of the smallest balance on deposit during the quarter.

1. Ara Colonna had $1,400, including interest, on deposit in the Woodburne Bank on July 1. He withdrew $600 on July 3, and deposited $250 on August 25. He made no other deposits or withdrawals that quarter. What was his balance on October 1, including interest at 5½% per year, compounded quarterly? **$1,061**

2. The Greenbelt Savings Bank pays interest on passbook accounts at an annual rate of 6%, compounded and added to accounts at each quarter. On January 2, Dinah Gavin had $575 in her savings account at the Greenbelt Bank. She deposited $120 on January 15, and $80 on February 15. She withdrew $50 on March 18. She made no other deposits or withdrawals during the quarter. What was her balance on April 1 after the interest was credited?

3. The Trumbull Savings and Loan Association pays interest of 7% per year, compounded quarterly. On October 1, Herbert Plante had $4,300 on deposit with the Association, including interest to date. During the quarter, Herbert deposited $100 on October 15, and $350 on November 30. He made withdrawals of $50 on November 1 and $200 on December 20. What was his balance on January 2 after interest was credited?

Terms to Remember

compound interest   compounding interest   passbook

a. Adding interest to a principal to make a new principal
b. Shows withdrawals, deposits, interest, and balances
c. The amount of money earned by compounding interest

Review 64

1. a. What amount is 0.0752 × $12,000?
   b. What is 40% of 48 m²?
   c. What is the banker's interest for 90 days at 10% on $1,800?
   d. What is the exact interest to the nearest cent on $1,000 @ 6% for 40 days?
   e. $24.60 increased by 75% of itself gives what amount?

2. On July 1, Josie Fenn opened a savings account with a deposit of $600. The account paid 6% interest per year, compounded and credited each quarter on whole dollars only. She made no other deposits or withdrawals for the next year.
   a. What was her balance on the next July 1?
   b. How much interest had she earned in a year?

3. Reba and Rafe Kellogg are married and file a joint income tax return. Their taxable income last year was $20,185. Using the tax table on page 237, what was their tax last year?

★ 4. Al Jarro's checkbook balance on June 30 was $1,303.26. His bank statement balance for June 30 was $1,194.04. His check No. 169 for $265.78 was outstanding on that date, and his deposit of $350 on June 30 did not show on the bank statement. He had failed to record his check No. 157 for $25 in his check register. Make a reconciliation statement for Al.

SAVINGS CERTIFICATES

You may want to put some of your savings into special accounts rather than into a passbook savings account. These special accounts, often called *savings certificates*, may also be called time deposits, certificates of deposit, money-market certificates, or small-saver certificates.

Special accounts usually pay a higher rate of interest than regular passbook savings accounts. The rate may be as much as two or three times the regular passbook rate. To get the higher rate of interest, you must meet certain requirements:

(1) You must deposit a certain minimum amount, such as $100, $250, $500, $1,000, $5,000, or $10,000. You may deposit more than the minimum if you wish.

(2) You must leave the money on deposit for a stated minimum time, such as 3 months, 6 months, 1 year, $2\frac{1}{2}$ years (30 months), 4 years, 6 years, or 8 years.

(3) You must have the bank's permission to withdraw any of the money during the stated time for which it was deposited. If you withdraw any money early, you must pay a penalty. The penalty involves the loss of interest for some specified time, figured on the amount of money you withdraw.

Special accounts are regulated by federal or state government. Deposits are generally insured and are considered quite safe.

Comparing Certificate Interest and Passbook Interest. To help decide which investment is better for you, you need to compare the interest on special savings accounts with the interest on regular passbook accounts. The extra interest earned on the higher-paying accounts may be worth some inconvenience or risk of penalty.

Written Practice 1

1. Gale West had $2,500 on deposit in a regular passbook savings account. Gale figured that she could invest $1,500 of that money in a certificate of deposit that would pay her $185.40 interest per year. She had been earning $92.03 a year on the $1,500 in her passbook account. How much more interest per year would she earn by buying the certificate? **$93.37**

2. If Anton Fermi puts $3,000 into a regular savings account at $5\frac{1}{2}\%$ compound interest, his annual interest will be $280.72. If he puts the money into a special time deposit, his interest will be $647 a year. How much more interest will he earn per year on the time deposit?

3. You have $10,000 to invest. In a passbook savings account you can earn interest at $5\frac{1}{2}\%$ per year, compounded quarterly on whole dollars. In a money-market certificate, you can earn $582.50 interest in six months.
   a. How much interest can you earn in 6 months on the passbook savings account? **$276.88**
   b. How much more interest would you earn in 6 months on the money-market certificate than on the passbook savings account? **$305.62**

4. On passbook savings accounts, the Bluefield Bank pays 6% interest per year, compounded quarterly on whole dollars. On 6-month certificates for $15,000, the bank pays $637.50 simple interest for 6 months.
   a. How much interest can you earn in 6 months on $15,000 invested in a passbook savings account?
   b. How much more would you earn in 6 months on $15,000 invested in a certificate rather than in a passbook savings account?

5. You have $3,000 in a passbook savings account that is earning $39.38 each quarter. If you invest the $3,000 in a 3-month savings certificate, you will earn simple interest at the rate of 8% a year, figured and paid at the end of 3 months.
   a. How much interest can you earn on a 3-month savings certificate?
   b. How much more would you earn in a quarter by investing the money in a certificate rather than in a passbook savings account?

6. Your bank pays $5\frac{1}{2}\%$ interest on passbook savings, compounded quarterly on whole dollars. Your bank pays 13.56% per year simple interest on a savings certificate. How much more would you earn in a year on $6,000 invested in a certificate rather than in a passbook account?

7. You plan to invest $10,000 in a 6-month certificate that pays interest at the rate of 12% per year. At the end of 6 months, you will reinvest the principal and the interest for another 6 months at 12% a year. How much interest will you earn in a year by doing that?

Penalties on Savings Certificates. The penalty for early withdrawal of money from a savings certificate may be heavy. You may lose 3 months' or 6 months' interest on the money you withdraw from a certificate before it is due. For example, Fay Turko has $2,000 invested in a 30-month savings certificate that is earning interest at 10% a year. The penalty for early withdrawal of any part of the principal is the loss of 6 months' simple interest at 10% on the amount withdrawn. So, if Fay withdraws $500 before the certificate is due, the penalty will be $25 ($500 × 0.10 × $\frac{1}{2}$ = $25).

Sometimes a further penalty may be added to the loss of 3 months' or 6 months' interest. For example, the interest rate on the amount withdrawn may be reduced to the passbook rate for the time that money was on deposit.

The penalty for withdrawing money may be greater than the amount of interest you have earned. If the penalty is greater than the interest, you lose some of your principal. With such heavy penalties, you need to be very sure of what you are doing before you invest in savings certificates or before you withdraw money from them.

Written Practice 2

1. Otis Ulster has $10,000 on deposit in a 6-month money-market certificate. If he withdraws any of the $10,000 before the certificate is due, he will be penalized 3 months' simple interest at 12% per year on the amount withdrawn. What will be the amount of the penalty if he withdraws:
   a. $5,000? **$150**
   b. $10,000? **$300**

2. You are thinking about withdrawing part or all of your money from an $8,000 certificate before it is due. The penalty for early withdrawal is the loss of 6 months' simple interest at 10% per year. What is the penalty in dollars if you withdraw:
   a. $3,000?
   b. $4,000?

Interest earned less the penalty equals net interest

3. Velda Banks has held a $10,000, 6-month certificate for 4 months and has earned $500 in interest. She wants the $10,000 now for other uses, but will be penalized 3 months' simple interest at 15% per year on the principal if she withdraws the money early.
   a. What is the amount of the penalty for early withdrawal?
   b. What will be her net interest if she cashes the certificate early? **$125**

4. You need $6,000 in cash to pay bills. You own a $6,000 savings certificate that has earned $875 in interest up to now. If you withdraw all the principal from the certificate, you will be penalized 6 months' interest at 9% on the $6,000 principal.
   a. What will be the amount of the penalty?
   b. What will be your net interest?

5. Bobby Lamarr invested $10,000 in a 6-month savings certificate. He held the certificate for 2 months, then withdrew the whole $10,000. Bobby had earned $141.67 interest for the 2 months. His penalty for early withdrawal was the loss of 3 months' interest at $8\frac{1}{2}\%$ per year on $10,000.
   a. What was the amount of the penalty?
   b. How much more was the penalty than the interest he had earned?   **$70.83**

6. Mildred Volks invested $3,000 in a 30-month savings certificate paying 10% annual interest. After earning $128 in interest, she withdrew all the money. Mildred paid a penalty of 6 months' interest at 10% per year on the $3,000. How much more interest did she lose by the penalty than she had earned on the investment?

Review 65

1. a. $21 is what percent less than $35?
   b. $135 increased by $16\frac{2}{3}\%$ of itself is what amount?
   c. What is $137\frac{1}{2}\%$ of 120 liters?
   d. What is the simple interest on $500 at 9% for 6 months?
   e. What is the banker's interest for 45 days on $4,000 at 12%?
   ★f. $120 is 15% of what amount?

2. On passbook accounts, the Coldstream Bank pays 6% interest compounded quarterly on whole dollar amounts. The bank pays 15% simple interest per year on money-market certificates. On an investment of $10,000 for 6 months:
   a. What would be the interest in a passbook savings account?
   b. What would be the interest on a money-market certificate?
   c. How much more interest would be earned on the money-market certificate?

3. You have earned $562.50 interest on a $5,000 savings certificate. You are cashing the certificate now and must pay a penalty of 6 months' simple interest at 9% per year on the $5,000.
   a. What is the amount of the penalty?
   b. What net amount of interest did you make on your investment?

4. Your bank statement shows a balance of $652.60 for April 30. The statement shows a service charge of $2.50 for the month and an interest credit of $1.42 that are not in your check register. You find that two checks are outstanding, No. 38 for $89.95 and No. 42 for $7.50. Your check register balance is $556.23. Prepare a reconciliation statement.

5. Maria Sandia is retiring at age 62 with an average indexed monthly wage of $500. Her only dependent is a child. Using the table of social security benefits on page 246:
   a. What will be Maria's monthly benefit?
   b. What will be the child's monthly benefit?

★6. Woody Erson is single and has no dependents. His taxable income last year was $55,300. Using Schedule X on page 240, what was Woody's income tax last year?

BONDS

You may want to invest some of your savings in bonds rather than in savings accounts. Bonds are sold by governments and by corporations as a way of borrowing large amounts of money for long periods of time. When you buy a bond, you are lending your money to the issuer of the bond. The bond is the evidence of your loan.

A **bond** is a written promise to pay a sum of money, with interest, at a certain time. The amount to be paid is printed on the face of the bond and is called the **face**, or face value. The date when the money is to be paid is called the **maturity date**.

When you have finished studying this unit about bonds, you should be able to:

- figure the cost of U.S. savings bonds
- find the interest on U.S. savings bonds
- figure bond premium and discount
- figure market price of bonds
- find broker's commission
- figure investment in bonds, with and without broker's commission
- find the income and rate of income from a bond investment
- read, write, speak, and recognize the meanings of some terms related to buying and selling bonds

U.S. SAVINGS BONDS

section
66

Many kinds of bonds are issued by federal, state, and local government units. People with little money to invest often buy **savings bonds** that are issued by the U.S. Treasury Department. Many other kinds of bonds pay more interest, but Series EE savings bonds can be bought for as little as $25 each.

Savings bonds may be bought easily at banks and savings and loan associations, or through payroll savings plans offered by many employers. Savings bonds are a safe investment. Money can be withdrawn after 6 months by cashing them. The interest earned on the bonds is exempt from state and local taxes.

When you buy a Series EE savings bond, you pay only one-half its face value. The interest earned by the bond is added to the purchase price until, at maturity, the bond is worth its full face value. If you cash the bond before maturity, you get back the purchase price, plus interest earned at less than the full rate.

For example, suppose you buy a U.S. savings bond that has a face value of $50 and that will mature in 9 years. You pay only $25 for it. Interest will be added to the $25 purchase price until, when it matures in 9 years, the bond will be worth the face value of $50. If you hold the bond for the full 9 years, it will have earned 8% interest, compounded semiannually. If you cash the bond before maturity, you will get less than $50. The amount you get will depend on how long you have held the bond, and the interest you have earned will be only 5.5% to 8%.

A U.S. savings bond

**Written
Practice 1**

1. You have $1,000 to invest. For $25 each, you can buy U.S. savings bonds that have a face value of $50 each.
   a. How many savings bonds can you buy? **40**
   b. What would be the total maturity value of the bonds you could buy? **$2,000**
   c. How much total interest would you earn if you held the bonds to maturity? **$1,000**

2. U.S. savings bonds with a maturity value of $75 each are sold for $37.50 each. Freddy Malone buys 12 of those bonds.
   a. How much do the 12 bonds cost?
   b. What will be the maturity value of the 12 bonds?
   c. If Freddy holds the bonds to maturity, how much interest will he get from them?

3. Noreen Kilgore is having her employer deduct $2 a week from her pay to buy U.S. savings bonds. In how many weeks will her total deduction be enough to buy a $50 bond that costs $25? **13 weeks**

4. Liz Portala's payroll deduction for buying U.S. savings bonds is $5.50 per week for each week of a year.
   a. How many whole bonds costing $25 each will she have bought in a year?
   b. How much money will she have toward the purchase of another bond?

5. Quentin Okola's employer is deducting $40 per week from Quentin's pay to buy savings bonds for him.
   a. How much will the employer deduct in a full year of 52 weeks?
   b. How many bonds costing $37.50 each can be purchased with that amount?
   c. If each bond purchased has a face value of $75, what is the total face value of the bonds purchased in a year?

6. Philip Rome's goal is to buy 30 savings bonds per year through a payroll savings plan. Each bond will cost $25. What amount should Philip's employer deduct from his salary every month to make that goal?

7. In one year, Sophia Roth wants to buy savings bonds worth $3,000 at face value. If the cost of the bonds is $\frac{1}{2}$ their face value, how much must Sophia invest in the bonds per month?

Rate of interest equals interest earned divided by the principal

8. Ward Lavery paid $25 for a savings bond. When he cashed it 4 years later, he was paid $32 for it.
   a. How much interest had he earned in 4 years? $7
   b. How much interest had he earned per year? $1.75
   c. What annual rate of interest had he earned? 7%

9. Maud Saginaw bought a $100 face-value savings bond for $50. She got $56 when she cashed the bond after holding it for only 2 years.
   a. How much interest per year had she earned on the bond?
   b. What annual rate of interest had she earned?

10. After holding a savings bond for 5 years, Yuki Kunio cashed the bond and got $34.40 for it. He had paid $25 for the bond when he bought it. What annual rate of interest had he earned on the bond, to the nearest tenth of a percent?

Terms to Remember

| bond | face | maturity date | savings bond |

a. The date when a bond is to be paid
b. A government or corporation's promise to pay a sum of money, with interest, at a certain time
c. A United States Treasury bond
d. The value printed on the face of a bond

Review 66

1. a. Multiply $18,000 by 0.73105
   b. Divide 33.075 by 630
   c. What amount is $16\frac{2}{3}\%$ less than $72?
   d. $108.50 is what percent smaller than $124?
   e. How many liters are there in 6 bottles holding 750 mL each?
   f. What is the simple interest on $650 for 45 days at 12%?
   g. What is the exact interest on $2,600 for $2\frac{1}{2}$ years at 14%?

2. Bill Alam has $8 deducted from his paycheck every 2 weeks for savings bonds. How many whole bonds costing $25 each will he have at the end of one year?

3. In one year, Geraldine Kurtz bought 10 savings bonds that cost $25 each. When she cashed the bonds a year later, she received $264 for them.
   a. How much interest had she earned on the bonds?
   b. What rate of interest, to the nearest tenth of a percent, had she earned on the bonds for the year?

4. On May 31, Ilsa Andersen's checkbook balance was $109.64. Her bank statement balance on that date was $133.89. Checks No. 179 for $7.25 and No. 184 for $19.50 were outstanding. A service charge of $2.50 was shown on the statement but not in the checkbook. Make a reconciliation statement for Ilsa.

CORPORATION BONDS

Many corporations borrow money by selling bonds. Corporation bonds often have a face value of $1,000.

To assure bondholders that their money will be repaid, corporations often back their bonds with some kind of security. The security may be a mortgage on the company's land, building, or equipment. If the corporation fails to repay the bonds as agreed, the mortgaged property will be sold to get money to pay the bondholders. A corporation's bond is shown below.

$1000   **$1000**

CC

COMTROL CORPORATION

FIRST MORTGAGE 9% BOND SERIES H
DUE FEBRUARY 1, 1990

Comtrol Corporation an Indiana Corporation (hereinafter called the Company) for value received hereby promises to pay to   JILL C. BUSWELL   or registered assigns, on the first day of February, 1990, the sum of   *ONE THOUSAND DOLLARS*

and to pay to the registered owner interest on said sum from the date hereof until said sum shall be paid at the rate of nine percentum (9%) per annum payable semi-annually on the first day of February and the first day of August in each year. Both the principal of and the interest on this bond shall be payable at the office or agency of the company in the city of Indianapolis, state of Indiana, or at the option of the company in the borough of Manhattan, the city of New York, state of New York, in any coin or currency of the United States of America which at the time of payment is legal tender for the payment of public and private debts.

This bond shall not be entitled to any security or benefit under the mortgage or be valid or become obligatory for any purpose unless and until it shall have been authenticated by the execution of the corporate trustee or its successor in trust under the mortgage of the certificate endorsed herein.

In Witness whereof ....
Comtrol Corporation has caused this bond to be executed in its name by its president or one of its vice-presidents and has caused its corporate seal to hereto be affixed by its secretary or one of its assistant secretaries as of the first day of February, 1970.

COMTROL CORPORATION

NO. 50623

A corporation's mortgage bond

Selling Bonds. When a corporation borrows money by selling bonds, the whole issue of bonds may be sold to an investment bank. The investment bank then resells the bonds to individual buyers for a slightly higher price.

For example, suppose the Comtrol Corporation issues 50,000 bonds, each with a face value of $1,000. An investment bank might buy all 50,000 bonds at $996 each, then sell them to investors at the face value of $1,000.

Par Value and Market Value. The face value of a bond is often called its **par value**. Par value is the amount, printed on the face of the bond, that the borrower promises to pay the bondholder on the maturity date.

The **market value**, or market price, of a bond is the price the bond is selling for at any time. The market value may or may not be the same as the par value. If the market value of a bond is *more* than its par value, the bond is selling at a **premium**. For example, a $1,000 par value bond selling for $1,025 is selling at a premium.

If the market value is *less* than the par value, the bond is selling at a **discount**. For example, a $1,000 bond selling at $990 is selling at a discount.

The amount of the premium or the discount is the difference between the market value and the par value.

Oral Practice 1

The market price of nine different $1,000 par value bonds is shown. You are to answer these questions for each bond:

a. Is the bond selling for a premium or for a discount?
b. What is the amount of the premium or the discount?

1. $1,100	**6.** $1,012.50
2. $925	**7.** $998
3. $1,060	**8.** $1,105
4. $890	**9.** $989.25
5. $975	**10.** $1,012.75

A bond quotation is a percent of par value

Bond Price Quotations. The market value, or market price, of a bond is quoted as a percent of par value. For example, suppose that Seaport Corporation's $1,000 par value bonds are quoted as selling at "92." The "92" means that the bond is selling for 92% of its par value. You find the market value by multiplying the par value by the percent.

$$0.92 \times \$1,000 = \$920 \text{ market value}$$

If the quoted price of a $1,000 bond is $105\frac{1}{2}$, the price of the bond is $1.05\frac{1}{2} \times \$1,000$, or $1,055.

Oral Practice 2

What is the market price, in dollars and cents, of a $1,000 bond selling at each of these quoted prices?

1. 98	**6.** $108\frac{1}{2}$
2. 102	**7.** $110\frac{1}{4}$
3. 115	**8.** $89\frac{3}{4}$
4. 94	**9.** $92\frac{1}{8}$
5. 86	**10.** $101\frac{3}{4}$

Written Practice 3

1. The quoted price of eight $1,000 bonds is shown below. For each bond, indicate (a) the market price, and (b) the amount of the premium or discount at which the bond is selling.

	Quoted Price	Market Price	Amount of Premium	Amount of Discount
a.	$103\frac{1}{2}$	$1,035	$35	
b.	107			
c.	95			$50
d.	$98\frac{1}{2}$			
e.	$104\frac{3}{4}$			
f.	$88\frac{1}{4}$			
g.	$102\frac{1}{8}$			
h.	$92\frac{5}{8}$			

2. Jartron Metals Corporation $1,000 bonds are quoted at $96\frac{1}{2}$.
   a. What is the price of the bonds in dollars and cents? $965
   b. What is the discount on the bonds in dollars and cents? $35

3. An investment bank is offering Central Energy Corporation $1,000 bonds at 101. What is the price of the bonds in dollars and cents?

4. Airspace Tek $1,000 bonds are offered for sale at $97\frac{3}{4}$. What is the discount on those bonds in dollars and cents?

Finding a Total Investment in Bonds Bought from an Investment Bank.
To find the total of an investment in bonds, you multiply the price of one bond by the number of bonds bought.

Example

Aggie Darcy bought four $1,000 Royer Chemical Company bonds at $99\frac{1}{4}$. What was her total investment in the bonds?

Solution

$99\frac{1}{4}\% = 0.9925$

$0.9925 \times \$1,000 = \$992.50$ market price per bond

$4 \times \$992.50 = \$3,970$ total investment in bonds

Written Practice 4

For Problems 1 through 4, find the amount of money invested in each bond purchase.

1. Fastrans Corporation, $1,000 bonds:

   a. 5 @ 106   b. 2 @ 96   c. 8 @ 101

2. Vidette Corporation, $1,000 bonds:

   a. 6 @ 93   b. 3 @ 107   c. 6 @ 89

3. Midwest Stores, $1,000 bonds

   a. 3 @ $108\frac{1}{2}$ **b.** 5 @ $97\frac{1}{4}$ **c.** 2 @ $96\frac{1}{8}$

4. Marvell Manufacturing, $1,000 bonds

   a. 25 @ 90   **b.** 15 @ 110   **c.** 30 @ $98\frac{3}{4}$

5. You plan to buy 5 Solweld Company $1,000 bonds that are quoted at $93\frac{3}{4}$ by an investment bank. What will be your total investment in the bonds?

6. Eric Valera bought twelve $1,000 bonds of the Zoneway Corporation. The quoted price of the bonds was $103\frac{1}{2}$. What was Eric's total investment in the bonds?

Terms to Remember

discount	market value	par value	premium

   a. Another name for face value of a bond
   b. The price at which a bond is sold
   c. Market value more than par value
   d. Market value less than par value

Review 67

1. **a.** Multiply $24,000 by 2.1746
   b. Multiply 5.5 by $3\frac{3}{5}$
   c. What is the banker's interest on $5,000 @ $9\frac{1}{2}$% for 180 days?
   d. What is 124.5 m² divided by 5?
   e. $40 simple interest on $2,000 for 1 year is what interest rate?

2. What is the discount on a $1,000 bond that is selling at $78\frac{1}{8}$?

3. What is your total investment in 15 $1,000 bonds bought from an investment bank at $103\frac{1}{2}$?

4. How many $75 U.S. Savings Bonds costing $37.50 each can be bought for $675?

5. Kirk Becket has $20,000 invested in a 6-month money-market certificate. He will be penalized 3 months' simple interest at 13% per year on any amount that he withdraws before the certificate is due. What will be the penalty if he withdraws $5,000 before the certificate is due?

★ 6. On July 1, Constance Almac had $1,675.40 in a savings account that paid interest at 6% a year, compounded quarterly on whole dollars of the minimum balance. On August 15 she deposited $200, and on September 10 she withdrew $50. What was her balance on October 1 after the interest was credited?

★ 7. **a.** $49.50 is $\frac{5}{8}$ of what amount?
   b. $196 is $33\frac{1}{3}$% more than what amount?

CORPORATION BONDS (concluded)

section 68

After a bond issue has been sold by an investment bank, anyone who wants to buy some of the bonds has to buy them from a bondholder who wants to sell. Or, a bondholder who wants to sell has to sell to someone who wants to buy.

Bonds are seldom sold directly by the seller to the buyer. Instead, bonds are sold through a **broker**, who is a dealer in stocks and bonds. The sale is handled this way:

Each buyer and seller places an order with a local broker to buy or sell certain bonds. Each broker then sends the order to an exchange, such as the New York Stock Exchange or the American Stock Exchange. The actual buying and selling of the bonds takes place at the exchange. The seller's broker gets the bonds from the seller and has the ownership transferred to the buyer.

Bond Quotation Tables. Bond sales are recorded at the exchanges as they are made. Each day's bond sales at the exchanges are reported the next day in the financial pages of many newspapers. Some bond quotations are shown in the table below.

Bonds			Current Yield	Sales in $1,000	High	Low	Last	Net Change
Alcoa	9s	95	12.9	33	71⅞	70	70	-¼
AAirl	4¼s	92	9.5	4	44¾	44½	44½	+⅝
ATT	13¼s	91	14	378	98	97¼	97½	-¾
Cmw E	14⅞s	87	15	35	101	100¾	100¾	-⅜
Det E	9⅞s	04	15	5	64½	64½	64½	-1¼
Exxon	6½s	98	11.3	69	57⅜	56½	57⅜	-⅛
Gdyr	8⅝s	95	12.2	5	70⅜	70⅜	70⅜	+2¾
IBM	9⅜s	04	12	650	76⅝	75½	75¾	-⅝
PacTT	15⅛s	88	15	224	100¾	100	100	-¾
RCA	9¼s	90	11	5	81⅛	81⅛	81⅛	—
Sears	8⅝s	95	12	10	70⅝	70½	70⅝	+1⅜
TWA	12s	05	15	11	114½	114¼	114½	+1

Corporation name usually abbreviated (Alcoa)
Annual interest rate (4¼s)
Year of maturity 2004 (04)
Rate of interest on current price (12.2)
Number of bonds sold (224)
Highest price of day
Lowest price of day
Last or closing price of day
Difference between last price of today and yesterday

Corporation bond quotations

Reading a Bond Quotation Table. The sales of Aluminum Company of America (Alcoa) bonds are shown first in the table. At the right of the name, the "9s" means that the bonds are paying 9% interest. The "95" means that 1995 is the year of maturity.

The "12.9" in the "Current Yield" column shows the annual percent of interest that a buyer would get at the current purchase price.

The "33" in the "Sales in $1,000" column shows that 33 bonds were sold that day.

The next three columns show the highest price, the lowest price, and the last or closing price paid that day for the bonds. The highest price was $71\frac{7}{8}$, or $718.75. The lowest price was 70, or $700. The last price, or closing price, was the same as the lowest price, 70, or $700.

Bond quotes are in percents

The "$-\frac{1}{4}$" in the "Net Change" column shows that the last price of the day, 70, was $\frac{1}{4}$ lower than the last price of the day before. So, the last price of the day before was $70 + \frac{1}{4}$, or $70\frac{1}{4}$.

Oral Practice 1

1. What annual rate of interest was paid on the American Airlines bonds listed in the table?

2. In what year are the American Telephone and Telegraph bonds listed in the table due to mature?

3. How many Commonwealth Edison bonds were sold on the day listed?

4. What was the highest price at which Detroit Edison bonds were sold?

5. What was the lowest price at which Exxon bonds were sold?

6. For the bonds listed in the table on page 286, what was the:
   a. highest price?
   b. lowest price?

7. For which bonds was the highest price the same as the lowest?

8. What was the last price of TWA bonds:
   a. for the day listed?
   b. for the day before the day listed?

9. What was the last price of the RCA bonds:
   a. for the day listed?
   b. for the day before the day listed?

10. If you bought 5 of the Pacific Telephone and Telegraph bonds at the lowest price listed, what would they cost you?

11. What would be the total investment in 5 Commonwealth Edison bonds bought at the highest price listed for the day?

Broker's Commission. When bonds are bought or sold through a broker, the broker charges a **broker's commission**, or brokerage fee. The commission is often a certain amount per bond, with a minimum charge per transaction. The amount charged may vary with the number of bonds bought or sold.

Finding Total Bond Investment, with Commission. When bonds are bought through a broker, the total investment is the market price of the bonds *plus* the broker's commission. Look at this example:

Example

Elinor Cortez bought three $1,000 New Century Corporation bonds through a broker at $90\frac{1}{2}$, plus $10 commission per bond. What was the amount of Elinor's investment in the bonds?

Solution

$90\frac{1}{2}\% = 0.905$
$0.905 \times \$1,000 = \$905$ market price per bond

$3 \times \$905 = \$2,715$ market price of 3 bonds
$3 \times \$\ 10 = \underline{\hspace{0.5cm}30}$ commission on 3 bonds
$\$2,745$ total investment

Written Practice 2

Purchase price plus commission equals total investment

Remember that quoted prices for bonds are percents of par

1. Dewey Jackson bought ten $1,000 bonds through a broker at $63\frac{1}{2}$. The broker charged $7.50 commission for each bond. What was Dewey's total investment in the bonds? **$6,425**

2. Joyce Kaplan buys twenty bonds at $42\frac{1}{4}$ each. The bonds have a par value of $1,000. The broker charges her $6 commission per bond.
   a. What is the purchase price of the bonds?
   b. What is the amount of the broker's commission?
   c. What is Joyce's total investment in the bonds?

3. You are planning to buy four $1,000 bonds at $85\frac{3}{4}$. The broker's commission will be $7.50 per bond. What will be your total investment?

4. Leslie Ramos bought six $1,000 bonds, but he paid only $741.75 for each bond. The commission on the purchase was $45. What was Leslie's total investment in the bonds?

5. Susanne Thane bought 15 bonds at $1,083.75 each, plus broker's commission of $6.50 per bond. What was her total investment?

6. Vada Bonita bought 3 Fairfax Corporation $1,000 par value bonds at 95. The broker's commission was $7.50 per bond, or a minimum charge of $35 on the transaction. What was Vada's total investment in the bonds, including commission?

7. Lara Fane bought five $1,000 bonds at $82\frac{1}{4}$, and four $1,000 bonds at $112\frac{1}{2}$. The broker's commission was $7.50 per bond. What was Lara's total investment?

8. Chi Li bought 10 bonds at $649.25, and five bonds at $938.75. The commission on the bonds was included in the purchase price. What was Chi Li's total investment in the bonds?

Terms to Remember

    broker   broker's commission

a. A fee charged by a bond dealer
b. a dealer in stocks and bonds

Review 68

1. a. $1,160 is what percent of $8,000?
   b. What is the interest on $4,000 for 270 days at 15%?
   c. $360 interest for 6 months on $12,000 is equal to what interest rate?
   d. What is 20% of 384 hectares?

2. Bryan Flynn bought five $1,000 corporation bonds at $92\frac{1}{2}$, plus commission of $7.50 per bond. What was Bryan's total investment in the bonds?

3. On April 1, Katrina Ahl deposited $300 in a savings account. Interest at 6% per year, on whole dollars only, was credited to her account each quarter. She made no other deposits or withdrawals that year.
   a. What was Katrina's account balance on January 2 of the next year?
   b. How much compound interest did she earn in 9 months?

4. Knute Tabert's bank statement balance on July 31 was $1,680.29. The statement showed interest earned of $5.42 that was not recorded in his check register. His check register balance on July 31 was $1,529.19. Knute found that one check for $145.68 was outstanding. Make a reconciliation statement for Knute.

BOND INCOME

Your income from owning bonds is the interest that is paid to you by the issuer of the bonds. Interest is usually paid semiannually, which is twice a year.

Bond Interest. Interest on a bond is figured on the par value as the principal. So, the formula for bond interest is:

Par Value × Rate × Time = Bond Interest

For example, the interest for one year on a $1,000, 9% bond is $90. ($1,000 × 0.09 = $90). If the interest is paid semiannually, the amount of each interest payment is $45 ($1,000 × 0.09 × $\frac{1}{2}$ = $45).

Finding Income from a Bond Investment. To find the income from an investment in bonds, you first find the interest on one bond. Then you multiply the interest on one bond by the number of bonds. For example, the annual income from ten $1,000, 12% bonds is $1,200.

$1,000 × 0.12 = $120 interest on 1 bond
10 × $120 = $1,200 income from 10 bonds

Written Practice 1

1. Find the annual bond income for each problem.

   a. Three $1,000, 8% bonds
   b. Five $1,000, 10% bonds
   c. Twenty $1,000, 13% bonds
   d. Fifteen $1,000, $9\frac{1}{2}$% bonds
   e. Twelve $1,000, $10\frac{3}{4}$% bonds
   f. Six $1,000, $12\frac{1}{4}$% bonds

2. What will be the yearly income from eight $1,000 bonds that pay 9% interest? **$720**

3. What is the annual income on twelve $1,000, $10\frac{1}{4}$% bonds?

4. What is the semiannual interest on a $1,000, 12% bond? **$60**

5. How much interest would you get every 6 months from five $1,000 bonds with interest at $7\frac{1}{2}$%, payable semiannually?

Written Practice 2

1. Zach Eckstein bought twelve $1,000 bonds at 85. He paid a commission of $7.50 per bond. The bonds pay interest at 9% a year.
   a. What is Zach's total investment in the bonds? **$10,290**
   b. What is his total annual income from the bonds? **$1,080**

2. You can buy five $1,000 bonds at $75\frac{1}{2}$. The commission will be $7.50 per bond. The bonds will pay interest at $8\frac{1}{2}$% per year.
   a. What would be your total investment in the bonds?
   b. What would be your annual income from the bonds?

3. Florita Jenner owns ten $1,000 bonds that she bought at $84\frac{3}{8}$, plus $7 commission per bond. Florita gets semiannual interest totaling $975 from the ten bonds.
   a. What is Florita's investment in the bonds?
   b. What is her annual income from the bonds?

Finding the Yield (Rate of Income) from a Bond Investment.

Before you buy bonds, you should figure the rate of income that you will get from owning them. **Yield**, or rate of income on bonds, is the percent you get by dividing annual income by total investment.

$$\text{Yield (Rate of Income)} = \frac{\text{Annual Income}}{\text{Total Investment}}$$

Example

What is the yield, or rate of income, on a $1,000, 8% bond bought at $63\frac{1}{4}$ plus $7.50 commission?

Solution

$0.6325 \times \$1,000 = \$632.50$ market price
$\underline{\hspace{2.5cm} 7.50}$ commission
$\$640.00$ total investment

$\$1,000 \times 0.08 = \$80$ annual income
$\frac{\$\ 80}{\$640} = 0.125 = 12.5\%$ yield (rate of income)

Written Practice 3

1. For each of these $1,000 bonds, find the rate of income (yield) on the investment. Round the rate to the nearest tenth of a percent.

	Interest Rate	Market Price	Commission	Rate of Income
a.	9%	$90\frac{1}{4}$	$ 7.50	9.9%
b.	10%	80	7.00	
c.	12%	102	8.00	
d.	$6\frac{1}{2}\%$	$74\frac{1}{2}$	6.00	
e.	$7\frac{1}{2}\%$	$55\frac{1}{8}$	10.75	

2. A $1,000 bond, paying interest at $8\frac{1}{2}\%$, was bought at $72\frac{1}{4}$, plus $7.50 commission. What was the rate of income on the investment, to the nearest tenth of a percent?   **11.6%**

3. Kathey Seville bought a $1,000 bond, paying 10% interest, for 112 plus a commission of $30. What was the rate of income (yield) on the investment, to the nearest tenth of a percent?

Yield is annual
income divided by
total investment

4. What is the yield, to the nearest tenth of a percent, on a $1,000, $5\frac{1}{2}$% bond bought at 48? (If no commission is stated, it is included in the price.)

5. A $1,000, $6\frac{1}{2}$% bond is bought at $76\frac{1}{2}$. What is the yield?

6. What is the yield, to the nearest tenth of a percent, on a 9% bond bought at 108? (If no par value is given, par is $1,000.)

7. What is the yield, to the nearest tenth of a percent, on a $10\frac{1}{2}$% bond bought at $98\frac{3}{4}$?

★Written Practice 4

1. a. How much annual income would you get from one $9\frac{1}{2}$% bond? (Remember that par is $1,000 if no par value is stated.)
   b. How many of those bonds would you have to own to get an annual income of $3,800?   40

2. Jetmore Products bonds can be bought at 95. The bonds pay 12% interest.
   a. How many of those bonds would Thomas Kovac have to buy to get an annual income from them of $6,000?
   b. What total investment would Thomas have to make in the bonds?

3. How much must be invested in $7\frac{1}{2}$% bonds selling at $82\frac{3}{8}$ to give an annual income of $7,500?

4. Lucy Harcourt can buy Witonka Company 10% bonds at $82\frac{3}{4}$. How much money must she invest to get an annual income of $5,000 from those bonds?

Review 69

1. a. Multiply $16,000 by 1.125
   b. Divide 180 km by 15
   c. 50 cm is what percent of 5 m?
   d. What is the interest on $12,000 at 8% for 60 days?
   e. $600 interest on $5,000 for one year is what rate of interest?
   f. $39.20 is what percent less than $49?
   ★g. $455 is 30% more than what amount?

2. Watt MacDuff bought ten $1,000, $8\frac{1}{2}$% Alamar Corporation bonds. The purchase price of the bonds was $63\frac{1}{4}$, plus $7.50 commission per bond.
   a. What was Watt's total investment in the bonds?
   b. What was his annual income from the bonds?

3. What is the yield, to the nearest tenth of a percent, on a $1,000, $9\frac{1}{2}$% bond that was bought at 105?

4. Sylvia Herrera's checkbook balance on November 30 was $768.24. On that date the bank statement balance was $565.44. In reconciling the bank balance, Sylvia found that check No. 88 for $63.95 was outstanding, and that a deposit of $248 made on November 30 was not shown on the statement. She had also failed to record check No. 77 for $18.75 in her check register. What was Sylvia's correct checkbook balance and available bank balance on November 30?

STOCKS

When corporations are formed, or when they expand, they need money for land, buildings, equipment, material, and labor. They may get some of the money they need by borrowing it with bonds, but they usually also sell shares of **stock** in the company. Anyone who buys stock in the company becomes a part owner of the business, and is called a **shareholder** or stockholder.

You may want to invest some of your savings in stock. If the company is successful, you will share in the profits and your stock will also increase in value.

When you have finished this unit, you should be able to:

- read a stock market report
- figure broker's commission on stock
- figure the total cost of a stock purchase
- find income from a stock investment
- find rate of income from a stock investment
- figure profit or loss on a sale of stock
- ★● find net gain or loss from buying and selling stock
- read, write, speak, and recognize the meanings of many terms related to buying, owning, and selling stock

A. G. Edwards & Sons, Inc.

INVESTING IN STOCK

Owning Stock. When you buy stock, you are issued a **stock certificate**. The certificate shows how many shares you own and is registered in your name by the corporation. An example of a certificate is shown below.

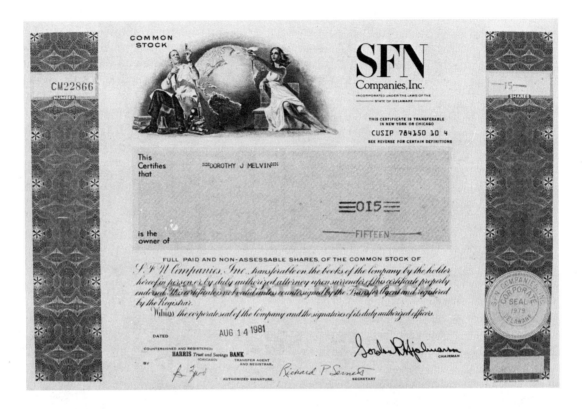

A stock certificate

When a corporation gets money by selling stock, it does not promise to repay the money as it does with bonds. Neither does it promise to pay any interest, as it does with bonds. Instead, the money paid for stock becomes a permanent part of the business.

As a shareholder, you are a part owner of the business. You will share **Shared profits are** in profits that are distributed to owners. Profits that are distributed to **called dividends** owners are called **dividends**. Dividends are often paid quarterly, but they may be paid semiannually or annually.

Par Value and Market Value of Stock. The value of a stock that is printed on the face of the certificate is its *par value*. All shares of an issue of stock have the same par value, such as $1, $10, $50, or $100. Sometimes stock is issued without a par value; it is called **no-par stock**.

After an issue of stock has been sold the first time, the shares are bought and sold at any price the buyer and seller agree on. The price at which stock is sold at any time is its *market price*, or market value.

Stock Price Quotations. Stocks are bought and sold through brokers and stock exchanges in the same way that bonds are traded. The market prices of stocks traded on the major exchanges each day are reported the next day in the financial pages of many newspapers.

The market price, or market value, of a share of stock is usually quoted in dollars per share. Amounts less than one dollar are shown as eighths of a dollar, or multiples of eighths of a dollar, such as $\frac{1}{8}$ for $12\frac{1}{2}$¢ and $\frac{1}{2}$ for 50¢.

For example, a stock market quotation of $35\frac{1}{8}$ means that the price of one share is $35.125. This is much different from a bond quotation of $35\frac{1}{8}$ which means $35\frac{1}{8}$% of par, or $351.25 on a $1,000 par value bond.

Stock prices are quoted in dollars per share

A market quote of 35⅛ means

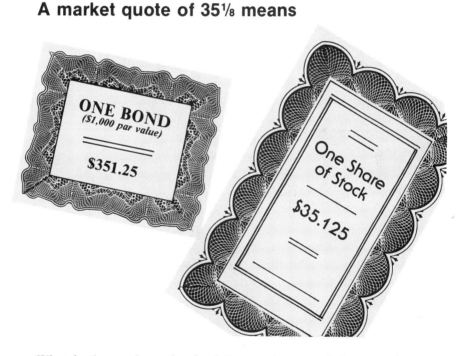

ONE BOND
($1,000 par value)

$351.25

One Share of Stock

$35.125

What is the market price in dollars and cents of these stock market quotations?

1. 22
2. $43\frac{1}{2}$
3. $8\frac{1}{4}$
4. 102
5. $56\frac{1}{8}$
6. $7\frac{3}{4}$

7. $101\frac{1}{2}$
8. $89\frac{7}{8}$
9. $15\frac{3}{8}$
10. $91\frac{1}{4}$
11. $105\frac{3}{4}$
12. $11\frac{1}{8}$

Daily Stock Market Report. Here is part of a daily stock market report:

	52 Week				Sales in				
	High	Low	Stock	Dividend	100s	High	Low	Last	Change
Highest and lowest prices for the last 52 weeks	56⅛	45	American Tel and Tel	5.40	4301	52⅛	51¼	51⅜	-1
	70	31⅛	Bausch and Lomb	1.56	135	62½	59¾	61	+1½
Corporation name	14¼	10	Detroit Edison	1.60	1752	10⅝	10	10	-⅝
	35¾	19⅛	Ford Motor Company	1.20	2403	19⅝	19	19	-⅜
Current dividend rate in dollars per share	88	46⅝	Homestake Mining	1.60	2035	74⅝	70½	72	+1¾
	105¼	65¼	Honeywell	3.00	536	102¾	100½	101⅛	+¼
Hundreds of shares sold in the day	52⅞	36¾	McDonalds	0.40	393	47	45⅛	45¾	-⅞
	89½	49¾	Mobil Oil	4.00	2330	81¼	79⅜	80	-¼
Highest price paid for a share that day	19⅝	14½	Sears Roebuck	1.36	373	15⅞	15¼	15⅝	---
	25	16⅜	U.S. Steel	2.00	687	22½	22⅛	22⅜	+⅛

Lowest price paid for a share that day

Last or closing price paid for a share that day

Difference between last price for that day and last price for the day before

A stock market report

Reading a Stock Market Report. The sales of American Telephone and Telegraph stock are shown first in the table above. The "52 Week High and Low" columns show the highest price ($56.125) and the lowest price ($45) at which the stock was traded during the preceding 52 weeks. At the right of the company name, the 5.40 in the "Dividend" column shows the current annual dividend paid per share, $5.40.

Stock quotes are in dollars

The 4301 in the "Sales in 100s" column shows the number of shares sold, 430,100 ($4,301 \times 100 = 430,100$).

The "High," "Low," and "Last" columns show the highest price ($52.125), the lowest price ($51.25), and the last or closing price ($51.375) paid that day for the stock.

The "−1" in the "Change" column shows the difference between the last price of the day and the last price of the day before. The day's last price (−1) is $1 less than the last price of the day before. Since the day's last price is $51\frac{3}{8}$ ($51.375), the last price of the day before must have been $51\frac{3}{8} + 1$, or $52\frac{3}{8}$ ($52.375).

Oral Practice 2

1. **a.** Of the stocks listed in the table, which stock sold at the highest price during the last 52 weeks?
   b. Which stock sold at the lowest price during the last 52 weeks?

2. a. Which stock is paying the highest annual dividend?
    b. What is that dividend in dollars and cents?

3. a. Which stock was least actively traded on the day of the report?
    b. How many shares of that stock were traded?

4. a. What stock had the highest price of the day? The lowest?
    b. What was the highest price of the day? The lowest?

5. What stock's closing price had changed most from the closing price of the day before? How much was the change?

6. What was the last price of the day before for these stocks:
    a. Bausch and Lomb?
    b. Ford Motor Company?
    c. Sears Roebuck?

Stockbrokers deal in stocks and bonds

Broker's Commission on Stock. When you buy or sell stock through a broker, you have to pay a *broker's commission*, or brokerage fee. Each brokerage firm sets its own fee. The fee often depends on the price of the stock and the number of shares you are buying. Large investors and good customers may get lower commission rates.

Finding Total Cost of a Stock Purchase. When you buy stock through a broker, your total cost or investment is the market price of the stock plus the broker's commission.

Market Price of Stock + Broker's Commission = Total Cost of Stock

---

Example

Mike Kolski bought 100 shares of Diamond Systems stock at $20\frac{1}{2}$. The broker's commission was $51.75. What was the total cost of the stock?

Solution

Market price of $20\frac{1}{2}$ is equal to $20.50 per share

Market price, $100 \times \$20.50$	$2,050.00
Broker's commission	51.75
Total cost of the stock	$2,101.75

Written Practice 3

1. Peg O'Rourke bought 300 shares of Ledyard Mining stock at $12\frac{1}{8}$. The broker charged $74.10 commission on the purchase.
    a. What was the market price of the stock?   **$3,637.50**
    b. What was the total cost of the stock?   **$3,711.60**

2. Juan Soto bought 25 shares of United Foods stock at $34\frac{3}{4}$. Commission on the purchase was $31.67. What was the total cost of the stock?

3. Julia Garcia bought 100 shares of General Computer stock at $106\frac{3}{8}$. She had to pay her broker that amount, plus a commission of $163.40. What total amount did she have to pay her broker?

4. Dolph Shands bought 20 shares of Forest Products stock at $11\frac{5}{8}$, and 56 shares of Dart Trucking at 34. The broker's commission on the purchase was $53.22. What was the total cost of the stock to Dolph?

5. Maria Campana's broker bought 80 shares of Hope Printing stock for her at $25\frac{1}{2}$, and charged $51.58 commission. What was the total cost of Maria's stock purchase?

6. What is the total investment in 150 shares of Allied Broadcasting stock bought at $26\frac{1}{4}$, plus $77.83 commission?

Terms to Remember

dividends	no-par stock	shareholder
stock	stock certificate	yield

a. Shows how many shares are owned
b. Stock without par value
c. The rate of interest on a bond investment
d. A part owner of a corporation; a stockholder
e. Profits distributed to shareholders
f. Any shares of ownership in a corporation

Review 70

1. **a.** Multiply $9,000 by 0.6504
   b. Divide 6.5 L by 5
   c. What amount is $37\frac{1}{2}\%$ less than $84.24?
   d. What is the interest at 12% on $2,500 for 60 days?
   e. 500 m is what percent of 2 km?

2. Dixon Firth bought 60 shares of Almoco stock at $28\frac{1}{2}$. Commission on the purchase was $46. What was the total cost of the stock?

3. Hetty Judge bought five $1,000, $7\frac{1}{2}\%$ bonds for 90, plus a commission of $50. What was the yield (rate of income) on her investment, to the nearest tenth of a percent?

4. Using the state tax rate schedule on page 243, what is the tax on taxable income of $10,600?

5. Lois Krug estimates these annual costs to go to college: tuition, $4,800; room and board, $3,600; fees and insurance, $650; clothing and personal, $650; transportation, $500; other, $750. What is her total estimated cost for 4 years of college?

6. Les Nogales sends a $4\frac{1}{4}$ pound parcel post package to a person who lives in Zone 4. Insurance costs 85¢. What is the total mailing cost? (Use the rate table on page 213.)

STOCK INCOME

As the owner of stock, you are paid dividends on it until you sell it. When you sell the stock, you may get more or less than you paid for it. If you get more, you make a profit on the sale. If you get less, you take a loss on the sale.

Kinds of Stock. Many corporations issue two kinds of stock: preferred stock and common stock. Both kinds indicate ownership in the corporation, but they differ in the way they share in profits.

**Preferred stock
gets a fixed rate of
dividend**

Preferred stock pays a fixed rate of dividend, such as 6% or $6 a share. The rate of dividend is set when the stock is issued. The company does not guarantee that any dividend will be paid. It does guarantee that, if any dividend is paid, it will be paid on preferred stock before it is paid on common stock. So, preferred stock is "preferred" as to the payment of dividends.

**Common stock has
no fixed rate of
dividend**

Common stock is the ordinary stock of a corporation. There is no guarantee that any dividend will be paid on common stock, or that any specific rate will be paid if a dividend is declared. On the other hand, there is no limit to the amount of dividend that may be paid on common stock after other dividends, expenses, and taxes have been paid.

Dividends. When a corporation wants to distribute some of its profits to shareholders, it declares a dividend. The dividend may be stated as a percent of the par value of the stock, or as a certain amount per share.

For example, suppose that a corporation wants to pay a dividend of 3% of the par value. If their shares have a par value of $100, the dividend on each share is 3% of $100, or $3 per share. So, the corporation can declare either a 3% dividend or a dividend of $3 per share, and the result will be the same. Dividends on no-par stock are declared as an amount per share.

Finding Income from a Stock Investment. Your income from an investment in stock is the dividends that you get. To find the amount of dividend you should get for any period of time, you multiply the dividend on one share by the number of shares you own.

Number of Shares × Dividend per Share = Total Dividend

Your annual income from a stock investment is the total of the dividends you get in a year.

Example 1

Tien Lin owns 100 shares of $100 par value Bradley Tubing stock. If the stock pays a dividend of $2\frac{1}{2}\%$, how much total dividend should she get?

Solution

$2\frac{1}{2}\% = 0.025$
$0.025 \times \$100 = \$2.50$ per share
$100 \times \$2.50 = \$250$ total dividend

Example 2

Ruby Samson owns 200 shares of Solar Energy stock that pays a quarterly dividend of $0.87\frac{1}{2}$ per share. What is Ruby's total annual income from the stock?

Solution

$200 \times \$0.87\frac{1}{2} = \$175$ dividend per quarter
$4 \times \$175 = \$700$ total yearly income from stock

Written Practice 1

1. Liz Kidd owns 100 shares of $100 par value preferred stock that pays $6\frac{1}{2}\%$ annually. What is her total income from the stock per year? **$650**

2. What will be your total income from 50 shares of $100 par value stock that you own if a dividend of $4\frac{3}{4}\%$ is declared?

3. Merv Freitag owns 200 shares of Altrak Company common stock. The stock pays a $1.12\frac{1}{2}$ dividend per quarter. What is Merv's annual income from the stock? **$900**

4. Glynis Moak's 150 shares of Southware no-par stock pays a quarterly dividend of 75¢ per share. What is her annual income from the stock?

5. Luisa Valdez owns 100 shares of common stock that pays $62\frac{1}{2}$¢ per share each quarter. She also owns 50 shares of a $100 par value preferred stock that pays $5\frac{1}{2}\%$ dividend per year. What is her total annual income from the stocks?

6. Ted McKay's 75 shares of Texon Oil stock pay a quarterly dividend of $0.45 per share. His 50 shares of Parenti Shipping pay an annual dividend of $4.25 per share. Which stock earns more annual income for Ted? How much more?

7. You can buy 300 shares of Delmarny stock that will pay an estimated quarterly dividend of $0.65 per share. Or, you can buy 200 shares of Printco stock that will pay an estimated quarterly dividend of $1.05 per share. Which stock would pay more estimated dividends per year? How much more?

Finding the Rate of Income from a Stock Investment. Suppose that you buy stocks at different prices and that they pay different dividends. You may want to compare them to find which one is the better investment. One way of comparing them is to figure and compare their *rate of income*.

To figure the rate of income on stock, you divide the annual dividend on the stock by the total cost of the stock.

$$\text{Rate of Income} = \frac{\text{Annual Dividend}}{\text{Total Cost of Stock}}$$

Example

Betty Baum owns 50 shares of stock that cost her $1,200. The stock pays an annual dividend of $100. What is the rate of income on her stock, to the nearest tenth of a percent?

Solution

$$\frac{\$100 \text{ annual dividend}}{\$1,200 \text{ total cost of stock}} = 0.0833 = 8.3\%$$

Written Practice 2

1. What is the rate of income, to the nearest tenth of a percent, on 100 shares of stock that cost a total of $5,000 and that pay a quarterly dividend of $0.85 per share? **6.8%**

2. A share of stock cost $68.50. It paid an annual dividend of $4.11. What was the rate of income on the stock?

3. A stock that costs $34.50 per share pays a quarterly dividend of 60¢. What is the rate of income on the stock, to the nearest whole percent?

You are finding what percent a number is of another number

4. Barbara Mazur owns some Model Drug stock for which she paid $1,400. The stock pays an annual dividend of $119. Barbara also owns some Argon Chemical stock that cost $4,810 and pays an annual dividend of $553.15. Which stock pays the greater rate of income? How much greater?

5. Laga Fastener stock sells for $48\frac{1}{4}$ per share and pays an annual dividend of $3.50. Combo Lock stock costs $22\frac{1}{2}$ and pays a dividend of $1.70 per year. Which stock pays a higher rate of income?

You Can Lose Your Shirt in the STOCK MARKET

You have used the term "net proceeds" with commission problems

Proceeds from Selling Stock. If you sell stock through a broker, you have to pay the broker's commission. The amount you get after paying the broker's commission is called *net proceeds.**

Market Price − Broker's Commission = Net Proceeds

Example

Beth Adams sold 50 shares of Carter Sportco stock through a broker at $46\frac{1}{2}$. The broker's commission was $56.50. What were Beth's net proceeds from the sale?

Solution	
Market price (50 × $46.50)	$2,325.00
Broker's commission	−56.50
Net proceeds	$2,268.50

Written Practice 3

1. Margot Hess sold 800 shares of Tomac Mining stock at $5\frac{5}{8}$. The commission on the sale was $104.95. What were Margot's net proceeds from the sale? **$4,395.05**

2. Yang Sun owns 250 shares of Southfield Furniture stock. She plans to sell the stock at $33\frac{3}{4}$. Her broker's commission will be $145. What net proceeds should she get from her broker after the sale?

3. Ricardo Silva sold 25 shares of Oakland Pipe at $63\frac{1}{4}$, and 100 shares of Lake Vans stock at $14\frac{7}{8}$. Silva's broker charged $70.28 commission. What net amount did Silva get from the sale?

4. You own 200 shares of stock. You are thinking of selling the stock at its quoted price of $36\frac{1}{2}$ and putting the net proceeds into a better investment. Your broker's commission on the sale would be $124.28. If you sell the stock, how much money would you have to reinvest?

5. Dody Cafaro needs to sell some stock to get cash for current expenses. She owns 40 shares of Metro Utility stock that she can sell at $17\frac{1}{2}$, less $28 commission and $1.53 for other fees and taxes. How much cash would Dody get from the sale? **$670.47**

Profit or Loss on a Sale of Stock. Your profit or loss on a sale of stock is the difference between the total cost of the stock and the net proceeds of the sale. If the net proceeds are greater than the cost of the stock, you have made a profit.

Net Proceeds − Total Cost = Profit

---

*A very small Securities and Exchange Commission (SEC) fee and, in one or two states, a stock transfer tax on the sale of stock may be included in the commission or charged separately. If charged separately, they also must be subtracted from the market price to find net proceeds.

If the net proceeds of the sale are less than the cost of the stock, you have taken a loss.

Total Cost − Net Proceeds = Loss

**Written
Practice 4**

1. Consuelo Guerra bought some shares of stock at a total cost of $5,874.50. She later sold the stock and the net proceeds of the sale were $6,239.25. What was Consuelo's profit on the sale?   **$364.75**

2. Troy Butler bought 100 shares of Foxcraft stock at $35\frac{1}{4}$, plus a total commission of $72.70. He later sold the stock at $43\frac{1}{2}$, less $83 commission. What was Troy's profit on the sale?

3. Luke Mapur received $1,672.40 from his broker as net proceeds from the sale of some stock. Luke had purchased the stock for $1,835.20. What was Luke's loss on the sale of the stock?   **$162.80**

4. Helen Columbo sold 200 shares of stock through a broker at 15. The broker charged $66.20 commission. Helen had bought the stock at $28\frac{1}{2}$, plus commission of $102.20. What was her loss on the sale?

5. You own 500 shares of stock for which you paid $8.75 a share, plus $84 commission. If you sell the stock now, you will get $9.25 a share, less commission, fees, and taxes of $86. Would you make a profit or a loss on the sale? How much?

★**Net Gain or Loss from Owning and Selling Stock.** In figuring your net gain or loss from owning and selling stock, you include any dividends that you have received while you owned the stock. If you had a profit from the sale of the stock, you add the profit and the dividends to find your net gain.

Suppose that you took a loss on the sale of the stock, but your dividends were greater than the loss on the sale. You subtract the loss on the sale from the amount of your dividends to find your net gain.

If you had a loss on the sale and your dividends were less than the loss, you had a net loss. You find the amount of the net loss by subtracting the dividends from the loss on the sale.

★**Written
Practice 5**

1. Victor Renkov bought 100 shares of stock for a total cost of $7,640. He kept the stock for a year and received quarterly dividends of $0.95 per share. Victor then sold the stock and his net proceeds on the sale were $8,275. What was his net gain from owning and selling the stock?

2. Penny Armot sold 50 shares of Victory Mills stock for net proceeds of $1,762.50. She had bought the stock two years before at a total cost of $1,587.50. While Penny owned the stock, she received eight quarterly dividends of 42¢ a share. What was her net gain from owning and selling the stock?

3. Boris Kaba paid $2,850 for some stock. While he owned the stock, he received $190 in dividends on it. He then sold the stock for $2,675.
   a. What was his loss on the sale of the stock?
   b. What was his net gain from owning and selling the stock? **$15**

4. Several years ago you bought some stock for $8,450. You had received $480 in dividends on the stock. If you sell it now, you will get $7,420 for it. What will be your net loss if you sell now?

Terms to Remember

common stock   **preferred stock**

a. Pays a specific rate of dividend, if any dividend is paid
b. Pays no specific rate of dividend

Review 71

1. a. Multiply $20\frac{1}{3}$ by $15\frac{1}{2}$
   b. $5 \text{ kg} - 4.2 \text{ kg} = ? \text{ kg}$
   c. Round $206.4045 to the nearest cent
   d. What is 25% of 110 m²?
   e. Find the amount that is 20% more than $450
   f. What is the simple interest on $8,000 for $2\frac{1}{2}$ years at 11%?

2. Dina Junco's 200 shares of Tileco stock pay a quarterly dividend of 48¢ a share. What is her annual income from the stock?

3. A share of stock that costs 75 pays an annual dividend of $6.20. What is the rate of income on the stock, to the nearest tenth of a percent?

4. Katy Parker bought 40 shares of stock a year ago for $855.40, including commission. She now plans to sell the stock for $990, less $35.50 commission.
   a. What will be her net proceeds from the sale of the stock?
   b. What will be her profit on the sale?

5. You own some Alcore stock for which you paid $1,200. The stock pays an annual dividend of $72. Your cousin owns some Carrier stock that cost $4,800 and pays an annual dividend of $240.
   a. Which stock pays the greater rate of income?
   b. How much greater?

6. Randy Waldorf bought 8 corporation bonds at $65\frac{1}{4}$, plus a commission of $7.50 per bond. What was his total investment in the bonds?

7. Your bank statement for February shows a balance of $298.27 on February 28. Your checkbook balance for February 28 is $274.05. You find that a check for $25.72 is outstanding. The bank statement shows a service charge of $1.50 that you don't have in your checkbook. Make a reconciliation statement.

Unit Fifteen

REAL ESTATE

Many investors put some of their savings into rental real estate such as houses, apartments, condominiums, stores, and offices. They invest in real estate with the hope that they will make a profit from the rental income and from increased value of the property.

Owning and renting real estate can produce a good return on the investment, but it may take a lot of work, time, and worry. To avoid those problems, some investors in real estate hire a rental agent or property manager to manage the property for them.

This unit is concerned with some of the common *financial* problems of owning and renting property. When you have completed this unit, you should be able to:

- figure gross and net income from renting real estate
- find the rate of income on a real estate investment
- figure rent to charge to give a desired income
- ★• figure maximum investment for a desired rate of return
- ★• find capital investment
- ★• find which investment gives the better income
- read, write, speak, and recognize the meanings of terms often used in real estate investment

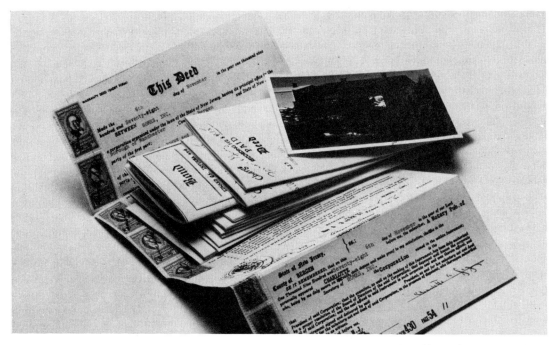

Merrill Lynch Realty Associates

INCOME FROM REAL ESTATE

section

72

Gross Income from Real Estate. If you own and rent real estate, your *gross income* is the rent you get from tenants. Rent is often charged by the month, but gross income from rent is usually figured on a yearly, or annual, basis. Sometimes, of course, rental property may be vacant and producing no income.

Written Practice 1

1. Emi Kim owns a two-family apartment house. She rents each apartment for $410 a month.
   a. What is Emi's monthly gross rental income?   **$820**
   b. What is her yearly gross rental income?   **$9,840**

2. Alec Vardin owns a two-family house. He lives in one apartment and rents the other apartment to a tenant. Alec charges the tenant $525 a month for the apartment, plus $30 a month for garage space. What is Alec's gross rental income per year?

3. Gus Kaiser invested in a four-family apartment building. He rented two of the apartments at $440 a month, and the other two at $475 a month. What was his gross yearly income from rent?

4. Rose Blanco invested some of her savings in a condominium in a resort area. During the first year, Rose lived in the condo herself for $1\frac{1}{2}$ months. She rented the condo for $5\frac{1}{2}$ months at $1,400 per month. The condo was vacant the rest of the year. What was Rose's gross rental income for the year?

5. Morris Swartz is considering buying an eight-unit office building as an investment. He estimates that each unit will rent for an average of $580 per month. He also estimates that, on the average, one unit will be vacant for 6 months of the year and he will have no income from it. What will be his estimated gross annual rental income from the building?

If I never had a vacancy, I'd charge less rent — or make more profit!

OFFICE SPACE
FOR RENT
CALL 434-6075

Net Income from Real Estate. When you own and rent real estate, you have many expenses of ownership. For example, if you borrow money to buy the property, you have to pay interest on the mortgage. You have to pay for repairs and maintenance, and for property taxes. The property may lose value, so you may have depreciation expense.

Owning property costs money!

You may have advertising expenses, legal fees, and cleaning costs to prepare the space for new tenants. If you use a rental agent or property manager, you may have to pay 8% to 10% of your gross income for those management services.

Your annual *net income*, or net profit, from the property is your annual gross income less all the annual expenses of owning and renting the property.

$$\begin{matrix} \text{Annual Gross} \\ \text{Income} \end{matrix} - \begin{matrix} \text{Annual Ownership} \\ \text{Expenses} \end{matrix} = \begin{matrix} \text{Annual Net} \\ \text{Income} \end{matrix}$$

Written Practice 2

1. Chen Loi's monthly rental income from a house was $800. His annual expenses were: interest, $3,600; depreciation, $1,400; repairs and maintenance, $700; taxes, $1,200; insurance, $350; other, $50. What was Chen's annual net income from the property? **$2,300**

2. Knute Ellers owns and rents a two-apartment building. He gets $425 rent per month for each apartment unit. Knute's annual expenses of ownership are $6,780. What is his net income from renting for a year?

3. Jane Wilbur bought a house and lot for $70,000, paying $25,000 down and mortgaging the rest. She rented the house for $900 a month. Her expenses for the first year were:

   10% interest on the mortgage of $45,000
   2% depreciation on the house, valued at $60,000
   Taxes, repairs, insurance, and other expenses, $2,900

   What was Jane's net income for the year?

4. Mary Chi owns a four-apartment building that cost her $100,000. She rents each apartment for $400 per month. Her expenses for a year are:

   12% interest on a $75,000 mortgage
   $2\frac{1}{2}$% depreciation on the building valued at $80,000
   Taxes, insurance, repairs, $5,000
   Agent's commission and other charges, $1,600

   What is Mary's net income per year from the property?

5. Adolph Velloz can buy a property for $60,000 that will pay $780 a month in rent. He estimates the yearly expenses of ownership as these:

   Interest on mortgage, 9% of $40,000
   Depreciation, 2% of $50,000
   Repairs and maintenance, $1\frac{1}{2}$% of $60,000
   Taxes and insurance, $2,000

   What would be his yearly net income from this property?

Finding Rate of Income on a Real Estate Investment. You find the rate of income on a real estate investment by dividing the annual net income by the cash investment.

$$\text{Rate of Income} = \frac{\text{Annual Net Income}}{\text{Cash Investment}}$$

In many cases, the owner's cash investment is only part of the total purchase price of the property. The owner borrows the rest of the purchase price with a mortgage.

Written Practice 3

1. Jun Nitobe invested $25,000 of his own money in a rental property, and borrowed the rest of the purchase price. He rented the property to a tenant for $840 a month. His ownership expenses were $7,700 a year. What was Jun's rate of income on the property, to the nearest tenth of a percent? **9.5%**

2. For a down payment of $20,000 of his own money, Lew Downes bought a two-family apartment building. He borrowed the rest of the purchase price with a mortgage. His annual ownership expenses were $13,500. Lew rented each of the apartments for $635 a month. What was Lew's rate of income on his investment, to the nearest tenth of a percent?

3. Marta Trafton gets $900 a month rent for a building that cost her $60,000. She invested only $30,000 of her own money in the building. Marta's annual ownership expenses on the building are 10% interest on a $30,000 mortgage, and other expenses totaling $4,400. What is Marta's rate of return on her investment, to the nearest tenth of a percent?

4. A condominium is rented by the owner for $1,000 a month. The owner's investment in the property is $40,000. The owner's annual expenses are: interest, $2,400; depreciation, $1,500; taxes, $1,100; other, $1,000. What is the owner's rate of income on the investment?

Some investments produce much more net income than others!

5. Juanita Carelos invested $10,000 of her own money in a mobile home. She lives in the home for 3 months of the year and rents it to tenants for 9 months of the year at $600 a month. Juanita's annual ownership expenses are $4,700. What is her rate of return on the investment?

6. Tien Woosung built a small office building for $100,000. She paid $30,000 cash and borrowed the rest on an 11% mortgage. During the first year, Tien rented each of the 4 rental spaces in the building at $395 per month. Tien's expenses for the year were:

> Interest at 11% on the $70,000 mortgage
> Depreciation at $2\frac{1}{2}$% on the building value of $80,000
> Other expenses, $5,800

What was Tien's rate of income on the investment, to the nearest percent?

Finding the Rent Needed for a Desired Rate of Income. If you own and rent property, you have to decide how much rent to charge for it. You have to find a rental charge that covers all your expenses and that gives you a fair return on your investment.

You can figure the amount of annual rent to charge by first deciding the percent of net income you need or want on your investment. Then you add the total of your annual ownership expenses and the desired annual net income to find the annual rental charge.

Annual Rental Charge = Annual Expenses + Annual Net Income

To find the monthly rental charge, you divide the annual rental charge by 12.

Example

You want to make 10% annual net income on your investment of $25,000 in a rental property. Your annual ownership expenses are $2,360. How much monthly rent should you charge?

Solution

10% of $25,000 investment = $2,500 desired annual net income
$2,360 expenses + $2,500 desired net income = $4,860 annual rental charge
$4,860 ÷ 12 = $405 monthly rent

Written Practice 4

1. Xavier Kosta has invested $30,000 in a rental property. His expenses to own the property are $5,220 per year. What monthly rent should he charge to make 12% per year on his investment? $735

2. You have $40,000 to invest and you want to make 9% on your investment. You estimate that, if you invest that amount in rental property, the annual expense to own the property would be $6,480. If you invest in the property, how much monthly rent would you have to charge to make your desired annual net income?

3. When prices and interest rates were low, Loretta Newell invested $10,000 in a two-family apartment house. Her annual ownership expenses average $4,860. She now wants to set the monthly rent so that she will make 15% on her original investment. What monthly rent must she charge for each apartment?

4. The owner of a house has invested $60,000 in it. Annual ownership expenses are taxes, $1,800; depreciation, 2% of the investment; repairs and maintenance, $600; insurance, $312. What monthly rent must the owner charge to cover the expenses and make 8% net income on the investment?

5. Norman Boyer buys a four-family apartment house for $120,000. He invests $40,000 of his own money in it and borrows $80,000 on a mortgage at 10%. His annual expenses in addition to the interest on the mortgage total $5,920. What monthly rent must he charge for each apartment to make 12% net income on his investment?

Review 72

1. **a.** Multiply $12,000 by 0.18204
   b. Divide 73.5 by 1,400
   c. Subtract 32.05 from 84.5
   d. Add 5.75 L and 0.5 L
   e. $25 is what fractional part greater than $20?
   f. What amount is 15% more than $800?
   g. What is the exact interest on $1,000 at 8% for 20 days?

2. An apartment house that Cornelia Bates owns produces monthly gross rental income of $2,200. Her annual ownership expenses are these: interest at 10% on a $100,000 mortgage; depreciation at $2\frac{1}{2}$% of the purchase price, $150,000; other expenses, $6,650. What is Cornelia's annual net income from the property?

3. Chad Arket has invested $35,000 in real estate that produces net income of $4,900 per year. What is Chad's rate of net income?

4. You own 100 shares of stock that you bought for $23.75 a share, plus $58.50 total commission. If you sell the stock now, you will get $24.50 a share, less commission, fees, and taxes totaling $64.40. Would you make a profit or a loss on the stock if you sell it now? How much?

5. Elseth Carton had health care expenses last year that totaled $2,498. All of the expenses were covered by major medical insurance, but the policy had a $200 deductible feature and an 80% coinsurance feature.
   a. How much of the total expenses did the insurance company pay?
   b. How much of the total did Elseth have to pay?

6. Your checkbook balance on November 30 was $720.85. Study of your bank statement for that date shows that (a) the bank balance was $758.52, (b) your check number 51 for $34.25 was outstanding, and (c) your account earned $3.42 interest for the month, which had to be added to the checkbook. What was your correct checkbook balance on December 1?

SPECIAL PROBLEMS OF REAL ESTATE INVESTMENT

★section

73

Before investing in real estate, you ought to find out how much annual net income you can expect from the property. When you know how much income you can expect, you can then figure the greatest amount of your own money that you should invest to give you a desired rate of income.

Greatest Investment for a Given Rate of Income. To find the greatest amount that you could invest in a property to make a given rate of income, you divide the annual net income by the annual rate of income.

$$\text{Cash Investment} = \frac{\text{Annual Net Income}}{\text{Rate of Income}}$$

Example

You are thinking of buying an apartment building that will produce net rental income of $4,500 a year. What is the greatest amount that you could invest in the building and make 12% income on your investment?

Solution

$4,500 ÷ 0.12 = $37,500 greatest investment

★Written
Practice 1

1. Isabel Vacarra wants to make 10% on money that she invests in real estate. What is the most that she should invest in a condominium that pays annual net rental income of $5,000?   **$50,000**

2. You are thinking of buying a small office building as an investment. You want to make at least 9% on your investment in the property. You can expect a maximum net rental income from the building of $7,200 a year. How much of your own money could you invest in the building and make your desired rate of income?

3. Each of the six units in an apartment building rents for $500 a month. Annual ownership expenses of the building total $28,850. If you want to make 11% on your investment, what is the greatest amount you should invest in buying this building?   **$65,000**

4. Wesley Hunter wants to invest some money in rental real estate, but he wants to be sure that he will make at least $10\frac{1}{2}$% on his investment. Wesley believes that a one-family house at 43 Pine Street can be rented for a maximum of $670 a month. If he buys that house and rents it, his annual cost of ownership will total $6,780. What is the greatest amount of his own money that he could invest in that house and make his desired rate of income?

★Total Capital Investment in Real Estate. To accurately figure your income on a property, you need to show your income as a percent of your total capital investment. Your *total capital investment* in real estate is your original investment plus any other amounts you have spent to increase the property value. Money that you spend for additions and improvements to the property should be added to your original investment to find your total capital investment.

$$\begin{array}{c} \textbf{Original} \\ \textbf{Investment} \end{array} + \begin{array}{c} \textbf{Additional} \\ \textbf{Investments} \end{array} = \begin{array}{c} \textbf{Total} \\ \textbf{Capital Investment} \end{array}$$

For example, suppose that you originally invested $40,000 in buying a two-family apartment house. You then spent another $20,000 to add garages to the apartments. Your total capital investment became $60,000. Original investment ($40,000) plus additional investment ($20,000) equals total capital investment ($60,000).

In figuring your additions to capital investment, you should *not* include expenses for ordinary repairs and replacements. Any money spent to repair, replace, or maintain the property in the condition in which you bought it is an expense rather than a capital addition. For example, money spent to repaint a house, to repair or replace the roof, to fix broken windows, or to reseed a lawn is an expense rather than an addition to capital.

"It's just repairs for flood damage — not a capital investment."

★Written Practice 2

1. Ilka Herr invested $50,000 in buying a small store. Before renting the building, Ilka spent $25,000 more to build a parking lot and to modernize the front of the store with display windows. She then rented the building and made a net annual income of $6,000.
   a. What was Ilka's rate of income on the *original* investment?   **12%**
   b. What was her total capital investment in the building?   **$75,000**
   c. What was her rate of income on the total capital investment?   **8%**

2. Akeo Makaha invested $30,000 of his own money to buy a small apartment building. After his original investment, he spent $10,000 for improvements. Akeo then rented the apartments and made a net income of $4,600 per year. What was his rate of income on the total investment?

3. Julio Gonzalez spent $42,000 of his savings to buy a rental house. He added a room to the house and finished part of the basement for a total cost of $5,500. He then rented the house for $650 a month. His annual ownership costs totaled $3,260 a year. What was his rate of income on the total capital investment, to the nearest tenth of a percent?   **9.6%**

4. Jim Fain invests $71,000 to buy a four-family house. He spends an additional $9,000 to modernize it. He then rents each apartment for $275 a month. His total annual ownership expenses are estimated at $6,250. What is Fain's rate of income on his total cash investment, to the nearest tenth of a percent?

5. Phyllis Zee can buy a building by investing $20,000 of her own money in it. She will have to invest another $5,000 in it for capital additions and improvements. She estimates that her ownership expenses will average $5,300 a year. How much rent will she have to charge per month to pay the expenses and make a net income of 10% on her total investment?

6. Dot Kaye is thinking of investing money in a rental building. She would have to spend $10,000 more than her original investment for capital improvements. After the improvements were made, she could rent the building for $1,100 a month. Her ownership costs would average $9,600 a year. If she wants to make 9% on her total capital investment, how much could Dot originally invest in the building before improving it?

★**Comparing Income from Real Estate Investments.** Before investing in real estate, you should compare the income or the rate of income that you could expect from alternative investments. Sometimes an investment that seems better-paying is not as good as another.

★**Written Practice 3**

1. Lim Yung wants to invest $30,000 in real estate. With that money, he can buy a two-family apartment house that will rent at $500 per month for each apartment. His estimated annual ownership expenses would total $8,900. As an alternative, he could buy a small office building with four office spaces, each of which would rent for $350 a month. His estimated ownership expenses for the office building would be $13,500 a year. From which building would he get a greater annual net income? How much greater?   **Office; $200**

2. Linda Spando estimates that $15,000 invested in Building *A* will give her an annual net income of $1,620. If she invests $24,000 in Building *B*, her annual net income would be $2,460. Which investment would give her a greater *rate* of net income? How much greater, to the nearest tenth of a percent?

3. Regaldo Rios is deciding between two investments in real estate. He could buy a four-family apartment building by investing $20,000 as a down payment. He would have to invest another $10,000 to modernize the apartments and would then rent each one for $375 a month. The yearly expenses of owning the apartments would be $14,200. His other choice is to buy a condominium by investing $20,000 in it. He could rent the condo at $1,050 per month and would have ownership expenses of $10,800 a year. Which investment would give a greater rate of net income? How much greater, to the nearest tenth of a percent?

★Review 73

1. **a.** $60 is equal to what number increased by $\frac{1}{9}$ of itself?
   b. Express $64.83\frac{1}{3}$ as a mixed number in simplest form
   c. $9.45 is $33\frac{1}{3}\%$ of what amount?
   d. What amount decreased by 22% of itself gives $460.20?
   e. Express $1\frac{5}{16}$ as a decimal correct to three decimal places
   f. $\frac{5}{8}$ of what amount is equal to $425?

2. Sarah Foster wants to earn 15% on an investment in real estate. What is the most that she should invest to buy a building that produces annual net income of $8,400?

3. George Amato invested $32,000 in a building, then built an addition that increased his capital investment by $8,000. When he rented it, the building produced $5,200 net income per year. What was George's rate of income on his total capital investment?

4. You can invest $25,000 in an apartment building that will produce $2,850 net income per year without further expense. Or, you can buy a house with a $25,000 down payment, invest another $9,000 in capital improvements, and make $4,216 net income per year from it. Which would give you a greater rate of income on your investment? How much greater?

5. Charlotte Kroll paid $2,605 for 80 shares of stock. She kept the stock for two years and collected eight quarterly dividends of 62¢ per share. She then sold the stock for $2,610. What was Charlotte's net gain or loss from owning and selling the stock?

6. The Gulfstream Savings and Loan pays interest on passbook accounts at an annual rate of 6%. Gulfstream compounds and adds the interest each quarter on whole dollars of the minimum balance during the quarter. Luis Aponte's account balance with Gulfstream on July 1 was $4,205.60. During the rest of that year, Luis deposited $500 on August 20, withdrew $75 on October 20, and withdrew $150.95 on December 15. What was his balance on January 1 after the interest was credited?

7. Mr. and Mrs. Ronan's adjusted gross income last year was $55,650. Their excess deductions totaled $1,650 and they claimed 3 exemptions at $1,000 each on their federal income tax return. What was their income tax for the year, using Schedule Y on page 240?

**Part III
Review**

1. **a.** Add $4\frac{1}{3}$, $8\frac{1}{4}$, $3\frac{1}{5}$
    b. Subtract $247\frac{2}{3}$ from $354\frac{1}{6}$
    c. Multiply $16\frac{1}{4} \times 12\frac{1}{2}$
    d. Divide $24\frac{1}{3}$ by $\frac{1}{2}$
    e. Multiply 0.45 by 0.627
    f. What is $\frac{1}{3}\%$ of $237?
    g. Show $\frac{7}{15}$ as a percent to the nearest tenth of a percent
    h. What is 28% of $420?
    i. Round 126.0439 to the nearest thousandth

2. Joanne Caron's regular pay rate is $9.60 an hour. During one week she worked 40 hours at regular time and 3 hours at time and a half pay. What was her gross pay for that week?

3. Dennis Lang's gross pay for a week was $275.60. He claims 4 withholding allowances. Use the table on page 35 to find his withholding tax.

4. Mitzi Andre earned $296 in one week. Her employer deducted social security tax on her wages at the rate of 0.067. What amount was deducted?

5. Barry Omana, a salesperson, is paid a salary of $960 a month and a commission of 4% on all sales. His sales for April were $16,000. What was his total pay for April?

6. Purvis Grant's combined wages and tips for five days were: $52.80; $49.70; $61.50; $56.45; and $50.65. What was his average pay per day?

7. What is the correct total sale price of 6 pairs of sox at $1.49, plus a 7% sales tax?

8. During one year, the Sandoval's rent and food expenses totaled $13,500. The ratio of their rent expense to their food expense was 5 to 4. How much did they spend for (a) rent; and (b) food?

9. A box of 9 cupcakes is priced at $1.65. At that rate, what is the price of a dozen?

10. You get a discount of $4.50 on a jacket that originally sold for $36. What fractional part of the original price is the discount?

11. Last year the Redwing family spent a total of $12,420 for housing and household expenses. What was their average monthly expense?

12. Two years ago, the Masamis used 1,200 gallons of heating oil at a total cost of $1,140. Last year, they used 1,050 gallons of heating oil at a total cost of $1,260.
    a. What percent less heating oil did they use last year than they used two years ago?
    b. By what percent was their total fuel oil cost greater last year than two years ago, to the nearest tenth of a percent?

13. Your electric meter reading in March was 0986 and in July it was 1408. The basic monthly charge for electricity is $6.25, plus $0.052 per KWH. What should be your total electric bill for the month, including sales tax at 6%?

14. Grace Huwan is spending $3,250 for energy-saving improvements to her home. She expects to save $500 a year in energy costs by the improvements. What is the payback period of the improvements?

15. For a 10-minute telephone call on a weekday, how much would you save by making a dial-direct call rather than a person-to-person call? (Use the table of telephone rates on page 167.)

16. To clean her carpets, Ione Ford rented a cleaner overnight for $6. She kept the cleaner for an extra 2 hours and had to pay $3.50 more for it. She used 2 quarts of cleaning fluid at $2.98 a bottle. Sales tax on the cleaner and fluid was at 5%. What was Ione's total cost?

17. Ready-made curtains will cost you $165.95. You can make curtains by buying 36 yards of fabric at $2.50 a yard, and other supplies costing $16.75. How much would you save by making the curtains?

18. Gib Bazik has been paying $340 a year for homeowner's insurance. By increasing the deductible amount, he cut the premium by 12%, and by installing smoke alarms he cut the original premium another 3%.
    a. How much did Gib save in premiums?
    b. What was his new premium?

19. Caesar Esko insured some property with Company Y for $70,000 and with Company Z for $50,000. What would be each company's share of a fire loss of $36,000?

20. Frances Kwong's real estate in Blue Ridge is assessed for $9,500. The school tax rate last year in Blue Ridge was $73.24 per $1,000. What was her school tax last year?

21. A car that you buy now for $8,500 will have an estimated trade-in value of $3,400 after 3 years. What is its annual rate of depreciation?

22. Lloyd McKenna's car operating expenses last year totaled $5,040. He drove the car 12,000 miles (19 312 km). What was his average operating cost for the car per mile (per km), to the nearest cent?

★23. On August 31, Oliva Navarro's bank statement balance was $770.20. Her checkbook balance was $596.25. A deposit of $145, made on August 31, was not on the statement. Her checks for $69.25 and $7.50 were outstanding. She had not recorded a deposit of $235, and she had recorded a check for $21.95 as $29.15 in her checkbook. Make a reconciliation statement for Oliva.

Part IV

Borrowing Money

At many times in your life, you may need or want to borrow money. If you do, you may get a loan from a friend or relative. Probably, though, you will borrow from a bank, savings and loan association, credit union, or consumer finance agency. Those businesses lend money for a profit. If you have life insurance, you might borrow from your insurance company.

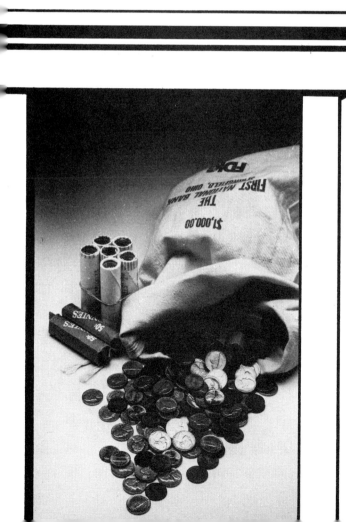

You may borrow money in another way by using credit. When you buy on credit and are given time to pay for the goods or services, you are borrowing someone else's money.

Sometimes you can borrow money for a short time or for special purposes without paying anything extra. Usually, though, you have to pay interest. Sometimes you have to pay other charges.

Part IV is concerned with some of the common problems of borrowing money by using notes, installment loans, and credit.

NOTES AND LOANS

When you borrow money from a person, a bank, or other business that lends money, you will probably have to sign a **promissory note.** The note is your written promise to repay the amount you borrowed and, usually, interest for the use of the money.

If you are to repay the loan in one payment, it is called a **single-payment loan.** If you are to repay the loan in several part-payments, or installments, the loan is called an **installment loan.**

This unit is concerned with borrowing by both single-payment loans and installment loans. When you have finished this unit, you should be able to:

- figure the amount due at maturity of several kinds of notes
- find the due date of a note
- find the number of days between dates on notes
★ • figure bank discount
★ • figure proceeds of discounted notes
- figure finance charges and total amount paid on installment loans
- find monthly payments on installment loans
- figure annual percentage rate on installment loans
- read, write, speak, and recognize the meanings of the terms shown in color

INTEREST-BEARING NOTES

section
74

Using Promissory Notes. Many different forms of printed notes are used, but most notes have the features of the note shown below.

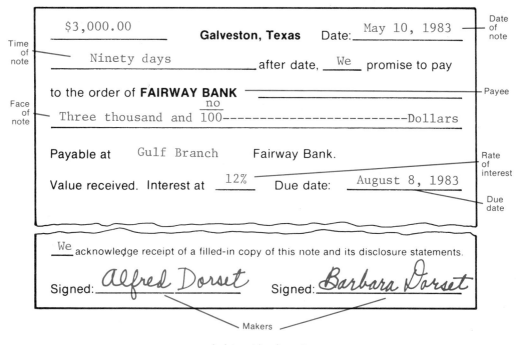

Time of note	Date of note
Face of note	Payee
	Rate of interest
	Due date

$3,000.00 **Galveston, Texas** Date: May 10, 1983

Ninety days _____ after date, __We__ promise to pay

to the order of **FAIRWAY BANK** _____ — Payee

Three thousand and $\frac{no}{100}$------------------------Dollars

Payable at Gulf Branch Fairway Bank.

Value received. Interest at 12% Due date: August 8, 1983

__We__ acknowledge receipt of a filled-in copy of this note and its disclosure statements.

Signed: *Alfred Dorset* Signed: *Barbara Dorset*

Makers

An interest-bearing note

On May 10, 1983, Alfred and Barbara Dorset borrowed $3,000 for ninety days from the Fairway Bank. They signed the note form that was furnished by the bank. The Dorsets are called the *makers* of the note. The Fairway Bank is the *payee* to whom the money must be repaid.

The day on which the Dorsets signed the note, May 10, 1983, is the **date of the note**. The time for which they borrowed the money, ninety days, is the **time of the note**. The amount borrowed, $3,000, is the **face of the note**, or *principal*. The interest to be paid, 12%, is the *rate of interest*, or just the *rate*. The date the money was to be repaid is the **due date**, or *date of maturity*.

An interest rate is a rate per year

The Dorset's note required them to pay interest, so the note is called an **interest-bearing note**.

Finding the Amount Due at Maturity. On the due date of the note, the Dorsets owed the face of $3,000, plus the interest on $3,000 for 90 days at 12%. The total amount of principal and interest owed on the due date of any note is called the **amount due at maturity**, or *maturity value*.

The way to figure the amount due at maturity is shown in the example on the next page.

Example

What is the amount due at maturity of the Dorset's note shown on page 319?

Solution

Face of note	$3,000
Interest $\left(\$3,000 \times 0.12 \times \dfrac{90}{360}\right)$	90
Amount due at maturity	$3,090

Written Practice 1

1. Chuck Grant borrowed $5,000 from the Becket Bank and signed a note promising to repay the money in two years with interest at a rate of 9% per year.
   a. What was the total amount of interest due in two years?　**$900**
   b. What was the amount due at maturity of the note?　**$5,900**

Interest rates are rates per year

2. You borrow $10,000 from a friend to help pay your expenses for further education. You sign a five-year note for the loan, with interest at 8%. When the note is due:
   a. How much interest will you owe?
   b. What total amount will you owe?

3. Hillary Plante borrowed $7,500 from her bank on a passbook loan. The note she signed required her to repay the loan in 6 months with 10% interest per year. She repaid the loan when it was due.
   a. What amount of interest did she pay?　**$375**
   b. What total amount did she pay at maturity?　**$7,875**

4. Juan Gomez signed a 3-month note with a face of $2,000. The loan required him to pay interest at 15%. What amount was due on the due date?

Use a 360-day year unless told otherwise

5. The Cree Bank loaned $850 to Dulsey Woodsong for 30 days. Dulsey had to sign a note for the loan, with interest at 14%.
   a. What was the interest on the loan?
   b. What amount was due on the loan at maturity?

6. You need $1,500 to pay some bills. You can borrow the money on a 90-day note with interest at 12%. If you borrow the money, how much will you have to pay back when the note matures?

7. Victor Kinnon needs to borrow $7,500 for 60 days. He can borrow the money at the First National Bank for 13% interest. The Mainland Bank will lend him the money at $13\frac{1}{2}$% interest. How much would Victor save by borrowing from the First National Bank rather than Mainland?

8. How much would you save on a 3-month loan of $12,000 by borrowing that amount at 14% rather than 16%?

Finding the Due Date When the Time Is in Years or Months.
The due date or date of maturity of a promissory note is often shown on the face of the note. For example, the due date of the Dorset's note on page 319 is August 8, 1983. If you want to check the accuracy of a due date, or if a due date is not shown on a note, you figure it this way:

Suppose that the time of a note is given in years or months. You find the due date by counting the given number of years or months from the date of the note. The due date is the same day of the month as the date of the note.

Example

What is the due date of a 3-month note dated October 15?

Solution	Explanation
October + 3 months = January October 15 + 3 months = January 15	The date of the note is October 15. Three months from October is January. The due date is the same day of the month as the date of the note. So, the due date is January 15.

To figure due dates, you need to know the number of days in the months

The month in which a note comes due may not have the same date as the date of the note. In that case, the due date is the last date of the month in which the note comes due.

For example, a 3-month note is dated March 31. Three months from March 31 would be June 31, *but June has only 30 days*. So, the due date of the note is June 30, the last date of that month.

I remember the days of the months by saying, 30 days has September, April, June, and November

I was taught to count them on my knuckles.

I've memorized them!

Oral Practice 2

What is the due date of each of these notes?

	Date	Time		Date	Time
1.	June 10, 1983	3 years	**6.**	June 30	2 months
2.	May 5, 1985	5 years	**7.**	August 31	1 month
3.	March 31, 1989	1 year	**8.**	May 31	6 months
4.	July 1	4 months	**9.**	December 31	2 months
5.	October 8	3 months	**10.**	February 28	5 months

Finding the Due Date When the Time Is in Days.
If the time of a note is given in days, you find the due date by counting ahead that number of days from the date of the note.

Example
What is the due date of a 90-day note dated October 15?

Solution	Explanation
90 days time of note −16 days left in October ——————— 74 days to count forward −30 days in November ——————— 44 days to count forward −31 days in December ——————— 13 days to count forward in January Due date: January 13 Check: 16 days + 30 days + 31 days + 13 days = 90 days	After October 15, 16 days are left in October. So, you subtract 16 days from 90 days, leaving 74 days to count forward. Subtract 30 days for November, leaving 44 days to count forward. Subtract 31 days for December, leaving 13 days to count forward in January. The due date of the note is January 13. Check your answer by adding the number of days you have counted in each month. The total should equal the time of the note.

Written Practice 3

Find the due date for the notes in Problems 1–8. In all problems, assume that February has 28 days.

	Date	Time			Date	Time
1.	March 20	60 days	May 19	**5.**	January 15	80 days
2.	June 6	90 days		**6.**	May 24	45 days
3.	February 25	30 days		**7.**	April 20	120 days
4.	November 2	75 days		**8.**	July 7	60 days

9. On February 18, Jacob Clum signed a 75-day note for $500. On what date was the note due?   May 4

10. A 90-day note, dated October 28, has a due date of January 16 on the face.
a. Is that due date correct?
b. What is the correct due date?

Written Practice 4

1. What is the due date of a 3-month note dated August 10?

2. Find the due date of a 45-day note dated January 14.

3. A 2-month note is dated July 31. What is the due date?

4. Leta Lim's 80-day note is dated November 30. What is the due date?

5. A note is dated June 25.
a. If the time of the note is 3 months, what is the due date?
b. If the time is 90 days, what is the due date?

Terms to Remember		
date of the note	due date	face of the note
installment loan	interest-bearing note	promissory note
single-payment loan	time of the note	amount due at maturity

a. A written promise to repay borrowed money, with or without interest

b. The date on which a note is signed

c. A loan that is repaid in one payment

d. The maturity date of a note

e. A loan that is repaid in several part-payments

f. The amount borrowed on a note

g. A note that requires payment of interest

h. The time for which money is borrowed on a note

i. The total principal and interest owed on the due date

Review 74

1. a. Multiply $12,500 by 0.08646

b. 750 mL is what percent of 3.75 L?

c. Round $99.43248 to the nearest tenth of a cent

d. What percent of $80 is $32?

e. Find the interest on $520 at 12% for 40 days

2. What amount is due at maturity on a $4,500, 60-day note, with interest at 15%?

3. What is the due date of a 120-day note that is dated June 15?

4. You have invested $20,000 in rental property. Your annual ownership expenses are $5,400. How much monthly rent must you charge to make 15% per year on your investment?

5. Andrea Perry owns 200 shares of Trent Airspace Corporation stock. She wants to sell the stock at $33\frac{1}{2}$. The broker's commission and other fees and taxes will total $124.75. What will be Andrea's net proceeds from selling the stock?

6. a. What is the annual income from fifteen Colorado Corporation $1,000 bonds that pay 9% interest?

b. What is the yield (rate of income) on those bonds if they were bought at 75?

7. On July 31, the balance in your check register is $784.32. The bank statement for that date shows a balance of $834.27. You find that two checks are outstanding: No. 467 for $15, and No. 474 for $37.95. The bank statement shows a service charge of $3 that is not in your record. Prepare a bank reconciliation statement in good form.

INTEREST-BEARING NOTES (concluded)

Suppose that you want to borrow money on a note, but you are not sure how long you will need the money. Your bank or other lender may agree to lend you the money for an indefinite time on a demand loan. To get the loan, you will have to sign a demand note.

Demand Notes. A **demand note** shows on its face that the loan is payable "on demand" rather than at the end of a fixed time such as 30, 60, or 90 days. You must pay a demand note at any time the lender demands payment but, if you wish, you can pay the note before the demand for payment is made. Demand notes usually bear interest, and you have to pay the interest every month or every quarter.

To get a demand loan, you often have to provide some kind of collateral as security. **Collateral** is personal property such as stocks, bonds, savings account passbooks, cash, or life insurance. If you do not repay the loan, the lender may get the money from your collateral.

$2,700.00   **Davenport, Iowa**   Date: August 20, 1983

On demand , I promise to pay

to the order of **RIVERSIDE NATIONAL BANK**

Two thousand seven hundred and $\overset{\text{no}}{100}$----------------------Dollars

Value received. Interest at 10 % per year. To protect the bank if I default on this loan, I have deposited with the bank, and give the bank a security interest in, the following property as collateral for this loan:

Description of Property

3 Graystone Corporation $1,000 bonds

By signing below, I acknowledge receipt of a completely filled-in copy of this note and disclosure statement.

Anabel Humber

A demand note, secured by collateral

Anabel Humber's note shows that she borrowed $2,700 on August 20. Her note was payable "on demand" and she had to pay interest at 10%. Anabel deposited three $1,000 bonds with the bank as security for the loan.

Finding the Amount Due on a Demand Note. The amount due when a demand note is paid is the face of the note plus interest. The interest is figured from the date of the note (or the date of the last interest payment) to the day the note is paid.

For example, on November 8 Anabel Humber paid her demand note shown on page 324. The amount due on the note was $2,760, figured this way:

Face of note	$2,700
Interest on $2,700 from August 20 to November 8 (80 days)	60
Amount due on November 8	$2,760

Finding the Number of Days Between Two Dates. To find the amount due on a demand note, you first have to find the time for which interest is to be paid. That time is the number of days between the date of the note (or of the last interest payment) and the date the note is paid. You can find the number of days between those two dates this way:

Example

Anabel Humber signed a demand note on August 20 and paid the note on November 8. For how many days was interest charged?

Solution		Explanation
Days left in August (31 − 20)	11	The note was dated August 20.
Days in September	30	August has 31 days, so interest was
Days in October	31	charged for the 11 days left in Au-
Days in November	8	gust. September has 30 days, and
Total days of interest	80	October has 31 days. The note was

paid on November 8. The sum of 11 days + 30 days + 31 days + 8 days is 80 days. So, interest was charged for 80 days.

Written Practice 1

1. A demand note, signed on October 2, was paid on December 14. For how many days was interest charged? **73**

2. On April 20, Isaac Palmer paid a demand note that he had signed on March 1. For how many days was interest charged?

3. Royann Solana signed a $2,000, 12% demand note on June 5. She paid the note on September 22. For how many days was interest charged?

4. Find the number of days from:

   a. September 8 to January 6   **120**
   b. December 17 to February 12
   c. April 18 to November 10
   d. January 19 to February 28

   e. March 12 to April 9
   f. July 3 to October 5
   g. June 30 to August 15
   h. May 27 to July 28

"How many days between these dates?"

Written Practice 2

1. On June 28, Theodore Olynko signed a demand note for $600 at 15% interest. He paid the note on August 7.
   a. For how many days was interest due? **40**
   b. How much interest did he owe?
   c. What was the total amount due on August 7? **$610**

2. Miriam Miranda borrowed $1,500 and signed a 9% interest-bearing demand note on March 8. She paid the note on May 19.
   a. How much interest did Miriam owe when she paid the note?
   b. What total amount did she owe on May 19?

3. You borrowed $4,000 at a bank on September 5 and signed an 11% interest-bearing demand note for that amount. You paid the principal and the interest on December 4. How much did you pay?

4. On January 14, Les Kahn paid in full a demand note for $8,000 with interest at 12% that he had signed on November 15. How much did he pay?

5. A demand note for $12,000, dated May 24 with interest at 8%, was paid in full on September 21. What amount was due on the note?

6. Liana Imoru signed a demand note for $6,000 on April 1. The note bore interest at 10%, payable quarterly. She paid quarterly interest of $151.67 on July 1, and $153.33 on October 1. On November 15, Liana paid the principal and the interest that was due.
   a. How much interest was due on November 15? **$75**
   b. What total amount was due on November 15?
   c. What total amount of interest did Liana pay on the loan?

Terms to Remember

collateral   demand note

a. Has no definite time of payment
b. Personal property used as security for a loan

Review 75

1. **a.** Divide $78.75 by 3.5
   b. What is 25% of 102 m²?
   c. What is the interest on $3,500 for 75 days at 16%?
   d. What is 115% of $340?
   e. What is the number of days from March 8 to May 3?

2. On July 10, Marco Parisi signed a demand note for $5,000. The note carried interest at 10%. What total amount did Marco owe when he paid the note on September 20?

3. What is the due date of a 3-month note that is dated March 31?

4. Lois Khan bought an apartment building for $120,000, paying $50,000 down and taking a mortgage for the rest. She rented each of the 6 apartments in the building for $425 a month. Her annual expenses were 9% interest on the mortgage, 3% depreciation based on the cost of the apartment building, and other expenses of $13,700. What was her net income per year from the building?

5. Claude Kreb bought 150 shares of Nevada Industrial stock at $37\frac{1}{8}$. The broker charged $101.05. What was the total cost of the stock purchase?

6. Emma Berry bought 4 Omaha Laboratory $1,000 bonds at $95\frac{3}{4}$, and 3 Pennsylvania Adhesives bonds at $102\frac{1}{2}$. The broker charged a commission of $7.50 per bond. What was Emma's total investment in the bonds?

7. Reuben Duro's total yearly payroll deduction for U.S. savings bonds is $7.50 per week for 52 weeks.
   a. How many whole bonds costing $50 each will he have bought in a year?
   b. How much money will be left toward the purchase of another bond?

8. On October 2, Sylvia Rice deposited $1,200 in a savings account. The account paid interest at 6% a year on whole dollars. Interest was compounded and added to the account quarterly on January 1, April 1, July 1, and October 1. She made no other deposits or withdrawals for a year. What was Sylvia's balance on the next October 1?

9. Mr. and Mrs. Garcia live in Central City. Central City's income tax rate is 1.2% of taxable income. Last year, the Garcias had taxable income of $32,920. What was their city income tax last year?

DISCOUNTING A NOTE

To get a short-term loan from a bank, you may have to pay the interest at the time the loan is made. The interest you pay in advance is called **bank discount**. Because you pay the interest in advance, no interest rate is shown on the note. When no interest rate is shown, a note is called a **non-interest-bearing note**.

The bank collects bank discount from you by deducting it from the face of the note. You get the face amount less the discount. When you repay the loan, you pay only the face amount because you have already paid the interest. Making a loan this way is called *discounting a note*.

The percent of discount charged by the bank is called the **discount rate** or *rate of discount*. The amount that you get is called the **proceeds**

Example

Louise Belak borrowed $10,000 for 90 days from the Frontier Bank and signed a non-interest-bearing note for that amount. The bank discounted the loan at 12%. What proceeds did Louise get?

Solution

Face of note	$10,000
Discount on $10,000 @ 12% for 90 days	300
Proceeds	$ 9,700

★Written Practice 1

1. Chin Feng borrowed $3,000 from the State Bank for 60 days. The bank discounted the note at 10% and gave Chin the proceeds.
   a. How much money did Chin get when the loan was made? **$2,950**
   b. How much money did Chin have to pay when the note was due?

2. You borrow $4,000 for 45 days. The lender discounts your note at 16%. What are your proceeds from the loan?

3. Daniel Evans can borrow $7,000 for 45 days from Bank A on his 15% interest-bearing note. Or, Daniel can borrow $7,000 from Bank Z on his 45-day non-interest-bearing note discounted at 15%.
   a. What amount would Daniel get from Bank A on the day of the loan?
   b. What proceeds would Daniel get from Bank Z?
   c. How much would Daniel have to pay Bank A when the note is due?
   d. How much would he have to pay Bank Z when the note is due?

4. Fuji Wakua borrowed $1,000 from the Citadel Bank on a 75-day note bearing interest at 9% a year. He also borrowed $1,000 from the Redwood Bank on his 75-day non-interest-bearing note discounted at 9% a year.
   a. Which bank gave Fuji more money to use for the time of the loan? How much more?
   b. How much more money did Fuji owe the Citadel Bank than he owed the Redwood Bank when the notes were due?

⋆**Effect of Discounting a Note.** Some lenders lend money on a discount basis rather than an interest basis because they make more profit that way. When a lender discounts a note, the discount money is collected immediately. The lender can then lend that money to someone else and make another profit. If the lender had loaned the money on an interest basis, the interest would not be available to re-lend until the note was paid.

Another effect of discounting a loan is to increase the actual rate charged. The discount is figured on the face of the loan at the stated rate, but the amount actually loaned (the proceeds) is smaller than the face of the loan. That makes the actual rate higher than the stated rate.

For example, when the Frontier Bank loaned Louise Belak $10,000 for 90 days, the bank charged 12% discount on $10,000. The discount of $300 was collected when the loan was made. By discounting the note, the bank actually loaned only $9,700 ($10,000 − $300 = $9,700). The actual annual rate charged was $\frac{\$300 \times 4}{\$9,700}$, or $\frac{\$1,200}{\$9,700}$ = 12.4%. So, Louise Belak got only $9,700 rather than $10,000, and she paid a rate of 12.4% rather than 12% for the loan.

When we discount
your note:

• You pay the discount
  immediately
• You get the face
  minus the discount
• Your actual rate is
  higher than the
  stated rate.

DISCOUNT CLERK

⋆**Written Practice 2**

To find the rate, first find the yearly interest

1. A bank discounted at 14% Helga Flan's 30-day non-interest-bearing note for $6,000.
   a. What proceeds did Helga get from the note?   **$5,930**
   b. To the nearest tenth of a percent, what actual annual rate did Helga pay for the loan?   **14.2%**

2. You borrow $2,400 for 60 days from a bank. The bank discounts the loan at 16%.
   a. How much money did you actually have to use for 60 days?
   b. What actual rate per year did you pay, to the nearest tenth of a percent?

3. Fidel Cadiz needs to borrow $5,000 for 90 days. A lender will discount his 90-day note at 12%. If Fidel takes the loan,
   a. what amount of money will he get?
   b. what actual annual rate will he pay, to the nearest tenth of a percent?

4. At the Midland Bank, Andora Zarr can borrow $10,000 for 90 days on her note discounted at 10%. Or, she can borrow $10,000 from the Concho Bank on her 90-day interest-bearing note at 10½%.
   a. From which bank will she get more money on the day of the loan? How much more?   **Concho; $250**
   b. Which bank is charging the higher actual rate? How much higher, to the nearest tenth of a percent?   **Concho; 0.2%**

★Terms to Remember

bank discount	discount rate
non-interest-bearing note	proceeds

a. A percent of discount
b. A note that shows no interest
c. Face less discount
d. Interest charged in advance

★Review 76

1. **a.** Express $0.83\frac{1}{3}$ as a common fraction in lowest terms
   b. Express 3 hectares as square meters
   c. What amount decreased by 55% of itself is equal to $155.70?
   d. $198.60 is 30% of what amount?
   e. Find the number of days from March 31 to May 1

2. On February 28, Oki Mono discounted her own $2,500, 90-day note. The discount rate was 14%.
   a. What proceeds did Oki get?
   b. What amount did she owe on the due date?

3. The Motown Bank discounted at 12% Nils Tipton's $4,000, 60-day non-interest-bearing note.
   a. What were the proceeds of the note?
   b. What actual rate, to the nearest tenth of a percent, did Nils pay for the loan?

4. What is the due date of a 50-day note that is dated February 15, if the year is a leap year?

5. Ester Londos estimates that an investment of $30,000 in an apartment building would give her a net income of $3,900 a year. If she invested $40,000 in a condominium, Ester's annual net income would be $5,120. Which investment would give her a greater *rate* of income, and how much greater, to the nearest tenth of a percent?

6. Manuel Torres bought 100 shares of stock for a total cost of $4,605.20. He kept the stock for 18 months and received 6 quarterly dividends of 38¢ per share. Manuel then sold the stock for $4,572.75. What was his net gain or loss from owning and selling the stock?

INSTALLMENT LOANS

When you borrow money, you may want to repay the loan in several part payments instead of one large payment. A loan that is repaid in part payments is called an *installment loan*, or *consumer loan*. Each payment is called an **installment**. You may get installment loans from many banks, savings and loan associations, credit unions, and consumer finance companies.

Amount Financed and Finance Charge. The amount of credit that you are given on an installment loan is called the **amount financed**. The total of the interest and other charges that you pay for using the money is called the **finance charge**. For example, suppose that you borrow $5,000 and you repay that amount plus $750 for interest and other charges. The amount financed on your loan is $5,000. The finance charge is $750.

Interest
+Other Charges
―――――――――
Finance Charge

Repayment Schedules. On an installment loan, the borrower is usually given a schedule of payments, or a payment book, that shows how much is to be paid each month. Some repayment schedules require *decreasing payments* each month. Other schedules require *level payments* of the same amount each month.

Decreasing Payments. On some installment loans, equal parts of the face of the loan must be repaid each month, plus interest on the unpaid balance. That kind of plan has a series of decreasing payments. A decreasing payment schedule is shown below.

REPAYMENT SCHEDULE FOR AN $800, 4-INSTALLMENT LOAN WITH A FINANCE CHARGE OF 2% PER MONTH ON THE UNPAID BALANCE

End of Month	Unpaid Balance	Finance Charge of 2% on Unpaid Balance	Payment on Principal	Total Payment
1	$800	$16	$200	$216
2	600	12	200	212
3	400	8	200	208
4	200	4	200	204
Totals	――	$40	$800	$840

Finance charges are often a certain percent *per month*

As shown in the schedule, the finance charge of 2% *per month* was figured on the unpaid balance. Part of the principal was paid each month, so the unpaid balance was reduced for the next month. The decrease in interest each month caused the monthly payments to decrease.

The total finance charge on the loan was $40. The total payments of principal and finance charge on the loan were $840.

Written Practice 1

1. Make a repayment schedule of monthly payments for a loan of $1,500 to be repaid in 6 monthly installments. Show each installment as one-sixth of the principal, plus $2\frac{1}{2}\%$ finance charge per month on the unpaid balance. Use the schedule on page 331 as an example. **Total $1,631.25**

2. Yule Pike borrowed $600 for 4 months on an installment loan. He had to repay equal parts of the principal each month, plus a finance charge of $1\frac{1}{2}\%$ per month on the unpaid balance. Make a repayment schedule for the loan. Use the schedule on page 331 as an example.

3. Rachael Mann borrowed $2,000 from a bank and repaid it in 5 monthly payments of $400 plus a finance charge of 2% per month on the unpaid balance.
   a. What was the total finance charge on the loan?
   b. What was the total amount repaid to the bank?

4. A credit union loaned a member $1,200 for 3 months. The repayment schedule required repayment of one-third on the principal per month, plus a finance charge of 1% per month on the unpaid balance.
   a. What was the total finance charge on the loan?
   b. What total amount had to be paid to the credit union?

5. An 8-month loan of $4,000 requires repayment of $500 per month, plus a finance charge of 3% a month on the unpaid balance of the loan. What is the total finance charge on the loan?

Level Payments. Many lenders use a level-payment plan in which each payment is the same amount. Borrowers can easily remember the amount of their payments when every payment is the same amount.

To find the finance charge on a level-payment installment loan, you subtract the amount financed from the total of the payments.

$$\text{Total of the Payments} - \text{Amount Financed} = \text{Finance Charge}$$

For example, suppose that you borrow $600 from a finance company for 6 months. You repay the loan in 6 monthly payments of $109 each. The total of the payments is 6 × $109, or $654. The amount financed is $600, so the finance charge is $654 − $600, or $54.

Written Practice 2

1. Nadine Argos borrowed $750 and repaid the loan in 5 monthly payments of $159.50 each.
   a. What total amount did Nadine pay? **$797.50**
   b. What was the finance charge on her loan? **$47.50**

2. An installment loan of $3,000 was repaid in 8 monthly installments of $412.50 each.
   a. What total amount was repaid?
   b. What was the finance charge on the loan?

3. You can borrow $500 on an installment loan and repay it in 3 monthly payments of $184.18 each. If you take the loan:
   a. What total amount will you have to pay?
   b. What will be the finance charge on the loan?

4. Byron Borden repaid a $1,600 loan by making 10 monthly payments of $176 each. What was the finance charge on Byron's loan?

5. A loan of $2,000 was repaid in 9 monthly installments of $245.56. What was the finance charge on the loan?

Figuring Level-Payment Installments. The amount of each monthly payment needed to repay an interest-bearing note is figured in two steps:

(1) Add the amount financed (face of the note) and the finance charge (interest on the note) to find the total of the payments.
(2) Divide the total of the payments by the number of installments.

Example

You want to borrow $1,000 on a 12% interest-bearing note and repay it in 5 monthly installments. What will be the amount of each installment payment?

Solution

(1) Amount financed (face of note)	$1,000
Finance charge (interest on $1,000 at 12% for 5 months)	50
Total of the payments	$1,050

(2) $1,050 \div 5 = $210 each installment payment

Explanation

On an interest-bearing note, the amount financed is the face of the note ($1,000). The finance charge ($50) is the interest figured on the amount financed ($1,000) at the annual rate (12%) for the time the money is borrowed (5 months). The sum of the amount financed and the finance charge is the total of the payments ($1,050). The total of the payments ($1,050) is divided by the number of installment payments (5) to find the amount of each payment ($210).

Written Practice 3

1. The Tioga Bank loaned Anna Hauf $1,400 on a 10% interest-bearing note. Anna repaid the loan and interest in 6 monthly installments.
   a. How much was the finance charge on the loan? $70
   b. What was the total of the payments on the loan? $1,470
   c. What was the amount of each monthly payment? $245

2. Keenan O'Shay borrowed $800 on a note that bore interest at 15%. He repaid the loan and interest in 4 monthly installments.
   a. What was the finance charge on the loan?
   b. What total amount did Keenan pay?
   c. How much was each monthly payment?

3. If you borrow $1,800 from the personal loan department of your bank, you will have to pay interest of 12% per year on the loan. You will repay the loan and the finance charge in 9 monthly installments.
   a. What will be the total of your payments?
   b. What will be the amount of each monthly payment?

4. Riva Welk needs to borrow $3,200. She can get the money on an interest-bearing note at an annual rate of 9%. She will have to pay the loan in 8 monthly payments. How much will each payment be?

5. You can borrow $1,500 from the City Bank on an installment loan, with interest at 12% per year, repaying the loan in 4 monthly installments. You could borrow the same amount from the Apex Bank, with interest at 12% a year, but repaying the loan in 6 monthly installments.
   a. How much more would your total payments be at Apex Bank?
   b. How much less would each monthly installment be at Apex Bank?

All required costs of getting a loan must be included in the finance charge

Other Charges for Installment Loans.

Charges other than interest charges are sometimes made on a loan. For example, some lenders add a **service charge** to cover the costs of servicing and collecting loans. The lender may also charge for insurance to pay the loan if the borrower should die before paying the loan. All charges that must be paid to get a loan are added to the interest to find the total finance charge on a loan.

Example

Jim Bardole wants to borrow $600 on a 15% interest-bearing note and repay it in 6 monthly installments. The lender will add a service charge of $7.50 and require insurance on the loan at a premium of $3.
   (1) What will be the finance charge on the loan?
   (2) What will be the total of the payments on the loan?
   (3) What will be the amount of each installment payment?

Solution

(1) Finance charge:

Interest on $600 at 15% for 6 months	$45.00
Service charge	7.50
Insurance premium	3.00
Total finance charge	$55.50

(2) $600.00 + $55.50 = $655.50 total of the payments
(3) $655.50 ÷ 6 = $109.25 each installment payment

**Written
Practice 4**

1. Ada Ramos borrowed $400 on a note with interest at 10% a year. The lender added a service charge of $16. Ada agreed to repay the loan in 3 monthly installments.
   a. What was the total finance charge on the loan? $26
   b. What was the amount of each monthly installment? $142

2. You are borrowing $500 on a note with interest at 16% per year. The lender will require insurance at a cost of $2. You will repay the loan in 12 installments.
   a. What will be the total finance charge on the loan?
   b. What will be the amount of each monthly payment?

3. Sacha Akim got a loan of $1,200 on an 8% interest-bearing note. The lender charged $25 for service on the loan, and required Akim to pay $9.50 for insurance. Akim repaid the loan in 10 monthly payments. What was the total finance charge on Akim's loan?

4. Birgit Kimmel borrowed $2,100 on a note. The bank charged interest at 14% per year, plus a service charge of $12 and an insurance charge of $3. She was to repay the loan in 18 equal monthly installments. How much was each installment?

Terms to Remember

amount financed   finance charge
installment   service charge

   a. The total of interest and other charges paid for using money
   b. The amount of credit given on an installment loan
   c. A part-payment on a loan
   d. A charge to cover costs of servicing and collecting loans

Review 77

1. a. $55.60 is what fractional part less than $69.50?
   b. Subtract 2.75 L from 5.5 L
   c. What is the due date of a 2-month note dated September 30?
   d. What is the number of days from July 13 to September 9?

2. A 5-month loan of $600 requires a payment of $120 a month, plus a finance charge of 2% per month on the unpaid balance. What is the total finance charge on the loan?

3. A $900 loan was repaid in 10 monthly payments of $101.25. What was the finance charge on the loan?

4. Rudy Zwick borrowed $2,000 on a 12-installment loan. The lender charged interest at 14% per year and required insurance at a premium cost of $9. What was the amount of Rudy's monthly payments?

INSTALLMENT LOAN RATES

Comparing the finance charge rates that you would have to pay is helpful in deciding which of several loans would be best for you. But, you may not find it easy to figure the actual finance charge rates on level-payment installment loans. The finance charge on the loan may include service charges and other charges that are not included in the stated interest rate. Also, though interest is figured on the face of the note, you do not have the whole face amount to use for the time of the loan. You repay part of the principal of the loan with each installment, so you reduce the amount of money that you have to use. The average amount that you have to use on an installment loan is only slightly more than half the face amount, so your actual interest rate may be nearly double the stated rate.

For those and other reasons, lenders are now required by law to show on the loan agreement all finance charges and the annual percentage rate of the loan. The **annual percentage rate (APR)** of the loan is the percent that shows the ratio of the total finance charge to the amount financed. The APR is an excellent guide to the actual cost of loans, so you should know what it means and how it is figured.

The annual percentage rate (APR) on a loan can be figured with a formula, but it can be found more easily with a table. Only two steps are needed to find the APR with a table:

(1) Figure the finance charge per $100 of the amount financed.
(2) Find that finance charge per $100 in a table and read the equivalent rate.

Figuring the Finance Charge per $100 of the Amount Financed.

To find the **finance charge per $100** of the amount financed, you multiply the finance charge by 100, then divide that product by the amount financed.

$$\text{Finance Charge per \$100} = \frac{\text{Finance Charge} \times 100}{\text{Amount Financed}}$$

Round the finance charge per $100 to the nearest cent

For example, suppose that the finance charge is $52.81 on a loan of $650. The finance charge per $100 of the amount financed is $8.12.

$$\frac{\$52.81 \times 100}{\$650} = \frac{\$5,281}{\$650} = \$8.124, \text{ or } \$8.12$$

Written Practice 1

1. On a $520 loan, Arne Kisky paid a finance charge of $19.83. What was the finance charge per $100 of the amount financed? **$3.81**

2. Louella Cooper paid a finance charge of $21.60 on a loan of $800. What was the finance charge per $100 of the amount financed?

3. Find the finance charge per $100 on a $400 loan on which the finance charge is $15.50.

4. What is the finance charge per $100 on a loan of $1,500 on which the finance charge is $150?

5. Daryl Alger borrowed $900 and repaid it in 6 monthly payments of $160.50 each.
   a. What was the finance charge on Daryl's loan? **$63**
   b. What was the amount financed? **$900**
   c. What was the finance charge per $100 of the amount financed? **$7**

6. A loan for $560 is to be repaid in 4 monthly installments of $145.60 each.
   a. What was the finance charge on the loan?
   b. What was the amount financed?
   c. What was the finance charge per $100 of the amount financed?

7. You borrow $2,000 and agree to repay it in 18 monthly payments of $126.10 each.
   a. What is the finance charge on the loan?
   b. What is the finance charge per $100 of the loan?

8. Eltha Biggs borrowed $1,200 and agreed to repay that amount, plus interest at 12% per year, in 8 equal monthly payments. What was the finance charge per $100 of the amount financed?

Finding the Annual Percentage Rate. After you have found the finance charge per $100 of the amount financed, you can find the equivalent percentage rate with a table. Parts of an APR table are shown below.

ANNUAL PERCENTAGE RATE (APR) TABLE
FOR MONTHLY PAYMENT PLANS

Number of Payments	Annual Percentage Rate										
	$12\frac{3}{4}\%$	13%	$13\frac{1}{4}\%$	$13\frac{1}{2}\%$	$13\frac{3}{4}\%$	14%	$14\frac{1}{4}\%$	$14\frac{1}{2}\%$	$14\frac{3}{4}\%$	15%	$15\frac{1}{4}\%$
	Finance Charge per $100 of Amount Financed										
3	2.13	2.17	2.22	2.26	2.30	2.34	2.38	2.43	2.47	2.51	2.55
6	3.75	3.83	3.90	3.97	4.05	4.12	4.20	4.27	4.35	4.42	4.49
9	5.39	5.49	5.60	5.71	5.82	5.92	6.03	6.14	6.25	6.35	6.46
12	7.04	7.18	7.32	7.46	7.60	7.74	7.89	8.03	8.17	8.31	8.45
15	8.71	8.88	9.06	9.23	9.41	9.59	9.76	9.94	10.11	10.29	10.47

Number of Payments	Annual Percentage Rate										
	$26\frac{3}{4}\%$	27%	$27\frac{1}{4}\%$	$27\frac{1}{2}\%$	$27\frac{3}{4}\%$	28%	$28\frac{1}{4}\%$	$28\frac{1}{2}\%$	$28\frac{3}{4}\%$	29%	$29\frac{1}{4}\%$
	Finance Charge per $100 of Amount Financed										
3	4.49	4.53	4.58	4.62	4.66	4.70	4.74	4.79	4.83	4.87	4.91
6	7.95	8.02	8.10	8.17	8.25	8.32	8.40	8.48	8.55	8.63	8.70
9	11.47	11.58	11.69	11.80	11.91	12.03	12.14	12.25	12.36	12.47	12.58
12	15.07	15.22	15.37	15.51	15.66	15.81	15.95	16.10	16.25	16.40	16.54
15	18.75	18.93	19.12	19.30	19.48	19.67	19.85	20.04	20.22	20.41	20.59

To find the annual percentage rate, you read across the line for the given number of monthly payments. When you find the amount nearest to the given finance charge per $100, you read the percent at the head of the column. That percent is the annual percentage rate of the loan.

For example, suppose that the finance charge per $100 of a 3-payment loan is $2.35. You read across the 3-payment line to $2.34, which is the amount nearest to $2.35. The amount of $2.34 is in the 14% column, so the APR for the loan is 14%.

If the finance charge per $100 that you want to find is exactly half-way between amounts in columns, use the higher percentage rate.

Use the APR table on page 338 for these problems.

Written Practice 2

1. R. C. Kimm repaid a $700 loan in 6 monthly payments of $121.90 each.
   a. What was the finance charge on the loan?   **$31.40**
   b. What was the finance charge per $100 of the amount financed?   **$4.49**
   c. What was the annual percentage rate on the loan?

Round the finance
charge per $100 to
the nearest cent

2. Lebow Rebost borrowed $1,400 and repaid the loan in 12 monthly payments of $134.42 each.
   a. What was the finance charge on the loan?
   b. What was the finance charge per $100?
   c. What was the annual percentage rate (APR) on the loan?

3. Mona Leroux paid $124.76 a month for 9 months to repay a $1,000 loan.
   a. What was the finance charge per $100 on the loan?
   b. What was the APR on the loan?

4. Osami Kwan repaid a $2,000 loan in 15 payments of $147.05 each. What was the APR on Osami's loan?   **15%**

5. You can borrow $600 and repay the loan in 3 monthly payments of $204.60 each. What is the APR on the loan?

Terms to Remember

annual percentage rate (APR)   finance charge per $100

   a. The ratio of the finance charge to the total amount financed
   b. (Finance charge × 100) ÷ amount financed

Review 78

1. a. How many liters of fluid are there in eight, 250 mL cans?
   b. $125 is what percent of $50?
   c. $340 is what part greater than $255?
   d. Find the number of days from September 21 to December 21

2. Ailene Novo repaid a $900 loan in 9 monthly payments of $112.47 each. Using the table on page 338, what was the annual percentage rate (APR) on her loan?

3. A demand note for $3,000, dated April 15, with interest at 12%, was paid in full on June 14. What total amount was paid?

4. Emilio Arroyo borrowed $500 on a 3-month promissory note, with interest at 15%. What amount did he owe when the note was due?

5. You have $25,000 to invest and you want to make 12% on your investment. If you invest the money in rental real estate, the annual expenses of owning and renting the property would be $8,400. How much monthly rent would you have to charge to cover the expenses and your desired income from the property?

6. What is the rate of income, or yield, on a $1,000, 9% bond bought at 72, plus a commission of $30?

USING CREDIT

You may want to pay cash for many of your purchases. You may prefer to buy other goods and services on credit through your regular charge account, credit card, or install-ment plan. Whatever method you choose, you need to figure and compare the costs and savings of the alternative ways of paying for your purchases.

In this unit you will meet some of the common problems in figuring the costs and savings of charge accounts, cash discounts, credit cards, and installment plans. When you have finished this unit, you should be able to:

- figure savings through buying on credit and with cash discounts
- find the costs of credit card purchases and cash advances
- find the costs of installment purchases
- figure the annual percentage rate on in-stallment purchases
- read, write, speak, and recognize the meanings of the terms shown in color

CHARGE ACCOUNTS AND CREDIT CARDS

Charge Accounts. If you are a regular customer with a good credit standing, many retail stores will let you open a **charge account** and buy on credit. That is, you can "buy now and pay later." You may have as much as 30 days from the billing date to pay for purchases at no extra cost. In effect, you can use the seller's money at no interest cost for 30 days or more from the time of the purchase. For credit beyond the 30 days, most retailers charge interest and show it as a finance charge on your bill.

To reduce their costs of giving credit, many manufacturers and wholesalers give a **cash discount** to a retailer who pays for a purchase at the time of the sale, or soon after. As a consumer, you may be able to get cash discounts from some retailers. Cash discounts may range from 1% to 7% of the purchase price, so you can make a substantial saving. Sometimes you can save by borrowing the money you need to get a cash discount.

SAVE $ $ $
We give
discounts
for **CASH**

Written Practice 1

1. You are buying merchandise for $300. You can pay cash for it, or you can charge it to your account for 30 days at no extra cost. If you charge the purchase, you can earn interest for 30 days at 6% per year on the money in your savings account. How much would you save by buying the merchandise on credit rather than for cash?   **$1.50**

2. Last year, the Korn family bought merchandise worth $4,000 on 30-day credit at no extra charge. They earned 12% per year on that money by investing it for 30 days. How much did they gain by buying on credit rather than for cash?

3. The Brownell Store makes no charge for credit within 30 days of the billing date, but adds a 2% finance charge on bills not paid until 30 to 60 days after the billing date. Ethyl Golden bought furniture costing $1,565 at the Brownell Store and paid the bill 45 days after the billing date. What total amount did she have to pay?   **$1,596.30**

Take time to
pay! Open a
charge account
with us. 30-day
credit
free!

4. You can charge an $800 purchase at no extra cost, or you can pay cash for it and get a 5% discount.
   a. What is the cash price?   **$760**
   b. How much would you save by paying cash?

5. You are buying an electric appliance for $1,200. You can charge it for 30 days at no extra cost, or pay cash and get a discount of 3%. If you charge the item, you can earn interest on the purchase price for 30 days at 6%.
   a. What is the net cost if you pay cash?
   b. What is the net cost if you charge the purchase?
   c. How much would you save by buying the less expensive way?

6. You can buy a TV set on 30-day credit for $500, or you can buy the set for $475 cash. What percent of the credit price would you save by paying cash?

Credit price
−Cash discount
Amount borrowed

7. Howie Knox can buy a boat for $2,300 and take 30 days to pay for it. If he pays cash, he will get a discount of 2% from the credit price. Howie doesn't have the cash, but he can borrow the cash price amount at 10% for 30 days. How much would he save by borrowing and paying cash?

8. You want to buy new carpet that will cost $1,875 if you take 30 days to pay for it. You will get a 3% discount from that price if you pay cash when the carpet is installed. You don't have the cash but you can borrow the necessary amount for 30 days by paying 12% annual interest. How much would you save by borrowing and paying cash?

Credit Cards. Instead of granting their own credit, many sellers accept bank credit cards such as Visa and MasterCard. Some merchants will also accept travel and entertainment credit cards, such as American Express, Diners' Club, or Carte Blanche.

A **credit card** is used to identify a customer who is entitled to be given credit. If you use a credit card for a purchase, the merchant sends the sales slip that you sign to the credit card agency. The issuing agency then credits the merchant with that amount, less a charge for the service. Many merchants like the credit card system because they get their money quickly and they don't have to check the credit standing of customers. Also, their recordkeeping and collection costs are reduced.

Before you are issued a credit card by a bank or other agency, you have to sign an application form. On the form you give information about your financial standing, and you authorize the issuer to investigate your credit record.

Some credit card agencies now charge an annual fee of $15 to $50 for the card service. Bank credit cards usually limit the credit to $1,000, $2,000, $3,000, or more. Travel and entertainment cards usually have no credit limit.

Most credit card issuers send a monthly statement to the cardholder. The statement shows all charges and credits during the billing period, and a new balance owed. The cardholder is generally given several weeks from the billing date in which to pay the entire bill without any finance charge. But, some bank cards charge a fee for each purchase, and some charge interest from the date of the purchase.

The agreement that the cardholder signs, and the monthly statement, usually show the minimum amount that must be paid each month if the whole bill is not paid. The finance charge that will be added if the bill is not paid on time is also shown, usually as a percent of the unpaid monthly balance. Collection costs may be charged if the bill is not paid as agreed.

Most bank credit cards also allow the cardholder to borrow money by using a *cash advance* slip or special check form. Interest on a cash advance is charged from the date of the loan at a daily interest rate.

The front of Lida Panetta's MasterCard statement for a month is shown below. Much other information about the way purchases and cash advances are handled is shown on the back of the statement.

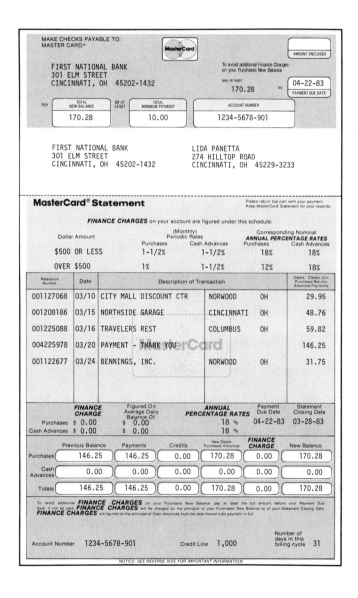

A bank credit card statement

Written Practice 2

Mario Mercato's credit card statement shows these facts. You are to use the facts to answer the questions that follow.

(1) The date of the statement (date of bill) is June 15. The payment due date is July 10.

(2) Mario's credit limit is $2,000.

(3) The previous balance was paid by the due date.

(4) Six purchases totaling $414 were made during the billing period, and an *annual* credit card fee of $18 was charged to the account.

(5) The new balance of the account is $432.

(6) No cash advances were made during the billing period.

(7) No finance charge will be added if the balance is paid by the due date.

1. How many days from the date of bill does Mario have to pay the bill without a finance charge?

2. What is the average of the credit card fee per month?

Credit limit
−New balance

Credit available

3. How much credit does Mario have available on his account until the new balance is paid?   **$1,568**

4. If Mario does not pay the bill by the due date, a finance charge of $1\frac{3}{4}\%$ per month will be charged on the average daily balance of the account. If the average daily balance of his account is $220, what will be Mario's finance charge for one month?   **$3.85**

5. If Mario does not want to pay the entire bill by the due date, he may pay an installment of as little as $\frac{1}{36}$ of the balance. What is the least amount that he must pay?

6. If Mario fails to pay the bill, collection costs of 20% of the balance will be charged. What would be the amount of the collection costs?

0.04931% is a
decimal rate of
0.0004931

7. The daily finance charge for cash advances on his card is 0.04931%. What would be the finance charge for 40 days on a cash advance of $500 on Mario's card?   **$9.86**

Written Practice 3

1. Jan Audi had a new balance on her credit card statement of $260.48. She did not pay that amount by the due date, so a finance charge of $1\frac{1}{2}\%$ was added on the next statement. How much was the finance charge?

2. Lin Loi's credit card costs $18 a year, plus 12¢ per transaction. She averages 8 transactions a month. What is her annual credit card cost?

3. Lars Nord borrowed $300 on his credit card by a cash advance. He paid the loan in 60 days at a daily finance charge of 0.08285%. What was the amount of the finance charge on the loan?

4. Credit Card *A* has an annual fee of $15, and a finance charge of 18% per year on unpaid balances. Credit Card *B* has no annual fee, but has a finance charge of 21% per year on unpaid balances. If your unpaid balance, subject to finance charges, averages $300 per year:
   a. How much would Card *A* cost you per year? **$69**
   b. How much would Card *B* cost you per year?

5. Peg Upton averages 75 credit card transactions per year, and her average balance subject to finance charges is $200 per year. If she uses Credit Card *X*, she will pay 15¢ per transaction, plus a 21% annual finance charge on her average balance subject to finance charges. If she uses Card *Z*, she will pay an annual fee of $12, plus a finance charge of 24% on her average balance. What would be the annual cost for:
   a. Credit Card *X*?
   b. Credit Card *Z*?

6. You have 2 credit cards. On each card, the finance charge per year is 21% of the first $500 of the unpaid balance, and 15% on amounts over $500 of the unpaid balance. If you make total purchases of $1,000 in a *month*, how much less will the finance charges be if a total of $1,000 is charged on one card rather than $500 on each card? **$2.50**

Terms to Remember

cash discount   **charge account**   **credit card**

a. The privilege of buying on a store's own credit
b. Identifies a customer who is to be given credit
c. Given for paying at the time of the purchase, or soon after

Review 79

1. **a.** Show 0.65 as a common fraction in lowest terms
   b. What amount is 40% less than $89.50?
   c. What is 10% more than 156 m²?
   d. What is the number of days from November 25 to February 25?

2. You can pay $349.50 for a new stove and take 30 days to pay for it on your charge account. If you pay cash for it, you will get a 2% discount. How much would you save by paying cash?

3. The new balance on Dora Lentz's credit card statement is $178.64. If she does not pay the balance by the due date, a finance charge of $1\frac{3}{4}$% will be added to her next statement. What would be the amount of the finance charge?

4. You can borrow money by taking a cash advance on your credit card. The daily finance charge rate on cash advances is 0.04932%. What would be the finance charge if your borrowed $400 for 20 days on the card?

INSTALLMENT BUYING

Furniture, furnishings, stereos, TVs, appliances, cars, motorcycles, recreation vehicles, boats, and many other items often cost too much to buy for cash or on short-term credit. You may want to buy expensive items such as those on the **installment plan**, or time payment plan. When you buy on the installment plan, you use the seller's money and pay it back in a series of part payments called installments.

Finance Charge on Installment Purchases. The total price that you pay for an installment purchase is usually higher than the cash price because you have to pay interest for using the seller's money. Also, other charges may be added for items such as credit life insurance. All charges made by the seller above the cash price have to be included in the finance charge and shown on the installment contract.

Down Payment and Installment Payments. When you buy on an installment plan, you may have to pay part of the price at the time of the purchase. The amount that you pay immediately is called a **down payment**. You also have to sign an installment contract and agree to repay the balance of the purchase price and finance charge in a series of equal weekly or monthly payments.

INSTALLMENT CONTRACT AND SECURITY AGREEMENT

Sergio Sound Systems, Inc.
The South Mall • Amarillo, TX 79199

I (we) the undersigned buyer(s) buy from, and grant a security interest, to SERGIO SOUND SYSTEMS, INC. in this property:

Buyer's Name *Julio Martinez*
Buyer's Address *67 Range Road*
City *Amarillo*　　　State *TX*　　Zip *79198*

Quantity	Description	Amount
1	Model 43K269 SS See-Hear-Record Home-Center System, installed	1,395 00
Description of Trade-in:		
		None
	Sales Tax	55 80
	Total	1,450 80

1	Cash Price	$1,395.00
2	Less: Down Payment $295	
3	Trade-in $ —	
4	Total Down	$295.00
5	Unpaid Balance of Cash Price	$1,100.00
6	Other charges: *Sales Tax*	$55.80
7	AMOUNT FINANCED	$1,155.80
8	FINANCE CHARGE	$244.70
9	Total of Payments	$1,400.50
10	Deferred Payment Price (1 + 6 + 8)	$1,695.50
11	ANNUAL PERCENTAGE RATE	25 1/4 %

Insurance Agreement

Credit life insurance is available at a cost of $*18* for the term of the credit. The purchase of insurance is voluntary and not required for credit.

I want insurance.

Signed:_____ Date:_____

I do not want insurance.

Signed: *Julio Martinez*　　Date: *5/1/83*

Signed:_____ Date:_____

The Buyer(s) agrees to pay to SERGIO SOUND SYSTEMS, INC. at their store the "Total of Payments" shown above in *17* monthly installments of *$77.80* and a final installment of *$77.90*. The first installment is due *June 1, 1983* and all other payments are due on the same day of the month until paid in full. The finance charge applies from *May 1, 1983*.

Signed: *Julio Martinez*　　Date: *5/1/83*

Notice to Buyer: You should get a copy of this contract when you sign. You can pay in advance the unpaid balance of this contract and get a partial refund of the finance charge based on the "Actuarial Method."

An installment contract

The way to solve some common types of installment problems is shown in this example:

Example

The Poncas are buying new kitchen appliances. The cash price is $1,600. The installment terms are $100 down and the balance in 24 monthly payments of $80 each.

(1) What is the installment price of the appliances?
(2) What is the finance charge on the purchase?
(3) To the nearest whole percent, how much greater is the installment price than the cash price?

Solution		**Explanation**
(1) Down payment	$ 100	(1) Add the down payment and the total of the installment payments to find the installment price.
Installments (24 × $80)	+1,920	
Installment price	$2,020	
(2) Installment price	$2,020	(2) Subtract the cash price from the installment price to find the finance charge.
Cash price	−1,600	
Finance charge	$ 420	
(3) $\dfrac{\text{Finance Charge}}{\text{Cash Price}} = \dfrac{\$420}{\$1,600} =$		(3) Divide the finance charge by the cash price to find the percent by which the installment price is greater.
$0.262 = 26\%$ **Ans.**		

Written Practice 1

1. A furnace sells for $800 cash, or $50 down plus 12 monthly payments of $71.25 each.
   a. What is the installment price of the furnace? **$905**
   b. What is the finance charge? **$105**
   c. By what percent is the installment price greater than the cash price, to the nearest whole percent? **13%**

2. Ollie Garr bought a motorcycle for $300 down and 18 monthly payments of $121.10. He could have bought the cycle for $2,000 cash.
   a. What total price did he pay on the installment plan?
   b. How much finance charge did he pay?
   c. To the nearest whole percent, how much more did he pay by buying on the installment plan rather than paying cash?

3. Lisa Ichiro can buy a camera for $25 down and 30 weekly payments of $8.25 each. The camera would cost $250 cash.
   a. What is the installment price of the camera?
   b. What is the finance charge on the camera?
   c. By what percent is the installment price greater?

4. A bracelet sells for $75 cash, or for $5 down and 25 weekly installments of $3.60 each.
   a. What is the finance charge on the installment purchase?
   b. To the nearest whole percent, how much greater is the installment price than the cash price?

5. The installment price of a mower is $100 down and 15 monthly payments of $69.45 each. The cash price is $950. To the nearest whole percent, how much greater is the installment price than the cash price?

6. Geoff Judson can buy an electric guitar with no down payment and 6 monthly payments of $43.75. Or, he can buy the guitar for $225 cash. To the nearest *tenth* of a percent, how much greater is the installment price than the cash price?

Written Practice 2

1. The total installment price of a motorboat is $3,690. The terms are $400 down and $164.50 a month. For how many months would the installments have to be paid?   **20**

2. On the installment plan, the total cost of a suit is $149.60. The terms are $30 down and weekly payments of $4.60. How many weekly payments would be needed to pay the total price?

3. To buy a typewriter for an installment price of $382.50, you would have to make no down payment but you would have to pay $21.25 a month. For how many months would you have to make the payments?

4. To buy a car for an installment price of $9,932, Rosetta Velez can make a $500 down payment and pay the balance in 36 monthly installments. What would be the amount of each installment?   **$262**

5. The installment price of a ring is $989. It can bought with $99.80 down and the balance in 52 weekly payments. How much would each payment be?

6. The cash price of a stereo tape player is $745. If you buy it on the installment plan, you must pay $75 down. A finance charge of $97.16 will then be added to the unpaid balance, and that amount must be paid in 12 equal monthly installments. What will be the amount of each monthly installment?

Annual Percentage Rate on Installment Purchases. When you buy on the installment plan, the finance charge is the total of the interest and any other charges you are required to pay. The amount financed is the cash price less any down payment.

The law requires that the finance charge, the amount financed, and the annual percentage rate (APR) be shown on the installment contract that you sign. The annual percentage rate is figured with tables in the same way as the APR on an installment loan.

Look at the example on the next page to see how the APR on an installment purchase is figured.

Example

The cash price of a mower is $875. The installment price is $75 down and $76 a month for 12 months. What annual percentage rate (APR) does the installment buyer pay?

Solution

$75 + (12 × $76) = $987 installment price
$987 − $875 = $112 finance charge
$875 − $75 = $800 amount financed
(100 × $112) ÷ $800 = $14 finance charge per $100
Annual percentage rate = 25% **Ans.**

Explanation

The installment price is the sum of the down payment and the total monthly payments. The finance charge is the installment price less the cash price. The amount financed is the cash price less the down payment. The finance charge per $100 is the finance charge multiplied by 100, with that product then divided by the amount financed. The finance charge of $14 per $100 on the 12-payment line of the APR table below is nearest to $14.05, which is in the 25% column. So, the APR is 25%.

ANNUAL PERCENTAGE RATE (APR) TABLE
FOR MONTHLY PAYMENT PLANS

Number of Payments	Annual Percentage Rate										
	23%	$23\frac{1}{4}$%	$23\frac{1}{2}$%	$23\frac{3}{4}$%	24%	$24\frac{1}{4}$%	$24\frac{1}{2}$%	$24\frac{3}{4}$%	25%	$25\frac{1}{4}$%	$25\frac{1}{2}$%
	Finance Charge per $100 of Amount Financed										
6	6.81	6.89	6.96	7.04	7.12	7.19	7.27	7.34	7.42	7.49	7.57
12	12.89	13.04	13.18	13.33	13.47	13.62	13.76	13.91	14.05	14.20	14.34
18	19.19	19.41	19.62	19.84	20.06	20.28	20.50	20.72	20.95	21.17	21.39
24	25.70	25.99	26.29	26.59	26.89	27.19	27.49	27.79	28.09	28.39	28.69
30	32.42	32.80	33.18	33.57	33.95	34.33	34.72	35.10	35.49	35.88	36.26
36	39.35	39.82	40.29	40.77	41.24	41.71	42.19	42.66	43.14	43.61	44.09

Use the table above for these problems.

Written Practice 3

1. You can buy a bicycle for $130 cash or for $15 down and 6 monthly installments of $20.53 each. What annual percentage rate (APR) would you pay on the installment plan?   24%

2. Ying Ho can buy a color TV for $95 down and 24 monthly payments of $26.20. The cash price of the TV is $595. What is the annual percentage rate (APR) on the installment plan?

3. Yvette Jardins bought a home computer for $300 down and 30 monthly payments of $58.88 each. She could have bought the computer for $1,600 cash. What was the APR on Yvette's purchase?

4. The cash price of a camper is $4,800. It can be bought on the install-ment plan with no down payment and $187 a month for 36 months. What is the APR on the installment plan? $23\frac{1}{2}\%$

5. An electric piano costs $2,200 cash. If bought on an 18-month install-ment plan, a down payment of $200 and monthly payments of $133.90 are required. What annual percentage rate is paid by the installment buyer of the piano?

6. At Furnish Your World, a davenport can be bought for $975 cash, or $100 down and 18 monthly payments of $57.95 each. At Carlinco, the same davenport can be bought for $950 cash, or with no money down and 24 monthly payments of $50.60 each. To the nearest quarter per-cent, how much less is the APR at Furnish Your World?

Terms to Remember

down payment   **installment plan**

a. Money paid at the time of making an installment purchase
b. Paying for a purchase in a series of part payments

Review 80

1. a. 700 kg is what fractional part greater than 560 kg?
   b. $98.75 minus 20% of itself is what amount?
   c. What is the number of days from May 18 to July 25?
   d. Find the interest on $646.25 at 11% for 45 days
   e. What percent of $120 is $72?

2. The installment price of a pendant is $10 down and $3 a week for 25 weeks. The cash price of the pendant is $79. To the nearest whole percent, how much greater is the installment price than the cash price of the pendant?

3. The installment price of a freezer is $695. The terms are $95 down and monthly payments of $30 each. How many monthly payments are needed to pay for the freezer?

4. The installment terms on a radar range are $75 down and 12 monthly payments of $37.68 each. The cash price of the range is $475. Using the APR table on page 349, what is the annual percentage rate on the in-stallment plan?

5. The new balance on your credit card statement is $164.80. You pay $10 of that amount, but a finance charge of $1\frac{3}{4}\%$ is added to the remaining balance. What is the amount of the finance charge?

6. Ethan Sammons borrowed $650 on an installment loan for a year. The lender charged 14% interest, plus a service charge of $7.50 and an in-surance fee of $4.50. He paid the loan in 12 monthly installments.
   a. What was the finance charge on the loan?
   b. What was the amount of each installment?

Part IV Review

1. **a.** Express $\frac{7}{8}$ as a decimal, correct to the nearest hundredth
   b. 4 t is what percent of 2 t?
   c. What is the number of days from August 21 to November 1?
   d. What is the due date of a 120-day note dated April 5?
   e. What is the exact interest on $2,000 for 75 days at 8%?
   f. $300 is what percent less than $500?
   g. $3,429 increased by $\frac{1}{6}$ of itself is what amount?

2. The Eastport Savings and Loan pays $5\frac{1}{2}$% interest per year, figuring and adding the interest each quarter on whole dollars only. How much interest would that savings and loan pay in one year on an $800 deposit?

3. You have held a $10,000 6-month money market certificate for 5 months and have earned $500 in interest on it. If you cash the certificate now, you will be penalized 3 month's simple interest at 12% per year on the principal.
   a. What is the amount of the penalty?
   b. How much net interest would you have earned if you cash the certificate now?

4. Adeline Dombrey is having her employer deduct $12.50 per week from her wages to buy U.S. savings bonds. How many bonds costing $25 each is she buying per year?

5. Arak Sahab bought 5 corporation bonds at $92\frac{3}{8}$. The broker charged $7.50 commission per bond. What was Arak's total investment in the corporation bonds?

6. A stock that is listed at 25 pays a quarterly dividend of 50¢. What is the annual rate of income of the stock?

7. Barbara Morton wants to make an annual net income of 14% on an investment of $30,000 in real estate. The annual ownership expenses are $4,620. How much rent per month must she charge?

8. Ling Yen repaid a $1,500 loan in 12 monthly payments of $135.04 each. Using the table on page 338, what was the APR on the loan?

9. Your checkbook balance on November 30 was $826.44. Your bank statement for that date showed a balance of $866.31. A check for $36.42 was outstanding, and the bank had credited $3.45 interest on your account for November. Make a reconciliation statement for your account, showing the correct checkbook balance and the available bank balance.

10. What is the finance charge on a credit card cash advance of $200 for 35 days at a daily rate of 0.04931%?

11. Last year, Violet Gage's two-year college expenses were these: tuition, $1,450; fees and insurance, $180; books and supplies, $320; transportation, $1,300; personal, $800. If her expenses this year are 8% higher than last year's, how much will her total expenses be for this year?

12. You borrowed $1,600 on an installment loan and repaid it in 12 payments of $143.35 each.
    a. What total amount did you repay?
    b. What was the finance charge on the loan?

★13. On June 30, your checkbook balance was $482.05, and the bank statement balance was $299.79. Checks No. 146 for $16.45, and No. 148 for $30.79 were outstanding. A deposit of $225 had been made too late to show in the statement. You had written a check for $19.45 but had recorded it in your checkbook as $14.95. Make a reconciliation statement in good form as of June 30.

★14. Delia Toros borrowed $600 on a note. The bank discounted the loan at 15% for 90 days. What proceeds did Delia get from the loan?

★15. Alfred Fairly wants to make 12% on an investment in real estate. What is the most that he should invest in a building that produces net income of $9,600 per year?

★16. Glenn Morris had an adjusted gross income of $56,400 last year. His deductions totaled $3,500, and his zero bracket amount was $2,300. Glenn claimed 2 exemptions at $1,000 each. Using Schedule Z on page 240, what was his federal income tax last year?

★17. a. $168.75 is 45% of what amount?

    b. What amount decreased by 28% of itself equals $57.24?

    c. $62.50 is 25% more than what amount?

    d. Express $3\frac{3}{8}$ as a decimal, correct to two places

    e. What amount increased by $\frac{2}{3}$ of itself is equal to $120?

    f. $\frac{7}{8}$ of what amount equals $56?

Part V

Understanding Business Operations

To be an effective money earner, spender, saver, investor, and borrower, you must understand and use a variety of information about business operations and conditions. Much of that information is shown in special forms such as balance sheets, income statements, and graphs.

This part of the book will help you learn to use those forms of business information.

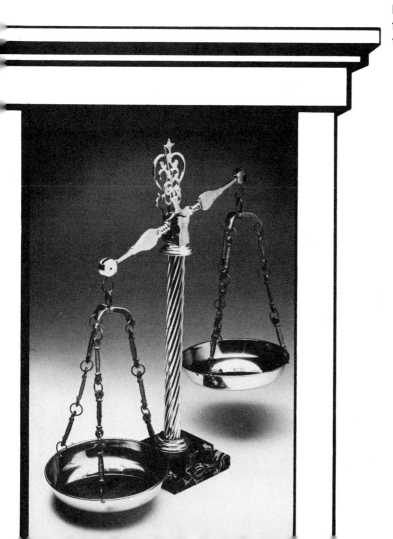

BUSINESS STATEMENTS

Most American private businesses are operated to make a profit for the owners. Unless a private, profit-making business regularly makes a profit, it can't continue to operate for very long. For that reason, business owners, managers, and investors need to make frequent checks on the condition and profitability of their business.

Unit Eighteen is concerned with two reports that are often used to analyze the condition of a business: the balance sheet and the income statement. A balance sheet shows the financial condition of a business at a point in time. An income statement reports business operations over a period of time and shows the profit or loss that resulted from those business operations.

When you have completed this unit, you should be able to:

- figure owner's net worth or capital
- make a simple balance sheet
- figure net sales, cost of merchandise sold, gross profit on sales, operating expenses, and net income or net loss
- analyze simple income statements
- read, write, speak, and recognize the meanings of many terms used with balance sheets and income statements

THE BALANCE SHEET

section 81

From time to time, businesses, individuals, and families need to find out how much money they are worth. To do this, they count up the value of everything they own. Then they figure how much of that value is owed to other people (outsiders) and how much of the value is theirs (owners). The formal report of this process is called a **balance sheet** or, sometimes, a *statement of net worth*. A balance sheet is made up in this form:

Assets (value of things owned) = Liabilities (claims of outsiders) + Capital (claims of owners)

Things owned are assets

Assets. Most successful businesses own many kinds of property. They have cash to make change and pay expenses. They have money owed to them as *accounts receivable* or *notes receivable*. Trading businesses have merchandise to sell. Most businesses also own land and buildings, equipment, and supplies. All these things of value that are owned by the business are called **assets**.

For a satisfying personal and family life, most individuals and families also own things of value. They may own cash, clothing, furniture and furnishings, homes, cars, other equipment, and supplies. These individually owned or family owned items are also called *assets*.

Outsiders' claims are liabilities

Liabilities and Capital. Although a business, a person, or a family owns its assets, outsiders may have claims to those assets. The claims of outsiders to assets are called **liabilities**.

For example, suppose that the Boxley Company buys some equipment for $10,000 on credit from a supplier. The supplier, as a creditor, has a claim for $10,000 against the assets of the Boxley Company until the money is paid. That claim is a liability of the Boxley Company.

Owner's claim is capital

The owner's claim to assets is often called **capital**, *owner's equity*, or *net worth*. If there are no liabilities, the owner's capital is the total value of the assets. For example, suppose that the assets of Ruth Brown's Fabric Shop are $100,000. If there are no liabilities, Ruth Brown can claim all the assets, so her capital is $100,000.

Assets, $100,000 = Capital, $100,000

What are the assets of this fabric store?

If outsiders have claims against the assets (liabilities), the owner's capital is the difference between the liabilities and the assets. For example, suppose that Ray Mott's Hobby Shop has assets of $100,000 and liabilities of $20,000. Ray Mott's capital is the difference, $80,000.

Assets, $100,000 − Liabilities, $20,000 = Capital, $80,000

Written Practice 1

Assets = Liabilities + Capital

Assets − Liabilities = Capital

Capital and net worth mean the same

1. The Send-It-Now Card Center has these assets: cash, $8,460; merchandise, $17,750; equipment, $8,450; supplies, $780. The store owes $950 to Pioneer Printing Company and $125 to Central Power and Light. What is the owner's capital? **$34,365**

2. The Kenwood Corporation has assets worth $250,000 and liabilities of $75,000. What is the capital or net worth of the business?

3. The Marosek family has assets worth $43,250 and no liabilities. What is the family's net worth?

4. Today the Goldmark Corporation has these assets: cash, $121,460; accounts receivable, $86,275; materials, $143,680; equipment and supplies, $472,568; land and building, $780,000. The corporation has these liabilities: Fourth National Bank, $240,100; Far West Lumber Company, $42,500. What is the corporation's capital today?

5. On December 31 last year, Pat Kono had these personal assets: checking account, $729.40; savings account, $2,641; clothing, $830; car, $5,395; other, $4,000. Pat owed $1,000 on the car and $129 on her credit card account. What was Pat's net worth?

The Balance Sheet. A balance sheet is a formal report or statement showing financial (money) worth on a certain date. The balance sheet for Rita Alber's Fixit Service as of December 31, 1983, is shown below:

Fixit Service,
Balance Sheet
December 31, 19--

Assets		Liabilities	
Cash............................	$ 7,475	Ektron Supply Company ..	$ 1,200
Parts and Materials..........	3,085	Appliance Wholesalers.....	730
Tools and Equipment.......	5,250	Total Liabilities	$ 1,930
Delivery Van..................	8,000	**Capital**	
Supplies	1,620	Rita Alber, Capital	23,500
		Total Liabilities and	
Total Assets..................	$25,430	Capital	$25,430

A balance sheet

As shown in the Fixit Service balance sheet, the value of everything owned by the business (assets) is listed on the left side. The claims of creditors (liabilities) and the claim of the owner (capital) to those assets are shown on the right side.

Regardless of the size of the business and the form or the detail of the balance sheet, the total value of the assets is always equal to the total claims to those assets.

Assets = Liabilities + Capital

Written Practice 2

1. On June 30 last year, Roy Polk's Spice Shop had the assets and liabilities shown below. Make a balance sheet for the shop on that date.

Assets		Liabilities	
Cash	$ 5,235	City Wholesalers, Inc.	$ 1,624
Merchandise.............	15,410	Spice Imports, Ltd. ...	538
Equipment...............	5,062		
Supplies	825		
Building..................	30,000		$56,532

2. Make a balance sheet for Shirley's Cleaning Service as of December 31 of last year. On that date, Shirley Rubin's business had these assets: cash, $1,380; cleaning equipment, $4,890; trucks, $18,400; supplies, $2,675. On that date, the cleaning service owed Koko Truck Sales $14,254, and Qwikway Supply Company $365.

Money owed for a credit purchase is called an account payable

3. Kingly Products had these assets on December 31 of last year: cash, $65,680; accounts receivable, $83,290; materials, $120,000; manufacturing equipment, $750,000; land and building, $500,000. Their liabilities on that date were: accounts payable, $89,250; taxes payable, $18,625. Make a balance sheet for Kingly Products as of December 31.

4. The Carlson family's partly completed statement of net worth (balance sheet) for December 31 of the recent year is shown below:

Assets		Liabilities	
Cash (Checking and Saving)............................	$ 8,375	Worthmore Stores...........	$ 475
Rent Paid for January.......	450	Motor Finance Corp.........	3,500
Furniture and Equipment..	15,000	Charge-It Credit Card	143
Clothing and Personal	2,600	Total Liabilities	$?
Cars	8,200		
		Net Worth	
		Carlson Family Net Worth	?
Total Assets..................	$?	Total Liab. and Net Worth	$?

What are the following totals for the Carlson family:

a. total assets?   c. net worth?
b. total liabilities?   d. total liabilities and net worth?

5. The Medina family had these assets on June 30 of last year: cash, $872; savings bonds and certificates, $14,500; home, $52,500; furniture and furnishings, $12,800; clothing, $2,780; cars, $7,895; other, $1,600. Their only liability on June 30 was a mortgage with Kiowa Savings and Loan for $23,400. Make a balance sheet (statement of net worth) for the Medina family as of June 30.

Terms to Remember

| assets | balance sheet | capital | liabilities |

a. A formal report showing financial (money) worth
b. Things of value owned by a business, person, or family
c. The owner's claim to the value of assets
d. The claims of creditors to the value of assets

Review 81

1. a. 16 kL less 25% of itself is what amount?
   b. 65% of $320 is what amount?
   c. Change $\frac{5}{6}$ to a percent
   d. What is the fractional equivalent of $62\frac{1}{2}\%$?
   e. What is the number of days from January 1 to February 28?

2. On December 31 of last year, Ken's Music Store had these assets: cash, $12,425; merchandise inventory, $43,000; equipment, $6,500; supplies, $650. The store owed $175 to OK Realty Corporation, and $1,365 to Musico Publishers. Make a balance sheet for the store as of that date.

3. Marjorie Kleinert bought a freezer for $49.50 down and 18 monthly payments of $30.25 each. The cash price of the freezer was $495.
   a. What was the installment price of the freezer?
   b. What was the finance charge on the freezer?
   c. By what percent was the installment price of the freezer greater than the cash price?

4. You want to buy some new furniture. The furniture will cost $2,000 if you buy it on a regular charge account and pay for it in 30 days. If you pay cash, you will get a 5% discount. How much would you save by borrowing the cash price at 10% for 30 days and paying cash for the furniture?

5. The Federated Bank loaned Claus Koppel $800 on a 15% interest-bearing note. Claus repaid the note and interest in 10 equal monthly installments.
   a. What was the finance charge on the loan?
   b. What was the total that Claus repaid?
   c. What was the amount of each installment?

6. A demand note dated March 10 was paid on October 8. For how many days had the note been in effect?

THE INCOME STATEMENT

In a profit-making business, goods or services must be sold at a price that will cover all costs of goods and materials, expenses of operation, and an adequate profit. This means that, from time to time, the business operators need to find out how much profit or loss the business has made. This is done by drawing up a summary statement showing the business income, costs, expenses, and profit or loss. The summary statement is called an **income statement**, or *profit and loss statement*.

Income statements are usually prepared at regular times such as the end of a month, quarter, or year. The Tots and Teens Shop income statement for the month of December is shown below:

Tots and Teens Shop
Income Statement
For the Month Ended December 31, 19--

Revenue:		
Sales...	$32,450	
Less Sales Returns and Allowances	2,450	
Net Sales..		$30,000
Cost of Merchandise Sold:		
Merchandise Inventory, December 1....................	$48,000	
Purchases	6,000	
Merchandise Available for Sale..........................	$54,000	
Less Merchandise Inventory, December 31...........	34,400	
Cost of Merchandise Sold		19,600
Gross Profit on Sales...		$10,400
Operating Expenses:		
Advertising Expense...	$ 800	
Depreciation of Equipment	300	
Insurance Expense	250	
Miscellaneous Expense	300	
Rent Expense...	1,400	
Salaries and Wages Expense	4,250	
Supplies Expense..	400	
Utilities Expense...	600	
Total Operating Expenses...............................		8,300
Net Income...		$ 2,100

An income statement

As shown in the Tots and Teens Shop statement, the main parts of an income statement for a retailing business are revenue, or income from sales; cost of merchandise sold; gross profit on sales; operating expenses; and net income or net loss.

Net Sales.
In a retailing business, the main source of *revenue*, or income, is the sale of merchandise. The total value of merchandise sold over a period of time is called the *sales* for that period. Usually some of the merchandise that is sold is returned because it is unwanted or unsatisfactory, and the customer's money is refunded. When these *sales returns and allowances* are subtracted from the sales, the remaining amount is called **net sales**

Sales − Sales Returns and Allowances = Net Sales

For example, the Tots and Teens Shop had sales in December of $32,450, and sales returns and allowances of $2,450. The net sales for December were $30,000 (Sales, $32,450 − Sales Returns and Allowances, $2,450 = Net Sales, $30,000).

Written Practice 1

1. The sales for the first quarter of a year at Homeway Hardware Store totaled $275,405. Sales returns and allowances for that quarter were $7,187. What were the store's net sales for the quarter? **$268,218**

2. A store's June sales totaled $706,824. Sales returns and allowances totaled $22,618. What were the store's net sales for June?

3. Lucca's Sport Shop had total sales last year of $425,634. Returns and allowances were $26,725. What were the year's net sales?

Cost of Merchandise Sold.
To find gross profit on sales, the value of the merchandise that was sold must be found, expressed in terms of its cost. Keeping track of the cost of all items as they are sold is too hard, so most merchants find the **cost of the merchandise sold** (by starting with the beginning merchandise inventory).

An **inventory** is a list of goods on hand and their value. The merchants add the value of merchandise on hand at the beginning of the period (*beginning inventory*) and the cost of merchandise purchased during the period (*purchases*). That sum is the amount of *merchandise available for sale* during the period. From the merchandise available for sale, they subtract the value of merchandise on hand at the end of the period (*ending inventory*). The difference is the cost of merchandise sold.

Beginning Inventory + Purchases = Merchandise Available for Sale

Merchandise Available for Sale − Ending Inventory = Cost of Merchandise Sold

For example, the Tots and Teens Shop's inventory of merchandise on December 1 was $48,000, expressed at cost value. Purchases of merchandise during December totaled $6,000, at cost. On December 31, the inventory of unsold merchandise was $34,400, at cost. So, the cost of the merchandise that was sold during December was $19,600.

Merchandise Inventory, December 1...............	$48,000
Purchases in December	6,000
Merchandise Available for Sale in December	$54,000
Merchandise Inventory, December 31	34,400
Cost of Merchandise Sold in December	$19,600

Written Practice 2

1. Find the merchandise available for sale and the cost of merchandise sold for August:

Merchandise Inventory, August 1......	$124,306	
Purchases.....................................	65,768	
Merchandise Available for Sale.........	?	$190,074
Merchandise inventory, August 31	105,320	
Cost of Merchandise Sold................	?	$ 84,754

2. The Green Thumb Shop's merchandise inventory on April 1 was $42,078. Purchases of merchandise in April, May, and June totaled $36,475. The merchandise inventory on July 1 was $18,245.
   a. How much merchandise was available for sale in the quarter?
   b. What was the cost of merchandise sold in the quarter?

3. On January 1 of last year, the Novelty Shop had a merchandise inventory of $24,680. Purchases during the year totaled $38,705. The merchandise inventory on December 31 last year was $25,100. What was the cost of the merchandise sold during the year?

Gross Profit on Sales. Gross profit on sales, or *margin*, is the difference between net sales and the cost of merchandise sold.

$$\textbf{Net Sales} - \frac{\textbf{Cost of}}{\textbf{Merchandise Sold}} = \frac{\textbf{Gross Profit}}{\textbf{on Sales}}$$

For example, the Tots and Teens Shop's net sales for December were $30,000. The cost of merchandise sold was $19,600. So, the gross profit on sales for December was $10,400 ($30,000 − $19,600 = $10,400).

Written Practice 3

1. The Bootery's net sales last year totaled $1,025,400. Their cost of merchandise sold for the year was $706,200. What was the Bootery's gross profit on sales? $319,200

2. The Art Shop had net sales last month of $72,680. Their cost of merchandise sold was $51,150. What was their gross profit on sales?

3. Goods that cost $18,740 were sold for $29,036. What was the gross profit on sales?

4. A store's net sales for a year were $123,640. The store's merchandise inventory on January 1 was $26,475. During the year, merchandise was purchased for $78,250. The inventory on December 31 was $23,384.
   a. What was the cost of merchandise sold for the year?
   b. What was the gross profit on sales?

5. A retail store had a merchandise inventory of $120,800 on January 1 and $115,475 on December 31. Merchandise costing $422,650 was purchased during the year. Net sales for the year were $615,842.
   a. What was the cost of merchandise sold for the year?
   b. What was the gross profit on sales?

Net Income and Net Loss. All businesses have many expenses such as salaries, wages, rent, insurance, utilities, taxes, depreciation, supplies, and advertising. Those expenses are called **operating expenses**, or *overhead*. Operating expenses decrease the profits of a business, so they are subtracted from gross profit. When operating expenses are subtracted from gross profit, the amount that is left is called **net income**, or *net profit*.

Gross Profit − Operating Expenses = Net Income

For example, the Tots and Teens Shop (page 359) had a gross profit of $10,400. When the shop's operating expenses of $8,300 were subtracted, the net income was $2,100 ($10,400 − $8,300 = $2,100).

If operating expenses are greater than gross profit, the gross profit is subtracted from operating expenses. The difference is a **net loss**

Operating Expenses − Gross Profit = Net Loss

Written Practice 4

1. Last year, the Towel Shop had a gross profit of $162,300. The operating expenses for the year totaled $139,570. What was the shop's net income? **$22,730**

2. In January, a business had operating expenses of $13,795. The gross profit was $14,980. What was the net income for January?

3. If operating expenses are $12,074 and gross profit is $11,265, what is the net loss? **$809**

Written Practice 5

1. During one year, a store had net sales of $560,000. Cost of merchandise sold for the year was $308,000. Operating expenses were $210,000.
   a. What was the store's gross profit for the year? **$252,000**
   b. What was the store's net profit for the year? **$42,000**

2. The year's records of a business show net sales of $1,247,600. The merchandise inventory on January 1 was $212,500, and on December 31 it was $198,400. Purchases for the year were $744,750, and operating expenses were $417,946. What was the amount of the:
   a. cost of merchandise sold?
   b. gross profit?
   c. net income?

3. In one year a store's sales were $392,195, and sales returns and allowances were $11,769. The merchandise inventory on January 1 was $120,804, and on December 31, $125,670. Purchases totaled $235,460. Operating expenses were $122,300. What was the store's net income or net loss for the year?

Analyzing an Income Statement. Analyzing an income statement, and comparing it with other statements, will help to reveal the condition of a business. One way to analyze an income statement is to find what percent each major item is of net sales. In figuring the percentages, the items are compared with net sales as 100%. For example, if cost of merchandise sold is $19,600, and net sales are $30,000, the cost of merchandise sold is 65% of net sales ($19,600 ÷ $30,000 = 0.653, or 65%).

The percentage analysis of the Tots and Teens Shop statement, shown on page 359, is an example:

	Amount	Percent of Net Sales
Net Sales	$30,000	100%
Cost of Merchandise Sold......	19,600	65
Gross Profit on Sales	$10,400	35
Operating Expenses	8,300	28
Net Income	$ 2,100	7

Percents are rounded to the nearest whole percent

Written Practice 6

What is the percentage for each item in Problems 1 and 2?

	1. Amount	Percent		2. Amount	Percent
Net Sales.......................	$350,000	*?*	100	$40,000	*?*
Cost of Merchandise Sold .	210,000	*?*	60	23,200	*?*
Gross Profit on Sales........	$140,000	*?*	40	$16,800	*?*
Operating Expenses.........	112,500	*?*		14,600	*?*
Net Income....................	$ 27,500	*?*		$ 2,200	*?*

3. In a recent year, the Lens and Film Shop's income statement showed net sales of $650,000; cost of merchandise sold, $440,000; gross profit on sales, $210,000; operating expenses, $150,000; and net income, $60,000. Find the percent of net sales for:
   a. cost of merchandise sold.
   b. gross profit on sales.
   c. operating expenses.
   d. net income.

4. The Brake and Muffler Shop's net sales last year were $832,000, and the operating expenses were $241,280. What percent of the shop's net sales were the operating expenses?

5. Store *A* made a net income of $22,500 on net sales of $450,000. Store *B* made a net income of $26,000 on net sales of $400,000.
   a. What was the percent of net income on net sales for Store *A*?
   b. What was the percent of net income on net sales for Store *B*?
   c. Which store had the higher rate of net income on net sales?

Terms to Remember

cost of merchandise sold	**gross profit on sales**	**income statement**
inventory	**net income or net loss**	**net sales**
operating expenses		

a. A summary of income, costs, expenses, and profit or loss
b. Sales less sales returns and allowances
c. Amount of merchandise sold, in terms of cost
d. A list of goods and their value
e. Difference between net sales and cost of merchandise sold
f. Overhead
g. Difference between gross profit and operating expenses

Review 82

1. a. What is $\frac{5}{6}$ of $84.96?
   b. 1 575 m decreased by $\frac{1}{3}$ equals how many meters?
   c. Round 0.58206 to the nearest thousandth
   d. What amount is equal to $25 increased by $\frac{1}{5}$ of itself?

2. A store's sales for the year totaled $562,084. Sales returns and allowances for the year were $19,673. What were the store's net sales for the year?

3. On January 1 last year, the Linen Shop had a merchandise inventory of $83,246. Purchases for the year totaled $208,115. Merchandise inventory on December 31 was $76,025. What was the shop's cost of merchandise sold for the year?

4. The Camerama Shop's net sales last year were $491,606. The cost of merchandise sold was $270,384, and the operating expenses were $176,978. What was the shop's net income for the year?

GRAPHS

Business, governments, social groups, families, and persons often present information in graphs. A *graph* is a way of reporting numerical information in picture form. Graphs are helpful in showing trends, analyzing data, and making comparisons.

Good graphs have brief but complete titles that clearly tell what data are presented. Good graphs also are clearly labeled to show what is being measured and the scale of measurement that is used.

When you have finished this unit on graphs, you should be able to:

- interpret data in line, vertical bar, horizontal bar, rectangle, and circle graphs
- make simple graphs
- read, write, speak, and recognize the meanings of the terms shown in color

LINE AND BAR GRAPHS

Line Graphs. In a **line graph**, the dots representing the values are connected by straight lines. The line graph below shows the amount of Dorothy Barzak's electric bills by months, January through December, for the year 1983.

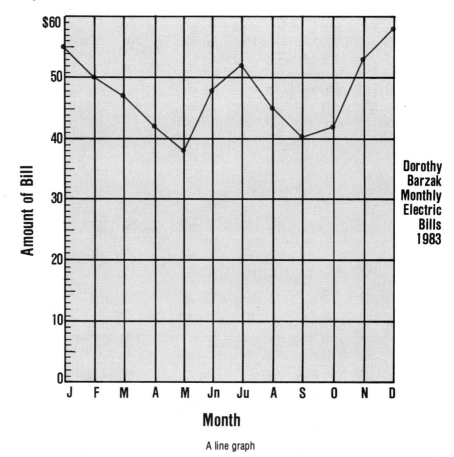

A line graph

The time scale is shown at the bottom of the graph. The months are shown from left to right. The dollar scale is shown at the left and runs from bottom to top. All amounts are rounded to the nearest dollar.

The line was made by first locating the dots to show each month's bills. Then, the dots were joined by using a ruler.

Oral Practice 1

1. What were the amounts of the bills for each of the first 3 months?

2. In what month was the bill smallest? What was the amount?

3. In what month was the bill largest? What was the amount?

4. In which two months were the bills the same?

5. What was the difference between the smallest and largest bills?

6. In how many months were the bills $50 or more?

Line graphs with two or more different kinds or colors of lines may be used to compare items. For example, the Kirth family's budgeted and actual food expenses for 12 weeks are shown in the two-line graph below. Their budgeted expenses are shown by the broken line. Their actual expenses are shown by the solid line. For convenience, expense amounts are rounded to the nearest $5.

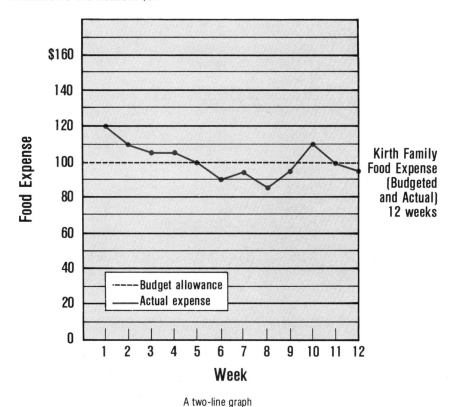

A two-line graph

Oral Practice 2

1. What was the Kirth's budgeted weekly food allowance?

2. What was the Kirth's greatest actual weekly food expense?

3. What was the Kirth's least weekly food expense?

4. In how many weeks did the Kirths exceed their food allowance?

5. In how many weeks did the Kirths stay within their allowance?

6. In how many weeks did the Kirths spend their exact budgeted amount?

7. In what week was the Kirth's actual food expense most different from their budget allowance?

Written Practice 3

Use graph paper with 8 or 10 blocks to the inch.

1. Make a line graph showing these facts:

Delia Bando's Car
Depreciated Value Over 6 Years

Time	Value	Time	Value
At purchase	$7,000	End of year 4	$3,400
End of year 1	6,100	End of year 5	2,500
End of year 2	5,200	End of year 6	1,600
End of year 3	4,300		

Make each vertical block equal to $100 of value. Use every tenth vertical line for the years.

2. Make a line graph showing Edwin MacCabe's monthly sales commissions for last year. His commissions were:

January	$2,100	May	$2,300	September	$1,800
February	1,850	June	2,600	October	1,900
March	1,900	July	1,600	November	2,250
April	2,200	August	1,000	December	2,500

Make each vertical block equal to $50 of commissions. Use every fifth vertical line for the months.

Use different kinds or colors of lines for the two lines

3. Make a two-line graph showing this information:

Nu-Way Corporation
Sales by Months, 1982 and 1983

Sales	1982	1983	Sales	1982	1983
January	$32,000	$39,000	July	$36,000	$46,000
February	34,000	42,000	August	24,500	43,000
March	35,000	45,500	September	28,000	37,000
April	38,500	48,000	October	32,000	34,000
May	32,000	50,500	November	39,000	33,000
June	30,000	47,000	December	41,000	33,000

Make each vertical block equal to $1,000 in sales. Use every fifth line for the months.

Bar Graphs. A bar graph is often used to compare the amounts or sizes of items. One bar is used for each item, and the length of the bar is proportional to the amount or size of the item. All bars, and the spaces between bars, are of the same width.

A **vertical bar graph** has bars in an upright or vertical position. A **horizontal bar graph** has bars running across (horizontally).

The Senior Play graph shown below is an example of a vertical bar graph. A bar is shown for each day of the school week, Monday through Friday. The height of the bar shows the number of tickets sold that day. The scale for measuring the bars is at the left of the graph.

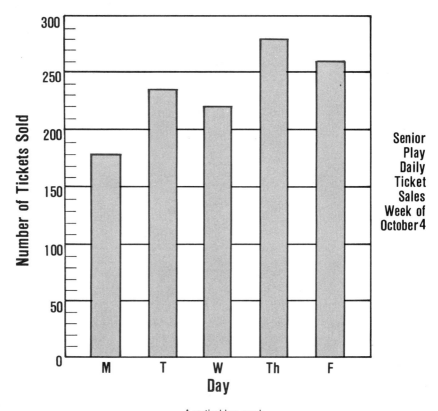

Senior
Play
Daily
Ticket
Sales
Week of
October 4

A vertical bar graph

1. What is the value of each vertical block in the Senior Play graph?

2. On what day were the most tickets sold? How many were sold that day?

3. On what day were the fewest tickets sold? How many were sold that day?

4. On what two days were the sales most nearly the same?

5. What total number of tickets were sold on Thursday and Friday?

Angela Navarro's cash payments graph, shown on page 370, is an example of a horizontal bar graph. It looks like a vertical bar graph that has been tipped on its side so the bars run across rather than up and down.

Angela Navarro's graph shows the relative amounts of her income that she spent for six kinds of expenses and for savings. For ease in graphing, the amounts were rounded to the nearest $100.

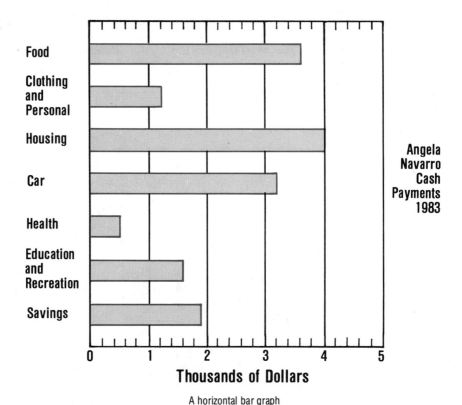

A horizontal bar graph

Oral Practice 5

1. For what two kinds of expenses did Angela spend the most?

2. What were Angela's total expenses for food and housing?

3. For what did Angela spend the third largest amount?

4. How much of her payments went to savings?

5. How much more did she spend for clothing and personal than for health?

For these problems, use graph paper with 8 or 10 blocks to the inch.

Written Practice 6

1. Make a vertical bar graph for the Exmark Company to show the average weekly pay of their factory workers for the years 1978–1983. Show these facts:

Year	Average Pay	Year	Average Pay
1978	$230.00	1981	$295.00
1979	250.00	1982	305.00
1980	255.00	1983	342.50

Make each vertical block equal to $5 of pay. Label $50 and each multiple of $50 on the scale at the left. Make the bars 5 blocks wide, and leave 5 blocks between bars. Label each bar with the year.

2. Toshi Wakichi is an assembler in an electronics plant. She is paid on the basis of the number of units she assembles each day. During the week of May 5, she assembled these numbers of units: Monday, 55; Tuesday, 48; Wednesday, 29; Thursday, 58; Friday, 52. Make a vertical bar graph showing Toshi's production for the week. Make each vertical block equal to one unit. Make the bars, and the spaces between the bars, 5 blocks wide.

3. Make a horizontal bar graph for Discount Appliances. Show these numbers of appliances sold by 5 salespersons during the October of last year:

Salesperson	Appliances Sold	Salesperson	Appliances Sold
Batto	42	Loudis	35
Deems	27	Makao	50
Flores	56		

Make each horizontal block equal to 1 appliance sold, but indicate the number on each tenth vertical line only. On the left side of the graph, label each bar with the salesperson's name. Make each bar 5 blocks wide, and leave 5 blocks between bars.

Terms to Remember

horizontal bar graph   **line graph**   **vertical bar graph**

a. Dots showing values are connected by straight line
b. Values are shown by bars in an upright position
c. Values are shown by bars running across

Review 83

1. a. 15 m² is what percent of 20 m²?
   b. What part of $192 is $120?
   c. Express $137\frac{1}{2}\%$ as a decimal correct to the nearest hundredth
   d. What part greater than $40 is $60?

For Problems 2 and 3, use graph paper with 8 or 10 blocks per inch.

2. Make a line graph showing these amounts of Jean Turbo's electric bills for January through June of last year: January, $56.24; February, $54.92; March, $49.76; April, $46.73; May, $42.37; June, $38.49. Round all amounts to the nearest dollar. Allow one vertical block per dollar.

3. Make a vertical bar graph showing average attendance at basketball games held on Tuesday through Saturday evenings at the Central High School. Attendance was Tuesdays, 550; Wednesdays, 560; Thursdays, 380; Fridays, 720; Saturdays, 700. Make each vertical block equal to 10 persons attending the games.

4. A restaurant's net sales for a month were $45,000. The operating expenses were $24,750. What percent of net sales were the operating expenses that month?

RECTANGLE AND CIRCLE GRAPHS

Rectangle Graphs. A rectangle graph is a vertical or horizontal rectangle that is divided into sections. Each section represents part of a whole and is proportional in size to the part of the whole that it represents. For example, suppose that a whole rectangle 5 inches long represents $100, and you want to mark off a section to represent $20. You would mark off $\frac{1}{5}$, or one inch of the rectangle $\left(\frac{\$20}{\$100}=\frac{1}{5};\frac{1}{5}\times 5 \text{ inches} = 1 \text{ inch}\right)$.

The values shown in rectangle graphs are often either dollars or percents. The vertical rectangle graph below shows the sales in dollars for each department of Pearly's Old-Time Sweet Shop during the month of April, 19--.

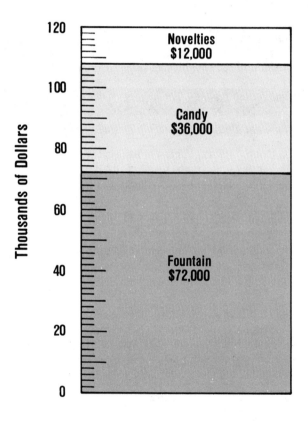

A vertical rectangle graph

The horizontal rectangle graph on page 373 shows the distribution of the federal, state, and local taxes paid by the Wing family in 1983. Each kind of tax is shown as a percent of the total amount of taxes that the Wing family paid.

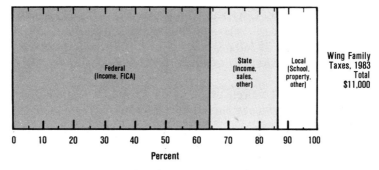

A horizontal rectangle graph

Written Practice 1

1. In the Pearly's Old-Time Sweet Shop graph on page 372:
   a. What were the total sales for the year?
   b. What percent of the total sales were the fountain sales? 60%
   c. What percent of the total sales were the candy sales?

2. In the Wing Family graph above:
   a. What percent of the family's total taxes was for state taxes? 22%
   b. What amount of federal taxes did they pay? $7,040
   c. What percent of local taxes did they pay?

For Problems 3, 4, and 5, use graph paper with 8 or 10 blocks per inch.

3. Make a vertical rectangle graph to show these parts of each dollar of sales by Trudy's Gift Shop last year:

Cost of Merchandise Sold	$0.58
Operating Expenses	0.28
Net Income	0.14
Sales	$1.00

   Make the rectangle $1\frac{1}{2}$ inches wide. Make each vertical block equal to $0.02.

4. Make a vertical rectangle graph to show these facts about the Booster Club's Card Sale that was held in January of the current year:

Cost of Cards	$ 500
Expenses	50
Net Income	450
Income from Sale	$1,000

   Make the rectangle 2 inches wide, and make each vertical block equal to $20.

5. Make a horizontal rectangle graph to show these expenses of operating Kurt Klein's car last year: gas and oil, 20%; repairs and maintenance, 8%; insurance, 12%; depreciation and interest on investment, 60%; total, 100%. Make the rectangle 2 inches high, and make each horizontal block equal to 2%.

Circle Graphs. Circle graphs, or "pie" graphs, are often used to show how parts relate to each other and to the whole. In a circle graph, the full circle of 360 degrees (360°) is the whole, or 100%. The full circle is divided into parts of the proper number of degrees to show the relative size of each part.

The circle graph below shows the same information about Pearly's Old-Time Sweet Shop that was shown in the rectangle graph on page 372.

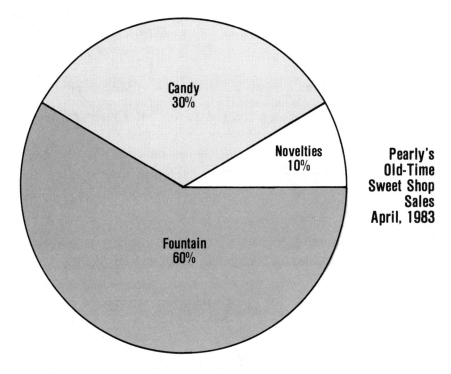

Pearly's
Old-Time
Sweet Shop
Sales
April, 1983

A circle graph

In making the circle graph, the dollar amounts were changed first to percents, then to degrees. For example, fountain sales were found to be 60% of sales ($72,000 ÷ $120,000 = 0.6, or 60%). The equivalent in degrees is 216° (0.60 × 360° = 216°).

The degrees in the other parts of the circle were found in the same way. The angles in the circle were then marked off with a protractor.

**Written
Practice 2**

1. Last year the Torkey Tool Company's production of four kinds of power tools was this:

| Drills | 35% | Saws | 20% |
| Grinders | 15% | Sanders | 30% |

a. On a circle graph showing total production, how many degrees should be used to show the production of each kind of power tool?

b. Make a circle graph showing the production of each kind of tool.

2. Analysis of the Buy-Rite Center's income statement for last year showed these facts:

Cost of Merchandise Sold	64%
Operating Expenses	30%
Net Income	6%
Net Sales	100%

Make a circle graph showing that analysis of net sales.

3. The Onawa family's total expenses for a vacation last year were distributed this way: flight, 35%; lodging, 25%; food, 20%; rental car, 8%; entertainment, 12%. Make a circle graph showing each expense and its percent.

Terms to Remember

circle graph   rectangle graph

a. May be either vertical or horizontal
b. Also called a "pie" graph

Review 84

1. a. What is the number of days from October 9 to December 29?
   b. 0.025 equals what percent?
   c. Express $\frac{1}{2}$% as a decimal
   d. Show $0.16\frac{2}{3}$ as a fraction in lowest terms
   e. 30 kg decreased by what percent of itself gives 20 kg?

2. Make a horizontal rectangle graph for the Food Discount Center showing this distribution of income from sales last year: net sales, 100%; cost of merchandise sold, 65%; operating expenses, 32%; net income, 3%. Make the rectangle 2 inches high, and each horizontal block equal to 2%.

3. Make a circle graph showing this distribution of Ellen Arden's investments as of today's date: savings accounts, 20%; stocks, 20%; bonds, 25%; real estate, 35%.

4. You can buy a kitchen appliance for $590 cash, or for $90 down and 24 monthly installments of $26.70 each. What annual percentage rate (APR) would you pay on the installment plan? (Use the APR table on page 349.)

5. The new balance of purchases on your credit card statement is $243.10. If you do not pay that balance by the due date, a finance charge of $1\frac{3}{4}$% will be added to the next bill. What would be the amount of the finance charge added to your bill?

6. What is the due date of a 120-day note dated July 10?

1. **a.** Show 0.43245 as a percent, correct to the nearest tenth
   b. $35 interest for 6 months on $500 is what interest rate?
   c. What is the exact interest on $5,000 for 60 days at 10%?
   d. What is the simple interest on $3,000 for 4 months at 15%?
   e. $\frac{1}{4}$% of $420 is what amount?
   ★**f.** Express 5.65 as a mixed number in simplest form

2. On July 1, Jacob Flenz opened a savings account with a deposit of $500. He made no other deposits or withdrawals during the next year. Interest was credited to the account each quarter on October 1, January 1, April 1, and July 1. Interest was paid at 6% on whole dollars only. How much did Jacob have in his account on July 1 of the next year?

3. On August 31, your checkbook balance was $198.65, and your bank statement balance was $240.27. The bank statement showed a $2.50 service charge and $1.02 in interest credited to your account for August. Your check No. 120 for $43.10 was outstanding. Make a reconciliation statement in good form as of August 31.

4. You bought 100 shares of Spacecorp stock at $25\frac{1}{2}$, plus a commission of $68.50. You later sold the stock at $28\frac{1}{4}$, less $71.10 commission. What was your profit on the stock?

5. Lin Yu bought eight $1,000 corporation bonds at $93\frac{1}{4}$, plus commission of $7.50 per bond. What was her total investment in the bonds?

6. Maria Sanchez invested $30,000 in rental property. She rented the property for $600 a month. Her ownership expenses were $3,000 a year. What was Maria's annual rate of income on her investment?

7. Ray Davis borrowed $4,000 from the Mechanic's Bank and signed a note promising to repay that amount, plus interest at 12%, in one year. What amount was due at maturity of the note?

8. You borrowed $1,500 on a 12% interest-bearing note. The lender added a service charge of $15 and charged $6 for insurance on the loan. You repaid the total amount in 12 monthly installments. What was the amount of each monthly payment?

9. On the installment plan, the total price of a trail bike is $599. The terms are $60 down and the balance in monthly payments of $26.95 each. How many monthly payments would be needed to pay the balance?

★10. You borrowed $900 from a bank for 90 days. The bank discounted your note at 15%. What amount of money did you get from the bank at the time of the loan?

TERMS

addend: a number to be added to another

addition: a process of combining numbers to give one number

adjusted gross income: an income tax term meaning gross income less adjustments to income

agent: a person who legally acts for, and makes contracts for, another

aliquot part of $1: an exact fractional part of $1

amount due at maturity: the total principal and interest owed on the due date of a note

amount financed: the amount of credit given on an installment loan or purchase

annual percentage rate (APR): the percent that shows the ratio of the finance charge to the amount financed

assessed value: a property value that is multiplied by a tax rate to find a property tax

assets: things of value owned by a business, person, or family

average: a number that represents a group of numbers

balance: the amount in an account at any time

balance sheet: a statement or report showing the assets, liabilities, and capital of a person or business on a certain date

bank discount: interest charged in advance

bank statement: a bank report sent to a checking account customer showing deposits, payments, other charges and credits, and the account balance

banker's interest: simple interest figured with a 360-day year; ordinary interest

banker's year: a 360-day year; a commercial year

beneficiary: the person or organization to whom life insurance benefits are paid

bodily injury insurance: car insurance covering injuries to persons other than the insured

bond: a government or corporation's promise to pay a sum of money, with interest, at a certain time

broker: a dealer in stocks, bonds, or real estate

broker's commission: a fee charged by a dealer in stocks, bonds, or real estate

budget: a plan for spending

canceled check: a check that has been paid and marked by the bank on which it was drawn

capital: the owner's claim to the value of assets; owner's equity; net worth

cash discount: a discount given for early payment of a bill

cash payments record: a record of all money spent

cash receipts record: a record of all money taken in

cash record summary: a review of cash receipts and cash payments

cash value: the amount that is returned if life insurance is canceled; cash surrender value

centimeter (cm): one-hundredth meter (0.01 m)

charge account: the privilege of buying on a store's own credit

check register: a record of a checking account, including deposits, checks, other charges or credits, and balances

circle graph: a circle showing how the parts relate to each other and the whole; a "pie" graph

coinsurance: a kind of health insurance that makes the insured share in expenses above a deductible amount

collateral: personal property used as security for a loan

collision insurance: insurance that covers damage to the insured's car from collision or upset

commission: money paid to an agent or salesperson based on the value or amount of goods bought or sold; broker's fee

common stock: the ordinary stock of a corporation, paying no specific dividend

compound interest: the amount of money earned by compounding interest; interest paid on interest after it has been added to form a new principal

compounding interest: adding interest to a principal to make a new principal

comprehensive damage insurance: insurance that covers damage to the insured's car from causes other than collision or upset

cost of merchandise sold: the amount of merchandise sold, in terms of cost; cost of goods sold

credit card: a card which identifies a customer who is to be given credit

cross product: the result of multiplying a numerator and denominator in a proportion

date of the note: the date on which a note is signed

decimal: a fraction with a denominator of 10, 100, 1,000, or other multiple of 10, that is written with a decimal point

deductible insurance: insurance in which the insured pays the first part of a loss

deductions: amounts subtracted from gross pay; expenses claimed to reduce income tax

demand note: a promissory note that has no definite time of payment

denominator: the numeral below the line in a fraction, showing the number of equal parts into which the whole is divided

deposit: money put into a checking or savings account

deposit slip: a form listing all items of a single deposit; a deposit ticket

depreciation: the loss of value caused by wear and aging

difference: the unknown addend in subtraction

discount: an amount off a full price; the difference between a lower market value and the par value of a bond; interest deducted in advance

discount rate: a percent of discount

dividend: the known product in division; part of a premium returned by an insurance company; profits distributed to corporation shareholders

division: the opposite process of multiplication; the process of finding the unknown factor when one factor and the product are known

divisor: the known factor in division; the number that shows the size or number of groups into which a dividend is to be split

double time pay: two times the regular pay rate

down payment: cash paid at the time of purchasing a home or making an installment purchase

due date: the maturity date of a note; the date on which a payment must be made

endowment life insurance: insurance that pays the face of the policy to a living insured at the end of a fixed time

equivalent fraction: a fraction that names the same number as another fraction

equivalent pay: pay expressed in terms of another amount of time

estimate: to find a rough or approximate answer

exact interest: simple interest figured with exact time and a 365-day year

exemption: an amount of income that is free from tax

expenses: money paid out; the cost of goods or services used

express: a service providing fast shipment for small and light goods

extension: the total price of the quantity of an item shown on a sales slip, found by multiplying the unit price and the quantity

face: the value printed on a bond; the amount borrowed on a note; the amount of insurance coverage

factor: the multiplicand or the multiplier

finance charge: the total of interest and other charges paid for using money

finance charge per \$100: (finance charge $\times$ 100) divided by the amount financed

fraction: a symbol with a numeral above and a numeral below a line; a common fraction; a fractional numeral

freight: a service for shipping heavy, bulky goods

fringe benefits: paid vacations, insurance, retirement plans, and other items of value above pay

graduated commission: a pay system in which the pay rate increases as sales increase

gram (g): one-thousandth kilogram (0.001 kg)

gross cost: the prime cost plus the agent's charges for commission and expenses

gross income: the total of all money earned; total income

gross pay: total pay

gross profit on sales: the difference between net sales and cost of merchandise sold

health insurance: insurance that reduces risks of loss from illness or injury

hectare (ha): a square hectometer (10 000 m²)

higher terms: an equivalent fraction having a larger numerator and denominator is in higher terms

homeowner's insurance: a "package" type of insurance bought by homeowners or renters

horizontal addition: the process of adding across

horizontal bar graph: a graph in which values are shown by bars running across

housing or household expense: a payment to provide shelter or home

improper fraction: a fraction having a numerator equal to or greater than the denominator

income: any money earned or received; revenue

income statement: a summary report of income, costs, expenses, and profit or loss; a profit and loss statement

installment: a part-payment on a loan or purchase

installment loan: a loan that is repaid in several part-payments

installment plan: a way of paying for a purchase in a series of part-payments

insured: the person whose life or property is insured

insurer: the insurance company

interest: money paid for the use of money

interest-bearing note: a note that requires payment of interest

inventory: a list of goods and their values

kiloliter (kL): one thousand liters (1 000 L)

kilometer (km): one thousand meters (1 000 m)

least common denominator: the smallest number divisible by the original denominators

liabilities: the claims of creditors to the value of assets

like fraction: fractions having the same denominator

limited-payment life insurance: insurance that covers the insured's entire life, but on which premiums are paid for a fixed time only

line graph: a graph on which dots showing the values are connected by straight lines

liter (L): the basic metric unit of capacity

lowest terms: a fraction is in lowest terms when both terms are divisible only by 1

markdown: an amount off a full price; a discount

market value: the price at which a stock or bond is sold; market price

maturity date: the date on which a note or bond is to be paid

medical payments insurance: car insurance that covers injuries to persons other than the insured, no matter who is at fault

meter (m): the basic metric unit of length

metric ton (t): one thousand kilograms (1 000 kg)

mill: one-tenth of a cent, or one-thousandth of a dollar

milligram (mg): one-thousandth gram (0.001 g)

milliliter (mL): one-thousandth liter (0.001 L)

millimeter (mm): one-thousandth meter (0.001 m)

minuend: the total of two addends from which, in subtraction, the subtrahend is taken to find the difference

mixed number: a number having both a whole number and a fraction, such as $2\frac{1}{4}$

mortgage: a written agreement that gives a lender the right to take a borrower's property if a loan is not paid

multiplicand: the number being multiplied; one of two factors of a product

multiplication: a short way of adding two or more equal numbers

multiplier: the number by which another is multiplied; one of the two factors of a product

net income: a self-employed person's profit; gross income less expenses or other deductions

net loss: the difference between gross profit and operating expenses when operating expenses are greater than gross profit

net pay: gross pay less deductions; take-home pay

net proceeds: the sale price or amount collected minus the agent's commission and expenses

net sales: sales less sales returns and allowances

non-interest-bearing note: a note that has no interest

no-par stock: stock issued without a stated value

number sentence: a statement that says two numbers are equal

numeral: a mark or name for a number

numerator: the numeral above the line in a fraction

operating expenses: salaries, rent, advertising, and other items which decrease profit; overhead

outstanding check: a check that has been written but not yet paid by the bank

overtime: time worked beyond regular time

overtime pay: extra money paid for working more than the usual time

par value: the face value of a bond or stock

parcel post: fourth-class mail

passbook: a record that shows withdrawals, deposits, interest, and balances of a savings account

percent: a term that means "per hundred," "parts per hundred," or "out of a hundred;" shows the comparison of a number to one hundred

piece: an item produced

piece rate: a pay rate based on items produced

policy: an insurance contract

preferred stock: stock that pays a specific rate of dividend

premium: the amount paid for insurance; a bond selling above par is selling "at a premium"

prime cost: the cost of goods before buying expenses or other expenses are added

principal: the person for whom an agent works; the face of a note; the amount on which interest is paid

proceeds: the face of a note less discount; the amount received from a sale

product: the result of multiplication

promissory note: a written promise to repay borrowed money, with or without interest, at a certain time; a note

proper fraction: a fraction having a numerator smaller than the denominator

property damage insurance: car insurance covering damage done to the property of others

property tax: a tax on real estate

proportion: a statement that two ratios are equal

quota: a fixed amount of sales above which commission is paid

quotient: the unknown factor, or answer, in division

rate of depreciation: the percent of depreciation found by dividing average annual depreciation by original cost

rate of interest: a part or percent of the principal paid for using money for one year

ratio: a way of comparing two numbers, as 3 to 5, $\frac{3}{5}$, 3 ÷ 5, or 3:5

reciprocal: a number that gives a product of 1 when multiplied with another; for example, $\frac{2}{3}$ is the reciprocal of $\frac{3}{2}$

reconciliation statement: a form to aid in making a checkbook balance and a bank statement balance agree

rectangle graph: a graph using a vertical or horizontal rectangle to show how parts relate to the whole and to each other

remainder: the leftover in division

regular time: the expected amount of work time per day or week

rent: money paid for the use of property

reverse addition: the process of adding in the opposite direction

round off: to drop unwanted digits from the right

salary: fixed pay for a week, month, or year

sales tax: a tax paid by the buyer of goods or services

savings bond: a kind of small-denomination U.S. Treasury bond

service charge: a bank charge for handling a checking account; an extra charge on an installment purchase

shareholder: a part-owner of a corporation; a stockholder

simple average: the average figured as the sum of the items divided by the number of items

simple interest: a way of figuring interest in which the principal stays the same for the time the money is used rather than increasing as interest is added to form a new principal, as is compound interest

single-payment loan: a loan that is repaid in one payment

Social Security (FICA): a U.S. government program that provides benefits for retired and disabled workers and their dependents

square centimeter (cm²): one ten-thousandth square meter (0.000 1 m²)

square kilometer (km²): one million square meters (1 000 000 m²)

square meter (m²): the basic metric unit of area

square millimeter (mm²): one millionth square meter (0.000 001 m²)

stock: the shares of ownership in a corporation

stock certificate: a paper issued to a shareholder showing how many shares are owned

straight commission: a pay system in which commission is the only pay

straight-line method: a way of figuring depreciation that spreads the total depreciation evenly over the life of the item

subtraction: the reverse of addition

subtrahend: a known addend that is subtracted from the total or minuend

sum: the result or answer in addition

take-home pay: gross pay less deductions; net pay

tax rate: a fraction in which the amount to be raised by tax is the numerator and the total assessed value is the denominator; often shown as a decimal, as dollars per $100 or $1,000, or as cents or mills per dollar

tax return: a form or report showing how income tax was figured

term life insurance: a kind of insurance that covers the insured for a short time only and has no savings feature

terms: the numerator and denominator of a fraction

time: the number of years or the fraction of a year for which interest is paid

time and a half pay: a pay rate that is $1\frac{1}{2}$ times the regular pay rate

time of the note: the number of years or fraction of a year for which money is borrowed on a note

tips: money given to service people "to insure prompt service"

total: the result or answer in addition

total income: the total of all money earned; gross income

transit number: a number that identifies a bank

uninsured motorists insurance: car insurance that, with medical payments coverage, covers the insured for injuries caused by another driver

unit price: the price of one unit, or of a group of units as one unit

unlike fractions: fractions that have different denominators

U.S. individual income tax: a federal tax on personal incomes

vertical addition: the process of adding up and down

vertical bar graph: a graph on which values are shown by bars in an upright position

wages: the total pay for a day or week of a worker who is paid by the hour

weighted average: an average that is figured as the sum of the products divided by the number of items

whole life insurance: a kind of insurance in which premiums are paid for the entire life of an insured; ordinary life insurance

withholding allowance: an amount that reduces the income tax; an exemption

withholding tax: an amount deducted from an employee's pay for income tax

yield: the rate of interest on a bond investment

INDEX